Grammar Links 3

A Theme-Based Course for Reference and Practice

Janis van Zante

Debra Daise
University of Colorado,
International English Center

Charl Norloff
University of Colorado,
International English Center

Randee Falk

M. Kathleen Mahnke
Series Editor
St. Michael's College

Houghton Mifflin Company   Boston   New York

Director of ESL Programs: Susan Maguire
Senior Associate Editor: Kathy Sands Boehmer
Editorial Assistant: Kevin M. Evans
Project Editor: Kellie Cardone
Production/Design Coordinator: Jennifer Meyer Dare
Senior Designer: Henry Rachlin
Manufacturing Manager: Florence Cadran
Senior Cover Design Coordinator: Deborah Azerrad Savona
Freelance Development Editor and Project Manager: Randee Falk

Cover Design: Rebecca Fagan
Cover Image: Arthur S. Aubry, Images® Copyright 1999 PhotoDisc, Inc.

Printed in the U.S.A.

Library of Congress Catalog Card Number: 98-72233

ISBN: 0-395-82892-9

6789-WEB-03

CONTENTS

INTRODUCTION

WELCOME TO GRAMMAR LINKS!

Grammar Links is a comprehensive three-level grammar reference and practice series for students of English as a second or foreign language. The series meets the needs of students from the beginning through the advanced level:

- *Grammar Links 1* . . . beginning/high beginning
- *Grammar Links 2* . . . intermediate
- *Grammar Links 3* . . . high intermediate/advanced

Each *Grammar Links* student text is accompanied by a workbook, an audiocassette package, a teacher's manual, and a CD-ROM for extra practice. In addition, the Houghton Mifflin ESL web site provides links to other web sites for grammar information and activities and for additional information about themes developed in the texts.

TO THE TEACHER

Series Approach

Recent research in applied linguistics tells us that when a well-designed communicative approach is coupled with a systematic treatment of grammatical form, the combination is a powerful pedagogical tool.

Grammar Links is such a tool. *Grammar Links* grammar explanations are clear, accurate, and carefully sequenced. All points introduced are practiced in exercises, and coverage is comprehensive and systematic. In addition, each grammar point is carefully recycled and reused in a variety of contexts.

The communicative framework of *Grammar Links* is that of the theme-based approach to language learning. Unlike other approaches, theme-based models promote the development of both cognitive and linguistic abilities through in-depth contextualization of language in a content area. In *Grammar Links*, content serves as more than a backdrop for communication; high-interest topics are presented and developed along with the grammar of each chapter. As a result, *Grammar Links* exercises and activities are content-driven as well as grammar-driven. While learning about adjective clauses in Book 3, for example, students explore various aspects of the discipline of psychology. While they are practicing gerunds and infinitives in Book 2, they read about successful American entrepreneurs. And, while practicing the simple present tense in Book 1, students learn about and discuss North American festivals and other celebrations. Throughout the series, students communicate about meaningful content, transferring their grammatical training to the English they need in their daily lives.

In short, the *Grammar Links* approach provides students with the best of all possible language learning environments—comprehensive, systematic treatment of grammar within a communicative, theme-based framework.

About the Books

Each book in the *Grammar Links* series is divided into approximately ten units. Each unit looks at a well-defined area of grammar, and each unit has an overall theme. The chapters within a unit each focus on some part of the targeted unit grammar, and each chapter develops some specific aspect of the unit theme. In this way, chapters in a unit are linked in terms of both grammar coverage and theme, providing a highly contextualized base on which students can build and refine their grammatical skills.

Grammar coverage has been carefully designed to spiral across levels. Structures introduced in one book are recycled and built upon in the next. Students not only learn increasingly sophisticated information about the structures but also practice these structures in increasingly challenging contexts. Themes show a similar progression across levels, from less academic in Book 1 and Book 2 to more academic in Book 3.

Grammar Links is flexible in many ways and can be easily adapted to the particular needs of users. Although its careful spiraling makes it ideal as a series, the comprehensive grammar coverage at each level means the individual books can also stand alone. The comprehensiveness and careful organization also make it possible for students to use their text as a reference after they have completed a course. The units in a book can be used in the order given or can be rearranged to fit the teacher's curriculum. Books can be used in their entirety or in part. In addition, the inclusion of ample practice allows teachers to be selective when choosing exercises and activities. All exercises are labeled for grammatical content, so that structures can be practiced more or less extensively, depending on class and individual needs.

Unit and Chapter Components

■ **Unit Objectives.** Each unit begins with a list of unit objectives so that teachers and students can preview the major grammar points covered in the unit. Objectives are accompanied by example sentences, which highlight the relevant structures.

■ **Unit Introduction.** A reading/listening selection introduces both the unit grammar and the unit theme. This material is followed by a quick comprehension check and a grammar consciousness-raising task, *Think about Grammar*. In *Think about Grammar* tasks, students figure out some aspect of grammar by looking at words and sentences from the selection and working together to answer questions about them. They induce grammatical rules themselves before having those rules given to them. *Think about Grammar* thus helps students become independent grammar learners by promoting critical thinking and discussion about grammar.

■ **Chapter Introduction.** Each chapter opens with a task. This task involves students in working receptively with the structures treated in the chapter and gives them the opportunity to begin thinking about the chapter theme.

■ **Grammar Briefings.** The grammar is presented in Grammar Briefings. Chapters generally have two or three Grammar Briefings, so that information is given in manageable chunks.

  • **Form and Function Charts.** The core of each Grammar Briefing is its **form** and **function** charts. In these charts, the form (the *what* of grammar) and the function (the *how, when,* and *why*) are presented in logical segments. These segments are manageable but large enough so that students can see connections between related grammar points—links and interactions that they cannot see and benefit from when grammar is broken up and presented in smaller pieces. Form and function are presented in separate charts when appropriate but together when the two are essentially inseparable. All grammatical descriptions in the form and function charts are comprehensive, concise, and clear. Sample sentences illustrate each point.

  • **Grammar Hotspots.** Grammar Hotspots are a special feature of *Grammar Links*. They occur at strategic points in each set of Grammar Briefings. Grammar Hotspots focus on aspects of grammar that students are likely to find particularly troublesome. Some hotspots contain reminders about material already presented in the form and function charts; others go beyond the charts.

- **Talking the Talk.** Talking the Talk is another special feature of the *Grammar Links* Grammar Briefings. Our choice of grammar is often determined by our audience, whether we are writing or speaking, the situations in which we find ourselves, and other sociocultural factors. Talking the Talk treats these factors. Students become aware of differences between formal and informal English, and between written and spoken English.

■ **Grammar Practice.** Each Grammar Briefing is followed by comprehensive and systematic practice of all grammar points introduced. The general progression within each Grammar Practice is from more controlled to less controlled, from easier to more difficult, and often from more receptive to more productive and/or more structured to more communicative. A wide variety of innovative exercise types is included in each of the four skill areas: listening, speaking, reading, and writing. The exercise types used are appropriate to the particular grammar points being practiced. For example, more drill-like exercises are often used for practice with form. More open-ended exercises often focus on function.

In many cases, drill-like practice of a particular grammar point is followed by open-ended communicative practice of the same point, often as pair or group work. Thus, a number of exercises have two parts.

The majority of exercises within each Grammar Practice section are related to the theme of the unit. However, some exercises depart from the theme to ensure that each grammar point is practiced in the most effective way.

■ **Unit Wrap-Ups.** Each unit ends with a series of activities that pull the unit grammar together and enable students to test, further practice, and apply what they have learned. The first of these is an error correction task, which covers the errors students most commonly make in using the structures presented in the unit. Following this is a series of innovative open-ended communicative tasks, which build on and go beyond the individual chapters.

■ **Appendices.** Extensive appendices supplement the grammar presented in the Grammar Briefings. They provide students with word lists, spelling and pronunciation rules, and other supplemental rules related to the structures taught. The appendices are a rich resource for students as they work through exercises and activities.

■ **Grammar Glossary.** A grammar glossary provides students and teachers with definitions of the grammar terms used in *Grammar Links* as well as example sentences to aid in understanding the meaning of each term.

Other Components

■ **Audiocassette.** All *Grammar Links* listening exercises and all unit introductions are recorded on cassette. The symbol ▄▄▄ appears next to the title of each recorded segment.

■ **Workbook.** Each *Grammar Links* student text is accompanied by a workbook. Workbooks contain a wide variety of exercise types and provide extensive supplemental self-study practice of each grammar point presented in the student texts. TOEFL® practice questions and student self-tests are also included in the workbooks.

■ **Teacher's Manual.** Each *Grammar Links* teacher's manual contains an introduction to the series, some general teaching guidelines, and the answer key and the tapescript for the student book.

■ **CD-ROM.** The *Grammar Links* CD provides further individualized practice and instruction for all grammar points presented in each student text (coming 2001).

■ **Links to the World Wide Web.** The Houghton Mifflin ESL Web site **http://www.hmco.com/college/ESL_site** provides links to other sites on the World Wide Web. These sites offer grammar information and practice, teacher resources, and information on topics and themes used in the texts. Links are updated frequently to ensure that students and teachers can access the best information available on the Web.

TO THE STUDENT

Grammar Links is a three-book series that gives you all the rules and practice you need to learn and use English grammar. Each unit in this book focuses on an area of grammar. Each unit also develops a theme—for example, business or travel. Units are divided into two or three chapters.

Grammar Links has many special features that will help you to learn the grammar and to use it in speaking, listening, reading, and writing.

FEATURE	BENEFIT
Interesting Themes	Help you link grammar to the real world—the world of everyday English
Introductory Readings/Listenings	Introduce you to the theme and the grammar of the unit
Think about Grammar Tasks	Help you become an independent grammar learner
Chapter Opener Tasks	Get you started using the grammar
Grammar Briefings	Give you clear grammar rules in charts, with helpful example sentences
Grammar Hotspots	Focus on especially difficult grammar points for learners of English—points you might want to spend extra time on
Talking the Talk	Helps you understand the differences between formal and informal English, and between written and spoken English
Grammar Practice	Gives you lots of practice, through listening, speaking, reading, and writing exercises and activities
Unit Wrap-up Tasks	Provide you with interesting communicative activities that cover everything you've learned in the unit
Grammar Glossary	Gives you definitions and example sentences for the most common words used to talk about English grammar. A handy reference for now and for later.

All of these features combine to make *Grammar Links* interesting and rewarding—and, I hope, FUN!

ACKNOWLEDGMENTS

I would like to thank all of the *Grammar Links* authors for their unwavering hard work in making this grammar series a success. I have learned much from each one of them, and I consider myself fortunate to have worked with such a dedicated and talented group of creative people.

I am also grateful to the staff at Houghton Mifflin, without whom this series would not have come about. Thanks to Kathy Sands Boehmer, Kevin Evans, Elaine Leary, Patricia Fossi, Henry Rachlin, and Kellie Cardone. I would also like to thank Kristine Clerkin, Editorial Director of the College Division, for her continued support and encouragement from conceptualization to realization of this very complex project.

Many thanks, as well, to Roderick Jacobs for his unwavering support and for his guidance in the early stages of the development of *Grammar Links.*

I owe a special debt of gratitude to Randee Falk, our project manager. Randee's commitment, care, creativity, and attention to detail were absolutely indispensable in making *Grammar Links* a success.

Finally, a very special thanks goes to Susan Maguire, Director of ESL Programs at Houghton Mifflin, for her vision, her sense of humor, her faith in all of us, her flexibility, her undying tenacity, and her willingness to take risks in order to move from the mundane to the truly inspirational!

M. Kathleen Mahnke, Series Editor

We would like to express our appreciation to our developmental editor and co-author, Randee Falk, for her commitment to creating a complete and accurate grammar text. Thank you, Randee, for your insights, care, and guidance throughout the project.

Janis van Zante, Debra Daise, and Charl Norloff

Many people made valuable contributions to this book. We would like to acknowledge and thank the following: the staff at Houghton Mifflin, for their constant patience and encouragement; each other and the other *Grammar Links* authors, for inspiration, advice, and continued friendship throughout the writing and production process; our students, who were accommodating testers of the material; the librarians at the Boulder Public Library, for their expertise and willingness to help, and Jessie Brundage of Boulder, for listening and understanding; and Keith Maurice, the Director of the International English Center at the University of Colorado.

In addition, we thank the following reviewers:

- Maureen Andrade, Brigham Young University, HI
- Victoria Badalamenti, LaGuardia Community College, NY
- Charlotte Calobrisi, Northern Virginia Community College, VA
- Eileen Hanson, Middlesex County College, NJ
- Kathy Judd, Truman College, IL
- Maryellen Langhout, Truman College, IL
- Don Linder, Hunter College, NY
- Grace Low, University of Oregon, OR
- Dennis Oliver, Arizona State University, AZ
- Nancy Olivetti, Passaic Community College, NJ
- Joe Pettigrew, Boston University, MA
- Norman Prange, Cuyahoga Community College, OH
- Barbara Smith-Palinkas, English Language Institute, FL

Finally, we are immensely grateful for the support, encouragement, and patience of our close friends and families, especially Lakhdar Benkobi; Lenny Neufeld; Richard, Jonathan, and Joshua Norloff; and Peter van Zante.

Janis van Zante, Debra Daise, Charl Norloff, and Randee Falk

Unit One

Present and Past: Simple and Progressive

Topic Focus—Time I: *Natural Time and Clock Time*

UNIT OBJECTIVES

■ **the simple present and present progressive tenses**
(The earth ***revolves*** around the sun. We ***are studying*** the solar system this year.)

■ **verbs with stative meaning**
(We ***own*** several watches and quite a few clocks.)

■ **the simple past and past progressive tenses**
(Mr. Smiley ***observed*** a man last week. He ***was sleeping*** at 10 o'clock.)

■ **time clauses**
(***Before the United States had standard time,*** each town or city had its own time.)

■ ***used to* and *would***
(People ***used to tell*** time by the sun. They ***would follow*** the sun's shadow on a dial.)

INTRODUCTORY TASKS

Reading and Listening

[▭▪▪▪]　Read and listen to the passage "When Did Time Begin?" on page 3. Then complete the Comprehension Check.

Comprehension Check

Read each sentence. Circle **T** if the sentence is true or **F** if the sentence is false.

1. The Big Bang is a name for the beginning of the universe and time.   (**T**)   **F**

2. Earth is a part of the Milky Way galaxy.   **T**   **F**

3. First, the Milky Way formed, and then our solar system formed.   **T**   **F**

4. Biological rhythms existed in the past, but they don't exist anymore.   **T**   **F**

5. Clock time gives us natural time cycles.   **T**   **F**

WHEN DID TIME BEGIN?

__Did__ time __have__ a beginning?
If so, how __did__ it __begin__?
When did it begin?

Scientists (think) that our universe began from an unimaginably small point of space-time. About 15 billion years ago, this point suddenly **exploded** outward. We **call** this enormous explosion the Big Bang. **Did** time **exist** before the Big Bang? No one **knows**. But the Big Bang was the beginning of time as humans are able to understand it now.

At the moment of the Big Bang, the universe **began** to expand and change. It **is** still **expanding** and **is** still **changing**. By observing distant parts of the universe, scientists **are learning** more about its early history. About 10 billion years ago galaxies **were forming** from clouds of stars, dust, and gas. While our galaxy, the Milky Way, **was moving** through space, our solar system **formed** within it. Our solar system **includes** the sun and the planets that revolve around it. The motion of our planet, earth, **gives** us natural time cycles— days, nights, and seasons of the year. These cycles have rhythms, repeating themselves regularly, over and over again.

Natural time cycles **had** an important influence in the development of life on earth. From the beginning, the rhythms of life **were** based on earth's patterns of daylight and darkness and the seasons of the year. As a result, all living things, including human bodies, **follow** biological rhythms connected to these natural time cycles. Our daily cycle of sleeping and waking **is** one of our biological rhythms.

People everywhere **lived** in close harmony with the cycles of nature. They **followed** their biological rhythms, and they depended on natural time, measured by changes in the sun, moon, and stars. But now we **have** a mechanical measure of time, clock time, and people often **schedule** their lives according to it. **Are** you **feeling** sleepy or hungry now, even though the clock **says** it's not time to sleep or eat? What **is** your body **telling** you? Perhaps it**'s trying** to follow its natural biological rhythms instead of the clock.

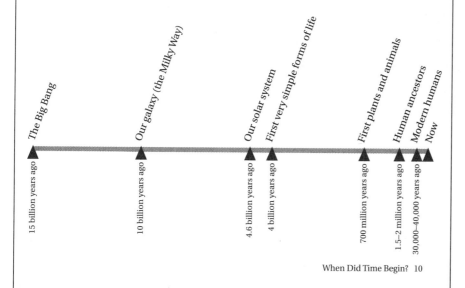

The Big Bang — 15 billion years ago

Our galaxy (the Milky Way) — 10 billion years ago

Our solar system — 4.6 billion years ago

First very simple forms of life — 4 billion years ago

First plants and animals — 700 million years ago

Human ancestors — 1.5–2 million years ago

Modern humans — 30,000–40,000 years ago

Now

Think about Grammar

A. Work with a partner. Look at the **boldfaced** verbs in the reading passage. If a verb describes an action or state that finished in the past or that was in progress at a time in the past, **underline** it. If a verb describes an action or state that includes the present or that is in progress in the present, **circle** it.

B. Some of the verbs that you underlined or circled describe an action or state in progress in the present or in the past. These verbs are in the present progressive or the past progressive tense. Look again at these verbs:

1. is expanding _____

2. is changing _____

3. are learning _____

4. were forming _____

5. was moving _____

6. are feeling _____

7. is telling _____

8. is trying _____

Progressive verbs all end in the same three letters. What are they? _____

Progressive verbs all have the same auxiliary (helping) verb. What is it? _____

Write *past progressive* or *present progressive* next to each of the verbs above.

C. The other verbs are in the simple present or the simple past tense. Look again at some of these verbs:

1. think _____

2. exploded _____

3. says _____

4. had _simple past_

5. began _s past_

6. were _____

7. followed _____

8. have _____

Write *simple present* or *simple past* next to each of the verbs above.

chapter

1

Simple Present and Present Progressive

Introductory Task: *True or False?*

A. Complete the questions based on the statements. Then move around the class, asking other students the questions. Make a small mark for each yes or no answer. After you have asked enough students, decide whether each statement is true or false.

1. Most people in the group use an alarm clock to wake up on weekdays.

    Do you __use an alarm clock to wake up on weekdays__ ? Yes: _____ No: _____

2. Only two people are wearing contact lenses at the moment.

    Are you __wearing contact lenses at the moment__ ? Yes: _____ No: _____

3. Everyone sleeps more than six hours every night.

    Do you _____? Yes: _____ No: _____

4. Three people are feeling sleepy now.

    Are you _____? Yes: _____ No: _____

5. Most people wear a digital watch every day.

    Do you _____? Yes: _____ No: _____

6. Right now, fewer than half of the students are thinking about time.

    Are you _____? Yes: _____ No: _____

B. As a class, compare results. Does everyone agree about which statements are true and which statements are false?

C. Work together in small groups to answer these questions.

1. Habits are things that people do regularly or routinely. Which statements

    describe people's habits? _____Statement 1_____ _____

    _____

    Are the verbs in these statements in the simple present or the present progressive? _____

2. Which statements describe things people are doing at this moment in time?

    _____ _____ _____

    Are these verbs in the simple present or the present progressive? _____

GRAMMAR BRIEFING 1: Simple Present and Present Progressive

The simple present is used to talk about habitual or repeated actions in the present and about things that are generally accepted as true. The present progressive (also called the present continuous) is used to talk about actions in progress at the moment of speaking or during a period of time extending through the present.

FORM Simple Present and Present Progressive

■ To form the simple present, use:

base form of verb (+ -s/-es for third person singular).*

To form negatives and questions in the simple present, use:

do/does + base form of verb.

* See Appendix 1 for spelling rules for the -s/-es form of the verb. See Appendix 2 for pronunciation rules for the third person singular form of the simple present tense.

■ To form the present progressive, use:

be + verb + -ing (present participle).*

* See Appendix 3 for spelling rules for the -ing form of the verb.

Affirmative Statements

Simple Present	Present Progressive
I **play** every day.	I **am** (**I'm**) **playing** now.
Joe **plays** every day.	He **is** (**He's**) **playing** now.
	We **are** (**We're**) **playing** now.

Negative Statements

Simple Present	Present Progressive
I **do not** (**don't**) **work** at night.	I **am not** (**I'm not**) **working** tonight.
You **do not** (**don't**) **work** at night.	You **are not** (You **aren't** / You**'re not**) **working** tonight.
She **does not** (**doesn't**) **work** on weekends.	She **is not** (She **isn't** / She**'s not**) **working** this weekend.

Yes/No Questions and Short Answers

Simple Present	Present Progressive
Q: **Do** they **work** every semester?	Q: **Am** I **working** this semester?
A: Yes, they **do**.	A: Yes, you **are**.
No, they **do not** (**don't**).	No, you **are not** (you **aren't** / you**'re not**).
Q: **Does** he **work** every evening?	Q: **Is** he **working** this evening?
A: Yes, he **does**.	A: Yes, he **is**.
No, he **does not** (**doesn't**).	No, he **is not** (he **isn't** / he**'s not**).
	Q: **Are** you **working** this evening?
	A: Yes, I **am**.
	No, I **am not** (**I'm not**).

Wh- Questions about the Predicate*

Simple Present	Present Progressive
Where **do** I **play**?	When **am** I **playing**?
How long **does** she **play**?	Why **is** Anna **playing**?
	Who **are** you **playing** with?

* The predicate is the verb and the words that come after it.

Wh- Questions about the Subject

Simple Present	Present Progressive
Who **works** with you?	Who **is working** with you?
What usually **happens**?	What **is happening**?

GRAMMAR HOTSPOT!

■ *Not* often contracts with *do* or *be* (e.g., *don't, aren't*). Be often contracts with subject pronouns (*he's, we're*). *Is* contracts with *wh-* words (*who's, what's*). In some formal writing, contractions are avoided.

■ When two verbs with the same subject are connected with *and* or *but,* it isn't necessary to repeat the subject.

   She **works** and **plays** every day.   She **works** but **doesn't play**.

■ When these verbs include a form of *be* (or of *have;* see Unit Two), it isn't necessary to repeat that form.

   She is **working** and **playing**.   She is **working** but **not playing**.

FUNCTION Simple Present and Present Progressive

Simple Present

■ Use the simple present to talk about habitual and repeated actions in the present.

   Farmers **get up** early every morning.

   They sometimes **go out** with friends.

■ Use the simple present to talk about things that are generally accepted as true, including scientific facts.

   Farmers **grow** crops.

   The earth **revolves** around the sun.

- The simple present is also used with verbs with stative meaning. (See Grammar Briefing 2, page 17.)

- Time expressions used with the simple present include *every day* (*week, month, year,* etc.), *on Mondays* (*weekends, holidays,* etc.), *in the morning* (*the fall, the first semester,* etc.), and *at noon* (*3:00 P.M., the end of the day,* etc.).

- Adverbs of frequency ([*almost*] *always, usually, often, sometimes, seldom, rarely,* [*almost*] *never,* etc.) are also often used with the simple present. (See Appendix 4 for the position of adverbs of frequency in a sentence.)

Present Progressive

- Use the present progressive to talk about actions in progress at this moment.

> Right now, the sun **is shining.**
>
> We **are listening** to the birds.

- Use the present progressive to talk about actions in progress through a period of time including the present. The actions began before now and will probably continue after now, but they do not have to be happening at this moment.

> Rosa **is taking** an astronomy course this semester.
>
> Scientists **are using** very sophisticated methods to measure time.

- The present progressive is sometimes used to emphasize the temporary nature of a situation. The simple present indicates a more permanent situation.

> They **are living** in Chicago this summer. (temporary situation)
>
> They **live** in New York. (more permanent situation)
>
> She**'s** not **earning** much money now. (temporary situation)
>
> She **doesn't earn** much money. (more permanent situation)

- The present progressive can be used with *always,* often to express a complaint.

> Dudley **is** always **arriving** late. I'm tired of waiting for him.
>
> Because he**'s** always **forgetting** things, his roommate gets upset.

- The time expressions *now, right now,* and *at the moment* can be used with the present progressive to talk about a point in time or an extended period. *Nowadays, at this time, at present, these days,* and *this week* (*month,* etc.) are used to talk about an extended period.

GRAMMAR PRACTICE 1: Simple Present and Present Progressive

☐ Simple Present—Form: A Conversation about Time

A student is interviewing a professor. Use the words in parentheses to complete the statements and questions in the simple present. Complete the short answers. Use contractions with subject pronouns and with *not*.

Q: Where __do you work__ (you, work)?
　　　　　　　　1

A: I ____work____ (work) in the astronomy department at this university.
　　　　2

Q: __Do you teach__ (you, teach) here?
　　　3

A: Yes, __I do__ .
　　　　　4

Q: _____ (you, teach) classes for beginning students?
　　　5

A: No, _____. I _____ (teach) mainly advanced students. I
　　　　　　6　　　　　　　　7

also _____ (do) research.
　　　　　8

Q: What _____ (your work, involve)?
　　　　　9

A: Well, very generally speaking, I _____ (think) about measuring time,
　　　　　　　　　　　　　　　10

motion, and space.

Q: I _____ (not, study) astronomy, so I _____ (have) some
　　　11　　　　　　　　　　　　　　12

very basic questions. How _____ (astronomy, be) connected to the
　　　　　　　　　　　　13

measurement of time?

A: Our ability to measure time _____ (come) from observing the
　　　　　　　　　　　　　　14

motions of the stars, the earth, and the moon.

Q: How _____ (we, measure) time?
　　　　15

A: We _____ (measure) time in two ways. We _____ (call)
　　　　16　　　　　　　　　　　　　　17

these measurements "natural time" and "clock time." The motions of the

earth _____ (give) us two units of natural time, the year and the day.
　　　　18

The motion of the moon _____ (give) us another natural time unit,
　　　　　　　　　　19

the lunar month.

Q: If we have natural time, why _____ (we, use) clock time?
                                              20

A: Natural time _____ (not, give) us small and precise enough units of
                            21

time.

Q: _____ (I, live) on natural time or clock time?
            22

A: You _____ (live) on both times. Your body and some of your
                    23

activities _____ (follow) regular natural cycles, or patterns. However,
                        24

in our culture, most of us _____ (have) the feeling that clock
                                          25

time _____ (control) our lives and routines.
              26

Q: Well, my teacher _____ (watch) the clock. And it _____
                                    27   28

(be) time for me to go to class. Thanks very much for the interview!

2 Adverbs of Frequency and Time Expressions with Simple Present: *Routines*

A. Use the adverbs of frequency and time expressions to write true statements about
your routines.

1. usually + in the evening ___*I usually drink a cup of hot tea in the evening.*___

2. often + in the morning _____.

3. seldom + at night _____.

4. always + once a day _____.

5. usually + once a week _____.

6. sometimes + on weekends _____.

7. always + every semester _____.

8. almost never + in the summer _____.

B. Now change one (any one) of the sentences so that it tells a lie. That is, the routine
it states should be possible but not true for you.

                              a glass of hot milk
Example: *"I usually drink ~~a cup of hot tea~~ in the evening."*

C. Work with a partner. Use the cues in **A** 2–8 to take turns asking about each other's
routines.

Example: Your partner asks: *What do you usually do in the evening?*

Answer the questions, pretending that the lie is one of your routines.

D. Which of your partner's routines is the lie? Find out by asking *yes/no* questions.

> Example: You ask your partner: *Is it true? Do you usually drink a glass of hot milk in the evening?*

> If the routine is a true one, your partner answers, *Yes, I do.* If the routine is the lie, your partner answers, *No, I don't. In fact, I usually drink a cup of hot tea in the evening.*

Try to detect the lie with as few questions as possible. Who is a better lie detector?

3 Simple Present—*Yes/No* and *Wh-* Questions: *Where Does Natural Time Come From?*

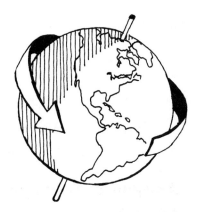

A. Write questions about the information in each paragraph. There are different questions you can ask, and different ways to ask the questions. Your *yes/no* questions can be phrased so the answer is *yes* or so the answer is *no*.

1. The earth and other planets move in orbits around the sun. It takes the earth about 365¼ days to orbit the sun. When we talk about the solar system, we call 365 days an "earth year."

Yes/No Questions: 1. Does the earth move around the sun? OR Does the sun move around the earth?

2. Does it take the earth about 365¼ days to orbit the sun? OR Does it take the earth about one day to orbit the sun?

Wh- Questions: 1. What is an "earth year"? OR What do we call 365 days? OR What do the earth and other planets do?

2. How long does it take the earth to orbit the sun? OR How long is an "earth year"?

2. The length of a planet's year depends on its distance from the sun. So on Venus years don't last as long as earth years, but on Mars years are longer than earth years. Venus makes one orbit of the sun in 224½ earth days. Mars travels around the sun once in 687 earth days.

Yes/No Questions: 1. _____?

2. _____?

Wh- Questions: 1. What _____?

2. How long _____?

3. How long _____?

3. As the planets orbit the sun, they also rotate. The earth rotates on its axis once every 24 hours. This rotation makes day and night on earth. When one side of the earth faces the sun, it is daytime on that side. When that side turns away from the sun, it is night.

Yes/No Questions: 1. _____?

2. _____?

Wh- Questions   1. How often _____?

2. What _____?

3. When _____?

B. With a partner, take turns asking and answering some of the questions you wrote in **A.**

Example: Your partner: What is an "earth year"?

You: An "earth year" is 365 days.

4 Present Progressive—Form: *Time Talk*

A. Use the words in parentheses to complete the statements and questions in the present progressive. Complete the short answer. Use contractions with subject pronouns and with *not.*

1. A mother and son:

A: Peter, why __aren't you doing__ (you, not, do) anything?
         ‾‾‾‾‾‾1‾‾‾‾‾

B: I __'m doing__ (do) something. I _____ (sit) here and
       ‾‾‾2‾‾‾   ‾‾‾3‾‾‾

_____ (think).
   ‾‾‾4‾‾‾

A: You _____ (not, think). You _____ (watch) television!
          ‾‾‾5‾‾‾   ‾‾‾6‾‾‾

B: I _____ (watch) a nature program. It _____ (help) me think
      ‾‾‾7‾‾‾   ‾‾‾8‾‾‾
about serious environmental problems.

A: That nature program _____ (not, help) you do your homework. You
                          ‾‾‾9‾‾‾

_____ (waste) time!
   ‾‾‾10‾‾‾

2. Three young men:

A: Hey, guys! What's up? Why _____ (you, sit) here on the sidewalk with
                               ‾‾‾1‾‾‾
all this stuff?

B: We _____ (wait) to buy concert tickets. The line _____
        ‾‾‾2‾‾‾   ‾‾‾3‾‾‾
(not, move) very fast.

C: We _____ (try) to entertain ourselves while we wait. We
      4

_____ (listen) to the radio and _____ (play) card games.
5   6

A: I get it. You _____ (kill) time.
              7

3. Three grandmothers:

A: How _____ (your children, get along) nowadays, Mildred?
        1

B: They _____ (get along) just fine. Jennie _____ (work) in
        2   3

Chicago, and Carl _____ (study) to be a lawyer. And the grandchil-
                        4

dren _____ (grow) fast!
      5

C: Good morning! _____ (I, interrupt) anything important?
            6

B: No, _____. We _____ (chat) about our families. Please
      7   8

join us.

C: Yes, indeed! You _____ (pass) the time of day.
           9

B. What is the difference between "wasting time," "killing time," and "passing the time of day"? In a small group, discuss these idioms and think of other examples of each.

5 Simple Present and Present Progressive—Meaning: *Watches*

Why is the simple present or the present progressive used in these sentences? For each boldfaced verb, choose a reason.

Simple Present

Habitual or repeated action

Scientific fact/thing generally accepted as true

Present Progressive

Action in progress at this moment

Action in progress through a period of time including the present

1. Tiny batteries **provide** the power for digital electronic watches.

    Scientific fact/thing generally accepted as true.

2. Please don't interrupt me! I**'m trying** to set my watch.

3. Megan never **wears** a watch.

4. Rachel's watch has been running slow for a while. Its battery **is wearing out.**

5. How often **do** you **look** at your watch each day?

6. Why **are** you **looking** at your watch? Are we late?

7. Our watches have beepers, so we sometimes **use** them as alarms.

8. Keith's watch **is beeping.** It's lunch time.

9. These days watches are status symbols. People **are wearing** expensive ones.

10. A watch is one type of chronometer. Chronometers **measure** time.

6 Simple Present versus Present Progressive: *Usually, but Not Today*

A. People sometimes change their routines temporarily. Work in pairs. Use the cues to write questions in the simple present. Then answer each question, using your own ideas and following the pattern in the example. In each answer, include *usually* and the time expression given and use the simple present and the present progressive.

1. *Q:* where / Arthur and Nancy / eat dinner ___Where do Arthur and Nancy eat dinner?___

   A: tonight ___They usually eat dinner at home, but tonight they're eating dinner at a restaurant.___

2. *Q:* what kind of clothes / Flora / wear _____?

   A: today _____.

3. *Q:* which language / Elena and Frank / speak _____?

   A: right now _____.

4. *Q:* how / Theresa / get to school _____?

   A: these days _____.

5. *Q:* when / the neighbors / go on vacation _____?

   A: this year _____.

B. Now work on your own. What about your own routines? Write **three** statements like those in **A** about temporary changes in your habits or situation. In each statement, include *usually* and a time expression such as *now, today, these days, this semester,* and *this year,* and use the simple present and the present progressive.

   Example: I usually live in Mexico, but this year I'm living in the United States.

7 Simple Present versus Present Progressive; Present Progressive with *Always: Dudley's Driving Me Crazy!*

A. Complete the e-mail message with the correct form of the verbs in parentheses—the simple present or the present progressive. Use contractions with subject pronouns and with *not*.

From: Chris

Sent: October 2 7:16 P.M.

To: Max

Subject: Dudley's Driving Me Crazy!

Hi, Max! College _____*is*_____ (be) great! I _____*'m enjoying*_____ (enjoy)
                        (1)   (2)
my classes this semester. Also, I _____*am getting*_____ (get) along well with all my
                                        (3)
housemates these days, except for Dudley. Everyday life with Dudley
_____*'s not going*_____ (not, go) very well just now. Let me tell you about his habits.
        (4)
First of all, Dudley often _____*eats*_____ (eat) other people's food and even
                                  (5)
_____*steals*_____ (steal) their cookies! Not only that, but he generally
        (6)
_____ (put) his dirty dishes in the sink for someone else to wash. In
            (7)
fact, Greg _____ (wash) Dudley's breakfast, lunch, and dinner dishes
                    (8)
now.

　　　Dudley and his friends _____ (make) noise constantly. At the
                                          (9)
moment, they _____ (play) his stereo very loudly. Also, they
                      (10)
_____ (talk) on the telephone all the time. Right now, they
        (11)
_____ (call and invite) more people over for a wild party.
        (12)
　　　On top of that, Dudley _____ (read) our mail sometimes. I
                                        (13)
_____ (type) this message quickly, just in case he comes in.
        (14)
　　　Finally, Dudley often _____ (borrow) our things without asking.
                                    (15)
He_____ (wear) my favorite sweater today.
        (16)
　　　Dudley won't change his bad habits. Slowly but surely, he
_____ (drive) me crazy! Your buddy, Chris
        (17)

B. Now imagine that you are one of Dudley's roommates. Dudley is driving you crazy, too. Use the information in Chris's message to complain to Dudley about his bad habits. Write **three** sentences. Use the present progressive and *always*.

　　Example: *You're always eating other people's food!*

8 Simple Present versus Present Progressive: *Studying the Universe and Time*

Matt just ran into an old friend from high school. Use the words in parentheses to complete the statements and questions in the simple present or the present progressive. Use contractions with subject pronouns and with *not*.

Matt: Hi, Ashley! It's good to see you again. What __are you doing__ (you, do) back
                                                    1

here? _____ (you, visit) your parents?
              2

Ashley: I _____ (live) at home with them this summer, and
                    3

I _____ (work) as a waitress at night. But I _____
              4   5

(look) for a day job, too, because part-time waitresses _____
                                                            6

(not, earn) enough money.

Matt: Why _____ (you, work) so hard this summer?
                7

Ashley: I _____ (try) to save money for my second year of
                8

college. _____ (you, go) to college these days?
                9

Matt: Not yet. At this point, I _____ (try) to figure out what subjects
                                        10

would interest me.

Ashley: I _____ (get) interested in astronomy and cosmology.
                11

Matt: Let's see, astronomers _____ (observe) the planets and the stars.
                                        12

But what _____ (cosmologists, do)?
                13

Ashley: They _____ (study) the universe as a whole. These days cosmolo-
                    14

gists _____ (try) to understand the beginning of the universe and
              15

the nature of time.

Matt: I often _____ (watch) those educational television programs
                    16

about the Big Bang and the expansion of the universe. The scientists on

them always _____ (ask) lots of really interesting questions
                    17

about the direction of time and the future of the universe.

Ashley: Maybe you should consider studying cosmology, too!

GRAMMAR BRIEFING 2: Verbs with Stative Meaning

Most verbs have an active meaning: they describe actions. Some verbs have stative meaning: they describe states. Verbs with stative meaning are usually used in the simple tenses.

FORM AND FUNCTION Verbs with Stative Meaning

■ Verbs with stative meaning occur in the simple tenses, rather than the progressive, even when used to talk about a particular moment in time.

> We **know** more about the moon these days.   **Not:** We ~~are knowing~~ more about the moon these days.
>
> The sky **seems** dark now.   **Not:** The sky ~~is seeming~~ dark now.

■ Verbs with stative meaning often concern thoughts, attitudes, emotions, possession, the senses, or description. Common verbs with stative meaning include:

Thoughts	Attitudes	Emotions	Possession	Senses	Description
believe	(dis)agree	fear	belong to	feel	appear
feel (= think)	doubt	(dis)like	have	hear	be
forget	hope	hate	owe	see	cost
know	mind	love	own	smell	look (like)
mean	need		possess	taste	seem
realize	prefer				sound (like)
remember	want				tend
suppose	wish				weigh
think					
understand					

Some of the verbs above have both a stative meaning and an active meaning.

Stative Meaning	Active Meaning
People **think** astronomy is exciting. (opinion)	People **are thinking** about solutions to environmental problems. (mental action)
She **doesn't see** well at night. (sense)	I**'m seeing** my professor to discuss the matter. (meeting with)
The air **smells** good. (sense)	They **are smelling** the roses. (action)
The pillow **feels** soft. (sense)	She**'s feeling** the temperature of the bath water. (action of touching)
They **look** happy. (description)	They **are looking** for their mother. (action)
He **weighs** 180 pounds. (state)	He **is weighing** himself on the scale. (action)
I **have** a good watch. (possession)	I**'m having** a good time. (experience)
She **has** blue eyes. (quality)	We**'re having** dinner at 8:00. (action)
You **are** a scientist. (quality)	You **are being** foolish about this. (behavior)

In their active meaning, these verbs can occur in the progressive and simple tenses.

> He **is thinking** about his future now.   He often **thinks** about his future.

TALKING the TALK

■   Sometimes certain verbs with stative meaning are used in the progressive, especially in conversation. The present progressive doesn't change the basic meaning of a sentence. However, it emphasizes emotion or a sense of a process or change.

Digital watches **cost** less these days.	Digital watches **are costing** less these days. (emphasis on change to lower cost)
They **love** it here.	They**'re loving** it here! (emphasis on how much they love it)

GRAMMAR HOTSPOT!

■   The verb *be* can have an active meaning, and occur in the progressive, when followed by an adjective describing a behavior that can change. Such adjectives include *bad, careful, foolish, good, impolite, kind, lazy, nice, patient, polite, rude,* and *silly.*

> Tom **is** tall. (Tallness is a state, not a behavior.)
>
> Tom **is** rude. (Tom is generally rude; speaker sees rudeness as a state of Tom's.)
>
> Tom **is being** rude. (Tom isn't generally rude; he is behaving in a rude way now.)

■   In addition to its uses shown in the chart on page 17, *feel* can be followed by an adjective describing health or emotions. Adjectives that do this include *fine, happy, lonely, sick, strange, tired,* and *well.* When used in this way, *feel* can occur in the simple or progressive.

> Peter **is feeling** pretty lonely today. = Peter **feels** pretty lonely today.
>
> Andrew **is feeling** sick. = Andrew **feels** sick.

GRAMMAR PRACTICE 2: Verbs with Stative Meaning

9   **Identifying Verbs with Active Meaning and Verbs with Stative Meaning:** *Astronomy Class I*

Work with a partner. Discuss the meanings of the boldfaced verbs. Mark the verbs that have active meaning with an **A** and the verbs that have stative meaning with an **S.** (Many of the verbs can have both active meaning and stative meaning. You will need to decide which meaning they have in the sentence they are in.)

Patricia: Walter's **taking** an astronomy class this semester. He often **complains** to
                          1   2

              me about it. He **thinks** it's difficult, and he's really **having** problems with it.
                                            3   4

Sylvia: Poor Walter. He's shy. He often **has** difficulty asking questions.
                       5   6

(Later . . .)

Walter: Please don't bother me! I'm **thinking** about astronomy. I'm **trying** to
                                                          7   8

              understand the homework.

Sylvia: Walter, you **need** help. Why **don't** you **see** the teacher during his office
                                        9   10

              hours?

Walter: Well, he always **seems** very busy. I'm sure that he **doesn't want** to answer
                                          11   12

              my questions.

Sylvia: Walter, you**'re being** foolish about this. He **has** time and patience, and he
                                      13   14

              enjoys helping students. Trust me.
                   15

Walter: Thanks, Sylvia. I **know** you're right. I'll see him tomorrow.
                                          16

10 Verbs with Stative Meaning and Verbs with Active Meaning: *Astronomy Class II*

Use the words in parentheses to complete the statements and questions in the simple present and present progressive. Complete the short answer. Use contractions with subject pronouns and with *not*.

1.

Teacher: I _____have_____ (have) something interesting to show you.

    I ____'m holding____ (hold) a rock that came from the moon.

    It _____ (belong) to the university museum now. Sylvia,

    let me hand the rock to you.

Sylvia: Wow, I ____don't____ (not, believe) this. I ___'m feeling___ (feel) a

    real moon rock! Actually, it ___doesn't feel___ (not, feel) much different

    from an earth rock.

Raymond: I _____ (want) to hold it now. I _____ (not, agree)

    with Sylvia. I ____think____ (think) that it ____feels____ (feel)

    lighter than an earth rock. It ____looks____ (look) different, too.

    It _____ (appear) to have a slightly different color.

Sylvia: Raymond, what _____ (you, do) to that rock now?

Raymond: I _____ (smell) it. It _____ (smell) different from

    an earth rock, too.

Sylvia: I _____ (doubt) that. Rocks _____ (not, smell).

    _____ (you, think) about tasting it, too?

Raymond: Yes, ____I____. I _____ (believe) in using all my

    senses to experience nature. I _____ (suppose) this

    rock ____is____ (be) pretty old, so it probably _____

    (not, taste) very good.

Sylvia: Raymond, you _____ (be) silly today!

2.

Martin: Sylvia, _____ (you, mind) answering a question?
                          1

Sylvia: What _____ (you, want) to know?
                        2

Martin: Why _____ (you, stand) on that scale?
                       3

Sylvia: I _____ (weigh) myself for homework.
                  4

Martin: I _____ (not, understand) how this can be your homework.
                 5

Sylvia: I _____ (try) to understand gravity.
                  6

Martin: Gravity _____ (hold) us on earth. It _____ (keep) the
                           7   8

earth in its orbit around the sun.

Sylvia: I _____ (know) that. And the moon _____ (have)
                  9   10

weaker gravity than the earth. I _____ (need) to figure out how
                                            11

much I _____ (weigh) on the moon now.
               12

Martin: How much _____ (you, weigh) on earth?
                            13

Sylvia: Martin, you _____ (be) usually very polite, but
                              14

that _____ (not, be) a polite question!
             15

Martin: I _____ (not, be) rude. I _____ (attempt) to help you
                 16   17

with your homework. Divide your earth weight by six. The

answer _____ (be) your moon weight.
                18

Sylvia: Great! I _____ (like) my moon weight!
                          19

Verbs with Stative Meaning and Verbs with Active Meaning: *Our Bodies in Time: The Sleep-Wake Cycle*

All humans naturally tend to be awake during the day and to sleep at night. However, some people tend to be "day people" (morning larks), while others tend to be "night people" (night owls). A typical lark and a typical owl are speaking about themselves at two different times of one day. Use the words in parentheses to complete their statements in the simple present or the present progressive. Use contractions with subject pronouns and with *not*.

Lark

"It's 7 A.M. I ___'m enjoying___ (enjoy) the sunrise.
          1

I ___'m feeling / feel___ (feel) wide awake now, and
          2

I _____ (look forward) to the morning.
          3

I _____ (want) to talk to other people now.
          4

I _____ (work) already because
          5

I _____ (have) a lot of energy. In fact,
          6

I _____ (think) about going jogging soon."
          7

Owl

"It's 7 A.M. I _____ (enjoy) my bed.
          8

I _____ (feel) really tired now, and
          9

I _____ (not, look forward) to the morning.
          10

I _____ (not, want) to talk to anyone yet.
          11

I _____ (not, move) yet because
          12

I _____ (not, have) much energy.
          13

I _____ (not, think) about exercising at
          14

this hour."

"It's 10 P.M. At this moment, I _____ (feel)
          1

exhausted and grumpy. In fact, I _____
          2

(fall) asleep. I _____ (need) to get into my
          3

nice, warm bed. I _____ (not, want) to go
          4

anywhere now."

"It's 10 P.M. I _____ (not, feel) sleepy at all
          5

now. I ___sta_____ (start) to feel alert, cheerful,
          6

and energetic! I _____ (study) hard now.
          7

I ___plan / planning___ (plan) to go out with some friends
          8

soon."

12 Verbs with Stative Meaning and Verbs with Active Meaning: *Are You a Lark or an Owl?*

A. Use the cues to write questions.

1. what time / you / tend / to wake up *What time do you tend to wake up?*

2. you / usually / wake up / without an alarm clock *Do you usually wake up without an alarm clock?*

3. how / you / usually / feel / early in the morning

4. at what time of day / you / have / the most energy

5. at what time of day / you / prefer / to work or study

6. how / you / usually / feel / late at night

7. when / you / like / to go to sleep at night

8. you / fall asleep / easily at night

B. Work with a partner. Use the questions you wrote in **A** to interview your partner. Then analyze your partner's tendencies. Is your partner a lark or an owl or in between?

C. Work with a partner whose tendencies are different from yours. Role-play a telephone conversation between a lark and an owl. Imagine that it is now 7 A.M. The lark tries to persuade the owl to go out and do something. Or imagine that it is now 10 P.M. The owl tries to persuade the lark to go out and do something.

Example: Lark: *Good morning!*

Owl: *Why are you calling so early? I'm still sleeping. I feel so tired.*

Lark: *I want to go out now. . . .*

chapter 2

Simple Past and Past Progressive

Introductory Task: *What Were You Doing?*

A. Work with a partner. Find out what your partner was doing at various times yesterday. Take turns using the cues to ask and answer questions. Use the past progressive in each question and answer.

> Example: Student A: *What were you doing yesterday at 6 A.M.?*
>
> Student B: *I was sleeping then. What were you doing yesterday at 6 A.M.?*
>
> Student A: *I was studying then.*

1. 6 A.M.

2. 9 A.M.

3. noon

4. 3 P.M.

5. 6 P.M.

6. 9 P.M.

B. Report to the class about the different things you and your partner were doing at the same time. Use the past progressive and *while*.

> Example: *At 6 A.M., while I was sleeping, Natalie was studying.*

C. Work on your own. Write short sentences about five things you did yesterday. Use the simple past.

> Example: *Yesterday, I studied English. I talked to a friend.*

1. _____

2. _____

3. _____

4. _____

5. _____

GRAMMAR BRIEFING 1: Simple Past and Past Progressive

The simple past is used to talk about actions and states that began and ended in the past. The past progressive (also called the past continuous) is used to talk about actions in progress in the past.

FORM Simple Past and Past Progressive

■ To form the simple past, use:

base form of verb + -ed.*

To form negatives and questions in the simple past, use:

did + base form of verb.

* See Appendix 5 for spelling rules for the -ed form of the verb. Some verbs have irregular forms in the simple past; see Appendix 7 for these irregular verbs. See Appendix 6 for pronunciation rules for the -ed form of the verb.

■ To form the past progressive, use:

the past of be + verb + -ing (present participle).*

* See Appendix 3 for spelling rules for verb + -ing.

Affirmative Statements

Simple Past	Past Progressive
I **played** every day.	I **was playing** then.
They **played** every day.	They **were playing** then.

Negative Statements

Simple Past	Past Progressive
He **did not (didn't) work** on weekends.	He **was not (wasn't) working** then.
You **did not (didn't) work** at night.	You **were not (weren't) working** then.

Yes/No Questions and Short Answers

Simple Past	Past Progressive
Q: **Did** she **work** every evening?	Q: **Was** she **working** that evening?
A: Yes, she **did.**	A: Yes, she **was.**
No, she **did not (didn't).**	No, she **was not (wasn't).**
Q: **Did** they **work** every evening?	Q: **Were** they **working** that evening?
A: Yes, they **did.**	A: Yes, they **were.**
No, they **did not (didn't).**	No, they **were not (weren't).**

Wh- Questions about the Predicate

Simple Past	Past Progressive
Where **did** Joan **work?**	When **was** Joan **working?**
How **did** we **work?**	How long **were** we **working?**

Wh- Questions about the Subject

Simple Past	Past Progressive
Who **worked** early?	Who **was working** with you?
What **happened?**	What **was happening** at that time?

FUNCTION Simple Past and Past Progressive

Simple Past

■ Use the simple past to talk about actions that began and ended in the past. The actions can be single actions, or they can be habitual or repeated actions. They can take place at a particular moment of time or over an extended period of time.

> She **left** her office at five o'clock. (moment of time, single action)
>
> They **milked** the cows every day. (repeated action)
>
> Those discoveries **took place** over many years. (extended time)

■ The simple past is used with verbs with stative meaning, to talk about states in the past. (See Grammar Briefing 2, page 32.)

> Galileo **was** a scientist. (state)

■ Time expressions used with the simple past include *yesterday, last Monday (week, year, etc.), a month (a year, a day, etc.) ago, in 1980 (January, the fall, etc.), on Monday (January 1, the weekend, etc.), at 8:00 A.M. (night, the end of the month, etc.)*.

■ Adverbs of frequency (*[almost] always, usually, often, sometimes, seldom, rarely, [almost] never*, etc.) are also used with the simple past. (See Appendix 4 for the position of adverbs of frequency in a sentence.)

Past Progressive

■ Use the past progressive to talk about actions in progress at a particular moment or over an extended period in the past. The past progressive emphasizes that the action was in progress.

> At nine o'clock last night, I **was studying** for a math test. (particular moment)
>
> During the early 1900s, when Einstein **was developing** his theory of relativity, he didn't use a laboratory. (extended period of time)

■ In contrast to the simple past, the past progressive doesn't specify whether the action was completed. The simple past emphasizes the completion of the action. Compare:

> She **was writing** a paper last night. (She might or might not have finished writing the paper.)
>
> She **wrote** a paper last night. (She finished writing the paper.)

■ Use the past progressive in narratives to provide background information. This information often sets the scene for the action that follows. The action that follows is in the simple past.

> The wind **was blowing** fiercely, and the rain **was beating** against the house. (background) Suddenly, the lights **went out.** (action)

- The past progressive is often used in time clauses with *when* and *while*. (See Grammar Briefing 2, page 32.)

    He **was doing** the dishes while she **was studying**.

- Time expressions used with the past progressive include *then, at that moment, at that time, during the fall (the past year, that period, etc.), last Monday (week, year).*

GRAMMAR PRACTICE 1: Simple Past and Past Progressive

Simple Past—Form: *Natural Time*

Long ago, before the Great Clock, time was measured by changes in the heavenly bodies: the slow sweep of stars across the night sky, the arc of the sun and variation in light, the waxing and waning of the moon, tides, seasons. Time was measured also by heartbeats, the rhythms of drowsiness and sleep, the recurrence of hunger . . . , the duration of loneliness.

                                                        Alan Lightman, *Einstein's Dreams*

Children in a modern "clock time" society have many questions about how people lived in the past. The following is a conversation between a child and her grandfather. Use the words in parentheses to complete the statements and questions in the simple past. Complete the short answers. Use contractions with *not*.

Child: Tell me about the old days, Grandpa. How ___did people live___ (people,
                                                                    1

live) a long time ago?

Grandfather: Life ___was___ (be) very different then.
                        2

Child: How _____ (people, spend) their time?
                    3

Grandfather: In those days, most people _____ (be) farmers. A
                                              4

farmer _____ (work) hard from early morning until night.
            5

Child: _____ (the farmers, have) alarm clocks?
            6

Grandfather: No, _____. They _____ (not, need) them. Their
                      7   8

life _____ (follow) nature's cycles of day and night.
        9

People _____ (wake up) at sunrise. They _____
              10   11

(not, stay up) late, because they _____ (not, have) electricity.
                                      12

Child: What _____ (the farmers, do) all year?
                  13

Grandfather: They _____ (take) care of their animals.
                              14

                They _____ (plant) their crops in the spring
                              15

                and _____ (harvest) them in the fall.
                              16

Child: _____ (you, be) alive in those days, Grandpa?
                17

Grandfather: No, _____. I _____ (grow up) in the industrial
                       18   19

                age, and I _____ (live) in a city.
                                   20

Child: How _____ (you, learn) about all this, Grandpa?
                    21

Grandfather: I _____ (learn) about it from *my* grandpa.
                       22

2 Simple Past—Irregular Verbs: *Clock Time*

A. Debbie's busy life is ruled by the clock. Yesterday her alarm clock rang at 5:45 A.M. and she raced through the day. Use the cues given to tell your version of what she did at each time listed below. Use the simple past.

begin working	have dinner with her sister
buy a newspaper	leave her office
drink a cup of instant coffee	make a phone call
drive to work	meet her boyfriend
eat some French fries and a cookie	put on her clothes and makeup
fall asleep	read some reports
feed the cat	see a movie with her boyfriend
feel tired	speak to her boss
get out of bed	take a shower
go out for tea with a coworker	write some letters

1. 5:55 A.M.: *She got out of bed at 5:55.*   11. 12:35 P.M.

2. 6:05   12. 1:00

3. 6:10   13. 2:00

4. 6:20   14. 3:45

5. 6:40   15. 5:00

6. 7:05   16. 6:00

7. 7:15   17. 8:15

8. 8:00   18. 8:20

9. 8:10   19. 10:30

10. 11:20   20. 11:00

B. Work with a partner. Compare your versions of Debbie's schedule by asking and answering *yes/no* and *wh-* questions.

> Example: Question: What time did Debbie get out of bed? Answer: She got out of bed at 5:55.
>
> Question: Did Debbie and her boyfriend see the movie at two o'clock? Answer: No, they didn't. They saw the movie at 8:20.

3 Past Progressive—Form: *Observing Mr. X*

A. Mr. Webster recently moved to Washington, D.C., and is just getting acquainted with his neighbor, Mr. Smiley. Use the words in parentheses to complete the statements and questions using the past progressive. Complete the short answers. Use contractions with *not*.

Q: It's nice to meet you, Mr. Smiley. What kind of work do you do?

A: Let's just say that I observe people from time to time. I work with other

observers. We report to the agency on our observations.

Q: Very interesting. What about last week? __Were you observing__ (you, observe)

1

anyone then?

A: Yes, __we were__ . We __were observing__ (observe) a man. The agency doesn't

2   3

allow us to mention names, so let's just call this man Mr. X.

Q: Aha! What _____ (Mr. X, do) last week?

4

A: Well, for example, last Monday at 11 A.M., Mr. X _____ (sleep). When

5

we checked at 4 P.M., though, he _____ (not, sleep) anymore.

6

Q: _____ (Mr. X, work) at 4:00?

7

A: No, _____ . But, he _____ (get) ready to start working.

8   9

He _____ (shave) off his beard. And by 6 P.M. he _____

10   11

(meet) with some other men.

Q: What _____ (they, talk) about?

12

A: I'm not sure. They _____ (speak) a foreign language.

13

They _____ (plan) something. Mr. X _____ (not, say) much.

14   15

Q: And at 8 P.M.? What _____ (this mystery man, do) then?

16

A: Mr. X _____ (eat) cereal and fruit.

17

Q: Cereal and fruit at dinner time? That's strange. And then?

A: Mr. X became very alert, and by midnight he ___was making___ (make) a lot of

    18

phone calls from a hotel room.

Q: Mr. Smiley, ___were you watching___ (you, watch) Mr. X last week because he

    19

___was acting___ (act) so suspiciously?

    20

A: No, _____. And, in fact, Mr. X ___was behaving___ (behave) in a com-

    21   22

pletely normal way, much as we thought he would.

Q: Phone calls at midnight aren't normal. Is Mr. X a spy? Are you a spy? Do you work

for the Central Intelligence Agency?

A: Not at all. I work for the U.S. aviation agency. Last week I ___was studying___

    23

(study) the effects of air travel across many time zones. Mr. X is a businessman

from Los Angeles. He flew to Austria Sunday night. While he ___was staying___

    24

(stay) there, he ___was experiencing___ (experience) jet lag. His body ___was living___

    25   26

(live) on Los Angeles time. That's normal!

B. While Mr. X was staying in Austria, he was thinking about home. What was happening in Los Angeles? What was his family doing? Write **three** sentences about what was happening at **each** time.

1. When it was 4 P.M. in Austria, it was 7 A.M. in Los Angeles.

    People were driving to work. OR *Mrs. X was fixing breakfast.*

2. When it was 1 A.M. in Austria, it was 4 P.M. in Los Angeles.

3. When it was 5 A.M. in Austria, it was 9 P.M. in Los Angeles.

4 Simple Past and Past Progressive in Narratives: *Setting the Scene and Telling the Story*

A. Write sentences in the past progressive to continue setting the scene for the action that follows.

1. My friends and I were having a party.

  1. ___People were laughing and singing.___

  2. ___People were dancing___

  3. ___drinking___

Suddenly, the music stopped. . . .

2. Henry was sitting at his desk.

1. _The clock was striking ___ the ___ ._____

2. _The ___ was ___ ___ _____

3. _The ___ was ___ _____

Then the door opened. . . .

B. Write sentences in the simple past to tell the actions in the story.

1. It was getting dark, and snow was beginning to fall. I was hurrying home.

1. _Then I heard footsteps behind me._____

2. _The ___ ___ ___ _____

3. _A strange ___ black ___ ___ me_____

2. Andrea was working in the art studio. She was painting and listening to the radio.

1. _The door ___ ___ ___ _____

2. _The light went out_____

3. _She fell ___ ___ ___ ___ ___ _____

C. Write a one-paragraph story of your own. Use the past progressive to set the scene and the simple past to tell the actions.

5 **Simple Past and Past Progressive—Meaning:** *Spring Forward*

The following statements were made by Nell. Read each statement and the sentence that follows it. If the sentence is true, mark it with a check mark (✓). If there isn't enough information to decide whether or not it is true, mark it with a question mark (?).

1. I **was explaining** something to a friend last week.

   Nell finished the explanation. ___?___

2. An event **happened** last April.

   The event ended in April. ___✓___

3. I **was teaching** English at the time it happened.

   Nell began teaching before that time. ___✓___

4. That Sunday, I didn't read the newspaper, watch television, or listen to the radio because I **was working** all day on grading papers and preparing for class.

   Nell finished her work on Sunday. ___?___

5. I **wrote** several letters that evening.

   Nell finished writing the letters. ___✓___

6. My students sometimes come a little late. But that Monday morning all of them **were sitting** in the classroom when I arrived.

   The students arrived before Nell did. ___✓___

7. They were tired of waiting and wanted to leave, so they **were writing** a note to me.

   The students finished the note. ___?___

8. They **explained** the reason. I felt really embarrassed about forgetting!

   They finished the explanation. ___✓___

Nell was late because she forgot something that starts on the first Sunday of every April in most of the United States. What is it?

GRAMMAR BRIEFING 2: Simple Past and Past Progressive in Time Clauses

The simple past and the past progressive are often used in time clauses to show the relationship between two or more actions or states.

FORM AND FUNCTION Simple Past and Past Progressive in Time Clauses

■ A clause is a group of related words that has a subject and a verb. A time clause begins with a time expression like *when, while, before,* or *after.* These expressions show the time relationship between the actions in the time clause and main clause of the sentence. The time clause can come before or after the main clause, with no difference in meaning. Use a comma between clauses when the time clause is first.

Time Clause	Main Clause		Main Clause	Time Clause
When he woke up,	he took a shower.	=	He took a shower	when he woke up.

do push up

Simple Past + Simple Past

■ Use two verbs in the simple past for two completed actions. Use *before, after, when,* or *while* in the time clause. These actions can occur one before the other or at the same time.

First Action	Second Action
When the alarm clock **rang,**	Charlie **woke up.**
After he **woke up,**	he quickly **took** a bath.
Charlie **fell** asleep	**before** he **got** to the dentist's office.

Second Action	First Action
Charlie **woke up**	**when** the alarm clock **rang.**
He quickly **took** a bath	**after** he **woke up.**
Before he **got** to the dentist's office,	Charlie **fell** asleep.

Same Time	Same Time
While Charlie **sat** in the chair,	the dentist **cleaned** his teeth.
He **felt** dizzy	**when** he **got** up.

Simple Past + Past Progressive

■ If an action began and ended while another action was in progress, use the past progressive for the action that was in progress and the simple past for the completed action. Either the past progressive or the simple past can be in the time clause. *When* can be used with the past progressive or the simple past. *While,* meaning "during a time," can only be used with the past progressive.

Action in Progress	Completed Action
While/When he **was working,**	Charlie **spilled** his coffee.
He **was working**	**when** he **spilled** his coffee.

Not: He was working ~~while~~ he spilled his coffee.

Past Progressive + Past Progressive

■ To talk about two actions that were in progress at the same time, use two past progressive verbs with *when* or *while.*

In Progress	In Progress
While/When she **was eating,**	she **was thinking** about her homework.

GRAMMAR PRACTICE 2: Simple Past and Past Progressive in Time Clauses

6   The Simple Past and Time Clauses: *Standard Time*

▄▄▄   Which event happened first? Listen once for the main ideas. Then listen again and check (✓) the correct answer.

Time Zones

Pacific Standard Time

Mountain Standard Time

Central Standard Time

Eastern Standard Time

● Boston

● Philadelphia

1. ☐ First, most people were farmers.

    ☐ First, it wasn't important for them to know the exact time.

    ☑ Both at the same time.

2. ☐ First, clock time became important.

    ☐ First, modern transportation and communications began to develop.

    ☐ Both at the same time.

3. ☐ First, the United States had standard time.

    ☐ First, each town or city had its own time.

    ☐ Both at the same time.

4. ☐ First, it was 7:00 A.M. in Philadelphia.

    ☐ First, it was 7:16 A.M. in Boston.

    ☐ Both at the same time.

5. ☐ First, the railroads spread throughout the country.

    ☐ First, the differences in times became a problem.

    ☐ Both at the same time.

6. ☐ First, the passengers traveled across the country

    ☐ First, they changed their watches.

    ☐ Both at the same time.

7. ☐ First, train schedules became confusing.

    ☐ First, railroad officials decided to set their clocks to a standard time.

    ☐ Both at the same time.

8. ☐ First, standard time started.

    ☐ First, officials divided the United States into four time zones.

    ☐ Both at the same time.

9. ☐ First, it was 7 A.M. in Philadelphia.

    ☐ First, it was 7 A.M. in Boston.

    ☐ Both at the same time.

7 The Simple Past and Past Progressive in Time Clauses; Combining Sentences: *Early Calendars*

Use the time expressions to combine the sentences into a sentence with **two** clauses. You must use the time word with the right clause. There are **two** ways to write each sentence. Use a comma when necessary.

1. Ancient peoples needed to be able to predict the seasons.
   Ancient peoples began to farm.
   + (after)

   After ancient peoples began to farm, they needed to be able to predict the seasons. OR *Ancient peoples needed to be able to predict the seasons after they began to farm.*

2. They learned to recognize the moon's patterns.
   They observed the moon's changes for a long time.   *Before (1) ,(2)*
   + (before)   *(2) before (1)*

3. They recorded the moon's cycles.   *while (2) ,(1)*
   They were observing the moon.
   + (while)   *(1) while (2)*

4. They made a calendar based on lunar months.
   They understood the cycles of the moon.
   + (after)

5. They were using the lunar calendar.
   They discovered that the lunar calendar didn't work well.   *They found a problem with the lunar calendar*
   + (when)
                                             (2) when (1)
6. A few years passed.   *when (1) ,(2)*
   The calendar and the seasons didn't match anymore.
   + (after) *(1), (2) / (2) ,after (1)*

7. The calendar became more accurate.
   They added days to the year.
   + (when) *(2), (1)   / (1) when (2)*

A lunar month averages 29½ days. A year equals 365¼ days. Approximately how many days did they need to add to 12 lunar months to make the calendar more accurate?

8 The Simple Past and Past Progressive in Time Clauses: *A Night Person's Bad Day*

A. Complete the statements with the simple past or past progressive form of the verbs in parentheses.

1. When Charlie's alarm clock ____rang____ (ring), he ____felt____ (feel) sleepy and confused.

2. After Charlie ____woke up____ (wake up), he ____remembered____ (remember) that he had an early appointment with the dentist.

3. Charlie ____dropped____ (drop) his watch into the tub while he ____was taking____ (take) his bath.

4. When Charlie ____rode____ (ride) the bus, he ____fell____ (fall) asleep

    and ____missed____ (miss) his stop.

5. While Charlie ____was running____ (run) back to the dentist's office,

    he ____tripped____ (trip) and ____hurt____ (hurt) his knee.

6. After the dentist ____ha____ (examine) Charlie's teeth,

    she _____ (tell) him that he had a cavity.

7. While Charlie ____was having____ lunch (drink) a cup of coffee, he ____spilled____ (spill) it on his new shirt.

8. Charlie finally ____started____ (start) to feel more alert before

    he ____left____ (leave) to go to work at the observatory.

9. After it ____got____ (get) dark, Charlie ____began____ (begin) to observe the stars.

10. When the clock _____ (strike) one, Charlie _____ (work) happily.

11. While he ____was looking____ (look) through the telescope, an

    idea ____hitted____ (hit) him: He was definitely a night person.

12. Before the sun ____came up____ (come up), Charlie ____made____ (make) a decision: He would always be an astronomer.

B. Think of times when things went wrong for you. Write **three** kinds of sentences about those times:

1. Write **two** sentences using *when, before,* or *after* and the simple past for two completed actions.

> Example: After I got to class, I realized that my homework was at home. OR
>
> I remembered the answer when the test was over.

[Handwritten: After I came into the room I regconised that I came to another one.

When I opened the book I found out that it was a wrong one.]

2. Write **two** sentences using *when* or *while* and the simple past and past progressive for an action that occurred when another action was in progress.

> Example: When I was traveling to the United States, the airline lost my
>
> luggage. OR I cut myself while I was shaving.

[Handwritten: When I locked the door, someone was sleeping inside.

While I was going down the stair I fell down.

When I wente home someone was trying to steal my TV.]

3. Write **two** sentences using *when* or *while* and the past progressive for two actions in progress at the same time. Then add sentences that tell what happened.

> Example: I was studying while I was eating lunch. I spilled my soup on my
>
> book. OR When I was driving to class, I was putting on my
>
> makeup. I almost had an accident.

[Handwritten: While I was sleeping the my brother was listening to music. Because the music was too loud so it woke me up.]

9   Simple Past, Past Progressive, and Time Clauses: *Legends of Discovery*

Use the words in parentheses to complete the statements in the simple past or the past progressive. In some cases, either tense may be possible.

1. Galileo Galilei ____was____ (be) an Italian scientist. He ____lived____

(live) from 1564 to 1642. Galileo ____made____ (make) one of his first discov-

eries while he ____was____ ____ing____ (attend) a service at the cathedral in Pisa.

During the service, he ____noticed____ (notice) a hanging lamp. Air

currents ____blew____ (blow) gently through the cathedral at the time, and the

lamp ____swung____ (swing) back and forth. While Galileo ____was watching____

(watch) the lamp, he ____realized____ (realize) that each swing took an equal

amount of time, no matter how wide it was. After he ____went____ (go)

home, he ____made____ (make) experiments, using weights and strings. In

this way, he ____discovered____ (discover) the principle of the pendulum (from a

Latin word meaning "hanging" or "swinging"). In 1656, a Dutch astronomer,

Christiaan Huygens, ____used____ (use) Galileo's discovery to build the first

pendulum clock.

2. Albert Einstein _____ (be) a physicist. He _____ (live) from
₁   ₂

1879 to 1955. During the early 1900s, Einstein _____ (develop) his
₃

theories about time and motion. When he _____ (experiment), he
₄

usually _____ (do) it by thinking. Once, while he _____
₅   ₆

(travel) on a train in Switzerland, he _____ (look) out the window at a
₇

clock. Then he _____ (let) his imagination carry out a new experi-
₈

ment with trains and clocks. While he _____ (imagine) a train travel-
₉

ing at the speed of light, he _____ (begin) to understand that time is
₁₀

not absolute—it is relative to different people moving at different speeds. The

movements of trains _____ (help) Einstein develop his general theory
₁₁

of relativity and other ideas about time, space, and motion.

GRAMMAR BRIEFING 3: *Used To*

Used to talks about actions and states that existed in the past but don't exist anymore.

FORM AND FUNCTION Used To

Form

■ Use *used to* + the base form of the verb in affirmative statements. In negative
statements and questions with *did*, use *use to*.

Affirmative Statements

We **used to believe** in the man in the moon.

Negative Statements

They **didn't use to have** clocks.   **Not:** They didn't ~~used to~~ have clocks.

Questions

Did you **use to play** every day?   **Not:** Did you ~~used to~~ play every day?
Where **did** you **use to play?**   **Not:** Where did you ~~used to~~ play?
Who **used to play** with you?

Function

■ Use *used to* to talk about actions and states that existed in the past but don't exist
anymore. In this way, *used to* emphasizes a contrast between the past and present.

People **used to use** the sun to tell time, but they don't anymore.

People **didn't use to have** digital watches, but now many do.

■ *Would* can sometimes be used instead of *used to* when repeated actions are involved. *Would* isn't used with states.

> When I was young, I **would go** swimming every chance I got.
>
> I **used to be** a good swimmer. **Not:** I ~~would be~~ a good swimmer.

GRAMMAR PRACTICE 3: *Used To*

10   *Used To—Form: Long, Long Ago*

a sundial

Rewrite the following sentences. Use *used to*.

1. People didn't know as much about the solar system and the universe as we do now.

   > People didn't use to know as much about the solar system and the universe as we do now.

2. What did people believe about the earth?

3. People believed the earth was the center of the universe.

4. They didn't know that the universe has no center.

5. How did people measure time?

6. People didn't have mechanical clocks or watches.

7. They used the natural motion of the sun to measure time with sundials.

8. The Greeks had water clocks for measuring time.

9. What other kinds of clocks did people use?

10. Some of them kept time with sand clocks, or hourglasses.

a water clock   an hourglass

11   *Used To and Would: When ~~I Was~~ a Child*

we were

A. Children often have mistaken ideas about the world and the things in it. Write **three** sentences about ideas you had as a child. Use *used to*.

> Example: I used to think that people in Australia were standing with their heads down and their feet up. OR I didn't use to understand what made the clock's hands move.

B. Write **three** pairs of sentences about things that you did in your childhood but don't do any longer. In each pair of sentences, use *used to* in the first sentence. Then use *would*, if possible, or *used to* in the next sentence.

> Example: I used to spend a lot of time with my grandmother in the summers. She would tell me about life in the old days.

When I was a child, I used to stay at home alone. My mother would tell me to go out.
When I was a child, I used to have a nap. My mother would examine whethe I slept or not.
                                              also
                                              few
when I was a child, I used to have a little friends.
When I was a child, I would read book all the time.

C. Some of your preferences and habits are probably different now than they were when you were a child. Write **three** sentences about the differences. Use *didn't use to* or *never used to.*

> Example: I *didn't use to drink coffee, but now I drink coffee every day.*

12   Used To; Wh- and Yes/No Questions: Did You Use To . . . ?

Work with a partner. Using the cues given, write three *yes/no* and three *wh-* questions to ask your partner about his or her past. Take turns asking and answering the questions.

drink	go	have	play	use	want
eat	hate	like	study	visit	wear

> Example: What *did you use to want to be?* OR *Did you use to want to be an astronomer?*

Now, tell the class one thing about your partner's past.

> Example: *Anna used to want to be a race car driver.*

UNIT WRAP-UP

Error Correction

Find and correct the errors in verb forms and tenses. Some errors can be corrected in more than one way. Including the example, there are **15** errors.

                        use
Astronomers didn't ~~used~~ to have powerful telescopes to look into space. ~~They~~

~~weren't able~~ to observe distant parts of the universe. Most scientists use^d to believe

that the universe was static. (In this case, the word "static" is meaning "not expand-

ing or contracting.") Then, in the 1920s an American astronomer, Edwin Hubble,

was h*[had]*aving the opportunity to use a big new telescope in California to observe

nearby galaxies. In 1929, he made a discovery that ~~changed scientists' ideas about~~

~~the universe.~~ The galaxies were mov*[moving]*eing away from each other. The universe were *[was]*

expanding. This meant that it i*[was]*s once very, very small. Hubble's discovery helped

cosmologists to develop the theory of the Big Bang.

     But in order to learn more about the beginning of the universe, scientists were

need*[need]*ing a telescope outside earth's atmosphere to provide a clear view of distant galaxies. After years of planning, a team of scientists and engineers at the National

sent

Aeronautics and Space Administration (NASA) ~~sended~~ a large telescope into space

named

in 1990. They ~~were naming~~ it the Hubble Space Telescope (HST) after Edwin

put

Hubble. After they ~~were putting~~ HST into orbit, they got an unpleasant surprise.

HST didn't work. Its mirrors didn't ~~focused~~ focus images correctly. Why was this? *while* They

were building HST, ~~while~~ they made an error ~~in its mirrors.~~ In 1993, astronauts

ed

correct the error. In simple terms, NASA corrected the telescope's vision by fitting it

with contact lenses. These days, HST ~~sending~~ clear, beautiful images to earth. So

now we are learning more about the expansion of the universe, the Big Bang, and

the beginning of time.

Task 1: What Was the Question?

The following are the answers that a student gave to questions asked in an interview.

A. Work with a partner. Write questions that fit the answers.

1. Q: ___How old are you?___   A: Twenty, almost twenty one.

2. Q: ___How many brother & sister do u have?___   A: One brother and two sisters.

3. Q: ___How " language can you speak?___   A: Two. My native language and English.

4. Q: ___What is your hobby___   A: Swim, play the guitar, and go to movies.

5. Q: ___Are u studying MBA?___   A: Yes, this semester I'm doing that.

6. Q: ___When did you start?___   A: Three years ago.

7. Q: ___What were you doing a year ago today?___   A: A year ago today, I was working and thinking about going back to school.

8. Q: ___Did you watch TV regularly?___   A: Yes, I used to, but not now.

B. Now work with a different partner. Use the questions you wrote in **A** to interview each other. Then report to the class. Tell the most interesting thing you learned about your partner.

Task 2: Origin Story

The Big Bang is the scientific account of the origin of the universe and the beginning of time. Read the beginning of an origin story from an Aboriginal people of Australia:

> In the beginning, the earth was an infinite cloudy plain. It was separated from both the sky and the sea and covered by shadowy twilight. Above the earth, there were no stars or sun or moon. On the surface of the earth, there were no plants or animals. But underneath the surface, the stars were twinkling, the sun was shining, and the moon was waxing and waning while all the forms of life were sleeping and waiting to come to life. Then, on the morning of the first day, the sun burst through the earth's surface and flooded the land with its light. . . .
>
> [Adapted from: Chatwin, Bruce. *The Songlines*. London: Jonathan Cape Ltd., 1987, p. 72]

Write a two-paragraph origin story. You can write a story that you know or make one up. Use the simple past and past progressive. Include at least two sentences with time clauses.

Task 3: Terratoo

A. Work in small groups. Imagine that you and your partners now live on Terratoo, an earth-like planet in a distant galaxy. Discuss what your imaginary planet is like and what is going on there. Decide on the answers to these questions about it:

1. Time: How long are the days, nights, seasons, and years? What other measures of time do you use?

2. The planet: How does it look? What is the weather like? What kinds of plants and animals live there?

3. Daily life: What kind of language do you speak? What kind of food do you eat? What do you like to do for fun?

4. Activities: What time is it on your part of the planet right now? What's happening? What are the people around you doing?

B. Describe your version of Terratoo to the class.

C. Now imagine that you must all go to live on one planet together. As a class, discuss the different versions of Terratoo and decide which version you want to live on.

Present and Past: Perfect and Perfect Progressive

Topic Focus—Time II: *The Pace of Life*

UNIT OBJECTIVES

■ **the present perfect and the present perfect progressive tenses**
(Millions of people *have* now *learned* to use computers. People *have been working* with them for years.)

■ **the present perfect tense versus the simple past tense**
(I *have been* to Egypt. I *went* there several years ago.)

■ **the past perfect and the past perfect progressive tenses**
(Before the industrial age, the pace of life *had*n't *changed* much. People *had been living* in the same way for many years.)

INTRODUCTORY TASKS

Reading and Listening

▪▪▪ Read and listen to the passage "The Pace of Life" on page 45. Then complete the Comprehension Check.

Comprehension Check

Read each sentence. Circle **T** if the sentence is true or **F** if the sentence is false.

1. The words *pace* and *speed* have similar meanings   (T)   F

2. People were living in the industrial age in the early 1900s.   T   F

3. The pace of life didn't begin to change until the information age began.   T   F

4. Computer use increased during the information revolution.   T   F

5. We are living in the information age now.   T   F

THE PACE OF LIFE

The pace, or speed, of life hasn't always been as fast as it is now.

In the last two hundred years, there **have been** revolutionary changes in technology. These changes led to the industrial age, which lasted from the early 1800s to the mid-1900s, and **have led** to the information age, which continues today. In the industrial age the pace of life became much faster, and that trend **has continued** in the information age.

The Industrial Revolution

Before the industrial revolution began in the early 1800s, people **had lived** according to the rhythms of nature. Generation after generation **had been living** as their parents **had lived**. People and information **had** never **moved** faster than the speed of a fast horse or sailing ship. The pace of life **had remained** much the same for thousands of years. But the introduction of industrial technology changed everything. By the late 1800s the speed of transportation and communications **had** greatly **increased**. And because the new technology **had made** it possible for people to do more in less time, the pace of life started to speed up, too.

The Information Revolution

Since the middle of the 1900s, **we have been experiencing** another revolution, the information revolution. Before the 1960s, very few people **had** ever **worked** with a computer. Since then, millions of people **have become** computer users. The information revolution **has given** us the ability to store, send, and receive huge amounts of information instantly. It **has** also **speeded up** the speed of change—lately, things **have been changing** faster than ever before. And it seems that time and life **have been moving** faster, too.

How **have** people **reacted** to the new technology and new speeds? Some people believe that the new technology **has brought** us many benefits and **made** our lives more convenient and exciting. Others believe that our lives **haven't improved** because the fast pace is unnatural and **has caused** us too much stress.

How **have** you **been feeling** about the pace of your life recently? **Has it been** too fast, just right, or too slow?

Think about Grammar

A. Read each pair of sentences. Some of the **boldfaced** verbs talk about actions or states that occurred before a time in the past. **Circle** these verbs. Some of the **boldfaced** verbs talk about actions or states that began in the past but continue to the present. **Underline** these verbs.

1. a. Since the information age began, people **have experienced** many changes.

   b. Before the industrial age began, people **had experienced** few changes.

2. a. By the late 1800s, the speed of communications **had gotten** much faster.

   b. Since the beginning of the information age, the speed of communications **has gotten** much faster.

3. a. In recent times, many people **have worked** with computers.

   b. Before the 1960s, only a few people **had worked** with computers.

4. a. The speed of technological change **has increased** since computers were introduced.

   b. The speed of technological change **had increased** by the 1990s.

5. a. Until the early 1800s, the pace of life **had stayed** slow.

   b. Lately, the pace of life **has stayed** fast.

B. Compare and discuss answers to **A** with a partner. The **circled** verbs are in the past perfect. The **underlined** verbs are in the present perfect. How are the past perfect and present perfect forms similar? How are they different?

Present Perfect and Present Perfect Progressive

chapter 3

Introductory Task: Quiz: *What Is Your Time Type?*

A. Answer the following questions with sentences with a verb in the present perfect. In each sentence, include the adverb of frequency that is most appropriate for you: *often, sometimes,* or *rarely.*

> Example: I have sometimes become irritated when I had to wait in line. OR I have rarely gotten annoyed when traffic was moving slowly.

1. How frequently have you become irritated when you had to wait in line?

   _____

2. How frequently have you gotten annoyed when traffic was moving slowly?

   _____

3. How frequently have you worried about being late for social events?

   _____

4. How frequently have you felt anxious when you didn't have anything to do?

   _____

5. How frequently have you wanted to make every moment of your life count?

   _____

6. How frequently have you wished that you could do more in the time that you have?

   _____

B. Work with a partner. Find out your partner's time type. Read your partner's answers and give **3** points for each answer with *often,* **2** points for each *sometimes,* and **1** point for each *rarely.* Then add up the points and look at Exercise page E-1 to learn what the score means.

C. Report to the class. What have you learned about your partner? Is your partner a "fast" or "slow" person?

GRAMMAR BRIEFING 1: Present Perfect and Present Perfect Progressive

The present perfect is used to talk about actions and states that occurred at an unspecified time in the past. Both the present perfect and the present perfect progressive (also called the present perfect continuous) are used to talk about actions that began in the past and continue to the present. Use of these tenses implies some connection to the present.

FORM Present Perfect and Present Perfect Progressive

■ To form the present perfect, use:

> simple present of *have* + past participle of verb.

For regular verbs, the past participle is the same as the simple past form.*

* See Appendix 7 for the past participles of irregular verbs.

■ To form the present perfect progressive, use:

> simple present of *have* + *been* (the past participle of *be*) + verb + *-ing* (present participle).*

* See Appendix 3 for spelling rules for the *-ing* form of the verb.

Affirmative Statements

Present Perfect	Present Perfect Progressive
I **have** (**I've**) **done** that.	I **have** (**I've**) **been doing** that.
She **has** (**She's**) **done** that.	She **has** (**She's**) **been doing** that.

Negative Statements

Present Perfect	Present Perfect Progressive
We **have not** (**haven't**) done that.	We **have not** (**haven't**) **been doing** that.
Bob **has not** (**hasn't**) **done** that.	Bob **has not** (**hasn't**) **been doing** that.

Yes/No Questions and Short Answers

Present Perfect	Present Perfect Progressive
Q: **Have** you **done** that?	Q: **Have** you **been doing** that?
A: Yes, I **have.**	A: Yes, I **have.**
No, I **have not** (**haven't**).	No, I **have not** (**haven't**).
Q: **Has** he **done** that?	Q: **Has** he **been doing** that?
A: Yes, he **has.**	A: Yes, he **has.**
No, he **has not** (**hasn't**).	No, he **has not** (**hasn't**).

Wh- Questions about the Predicate

Present Perfect	Present Perfect Progressive
What **have** they **done**?	What **have** they **been doing**?
Where **has** it **gone**?	Where **has** it **been going**?

Wh- Questions about the Subject

Present Perfect	Present Perfect Progressive
Who **has** (Who**'s**) **done** that?	Who **has** (Who**'s**) **been doing** that?
Which students **have done** that?	Which students **have been doing** that?

GRAMMAR HOTSPOT!

- Both *is* and *has* are contracted to *'s*. *'S = is* when it is followed by the present participle to form the present progressive. *'S = has* when it is followed by the past participle to form the present perfect or the present perfect progressive.

    She**'s climbing** Mt. Everest. (present progressive: *'s = is*)

    She**'s climbed** Mt. McKinley. (present perfect: *'s = has*)

    She**'s been climbing** mountains for a long time. (present perfect progressive: *'s = has*)

FUNCTION Present Perfect and Present Perfect Progressive

Present Perfect

- Use the present perfect to talk about actions and states that occurred at an unspecified time in the past. The actions can be single actions or repeated actions. The present perfect indicates that the past action or state is connected to the present in some way—for example, because it occurred recently, because the speaker thinks it could happen again, or because the past experience is relevant to the present situation.

    I**'ve** just **graduated** from college. (recent action)

    Have you ever **gone** to Europe? (speaker thinks it could still happen)

    I **have rewritten** that paper three times. (speaker thinks more rewriting is possible)

    I can do the job because I**'ve had** experience with those machines. (past experience is relevant to present situation)

- Time expressions used with the present perfect to indicate unspecified time in the past include *already, yet* (in questions and negatives), *so far, ever* (in questions and negatives), *never,* and *three times* (*many times,* etc.). Time expressions used to indicate unspecified time in the recent past include *just, recently,* and *lately.* (See Appendix 8 for more about time expressions and adverbs of frequency used with the present perfect.)

- Use the present perfect with *for, since,* or *all day* (*month, year,* etc.) to talk about actions and states that began in the past and continue to the present. These time expressions of duration tell how long the action or state has been occurring. *For* and *all* tell the length of time. (*For* can sometimes be omitted.) *Since* tells the beginning of the time period.

    I **have taught** (for) 10 years.

    She**'s liked** mountain climbing since she was a teenager.

    They**'ve lived** and **worked** here all their lives.

Present Perfect Progressive

■ Use the present perfect progressive alone or with *for, since,* or *all* to talk about actions that began in the past and continue to the present. The present perfect progressive often expresses a sense that the action is ongoing.

> The race car **has been circling** the track.
>
> I**'ve been snowboarding** for three years.
>
> We**'ve been singing** and **playing** in a band since 1996.
>
> Joe**'s been practicing** all month.

(See Appendix 8 for more about time expressions and adverbs of frequency used with the present perfect progressive.)

Present Perfect Progressive versus Present Perfect

■ There is generally a difference between the present perfect progressive and the present perfect: The present perfect progressive is used to talk about actions that are not yet completed; the present perfect is used to talk about actions that were completed at an unspecified time in the past.

> I**'ve been studying** chemistry. (I am still studying it.)
>
> I**'ve studied** chemistry. (I studied it at an unspecified time in the past.)

■ When a time expression of duration is used, there is often little or no meaning difference between the two tenses.

> It**'s been raining** all day. = It**'s rained** all day.
>
> I**'ve been living** here for 10 years. = I**'ve lived** here for 10 years.

• When the verb + object indicate progress toward a stated end result—for example, *write a novel, read a book, build a house*—only the present perfect progressive can be used with time expressions of duration. The present perfect cannot be used.

> She**'s been writing** a novel for five years. (end result = a written novel)
>
> **Not:** She's written a novel for five years.

■ Use the present perfect, not the present perfect progressive, when stating the number of times an action is repeated (*once, twice, five times,* etc.).

> I **have written** that paper many times.
>
> **Not:** I have been writing that paper many times.

■ Like other progressives, the present perfect progressive is not usually used with verbs with stative meaning. Use the present perfect instead.

> I **have known** him for many years.
>
> **Not:** I have been knowing him for many years.

> ### GRAMMAR PRACTICE 1: Present Perfect and Present Perfect Progressive

☐ Present Perfect—Form: *Panel Discussion on the Pace of Life*

At a recent conference in the United States, three participants presented their ideas in a discussion led by a moderator. Use the words in parentheses to complete the statements and questions in the present perfect. Complete the short answers. Use contractions with subject pronouns and with *not.*

Moderator: People used to live according to natural time, but they don't any-

more. What __has happened__ (happen) as a result?
                    1

__Have people lost__ (people, lose) their sense of natural time?
          2

Participant #1: Yes, __they have__. Natural time __hasn't changed__ (not,
                          3   4

change). However, people's ideas and feelings about

time _____ (change).
         5

Moderator: Why _____ (this, happen)?
                    6

Participant #2: Modern technology _____ (cause) many changes.
                                      7

Moderator: Time _____ (not, speed up), but it seems to go
                    8

faster. _____ (life, speed up)?
          9

Participant #3: Yes, _____. And some people _____ (not,
                        10   11

react) well to the fast pace of life. They _____ (feel) a lot
                                            12

of stress. The fast pace _____ (make) their lives too pres-
                          13

sured.

Participant #1: I agree. Lately, we Americans _____ (have) the feeling
                                                14

that we don't have enough time. Time _____ (become)
                                      15

more valuable to us than money.

Moderator: This is something that I _____ (think) about often.
                                      16

Americans _____ (always, want) new technology to help
              17

us save time. Now we have supersonic jets, microwave ovens, per-

sonal computers, electronic mail, and cell phones. _____
                                                    18

(we, save) time by using these?

Participant #2: No, _____. It's strange. It _____ (not, work out)
                        19   20

that way. In the end, the new technology _____ (take)
                                              21

more time than it _____ (give) us.
                      22

2   Present Perfect—Irregular Past Participles; Yes/No Questions: *The Right Experience?*

Your class has decided to go on a camping trip together in a mountain wilderness area. You need an experienced guide. Frank and Paul have applied for the job. Find out about their experience.

A. Work in pairs. Take turns. First, Student A uses the cues in Questions about Frank to ask *yes/no* questions. Student B uses the information about Frank on Exercise Page E–1 to give short answers. Then Student B asks *yes/no* questions using the cues in Questions about Paul. Student A uses the information about Paul on Exercise Page E–1 to give short answers. Use the present perfect and *ever* in the questions. Listen carefully to all answers.

Frank

Paul

Questions about Frank:

1. break his leg

> Student A: Has Frank ever broken his leg?
> Student B: Yes, he has.

2. draw a map

3. catch a fish

4. teach a rock-climbing class

5. feed a wild animal out of his hand

6. find his way in a snowstorm

7. drive a bus

8. run away from danger

9. see a mountain lion

10. lose his way

11. win a prize for physical fitness

12. fight a wild animal with his bare hands

Questions about Paul:

1. fall off a cliff

> Student B: Has Paul ever fallen off a cliff?
> Student A: No, he hasn't.

2. build a campfire

3. drink water from a rain puddle

4. ride a wild horse

5. eat an insect

6. sleep in a cave

7. forget to bring a compass

8. leave a camper behind

9. read many survival skills books

10. send a smoke signal for help

11. fly a helicopter

12. write an adventure story

B. Work in small groups. Do you prefer Frank or Paul to be the guide for your camping trip? Discuss their experience and decide who is better for your group. Then, as a class, compare your choices and decide whether Frank or Paul will guide you.

3   Present Perfect—*Wh-* Questions: *How Have You Used Your Time?*

A. Some researchers study how people use their time and how they feel about the pace of their lives. Imagine that a researcher has asked you to participate for a week in a study of how students use their time. Today is the fourth day of the week. The researcher has just given you a questionnaire about your activities so far this week. First, use the cues to write the questions. Then, add up the number of hours you have spent on each activity in the past four days and write the answers to the questions. Use the present perfect.

1. how many hours / sleep / so far this week

   How many hours have you slept so far this week?

   I have slept for _____ hours so far this week.
   [insert number]

2. how many hours / be in classes / so far this week

3. how many hours / study / so far this week

4. how many hours / work / so far this week

5. how many hours / do housework / so far this week

6. how many hours / watch television / so far this week

7. how many times / exercise or play sports / so far this week

8. how many movies / see / so far this week

9. what other activities / do / so far this week

B. Work with a partner. Use the cues and the present perfect of the verbs to ask each other questions about how you have used your time in the past four days and how you have felt about it.

1. which activities / take / the most time   Which activities have taken the most time ?

2. which activities / take/ the least time _____?

3. which activity / take / too much time _____?

4. which activity / you / not / have enough time for _____?

5. how / you /feel / about the pace of your life _____?

4 Present Perfect Progressive—Form; Using Present Perfect Progressive: *What Have People Been Doing?*

A. Use the words in parentheses to write statements and questions. Use the present perfect progressive except for verbs with stative meaning. Complete the short answers. Use contractions with subject pronouns and with *not*.

Lauren, who is from a small town, has been visiting the big city where her friend Shelly lives. They planned to meet in the park at noon. It's now 12:30.

Lauren: Hi, Shelly. You're out of breath. ___Have you been running___ ?
                                                      1. (you / run)

Shelly: Yes, __I have____. I'm sorry I'm late. _____?
                 2   3. (you / wait / long)

Lauren: No, _____. _____.
                  4   5. (I / wait / for only half an hour)

Shelly: _____?
          6. (what / you / do)

Lauren: _____. _____. _____.
          7. (I / watch / all the people)   8. (I / not / mind / waiting)   9. (it / be / interesting)

Shelly: Why? _____? _____?
               10. (what / the people / do)   11. (they / relax / in the park)

Lauren: No, _____. _____. Do you see that guy sitting on
                  12   13. (everyone / seem / very busy)

           the bench over there?

Shelly: The one with the laptop computer? _____?
                                             14. (he / work)

Lauren: Yes, _____. _____.
                  15   16. (he / eat / lunch / at the same time)

           _____. _____. Except for the traf-
           17. (that woman / make / calls on her cell phone)   18. (everything / move / fast)

           fic. _____. _____.
                19. (the traffic / not / move / at all)   20. (the drivers / honk / impatiently)

Shelly: _____. Let's go eat!
          21. (I / get / impatient for lunch)

B. Work with a partner. Role-play a situation like the one in **A.** Choose a place—for example, a park in a busy city or a café in a small town—and imagine that you have been waiting for your partner there. Describe what's been going on around you while you've been waiting. Use the present perfect progressive.

5 Present Perfect and Present Perfect Progressive—Meaning: *People, Places, and Paces I*

Work with a partner. Decide whether option **a** or **b** follows more logically from the first sentence. **Circle** the correct letter.

1. Bruce **has been working** on his report about economic influences on the pace of life.

    a. He finished a little while ago.

    (b.) He's still working.

2. The professor **has studied** the relationship between the pace of life in a city and the health of the people who live there.

   a. He finished the study at some point in the past.

   b. He's still studying.

3. Andy **has been learning** about the effect that climate has on the speed of life in a place.

   a. He is continuing to learn about this topic.

   b. He lost interest in this topic earlier.

4. Kathleen **has rushed** all day.

   a. She was really busy at some time earlier today, but not recently.

   b. She's still rushing.

5. We**'ve been adjusting** to the different pace here.

   a. We expect to adjust even more in the future.

   b. We don't expect that more adjustment will be necessary.

6. My brothers **have lived** in the city since they finished school.

   a. But they moved to the country a couple of months ago.

   b. But they're thinking of moving to the country in a couple of months.

7. I**'ve visited** my relatives in the country.

   a. I'm planning to go back to the city as soon as possible.

   b. It was relaxing, but I missed the excitement of the city.

8. I**'ve been wondering** why some people want a slower pace of life.

   a. Then I decided that was a difficult question.

   b. I still don't know why.

6 Present Perfect and Present Perfect Progressive—Use with Time Expressions: *The Information Age*

For each pair, decide whether the present perfect sentence and/or the present perfect progressive sentence can be completed with the time expression given. If the time expression cannot be used, do not complete the sentence.

1. Recently,

   a. <u>Recently,</u> technological speed has made the world seem too slow.

   b. <u>Recently,</u> technological speed has been making the world seem too slow.

2. since the 1950s

   a. Computer speeds have been increasing _____.

   b. Computer speeds have increased _____.

3. many times

   a. The speed of information processing has doubled _____.

   b. The speed of information processing has been doubling _____.

4. for the last three months

    a. The software developer has written a new program _____.

    b. The software developer has been writing a new program _____.

5. twice

    a. Their company has been buying faster computers _____ this year.

    b. Their company has bought faster computers _____ this year.

6. all night

    a. My computer is fast, but my brain isn't. I have been working _____.

    b. My computer is fast, but my brain isn't. I have worked _____.

7. for two years

    a. An engineer has designed a new computer chip _____.

    b. An engineer has been designing a new computer chip _____.

8. Lately,

    a. _____ technological improvements have affected our relationship with time.

    b. _____ technological improvements have been affecting our relationship with time.

7 Contractions with Present Progressive, Present Perfect, and Present Perfect Progressive: *Answering Questions*

Listen and complete the answer to each question. Use *is* or *has*. Then listen again to check your answers.

1. Lisa <u>has</u>.

2. The stress <u>is</u>.

3. Someone else _____.

4. I think her father _____.

5. His job _____.

6. I'm not sure, but something _____.

7. The computer _____.

8. Something _____.

9. Another person _____.

10. Her job _____.

11. I don't know, but something _____.

12. The boredom _____.

13. I think his mother _____.

14. Jason _____.

15. The printer _____.

16. Everything _____.

8   Present Perfect versus Present Perfect Progressive: *Living in the Past in the Present*

The Amish immigrated from Europe to North America in the 1700s. Since then, they have followed their religion and its traditions, and their way of life has changed very little. The following tells about an Amish couple, Jacob and Rebecca Fisher, at three times on a typical day. Use the words in parentheses to complete the sentences. Use the present perfect progressive where possible and the present perfect elsewhere. Use contractions with *not*.

10 A.M.: Jacob is working in a field on his farm. He

___has been working___ (work) since 8 A.M., but he ___hasn't finished___ (not, finish)
      1   2

plowing the field yet. This morning, he _____ (use) a team of mules to
                                             3

pull the plow. He also _____ (use) horses for farm work many times in the
                                  4

past. But because Amish farmers don't often use modern technology, Jacob

_____ (not, use) a tractor once. His twelve-year-old son, Amos, is with
   5

him in the field. He _____ (help) his father this morning. Since he was a
                    6

little boy, Amos _____ (help) his father many times. By doing this,
                   7

he _____ (learn) how to farm in the traditional way.
   8

Noon: Rebecca is working in the house. She _____ (sew) by hand all
                               9

morning. She _____ (make) a quilt for the past few weeks, and so far
            10

she _____ (finish) half of it. Each quilt takes hundreds of hours to make,
     11

and Rebecca _____ (make) several of them in her lifetime. For the past six
            12

months, Rebecca _____ (teach) her young daughter, Rachel, how to sew.
            13

Rachel _____ (not, make) a quilt yet, but she _____ (make)
    14   15

three dresses.

8 P.M.: The Fishers are returning home from a visit to friends. Jacob is driving them in

a buggy pulled by a horse. He _____ (drive) for half an hour. Jacob
                               16

_____ (ride) in a car several times in his life, but he _____ (not,
   17   18

drive) a car even once. He _____ (not, ever, want) to own a car. He
                              19

believes that cars and other forms of modern technology make it too easy for family

members to spend time away from one another. The Fishers _____
                                                              20

(always, prefer) to live their lives at a slow pace and keep their family close.

GRAMMAR BRIEFING 2: Present Perfect versus Simple Past

Both the present perfect and the simple past are used to talk about past time. The difference is in whether there is a connection to the present.

FUNCTION Present Perfect versus Simple Past

- The present perfect, unlike the simple past, expresses a connection to the present.

  > I **haven't seen** the Picasso exhibit. (implies connection to present—e.g., the exhibit is still there and I can go)

  > I **didn't see** the Picasso exhibit. (implies lack of present connection—e.g., the exhibit is finished and I can't go)

- If a past action or state continues to the present, use the present perfect, not the simple past.

  > I **have taught** for 10 years. (I still teach.)

  > I **taught** for 10 years. (I don't teach anymore.)

- If a past action or state cannot occur again, use the simple past, not the present perfect.

  > Marilyn Monroe **made** many movies. (She's dead—she can't make any more movies.)

  > Demi Moore **has made** many movies. (She can make more movies in the future.)

- If an action or state happened at a specified time, use the simple past. The present perfect can only be used to talk about actions and states that happened at unspecified times.

  > I **went** to France in 1989.

  > **Not:** I've gone to France in 1989.

  > When Jack moved here, he **got** a new job.

  > **Not:** When Jack moved here, he has gotten a new job.

- Often sentences with the present perfect and simple past are similar in meaning but the present perfect focuses on a connection to the present, while the simple past focuses on the completed action.

  > I've **enrolled** in English. (focus on connection to present, to the fact I'll be taking English)

  > I **enrolled** in English. (focus on the action of enrolling)

- The simple past can be used instead of the present perfect with many time expressions, including *just, already,* and *yet.*

  > **Did** you **eat** yet? = **Have** you **eaten** yet?

  > I already **ate**, but Carolyn **didn't**. = I've already **eaten**, but Carolyn **hasn't**.

GRAMMAR PRACTICE 2: Present Perfect versus Simple Past

9 Present Perfect—Meaning: *Keeping Time*

Think about the meanings of the present perfect. Decide which of the time expressions given can be used to complete the sentences. Write the correct letter or letters to complete each sentence.

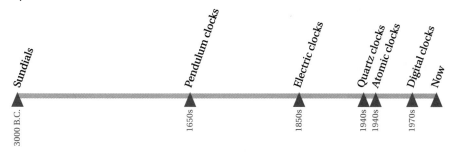

The Introduction of Time-Keeping Technology

1. The precise measurement of time is important to scientists, so they haven't used sundials to measure time _b, c_____

   a. in ancient times.
   b. since the invention of the pendulum clock.
   c. recently.

2. The pendulum clock has existed _____

   a. since Christiaan Huygens built the first one in 1656.
   b. in 1656.
   c. for a long time.

3. People have used electric clocks _____

   a. during the nineteenth century.
   b. in this century.
   c. last week.

4. Have people used quartz clocks _____

   a. before the 1930s?
   b. lately?
   c. at that time?

5. Scientists have used atomic clocks to measure time very accurately _____

   a. in recent decades.
   b. for several decades.
   c. since the late 1940s.

6. Digital clocks and watches have been popular _____

     a. when they were first introduced.

     b. since they were first introduced.

     c. recently.

7. Have you worn that digital watch _____

     a. yet?

     b. all day?

     c. yesterday?

▐▌ Present Perfect and Simple Past—Meaning: *People, Places, and Paces II*

Work with a partner. Decide whether option **a** or **b** follows more logically from the first sentence. **Circle** the correct letter.

1. Martha **lived** in the city for several years.

     ⓐ It was in the mid-1990s.

     b. She still lives there.

2. Susan **has lived** in the city for several years.

     a. It was in the mid-1990s.

     b. She still lives there.

3. Oliver **took** a course in time management.

     a. He went to class three days a week last semester.

     b. The course isn't over yet.

4. Melanie **has taken** a course in time management.

     a. The course isn't over yet.

     b. Now she can manage her time effectively and reduce stress in her life.

5. Mr. Fields **has had** a lot of stress in his life.

     a. He's still alive.

     b. He isn't alive anymore.

6. Mr. Antonelli **had** a lot of stress in his life.

     a. He's still alive.

     b. He isn't alive anymore.

7. Social scientists **have observed** the pace of life in cities and in smaller places.

     a. As a result of their observations, they know that the pace is faster in cities than in small towns.

     b. Their observations took place between 1992 and 1995.

8. Social scientists **observed** the pace of life in cities all over the world.

     a. Their observations are continuing now.

     b. Their observations took place in the early 1990s.

▮▮ **Present Perfect versus Simple Past: *Time Lines***

Use the words in parentheses and the information from the time lines to complete the
sentences. Use the present perfect or simple past.

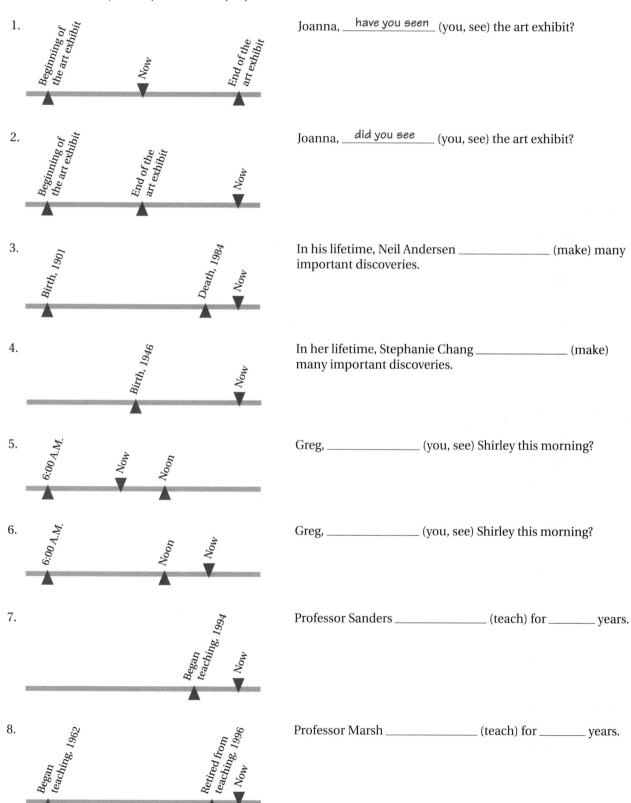

1. Joanna, ___have you seen___ (you, see) the art exhibit?

2. Joanna, ___did you see___ (you, see) the art exhibit?

3. In his lifetime, Neil Andersen _____ (make) many
    important discoveries.

4. In her lifetime, Stephanie Chang _____ (make)
    many important discoveries.

5. Greg, _____ (you, see) Shirley this morning?

6. Greg, _____ (you, see) Shirley this morning?

7. Professor Sanders _____ (teach) for _____ years.

8. Professor Marsh _____ (teach) for _____ years.

12   Present Perfect versus Simple Past: *Have You Ever...?*

Use the words in parentheses to complete the statements and questions. Use the present perfect where possible and use the simple past elsewhere. Use contractions with subject pronouns and with *not*.

Tyler: ___Have you ever been___ (you, ever, be) to a Shakespeare play?
         1

Annie: Yes, ___I have___. I ___'ve seen___ (see) several plays by Shakespeare.
              2   3

Tyler: How many plays ___did he write___ (he, write)?
                         4

Annie: I don't know exactly how many, but he _____ (write) a lot of them.
                                                      5

Tyler: _____ (you, ever, see) *Romeo and Juliet?*
         6

Annie: I _____ (not, see) the play yet, but I _____ (see) the
           7   8

movie.

Tyler: When _____ (you, see) the movie?
              9

Annie: I _____ (see) it for the first time in 1996. Actually,
          10

I _____ (watch) it on video several times since then, too.
  11

Leonardo Di Caprio _____ (play) the part of Romeo in the movie.
                   12

I _____ (be) in love with him since I first saw it.
  13

Tyler: _____ (Leonardo Di Caprio, make) many movies?
         14

Annie: He _____ (not, make) enough for me. I hope he makes another
            15

one soon!

13   Present Perfect and Simple Past: *Telling about Your Experiences*

A. Write **five** pairs of sentences about exciting, interesting, or unusual experiences you have had. Use the present perfect in the first sentence of each pair. Use the simple past in the second sentence to tell when the experience happened.

> Example: I have seen a comet. I saw the comet Hale-Bopp in 1997. OR I have been to New York City once. I went there when I was sixteen years old.

B. Write **four** sentences about exciting, interesting, or unusual experiences that you haven't had yet. Use the present perfect + *never*.

> Example: I've never traveled to Japan.

C. Work in small groups. Read your sentences to the group. Have the students in the group had very similar or very different experiences?

Past Perfect and Past Perfect Progressive

Introductory Task: *New Experiences*

A. Sam left his country to come to the United States last year. Since then, he has had many new experiences. For each of his new experiences, write a follow-up sentence in the past perfect (*had* + past participle of the verb). Use *never* and *before*.

1. Last year, Sam was away from his family.

   He had never been away from his family before.

2. In August, he flew in an airplane.

   He had never flown in an airplane before.

3. In September, he drank cranberry juice. _____

4. In December, he saw snow. _____

5. Last winter, he wore a heavy coat. _____

6. In February, he went skiing. _____

7. In March, he ate granola. _____

8. In May, he rode a horse. _____

B. Now write sentences about three new experiences you have had. Follow the pattern in **A.**

   Example: *Last year, I tasted caviar. I had never tasted caviar before.*

1. _____

2. _____

3. _____

Report to the class about your most interesting new experience.

GRAMMAR BRIEFING 1: Past Perfect and Past Perfect Progressive

The past perfect is used to talk about actions and states that occurred before other past actions or states. The past perfect progressive (also called the past perfect continuous) is used to talk about actions that began before and continued to or through other past actions.

FORM Past Perfect and Past Perfect Progressive

■ To form the past perfect, use:

> simple past of *have* + past participle of verb.*

* See Appendix 7 for the past participle forms of irregular verbs.

■ To form the past perfect progressive, use:

> simple past of *have* + *been* (the past participle of *be*) + verb + *-ing* (present participle).*

* See Appendix 3 for spelling rules for the *-ing* form of the verb.

Affirmative Statements

Past Perfect	Past Perfect Progressive
I **had** (**I'd**) **done** that before she arrived.	I **had** (**I'd**) **been doing** that before she arrived.

Negative Statements

Past Perfect	Past Perfect Progressive
You **had not** (**hadn't**) **done** that yet.	You **had not** (**hadn't**) **been doing** that yet.

Yes/No Questions and Short Answers

Past Perfect	Past Perfect Progressive
Q: **Had** they **done** that before she arrived?	Q: **Had** they **been doing** that before she arrived?
A: Yes, they **had.**	A: Yes, they **had.**
No, they **had not** (**hadn't**).	No, they **had not** (**hadn't**).

Wh- Questions about the Predicate

Past Perfect	Past Perfect Progressive
What **had** Joe **done** before she arrived?	What **had** Joe **been doing** before she arrived?

Wh- Questions about the Subject

Past Perfect	Past Perfect Progressive
Who **had done** that?	Who **had been doing** that?
Which students **had done** that?	Which students **had been doing** that?

FUNCTION Past Perfect and Past Perfect Progressive

Past Perfect

■ Use the past perfect to talk about actions or states that occurred before another past action, state, or time. The second time can be expressed in a past time expression. The second action or state can be expressed in a time clause with a verb in the simple past. (For more on sentences with time clauses, see Grammar Briefing 2, Chapter 2, page 32.)

> They **had started** down the mountain when the snowstorm **began.**
>
> Before they **were** halfway down, the snow **had covered** the trail.
>
> By 3:00, the weather **had cleared.**

■ When the time clause begins with *before* or *until*, the verb in the **main** clause is in the past perfect. When the time clause begins with *after,* the verb in the **time** clause is in the past perfect.

> She **hadn't realized** the importance of studying **until** she **failed** her exams.
>
> **After** he **had lived** and **studied** abroad, he **learned** more about himself.

■ With *before, after,* and *until*, the simple past is often used in place of the past perfect. The past perfect isn't needed because these time expressions make the order of the actions clear.

> He **studied** the language **before** he **left.** = He **had studied** the language **before** he **left.**

■ With *when,* the past perfect is often necessary to indicate the order of the actions.

> He **ate when** we **got** there. (First, we got there.)
>
> He **had eaten when** we **got** there. (First, he ate.)

■ The first and second actions or states don't have to be expressed in the same sentence.

> Ted **felt** afraid as he looked down the mountain. He **had never skied** before.
>
> He **didn't recognize** her. She **had changed.**

■ Use the past perfect with *for, since,* or *all day* (*year,* etc.) to talk about actions or states that began in the past and continue to another past action, state, or time.

> I**'d lived** in Peru for six months before she **arrived.**

■ Time expressions that are often used with the past perfect include *by then* (*three o'clock, the next day,* etc.), *already, just, yet* (in questions and negatives), *ever* (in questions and negatives), *never, still,* and *three times* (*many times,* etc.). (See Appendix 8 for more about time expressions and adverbs of frequency used with the past perfect.)

Past Perfect Progressive

■ Use the past perfect progressive to talk about actions that began before and continued to other actions, states, or times in the past. The second action or state is expressed with a verb in the simple past. As with the past perfect, sentences with a verb in the past perfect progressive often include a time clause and a main clause.

> Sleeping Beauty **had been spinning** thread **before** she **fell** asleep.
>
> She **had been sleeping** for 100 years **when** the prince **arrived.**

■ The past perfect progressive expresses a sense that the action was ongoing, and is often used with *for, since,* or *all day* (*night,* etc.).

> People **had been telling** the story and **waiting** for the prince **for** many years.

(See Appendix 8 for more about time expressions and adverbs of frequency used with the past perfect progressive.)

Past Perfect Progressive versus Past Perfect

■ The past perfect progressive is used to talk about actions that were in progress up to another past action or time. The past perfect is used to talk about actions that were completed at an unspecified time before another past action or time.

> He**'d been doing** his homework when they **arrived.** (in progress up to or before arrival)
>
> He**'d done** his homework when they **arrived.** (completed at an unspecified time before arrival)

■ When *for, since,* or *all* is used, there is often little or no meaning difference between the past perfect progressive and the past perfect. (However, with the past perfect progressive there may be emphasis on the duration of the action.)

> By then, I**'d been living** in Peru for five years. = By then, I**'d lived** in Peru for five years.

■ Like the present perfect progressive, the past perfect progressive is not used when stating the number of times an action is repeated. Only the past perfect is used.

> Patricia **had visited** Asia three times before she went to Europe.
>
> **Not:** Patricia ~~had been visiting~~ Asia three times before she went to Europe.

■ Like other progressives, the past perfect progressive is not usually used with verbs with stative meaning. Use the past perfect instead.

> He **had had** that job for many years before he retired.
>
> **Not:** He ~~had been having~~ that job for many years before he retired.

GRAMMAR HOTSPOT!

■ The past perfect is used when an action or state occurred before another action, state, or time in the past. When there is no second action, state, or time, the past perfect is not used.

> I **had given** him the key before he **left.**
>
> I **had given** him the key by then.
>
> Last night I **gave** him the key. **Not:** Last night I ~~had given~~ him the key.

GRAMMAR PRACTICE 1: Past Perfect and Past Perfect Progressive

1 Past Perfect—Form: *An Exchange Student—A Different Place*

Use the words in parentheses to complete the statements and questions in the past perfect. Complete the short answer. Use contractions with subject pronouns and with *not*.

Jim: Hey, Dan. I heard that you spent last year as an exchange student. Tell me

about your experiences. <u>Had you studied</u> (you, study) the language

                                               1

before you left?

Dan: Yes, <u>I had</u> . I <u>'d learned / learnt</u> (learn) it pretty well. And every-

            2   3

one in our group _____ (read) a lot of books about our host coun-

                              4

try. But the books _____ (not, prepare) us for everything. Most of

                             5

us _____ (not, live) in any country with a really different culture

             6

before. We experienced some differences there that we _____ (not,

                                       7

be) aware of before we left the United States.

Jim: What do you mean?

Dan: Well, until I went away, I _____ (not, understand) the importance

                                    8

of cultural differences in how people think about time. I guess

I _____ (always, think) that everyone else had the same ideas about

          9

time that I had. When I was there, I realized that I _____ (bring) my

                                      10

own culture's time sense with me. By the time I left, I _____ (have)

                                       11

lots of experiences that taught me a different way of thinking about time. For

example, one night I was really worried about being late.

Jim: Why were you worried? What _____ (happen)?

                            12

Dan: Another American and I _____ (meet) some students earlier that

                                 13

day, and they _____ (invite) us to a party at eight o'clock. The two

                        14

of us _____ (got) lost on the way to the party, and when we got

             15

there it was almost nine.

Jim: _____ (the other guests, already, arrive) by then?
                    16

Dan: No, _____. The host _____ (not, finish) getting ready for
                          17   18

the party yet. He was really surprised that we _____ (come) so
                                                                      19

early. By the end of the year, he _____ (teach) me a lot about his
                                                          20

culture's time customs. And now that I'm back, I'm experiencing culture shock

here. I'm always late!

2 Past Perfect and Simple Past: *"Rip Van Winkle"—A Different Time*

A. "Rip Van Winkle" is a well-known American story set in the late 1700s. While Rip
Van Winkle was out hunting one day, he drank a strange liquor and fell asleep. When
he woke up, he thought that he had slept for one night. But when he looked around,
he discovered that things had changed. Use the words in parentheses to complete
the sentences in the simple past and past perfect. Use contractions with *not.*

1. Rip's gun __*had gotten*__ (get) old and rusty, so it __*didn't work*__ (not, work)
   anymore.

2. His faithful dog _____ (be) no longer beside him. It _____
   (run away).

3. He _____ (look) at his beard. It _____ (grow) long and gray.

4. The clothes worn by the people in his village _____ (seem) strange to

   him because their fashions _____ (change).

5. He _____ (be) surprised at the terrible
   condition of his house.

   It _____ (fall apart).

6. His children _____ (grow up), so

   he _____ (not, recognize) them.

7. His daughter _____ (have) a new

   name because she _____ (get) married.

8. She _____ (have) a child in her

   arms. Rip _____ (become) a grandfather.

9. His wife _____ (not, be) there any longer.

   She _____ (die).

10. His friends and neighbors _____ (forget)

    him, so they _____ (think) he was a stranger.

11. The United States _____ (win) its independence. It _____ (be) no longer a British colony.

12. Finally, Rip _____ (discover) that he _____ (be) asleep for 20 years.

B. Write a one-paragraph story about the experiences of someone like Rip who awoke after sleeping for a long time. You can write a story that you know or make one up. Use past perfect and simple past.

3   Past Perfect and Simple Past—Combining Sentences: *A New Experience*

For each pair of sentences, decide the order of events. Then combine the two sentences into one sentence using the time word in parentheses, the simple past, and the past perfect. The order of events determines which verb is past perfect. There are **two** ways to write each sentence. Use a comma when the time clause comes first.

1. after: Sandra decided to study abroad. ____1____

   She applied to the university. ____2____

   After Sandra had decided to study abroad, she applied to the university.
   OR Sandra applied to the university after she had decided to study abroad.

2. after: She got her visa. _____

   She waited in line a long time. _____

3. before: She didn't fly in an airplane. _____

   She traveled to her host country. _____

4. until: She didn't experience another culture. _____

   She went to her host country. _____

5. before: She made a few embarrassing mistakes. _____

   She adapted to the customs of the new culture. _____

6. after: She studied hard and practiced often. _____

   She learned the language well. _____

7. when: She was in the country for a while. _____

   She became more flexible. _____

8. after: She understood her own culture much better. _____

   She stayed in her host country for a few months. _____

4 Past Perfect and Simple Past—Order of Actions: *Place and Time*

A. Listen to the sentences once for the main ideas. Then listen again and **circle** the letter of the state or action that occurred first.

1. (a.) Robert Levine taught at a university in the United States.

   b. He went to Brazil to teach as a visiting professor.

2. a. Professor Levine went to Brazil.

   b. He was aware of differences in time customs between the North American and Brazilian cultures.

3. a. The professor didn't realize that the cultural differences were so confusing.

   b. He arrived at the Brazilian university.

4. a. Many of the students came to class.

   b. He began to lecture at 10 A.M.

5. a. Professor Levine's students got ready to leave.

   b. The class ended.

6. a. Quite a few of the students asked questions and listened to him.

   b. The class ended.

7. a. Professor Levine was in Brazil for a while.

   b. He became interested in studying cultural differences in people's sense of time and in the pace of life.

8. a. He began to study differences in the pace of life.

   b. He compared North American and Brazilian ideas about what it means to be on time or to be late.

9. a. Professor Levine thought a lot about how to measure the pace of life.

   b. He and his students began making observations in cities all over the world.

10. a. They measured the walking and working speeds of people in many cities.

    b. Professor Levine analyzed the differences.

11. a. He evaluated the data.

    b. He found that there were differences in the pace of life on every level.

B. In his book *A Geography of Time,* Professor Levine has described cultural differences in the pace of life and in the way that people think about time. We often don't realize that people in another culture might not think about time in the same way that we do. Have you ever been confused by a different culture's sense of time? What happened? What had you thought before? What hadn't you realized until you had the experience? What did you learn about yourself and your own culture? Write a paragraph. Use the past perfect three or more times.

5 Past Perfect versus Simple Past: *Speed*

Use the words in parentheses to complete the sentences. Use the simple past or the past perfect. In cases where both tenses are possible, use the past perfect. Use contractions with *not*.

When Rip Van Winkle __woke up___ (wake up) around the year 1800, he
                           1

__discovered__ (discover) that he __had been__ (be) asleep for 20 years. After
      2   3

Rip _____ (return) to his village, he _____ (notice) personal
        4   5

and political changes, but he probably _____ (not, notice) any technolog-
                                              6

ical changes. Not much technological change _____ (happen) yet. In the
                                                   7

time of Rip Van Winkle, nothing _____ (move) faster than the speed of a
                                      8

sailing ship or a horse. The speed of transportation and communication

_____ (not, increase) very much since ancient times.
      9

In 1801, Thomas Jefferson _____ (be) president of the United States.
                                 10

The industrial revolution _____ (already, begin) in England by that time,
                                11

but it _____ (not, spread) to the United States yet.
          12

Sixty years later, in 1861, Abraham Lincoln _____ (be) president.
                                                   13

What _____ (happen) to the speed of transportation by then?
        14

It _____ (increase) by 20 times or more. The main reason
     15

_____ (be) that steamboats and trains _____ (begin) operating
      16   17

in many parts of the country. As a result, Americans of the 1860s _____
                                                                        18

(travel) rapidly to distant places.

How much faster _____ (communications, become) by Lincoln's
                       19

time? In 1801, it _____ (take) six weeks for a message from St. Louis to
                     20

reach Washington, D.C. However, by the 1850s, the telegraph, then a recent inven-

tion, _____ (become) an important means of communication. So, in the
         21

1860s, a message from St. Louis _____ (reach) Washington in a few sec-
                                      22

onds. This _____ (be) an even greater change, of course, than the change
              23

in the speed of transportation.

6 Simple Past and Past Perfect: *Milestones*

Childhood is often measured by important accomplishments or "milestones," such as learning how to read or to tell time. Think about ages by which you had or hadn't reached various milestones. Mark some of them on the time line below. Then write a paragraph about them. Use the simple past and the past perfect.

> Example: When I was a child, I learned quickly. I started first grade when I was six. Before I started first grade, I had already learned to read, but I had-n't learned how to write yet. When I was eight years old, I began playing soc-cer. By the time I was 10, I had become a very good soccer player . . .

Read your paragraph to the class.

7 Past Perfect Progressive—Form: *Once Upon a Time: Sleeping Beauty*

Use the words in parentheses to complete the statements and questions in the past perfect progressive. Complete the short answers. Use contractions with subject pronouns and with *not*.

Tina: Kate, do you remember the fairy tale about

Sleeping Beauty? I remember that an evil fairy

put a curse on the princess after she was born,

but I can't remember all of it. What

_____had been happening_____ (happen) before she
                1

fell asleep?

Kate: Sleeping Beauty _____had been growing up_____ (grow
                                       2

up) in her family's big castle. She

_____hadn't been worrying_____ (not, worry) about the
                3

curse. Just before she fell asleep, she had

found a tiny room in a tower in the castle where an

old woman _____ (spin) thread. Sleeping Beauty pricked her
              4

finger on the spindle, and the curse came true. She fell asleep in the tower.

Tina: Why _____ (her parents, not, protect) her from danger?
   5

   What _____ (they, do)?
   6

Kate: The king and queen _____ (visit) another kingdom, I think. They
   7

   had just returned.

Tina: _____ (the servants, watch) the princess?
   8

Kate: No, _____. They _____ (work). They _____
   9   10   11

   (not, pay) attention to Sleeping Beauty.

Tina: I want more details. What else _____ (go on) before they all fell
   12

   asleep?

Kate: The usual things, Tina. The dogs _____ (bark), the chickens
   13

   _____ (lay) eggs, and the flies _____ (crawl) on the wall.
   14   15

   Then Sleeping Beauty and everyone in the castle fell asleep.

Tina: Now I remember. A lot of time passed before the curse ended. Handsome

   princes _____ (come) to the castle walls, but none of them had
   16

   been able to get inside. Finally, after a hundred years, a brave and charming

   prince rode into the castle and found Sleeping Beauty. He kissed her, and she

   woke up.

A few days later:

Kate: What _____ (you, think) about before you asked me to help you
   17

   remember the story of Sleeping Beauty? _____ (you, dream) about
                                              18

   marrying a prince?

Tina: No, _____. Just before I asked you about the story,
   19

   I _____ (spend) too much time working and studying.
   20

   I _____ (feel) stressed, and I _____ (not, get) enough
   21   22

   sleep.

Kate: Now I understand. You _____ (imagine) stopping the frantic pace
   23

   of your life. You wanted to remember the story so that you could fantasize

   about falling into an enchanted sleep.

8 Past Perfect and Past Perfect Progressive—Meaning: *At the Stroke of Midnight*

Decide whether the past perfect or the past perfect progressive can be used in the following sentences. In some cases, only one is possible. In other cases, both are possible.

1. Cinderella's cruel stepmother came home. She saw Cinderella on her hands and knees on the floor. Half of the floor was clean and wet. When her stepmother came home,

   Cinderella _____ *b* _____ the floor.

   a. had scrubbed   b. had been scrubbing

2. Cinderella was very unhappy because her

   stepsisters _____ *a, b* _____ her unkindly for months.

   a. had treated   b. had been treating

3. Cinderella's fairy godmother appeared and looked
   closely at her. She saw tears in Cinderella's eyes.

   Cinderella _____.

   a. had cried   b. had been crying

4. The fairy godmother gave Cinderella a beautiful dress so that she could go to the

   prince's ball. When the clock struck midnight, Cinderella _____ for hours.

   a. had danced   b. had been dancing

5. Cinderella was shocked when the clock struck midnight. Long before,

   she _____ the time.

   a. had forgotten about   b. had been forgetting about

6. Cinderella rushed home, but then she realized that she had only one shoe.

   She _____ the other one.

   a. had lost   b. had been losing

7. Finally, the prince found Cinderella. He _____ her since he met her at the ball.

   a. had looked for   b. had been looking for

8. After they were married, Cinderella lived in the castle. On his birthday, the prince went into the kitchen. He saw Cinderella stirring flour, butter, sugar, and

   eggs. When the prince went into the kitchen, Cinderella _____ a cake for him.

   a. had made   b. had been making

9. Cinderella looked into the prince's library. He was holding a pen and looking thoughtfully at a piece of paper with a few words on it. When Cinderella looked

   into the library, the prince _____ a poem for her.

   a. had written   b. had been writing

10. The fairy godmother went to visit Cinderella and the prince last week. They

    thanked her and told her that they _____ very happily since their marriage.

    a. had lived   b. had been living

UNIT WRAP-UP

Error Correction

Find and correct the errors in verb forms and tenses. Some errors can be corrected in more than one way. Including the example, there are **13** errors.

Time for Life

For many years, John Robinson ~~had~~ **has** been interested in how people use their

time. He is now the director of the Americans' Use of Time Project. Robinson has

first asked Americans to take part in a use-of-time survey in 1965. He has been

repeating the surveys three times since then. Robinson has used the results of each

survey to answer two questions: How has Americans been spending their time

recently? How they've been feeling about it?

Ten thousand Americans had taken part in the 1995 use-of-time survey. In 1995,

the study participants have wrote down their activities in a "time diary" every day. In

addition, they reported on their feelings about their amount of free time.

After the participants had completed the 1995 survey, Robinson had analyzed

the results and compared them to previous survey results. He found some interest-

ing changes in people's use of time. Americans actually spent less time working in

1995 than they did in 1985. By 1995, they have gotten more free time. However,

many people believed that they had less time and felt more rushed and stressed. In

1997, Robinson has published a book, *Time for Life*, about the results of his surveys.

Why does it seem that we Americans have so little time for life nowadays?

According to Robinson, there are two reasons for this. First, since 1965, we spend

more and more of our free time watching television. Most of us usually say that tele-

vision is unnecessary or a waste of time. But in recent years we had spent more time

on it than any other free time activity. Second, since Robinson did his first survey,

we have been having many more opportunities and choices. We have been feeling

more rushed because we want to do everything.

Task 1: A Question Challenge

Work together in teams of two. Write questions for each of the answers below. The
questions must be logical and grammatically correct. Each team must write at least
three questions for each answer. The winning team is the one that writes the most correct questions within the time limit set by your teacher.

1. They've made new friends.

    What have the students done since the beginning of the semester?
    Why haven't Christina and Patrick been coming to our parties?
    Why are the visitors so happy?

2. Since I was a child.

3. Yes, they have many times.

4. For a very short time.

5. I've been setting my alarm clock.

6. Yes, she has been, but she hasn't been enjoying it.

7. We'd gotten lost.

8. Everything had speeded up.

9. Yes, he already had.

10. She'd been falling asleep.

11. No, when we arrived, they'd already finished.

Task 2: Things Have Changed Since I Was a Child

Things change very fast nowadays in almost every area. In your lifetime there have been many changes in areas such as science, technology, communications, transportation, business, politics, art, movies, music, fashion, and sports.

A. Work in small groups. Choose three areas that members of the group are interested in. For each one, think of changes that have happened in your lifetimes.

> Example, in communications: Most people hadn't used the Internet before the 1990s. The Internet has gotten much bigger and more important.

Be sure to talk about changes that have been happening recently.

> Example: People have been finding new ways to use the Internet.

Make a list of changes—past and ongoing—in each area that you discuss.

B. Work on your own. Choose an area that your group discussed. Write two paragraphs. In the first paragraph, describe changes that have happened in that area since you were younger. In the second paragraph, describe changes that have been happening recently. Be sure to include the past perfect, past perfect progressive, present perfect, and present perfect progressive.

Task 3: Your Psychological Clock

> When you sit with a nice girl for two hours, it seems like two minutes; when you sit on a hot stove for two minutes, it seems like two hours. That's relativity.
> —Albert Einstein
>
> Sad hours seem long.
>
> —William Shakespeare
> *Romeo and Juliet*

Have you ever had the feeling that time was racing by, dragging very slowly, moving in slow motion, or standing still? What caused this? Were you happy, sad, bored, busy, waiting, cold, hot, sick, nervous, frightened, or in love? Or have you ever had the feeling that you had experienced an event before it happened, even though you knew it wasn't possible? (This kind of experience is called *déjà vu*.)

Write a paragraph about a situation in which you experienced a changed feeling about the passage of time. Include the present perfect, past perfect, and past perfect progressive in your paragraph. For example:

> I'd been out on a date with a girl I really liked. We'd been having a very nice time, but the evening was passing much too quickly for me. It had been snowing all night, and I was driving home on a snowy street. Suddenly, a tree appeared right in front of the car. I stamped on the brake, but the car kept moving forward. Time seemed to stretch out in slow motion while the car slid into the tree. With a big jolt, the car hit the tree, I broke the steering wheel with my chin, and time jumped back to normal. I've never forgotten that experience.

Read your paragraph to the class.

Unit Three

Future; Phrasal Verbs; Tag Questions

Topic Focus: *Travel*

UNIT OBJECTIVES

- **expressing future time with *will* and *be going to***
  (Your tour *will* be an educational experience. A professional *is going to* drive the bus.)

- **expressing future time with the present progressive, the simple present, and *be about to***
  (Lisa *is touring* the Capitol on Tuesday afternoon. Her tour *starts* at one o'clock. It's now one o'clock, and the tour *is about to* start.)

- **the future progressive with *will* and *be going to***
  (The plane *will be taking* off soon. It *is going to be leaving* on time.)

- **the future perfect with *will* and *be going to***
  (The Mars mission *will have been completed* by 2005. Humans *aren't going to have gone* to Mars by then.)

- **the future perfect progressive with *will* and *be going to***
  (We *will have been preparing* for the Mars project for many years. People *aren't going to have been traveling* there regularly by then.)

- **phrasal verbs and verb-preposition combinations**
  (Roald Amundsen *set off* for the South Pole. He *was looking for* adventure.)

- **tag questions**
  (Columbus was an explorer, *wasn't he*?)

INTRODUCTORY TASKS

Reading and Listening

[···]   Read and listen to the advertisements and announcements on the Travel Bulletin Board on page 79. Then complete the Comprehension Check.

Comprehension Check

Read each sentence. Circle **T** if the sentence is true or **F** if the sentence is false.

1. Mesa Verde, the Grand Canyon, and Yellowstone are national parks. ⓣ F

2. The Mall of America is amazing because it has baseball stadiums and airplanes inside it. T F

3. The space-science researcher thinks we are almost ready to explore Mars. T F

4. According to "Destination Mars," earth's population problems can be solved now. T F

5. According to "Destination Mars," colonies exist on Mars. T F

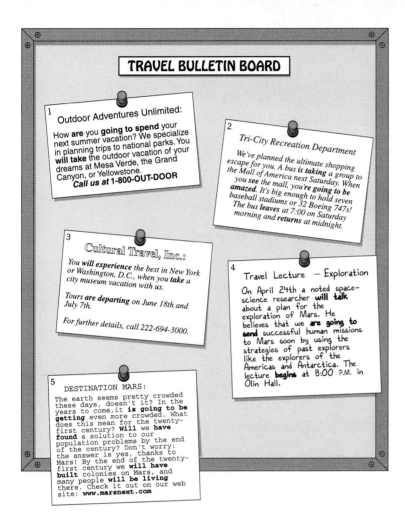

TRAVEL BULLETIN BOARD

1 Outdoor Adventures Unlimited:
How **are** you **going to spend** your next summer vacation? We specialize in planning trips to national parks. You **will take** the outdoor vacation of your dreams at Mesa Verde, the Grand Canyon, or Yellowstone.
Call us at **1-800-OUT-DOOR**

2 Tri-City Recreation Department
We've planned the ultimate shopping escape for you. A bus **is taking** a group to the Mall of America next Saturday. When you see the mall, you're **going to be amazed**. It's big enough to hold seven baseball stadiums or 32 Boeing 747s! The bus **leaves** at 7:00 on Saturday morning and **returns** at midnight.

3 Cultural Travel, Inc.:
You **will experience** the best in New York or Washington, D.C., when you **take** a city museum vacation with us.

Tours **are departing** on June 18th and July 7th.

For further details, call 222-694-3000.

4 Travel Lecture — Exploration
On April 24th a noted space-science researcher **will talk** about a plan for the exploration of Mars. He believes that we **are going to send** successful human missions to Mars soon by using the strategies of past explorers like the explorers of the Americas and Antarctica. The lecture **begins** at 8:00 P.M. in Olin Hall.

5 DESTINATION MARS:
The earth seems pretty crowded these days, doesn't it? In the years to come, it **is going to be getting** even more crowded. What does this mean for the twenty-first century? **Will** we **have found** a solution to our population problems by the end of the century? Don't worry: the answer is yes, thanks to Mars! By the end of the twenty-first century we **will have built** colonies on Mars, and many people **will be living** there. Check it out on our web site: **www.marsnext.com**

Think about Grammar

The **boldfaced** verbs in the reading express a future time meaning. Work with a partner.

A. Look at the **boldfaced** verbs in items 1, 2, 3, and 4 on the Travel Bulletin Board.

1. In 1–4, four different forms are used to express the future. Give an example of a

   verb in each form. _____ are going to spend _____

2. a. Which two of the forms also can express another time? _____

   b. What other time do they express? _____

B. Look at the **boldfaced** verbs in item 5 on the Travel Bulletin Board.

1. Which two verbs express actions that will be ongoing at some time in the future?

   _____

2. Which two verbs express actions that will have happened before a time in the future?

   _____

Future Time

A. Listen to the first part of the conversation. The speakers are talking about their future vacation plans. Then listen again and fill in the blanks with the verbs you hear.

A: This summer I _____'m taking_____ an outdoor vacation with my family.

1

We __'re going to go__ to a national park in Colorado.

2

B: That sounds great! When _____ you _____?

3

A: We _____ to Colorado on June fifteenth. What about you? Do you

4

have vacation plans?

B: I _____ to Washington, D.C., in July.

5

A: What _____ you _____ there?

6

B: I _____ National Gallery of Art and other museums.

7

A: _____ your brother _____ to Washington with you?

8

B: Oh, no. He hates museums. He _____ his vacation at a shopping mall.

9

B. Listen to the second part of the conversation. The speakers are making predictions about their vacations. Then listen again and fill in the blanks with the verbs you hear.

A: How can you spend a vacation in a shopping mall? Do you think

he _____'ll have_____ a good time?

1

B: It's not just any mall. It's the Mall of America. It has lots of things to do for fun, so

I think he __'s going to enjoy__ it. And he _____ cool, too, because the

2   3

mall _____ air-conditioned.

4

A: I hadn't thought about that. What _____ the weather _____

5

like in Washington in July?

B: It _____ probably _____ hot and humid. But I like hot

6

weather. . . . If I don't see you before you go, have a great vacation.

A: Thanks. It _____ interesting.

7

Forms used to talk about the future include *will, be going to,* and the present progressive.

Which two of these forms are used to talk about future plans? _____

_____

Which two are used to make predictions? _____ _____

GRAMMAR BRIEFING 1: *Will* and *Be Going To*

The modals *will* and *be going to* are used to talk about future time. They have similar functions but are not always interchangeable.

FORM *Will* and *Be Going To*

■ To talk about future time with *will* and *be going to,* use:

> *will* + base form of verb.
>
> simple present of *be* + *going to* + base form of verb.

Affirmative Statements

Will	Be Going To
I **will** (**I'll**) **leave** tomorrow.	I **am** (**I'm**) **going to leave** tomorrow.

Negative Statements

Will	Be Going To
We **will** not (**won't**) **leave** in July.	We **are** not (We**'re** not/We **aren't**) **going** to leave tomorrow.

Yes/No Questions and Short Answers

Will	Be Going To
Q: **Will** Jill **leave** this summer?	Q: **Is** Jill **going to take** a trip this summer?
A: Yes, she **will.**	A: Yes, she **is.**
No, she **won't.**	No, she **is not** (she **isn't**/she**'s not**).

Wh- Questions about the Predicate

Will	Be Going To
When **will** they **leave?**	When **are** they **going to leave?**

Wh- Questions about the Subject

Will	Be Going To
Which students **will leave** on vacation?	Which students **are going to leave** on vacation?

FUNCTION *Will* and *Be Going To*

- Use the modal *will* or *be going to* to make predictions and state expectations about the future. A prediction is a guess based on evidence or knowledge. An expectation is a belief that something will happen because it is usual or possible.

     He**'ll be** famous someday. = He**'s going to be** famous someday.

     The mail **will** probably **get** here around three o'clock. = The mail **is** probably **going to get** here around three o'clock.

- *Will* is usually used to express willingness and for purposes related to willingness. It is used to offer, to promise, to request (ask about willingness), and to refuse (express lack of willingness) to do something. (See Grammar Briefing 2, in Chapter 14, page 261, for other modals used to talk about the future.)

     If you want, I**'ll mail** those letters. (offer)

     We**'ll be** there promptly at 8:00 A.M. (promise)

     Will you **take** these packages to the post office? (request)

     She **won't tell** me what's bothering her. (refusal)

- *Be going to* is usually used to talk about an intention or plan.

     She**'s going to discuss** the problem with the travel agent.

     They**'re going to go** on vacation next month.

- *Be going to* is usually used to make a prediction about the immediate future. Often the prediction is based on evidence in the present situation.

     That boy**'s going to spill** his drink. Grab it! (he's not paying attention and is moving his arm toward the glass)

     Cool! The band **is going to play** again! (they're picking up their instruments and moving toward the stage)

- *Will* is often used in formal situations if both *will* and *be going to* could be used. For example, *will* is almost always used in written notices.

     The train **will depart** at ten o'clock. (formal announcement)

     The train**'s going to leave** at ten o'clock. (less formal)

- Time expressions used in talking about future time include *tomorrow, tonight, this afternoon* (*semester, year,* etc.), *next week* (*spring, Monday,* etc.), *on the first of the month* (*June tenth,* etc.), *in two hours* (*a few days,* etc.), and *at four o'clock* (*this time next year,* etc.).

FORM AND FUNCTION Expressing Future Time in Time Clauses

- Use a present tense in time clauses to talk about future actions or states. Expressions that begin time clauses include *before, after, when, as soon as, until,* and *by the time.* Use a future form in the main clause. (See Grammar Briefing 2, in Chapter 2, page 32 for more about time clauses.)

Before he **comes,** we**'ll eat** dinner.	**Not:** Before he ~~will come,~~ we**'ll eat** dinner.
When they**'re traveling,** they**'ll stay** in a hotel.	**Not:** When they**'**~~ll travel,~~ they**'ll stay** in a hotel.

TALKING the TALK

■ In speech, *going to* is usually pronounced "gonna." "Gonna" is not used in writing.

> *Joe:*   Where **are** you **gonna go** on your vacation?
>
> *Hal:*   We**'re gonna go** to Tahiti.

GRAMMAR PRACTICE 1: *Will* and *Be Going To*

1 *Will*—Form: *An Outdoor Vacation—Mesa Verde National Park*

A. Use *will* and the words in parentheses to complete the statements and questions. Complete the short answer. Use contractions with subject pronouns and with *not.*

Four Corners Heritage Tours

Durango, CO 81301

Utah   Colorado
Mesa Verde   • Durango
Arizona   New Mexico

Thank you for making a reservation to tour the ancient Native American

village, or "pueblo," at Mesa Verde National Park. We promise that you

_____*won't be*_____ (not, be) disappointed. Your tour _____*will be*_____ (be)
     (1)   (2)

an educational and enjoyable experience—one that we're sure you

_____ (not, forget)! This information sheet answers the questions
    (3)

that our guests frequently ask.

Q: At what time _____ (the tour, begin)?
                     (4)

A: The tour _____ (begin) at 8 A.M. The driver _____
               (5)   (6)

   (not, wait) for you, so please be ready. The trip from Durango to Mesa Verde

_____ (not, take) more than an hour.
    (7)

Q: _____ (my tour group, be) small?
    (8)

A: Yes, _____ . There _____ (not, be) more than eight
           (9)   (10)

   people in your group.

Q: What _____ (we, do) at Mesa Verde?
           (11)

A: You _____ (explore) "cliff dwellings" —homes built high on
        (12)

   the sides of steep, flat-topped mountains.

B. Write *wh-* questions about the **boldfaced** words in the answers. Use *will.*

1. Q: ___What will I need to bring?___
   A: You'll need to bring **a hat, sunblock, a jacket, and sturdy shoes.**

2. Q: _____?
   A: You'll need sturdy shoes **because you will be climbing up ladders to the cliff dwellings and hiking on steep trails around the pueblo.**

3. Q: _____?
   A: **Two graduate students in archaeology** will guide the tour.

4. Q: _____?
   A: The tour will last **about four hours.** After the tour, you'll have time to look around the Visitor Center.

5. Q: _____?
   A: The group will have lunch **in a scenic picnic area.** Lunch will include typical native foods.

6. Q: _____?
   A: The tour will cost **$120 per person.** The price includes transportation and lunch.

2 Be Going To—Form: A Shopping Vacation—The Mall of America

A. Use *be going to* and the words in parentheses to complete the statements and questions. Complete the short answer. Use contractions with subject pronouns.

Roger: Hey, Nick. I ___'m going to go___ (go) on a one-day vacation next Saturday. Do
                        1

you want to come along?

Nick: Where ___are you going to go___ (you, go)?
                        2

Roger: Believe it or not, I _____ (go) to the Mall of America, near
                        3

Minneapolis. You should come. It _____ (be) a lot of fun.
                                                        4

Nick: I don't believe it. Why _____ (you, go) so far just to go to a
                                        5

mall? _____ (you, shop) there?
              6

Roger: Yes, _____. Of course. The Mall of America is the biggest indoor
                        7

mall in the United States—it has over 500 stores.

Nick: Over 500 stores? No, no way. I hate shopping. I _____ (not, go)
                                                                        8

with you.

Roger: That's OK. My nephew Jeremy and his friend Tyrone _____

        (come). We _____ (visit) Camp Snoopy, a huge amusement park
                    10

        in the mall. Tyrone _____ (play) at the golf course there.
                              11

Nick: Golf! I _____ (think about) coming after all! Let me ask you some
                12

        questions.

B. Write *wh-* questions about the **boldfaced** words in the answers. Use *be going to*.

1. Q: <u> How are we going to get there?</u>
   A: We're going to get there **by bus.**

2. Q: _____?
   A: **Fifty people** are going to go on the trip.

3. Q: _____?
   A: The bus is going to leave **at 7 A.M.**

4. Q: _____?
   A: The trip to Minneapolis is going to take $2\frac{1}{2}$ **hours.**

5. Q: _____?
   A: We're going to eat lunch **at a restaurant in the mall.** There are over 70 places
      to eat at!

C. Work with a partner. Take turns using *be going to* to ask and answer questions about
your future plans. Use *tonight, tomorrow, next Saturday, next week, this winter, next summer,* and other time expressions.

        Example: *What are you going to do tonight? I'm going to go to a movie.*

3   *Will* and *Be Going To*—Predictions: *What Next?*

A. Work with a partner. Decide what you think will happen next in each of the following situations. Write **two** predictions for each situation. Use *will* for one prediction
and *be going to* for the other one.

1. Len and Miranda have spent their vacation at Mesa Verde. Now they're on a
   plane, trying to get home. The plane is sitting on the runway. It was ready to take
   off an hour ago, but snow has been falling steadily since then.

        *The passengers will get very nervous about the weather and ask to get off
        the plane.*
        Len and Miranda aren't going to make it home tonight.

2. Mr. and Mrs. Miller and their six-year-old son Ricky are at the Mall of America.
   Mr. and Mrs. Miller have decided to separate for a few hours and meet later. Mr.
   Miller thinks that Ricky is with his mother. Mrs. Miller thinks that Ricky is with
   his father. Ricky is all alone in the biggest mall in the country.

3. Vicky and Doug are driving to Grand Canyon National Park in Arizona. Doug decided to take a small road through the desert to save time. He made a wrong turn, and they've been lost for hours. It's dark and late, and they haven't seen anyone else for a long time. Suddenly, their car sputters to a stop, out of gas.

4. Penny and Beth are in a restaurant in Wyoming. They've been backpacking for a week at Yellowstone National Park, and they're very hungry. The waitress brought their soup, and Penny has eaten half of hers. Now she notices something moving in her soup bowl.

5. Brittany and Seth are having a great time together at the Mall of America. A few weeks ago Brittany promised to marry Seth, but since then she's secretly been seeing her old boyfriend again. As Brittany and Seth stroll through the mall, they see the wedding chapel there. It has a sign, "Chapel of Love. Have your dream day here."

B. Work with your partner to write two short paragraphs describing travel situations like the ones in **A.** Read your paragraphs to the class. The class should make predictions about each paragraph. Write the predictions on the board.

4 Will verus Be Going To: Before an Outdoor Vacation

Decide whether each item is expressing willingness or a plan. Complete the items with the words in parentheses and *will* or *be going to.* Use contractions with subject pronouns.

I.
Pam: Do you know where the newspaper is?

Ryan: It's still on the porch. I _____'ll get_____ (get) it for you.
                                        1
II.
Ryan: Pam, why are you reading travel articles?

Pam: I've been thinking about our summer vacation. I _____'m going to find_____ (find)
                                                            2

something exciting for us to do.

III.
Ryan: I want to make a phone call, but I can't find the phone book. _____
        (you, help) me look for it?   3

Pam: Sure. I _____ (help) you. Who _____ (you, call)?
                    4   5

Ryan: I _____ (call) the travel agent to make a reservation for our vacation.
            6
IV.
Pam: Ryan has just made reservations for our vacation.

Diane: Where _____ (you, go)?
                    7

Pam: We _____ (take) a raft trip in the Grand Canyon. _____
            8   9

(you, look after) our cat for us while we're gone?

5   *Will* and *Be Going To*—Function: *An Outdoor Adventure Vacation—Grand Canyon National Park*

Use *will* or *be going to* to express the functions in parentheses. If both forms can express the function, write both. Use contractions with subject pronouns and with *not*.

Before the raft trip:

Glenda: Welcome to Grand Canyon Raft Adventures. I know you _'ll/'re going to_ have

1 (prediction)

a really great trip.

Ryan: When ___are we going to___ start rafting?

2 (plan)

Glenda: At seven tomorrow morning. Please don't be late.

Ryan: We _____ be ready to start at seven.

3 (promise)

In the Grand Canyon:

Ryan: Do we have to wear our life jackets all the time?

Glenda: Yes, you do. The river _____ be very fast in some places.

4 (prediction)

Ryan: Oh, no! I dropped my paddle. It's floating away.

Glenda: Don't worry. I _____ get it.

5 (promise)

Pam: The river is moving really fast here!

Ryan: There's a big rock in the river. Hang on! We _____ hit it!

6 (prediction about immediate future)

Ryan: Glenda, that was exciting, but now we're wet and cold.

Glenda: If you want, I _____ make you some hot tea when we stop.

7 (offer)

After the raft trip, at a restaurant:

Waiter: Welcome to the Canyon View Restaurant. I recommend the Arizona Slider.

Pam: It sounds interesting. I _____ have it, please.

8 (request)

Waiter: It's made with rattlesnake meat and a spicy chili sauce.

Pam: Rattlesnake? I _____ (not) have it. Don't bring it.

9 (refusal)

Ryan: Pam, we _____ go home tomorrow. You _____ (not)

10 (intention)   11 (expectation)

have another chance to try rattlesnake for a long time.

Waiter: We also have a vegetarian dish called the Cactus Flower.

Pam: _____ you bring me that? It sounds perfect!

12 (request)

6 *Will* and *Be Going To: What Will They Say Next?*

You're staying at a motel that has only one television, in the lobby. You want to watch the weather forecast, but a man has the remote control. He watches each show for a few seconds and then changes channels. Although these changes come in the middle of sentences, you have a good idea of how each sentence ends. Listen once for the main ideas. Then listen again and **circle** *will* or *be going to* or both.

1. *Nature Program:*   . . . the universe [will/is going to] end in a Big Crunch.

2. *Quiz Show:*   . . . She [will/'s going to] have a baby.

3. *Soap Opera:*   . . . I ['ll/'m going to] change.

4. *News:*   . . . prices [will/are going to] rise.

5. *Hospital Drama:*   . . . Your son [is going to/will] be okay.

6. *Football Game:*   . . . Wilson [will/is going to] score a touchdown!

7. *Situation Comedy:*   . . . I [won't/'m not going to] eat your food anymore.

8. *Prison Drama:*   . . . A shovel? [Will you/Are you going to] dig a tunnel?

9. *Weather Forecast:*   . . . the sky [will/is going to] remain clear.

7 Expressing the Future in Sentences with Time Clauses: *A City Museum Vacation—The Cloisters*

A. The Cloisters is a museum in New York. Before a tour, the guide gives an introduction. Use the words in parentheses to complete the statements with the correct form of *will* or the simple present. Use contractions with subject pronouns.

1. Before we _____start_____ (start) the tour, I _____'ll describe_____ (describe) the museum to you.

2. When we _____ (tour) the museum, you _____ (see) three cloisters, or courtyards, three chapels, and many tapestries and other works of art from the Middle Ages.

3. We _____ (go) into the first cloister as soon as I _____ (finish) my introduction.

4. When you _____ (walk) through the cloister, you _____ (see) beautiful stone carvings.

5. I _____ (take) you into the first chapel after

   everyone _____ (look) at the carvings in the cloister.

6. You _____ (hear) a recording of music composed in the Middle Ages

   as soon as we _____ (enter) the chapel.

B. Combine the pairs of sentences into one sentence using the time word given, the simple present, and *be going to*. In each pair, the action in the first sentence happens first. There are **two** ways to write each sentence.

1. as soon as: We're going to leave the chapel.
                    We're going to look at the unicorn tapestries.

   > As soon as we leave the chapel, we're going to look at the unicorn tapestries.
   > OR We're going to look at the unicorn tapestries as soon as we leave the chapel.

2. before: I'm going to explain the meaning of the various symbols in the tapestries.
                    We're going to go on to see the rest of the museum.

3. after: I'm going to point out flowers and herbs that were grown during the Middle Ages.
                    We're going to go into the second cloister.

4. when: You're going to enter the room called the Treasury.
                    You're going to see many valuable objects used in religious services.

5. until: You aren't going to have an opportunity to take photographs.
                    We're going to go into the gardens outside the museum.

6. by the time: You're going to know much more about art in the Middle Ages.
                    You're going to go home.

8 Using *Will* and *Be Going To: I'll Give You the Guided Tour*

A. Imagine that you are going to give a tour of a place that you know very well, for example, your school, your home, or your room. Write a one-paragraph introduction to tell the members of the tour group what they will see. Use *will*, and use at least three sentences with time clauses.

   > Example: Welcome to my house. After I tell you a little about it, I'll show you the living room. You'll see a couch and other furniture there. Before we go into the kitchen, I'll show you our new television. . . .

B. Work in groups of three or four. The other students in your group are going to go on your tour. Tell them what they are going to see. Read them the paragraph that you wrote in **A,** but use *be going to* instead of *will*.

   > Example: Welcome to my house. After I tell you a little about it, I'm going to show you the living room. You're going to see . . .

Try pronouncing *going to* as "gonna."

GRAMMAR BRIEFING 2: Expressing the Future with Present Progressive, Simple Present, and *Be About To*

The present progressive, the simple present, and *be about to* can also express future time.

FUNCTION Present Progressive, Simple Present, and *Be About To*

Present Progressive

- The present progressive can be used to talk about planned future actions. A future time expression is stated or implied.

    We**'re meeting** her in Paris in a month.

    What **are** you **doing** tomorrow afternoon? I**'m buying** a bicycle.

Simple Present

- The simple present can be used to talk about future actions or states that are on a calendar or timetable. When the simple present is used, the actions or states usually have been previously scheduled and are not likely to change. A future time expression is stated or implied.

    What are you doing next week? I**'m** on vacation.

    The semester **ends** on December 17.

    What time **does** our flight **leave** tomorrow? It **leaves** at 9:00 A.M.

- The simple present is also used in time clauses instead of the future. (See Grammar Briefing 1, page 81.)

Be About To

- Use *be about to* to talk about the immediate or very near future.

    We**'re about to leave** for the airport. Our bags are in the car.

    They**'re about to decide** on their travel plans. They need to let the travel agent know by tomorrow.

- Time expressions are not usually used in sentences with *be about to*.

    Not: The plane is about to leave ~~in five minutes~~.

GRAMMAR HOTSPOT!

- Use *will* or *be going to* for predictions about unplanned events in the future. The present progressive and simple present are not used.

    It **will rain** tomorrow.   **Not:** It ~~rains~~ tomorrow.

    It**'s going to rain** tomorrow.   **Not:** It ~~'s raining~~ tomorrow.

GRAMMAR PRACTICE 2: Expressing the Future with Present Progressive, Simple Present, and *Be About To*

9   Future Time with Present Progressive Tense: *A City Museum Vacation—Washington, D.C.*

A.   You are a travel agent. Three coworkers—Lisa, Mike, and Theo—plan to spend three days in Washington, D.C., next week. They gave you a list of what they want to do and asked you to make the arrangements. Use the chart to organize their activities. They can spend half a day at each place, and no one can be in two places at the same time.

Wish List

~~Lisa—tour the Capitol~~

Mike—visit the Folger Shakespeare Library

Theo—attend an event at the Kennedy Center

Lisa and Mike—visit the Library of Congress

Mike and Theo—go to the National Air and Space Museum

Lisa and Theo—see the National Gallery of Art

Lisa, Mike, and Theo—explore the National Museum of Natural History

~~Lisa, Mike, and Theo—visit the National Zoo~~

Lisa, Mike, and Theo—tour the White House

B.   Work with a partner. Student A is the travel agent, and Student B is the secretary for the three coworkers. The travel agent calls the secretary to explain the arrangements. Use the information in your chart and the present progressive.

> Example: Student A:
>
> *On Tuesday morning, Lisa, Mike, and Theo are visiting the National Zoo. Then on Tuesday afternoon, Lisa is touring the Capitol, and....*

Then reverse roles.

C.   Work on your own. You can spend a three-day vacation anywhere you want. Plan your three days. Using the present progressive, write a paragraph about your plan.

> Example:
>
> *I'm visiting San Francisco next week. I'm going to Golden Gate Park on Monday morning. Then I'm having lunch at ...*

Tell the class your plan.

Tuesday	Wednesday	Thursday
Morning:	Morning:	Morning:
1. Lisa, Mike, and Theo – visit the National Zoo	1.	1.
2.	2.	2.
Afternoon: 1.	Afternoon: 1.	Afternoon:
1. Lisa – tour the Capitol	1.	1.
2.	2.	2.

▐▌ Present Progressive versus *Will: In Washington, D.C.*

Decide whether the conversations express a planned future action or a prediction.
Complete the conversations with the words in parentheses and the present progressive
or *will*. Use contractions with subject pronouns and with *not*.

1.   *Lisa:* I've decided to go to Washington, D.C., with Mike and Theo next week.

     Mariah: That sounds great! You_____*'ll have*_____ (have) a good time there.

2. *Lisa:* Did you listen to the weather forecast for Washington?

    Mike: Yes, I did. Bring your umbrella. It _____ (probably, rain) tomor-
    row.

3. *Airline Ticket Agent:* Good morning, sir. Do you have your tickets?

              Theo: Yes, I do. We _____ (go) to Washington, D.C.

4. *Theo:* Has Lisa chosen a place for dinner tonight?

    Mike: Yes, she has. We _____ (eat) at an Indian restaurant near
    Dupont Circle.

5. *Mike:* Do you see that man over there? Is he a senator?

    Lisa: Yes, he is now, but he isn't very popular in his home state. I think

    he _____ (lose) the election in November.

6. *Lisa:* There's the National Portrait Gallery. What does the poster on the

    door say?

    Theo: They _____ (have) a special exhibition next week.

7. *Mike:* Let's go to the National Archives. I want to see the Declaration of
    Independence.

    Theo: We don't have time to see everything. We _____ (go) home
    tomorrow.

8. *Lisa:* Where's Mike?

    Theo: I'm not sure. I hope he gets here soon. He _____ (miss) the
    plane.

9. *Theo:* Hey, Mike! We have to leave for the airport soon. Where's your bag?

    Mike: I _____ (not, leave) with you. I've decided to stay longer and
    see everything in Washington.

▮▮ Future Time with Simple Present Tense: *An Outdoor Vacation— Yellowstone National Park*

Work with a partner. Student A looks at the information on this page. Student B looks at the information on Exercise Page E–2. Ask *wh-* questions to get information to complete both schedules. Use simple present and these verbs: *start, begin, end, finish, open, close, leave,* and *return.*

> Example: Student A: *When does the summer season begin?* Student B: It *begins on April 15th.*

Yellowstone National Park Association

Here's the information you requested on next year's activities.

Park Information:

    Summer Season: _____ to October 22

Opening and Closing Dates:

    Madison Campground: May 1 – _____

    Visitor Centers and Museum: _____ – September 30

Yellowstone Institute Course Dates:

    Ecology of the Park: _____ – June 12

    Geology and Geysers: June 29 – _____

Tour Departure and Return Dates:

    Wildlife Observation: July 3 – _____

    High-Country Fishing: _____ – August 12

12   Future Time with *Be About To: Yellowstone Vacation*

Work with a partner. Write a sentence about each of the pictures. Use *be about to.*

1.   They're about to go on a trip.

4.

2.

5.

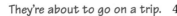

3.

6.

13   Expressing Future Time—*Vacation Finales*

Complete the following statements and questions using the words in parentheses and *be going to, be about to,* the present progressive for future time, and/or the simple present for future time. Write all the forms that are correct. Use contractions with subject pronouns and with *not.*

Museum Vacation:

A: The museum ___is going to close/is closing / closes___ (close) in fifteen minutes. I
                                    1

wish we didn't have to leave.

B: The museum _____ (have) a special exhibition next month. I read
                               2

about the plans for it. Artists _____ (give) demonstrations.
                                            3

A: That exhibition _____ (be) interesting. Let's come back for it!
                          4

Shopping Vacation:

A: Hurry up! You _____ (miss) the bus. It _____ (leave) in a

　　　　　　　　　　5　　　　　　　　　　　　　　　　　　　6

few minutes.

B: I want to stay. I haven't done and seen everything at the mall yet.

A: I know what you mean. I _____ (come back) for the Festival.

　　　　　　　　　　　　　　　7

It _____ (start) in two weeks. Come back with me.

　　　　8

Outdoor Vacation:

A: I'm depressed. We _____ (leave) tomorrow afternoon at three o'clock.

　　　　　　　　　　　　　9

B: I _____ (get up) early to see the sun rise over the Grand Canyon

　　　10

tomorrow. It _____ (rise) at 5:35 A.M.

　　　　　　　　11

The next day at 5:00 A.M. :

A: Look at the sky. It's really dark and cloudy. It _____ (rain).

　　　　　　　　　　　　　　　　　　　　12

B: We _____ (not, see) the sun rise this morning, I'm afraid. We'll have to

　　　13

come back to the Grand Canyon again.

Future Progressive, Future Perfect, and Future Perfect Progressive

Introductory Task: *Predictions about Transportation and Travel in the Future*

A. Work with a partner. Read the following statements. Some of the **boldfaced** verbs talk about actions that will be in progress at a time in the future. **Circle** them. Some of the **boldfaced** verbs talk about actions that will be completed at a time in the future. **Underline** them.

1. Twenty years from now, most international airlines (**will be using**) planes that fly faster than the speed of sound.

2. Twenty years from now, most students in the class **will have flown** faster than the speed of sound at least once.

3. Five years from now, most people in the United States **will be driving** cars that have computers connected to the Internet.

4. Ten years from now, at least one student in the class **is going to be driving** a car that steers itself.

5. By 2006, the National Aeronautics and Space Administration (NASA) **will have brought** a sample of Mars's soil to earth for testing.

6. By 2007, scientists **are going to have proven** that life existed on Mars in the past.

B. 1. The **circled** verbs in **A** are in the future progressive. List them: _____ will be using, _____

_____

2. The **underlined** verbs in **A** are in the future perfect. List them: _____ will have flown, _____

_____

3. Compare the lists. How are the future progressive and future perfect similar? How are they different?

C. Discuss the predictions in the sentences in **A.** Which ones do you think will prove to be accurate? Which ones do you think won't?

GRAMMAR BRIEFING 1: Future Progressive

The future progressive (also called the future continuous) is used to talk about actions that will be in progress in the future.

FORM Future Progressive

■ To form the future progressive, use:

> *will*
>
> the simple present of *be + going to + be* + verb + *-ing.**

* See Appendix 3 for spelling rules for verb + *-ing*.

Affirmative Statements

Future Progressive with *Will*	Future Progressive with *Be Going To*
I **will** (**I'll**) **be working** tomorrow.	I **am** (**I'm**) **going to be working** tomorrow.

Negative Statements

Future Progressive with *Will*	Future Progressive with *Be Going To*
We **will** not (**won't**) **be working** in July.	We **are** not (**We're** not/We **aren't**) **going to be working** in July.

Yes/No Questions and Short Answers

Future Progressive with *Will*	Future Progressive with *Be Going To*
Q: **Will** Jill **be working** this summer?	Q: **Is** Jill **going to be working** this summer?
A: Yes, she **will** (**will be**).	A: Yes, she **is** (**she's going to be**).
No, she **will not** (**won't/won't be**).	No, she **is not** (she **isn't**/she's **not**/she **isn't going to be**).

Wh- Questions about the Predicate

Future Progressive with *Will*	Future Progressive with *Be Going To*
When **will** they **be traveling?**	When **are** they **going to be traveling?**
Where **will** you **be traveling?**	Where **are** you **going to be traveling?**

Wh- Questions about the Subject

Will	*Be Going To*
Who **will be traveling?**	Who **is** (**Who's**) **going to be traveling?**
Which students **will be traveling?**	Which students **are going to be traveling?**

FUNCTION Future Progressive

■ Use the future progressive to talk about actions that will be in progress at a particular moment or over an extended period in the future. The future progressive emphasizes that an action will be in progress.

> At this time tomorrow, **I'll be relaxing** on the beach. (particular moment)
>
> She**'s going to be working** in Bangkok for the next few years. (extended period)

- The future progressive and the future with *will* or *be going to* can be used interchangeably to talk about actions over an extended period.

    We**'re going to live** in a new place. = We**'re going to be living** in a new place.

- To talk about a particular moment, use the future progressive for actions that began before and continue through that moment. Use the future with *will* or *be going to* for actions that begin at that moment.

    At ten o'clock tomorrow, I **will be flying** to Europe. (The plane will leave before ten o'clock.)

    At ten o'clock tomorrow, I **will fly** to Europe. (The plane will leave at ten o'clock.)

- Like other progressives, the future progressive is not usually used with verbs with stative meaning.

    We **will know** more about London after our trip.

    Not: We ~~will be knowing~~ more about London after our trip.

- The future progressive is often used in the main clause of sentences that have time clauses. (See Grammar Briefing 2, Chapter 2, page 32.) Remember that the verb in the time clause is in the present.

    She**'ll be flying** to London while we **are** at the meeting.

- Time expressions used with the future progressive include *tomorrow, tonight, this evening* (*month, year*, etc.), *next week* (*June, summer*, etc.), *on October 30* (*Tuesday, the 8th*, etc.), *in a few months* (*three days, a year*, etc.), and *at nine o'clock* (*this time next week*, etc.).

GRAMMAR PRACTICE 1: Future Progressive

1 Future Progressive with *Will*—Form: *The Flight of the Future*

It's possible that airlines will be using High-Speed Civil Transport (HSCT) planes in the future. What will the flights be like? Use the words in parentheses to complete the statements and questions in the future progressive with *will*. Complete the short answer. Use contractions with subject pronouns and with *not*.

Announcement: Flight 101 from Los Angeles to Tokyo <u>will be boarding</u> (board)
                                                                                    1

                  shortly.

A few minutes later:

   Passenger: This is my first HCST flight, so I'm a little nervous.

                 <u>Will the plane be taking off</u> (the plane, take off) soon?
                                            2

Flight Attendant: Yes, <u>it will/it will be</u>. Please fasten your seat belt, sir.
                                        3

   Passenger: How fast _____ (we, fly)? At what
                                   4

                 altitude _____ (the plane, cruise)?
                                   5

Flight Attendant: The pilot _____ (give) you that information soon.

   Pilot: Welcome aboard. We _____ (take off) in a few minutes.

   Then we _____ (climb) to an altitude of 60,000 feet.

   The plane _____ (not, break) the sound barrier until

   we are over the ocean. After that, we _____ (cruise) at

   1,800 miles per hour—almost two and a half times the speed of

   sound. Sit back and relax. The flight attendants _____

   (come) through the cabin to make sure that you're comfortable.

Passenger: Excuse me. _____ (you, show) a movie soon?

Flight Attendant: No, _____. We _____ (not, show) a movie

   because you can choose any movie you want to watch on your

   private monitor.

Three and a half hours after takeoff:

   Pilot: Please fasten your seatbelt. About ten minutes from now,

   we _____ (arrive) at Tokyo's Narita Airport.

2   Future Progressive with *Be Going To*—Form: *The Car of the Future*

At a university's robotics institute, engineers have been working on automated systems to make cars safer and more efficient. The following is a conversation between an engineer and a reporter. Use the words in parentheses to complete the statements and questions in the future progressive with *be going to*. Complete the short answers. Use contractions with subject pronouns.

A: What kind of cars __are people going to be driving__ (people, drive) in the future?

B: In the future, people __aren't going to be doing__ (not, do) much of the driving.

   Cars _____ (use) computer technology to drive themselves.

A: What _____ (you, show) me today?

B: I _____ (demonstrate) a computer-based system called Ralph. Ralph

   is short for Rapidly Adapting Lateral Position Handler. We _____

   (take) an automated car for a test drive. Let's go . . .

A: _____ (the car, drive) itself all the time?

B: No, _____ . I _____ (steer) it at first. But once I switch to the
            8   9

automated system, I _____ (not, control) its steering or speed.
                          10

Ralph _____ (use) its tiny video cameras and sensors to "see" the
        11

road. . . . OK. Now Ralph _____ (take over).
                              12

A: There's a car ahead of us. How _____ (Ralph, react to) it?
                                       13

B: In a few seconds, Ralph _____ (change) lanes.
                                 14

A: You seem very relaxed. _____ (you, fall asleep) soon?
                                15

B: No, _____ . Don't worry. Ralph is good, but it isn't perfect yet. Until it
           16

is, I _____ (keep) my eyes on the road.
        17

3 Using the Future Progressive: *Making Predictions about Transportation of the Future*

A. How are people going to be traveling in the future? What kinds of transportation
will we be using? Write **six** sentences about your predictions for the transportation
of the future. Use the future progressive with both *will* and *be going to*. Use *not* in at
least two sentences. Use time expressions in at least three sentences.

> Example: In twenty years, people will be traveling in high-speed buses that
> float above the road.
>
> OR   People won't be using transportation much; instead, they're going
>   to be using their computers to take virtual reality trips.

B. Work in groups of three or four. Discuss your predictions and decide on four predictions that everyone likes best. Tell these predictions to the class.

4 Future versus Future Progressive: *Coming and Going*

Work with a partner. Choose the form or forms—future, future progressive, or both—
that can be used to complete the statements.

1. We plan to drive to Denver tomorrow. We _____ a, b _____ for eight hours.

   a. 're going to drive   b. 're going to be driving

2. My vacation starts on Saturday. At this time next week, I _____ a
   wonderful time in Hawaii.

   a. 'll have   b. 'll be having

3. I haven't gotten my itinerary from the travel agent yet. I _____ it
   tomorrow.

   a. 'll have   b. 'll be having

4. I don't want to go to the beach until you come. When you come,

we _____ to the beach together.

    a. 'll go   b. 'll be going

5. Lily's making plans for her vacation. She _____ in a youth hostel for a week.

      a. 's going to stay   b. 's going to be staying

6. You're packing a lot of heavy things. Your bag _____ too much.

    a. is going to weigh   b. is going to be weighing

7. Casey is coming home late tonight, so we can't wait for him. When he comes,

we _____.

      a. 're going to eat   b. 're going to be eating

8. Vincent is coming home late tonight, but we'll wait for him. When he comes,

we _____.

      a. 're going to eat   b. 're going to be eating

9. My boyfriend promised to meet me at the airport. When I get there,

he _____.

      a. 'll wait   b. 'll be waiting

5   Future Progressive in Sentences with Time Clauses: *"Smart" Cars*

A. Although "smart" cars won't steer themselves, they'll be equipped with information technology. A car salesman is trying to persuade a customer to buy one. Use the words in parentheses to complete the sentences. Use the future progressive with *will* and the simple present. Use contractions with subject pronouns.

1. Before you _____begin_____ (begin) a trip, the car's computer

   ___will be downloading___ (download) useful information from the Internet.

2. While the driver _____ (steer) the car, the computer _____
   (monitor) traffic conditions.

3. The computer _____ (respond) to your voice commands while

   you _____ (keep) your eyes on the road.

4. The car's computer _____ (search for) a new route before the

   car _____ (get) stuck in a traffic jam.

5. While the car _____ (be) in motion, a satellite _____
   (keep) track of its position.

6. When you _____ (look) at the computer screen, it _____
   (display) a map of your location.

7. The computer _____ (send) your e-mail and faxes while

   it _____ (play) your favorite music.

8. _____ (you, drive) one of our "smart" cars as soon as

   they _____ (be) available?

B. Think of some type of futuristic technology, for example, a communication device, an
appliance, a vehicle, a computer program, or a robot. Write a paragraph that tries to
persuade someone to buy it. Include at least four sentences with the future progressive and a time clause.

> Example: Your Roboready will do everything you want it to do. Before you
> wake up, Roboready will be making your breakfast. Roboready will be cleaning
> the kitchen while you get ready for school. . . .

Read your paragraph to the class. Whose paragraph is the most persuasive?

GRAMMAR BRIEFING 2: Future Perfect and Future Perfect Progressive

The future perfect is used to talk about actions and states that will occur before a future action, state, or time. Both the future perfect and the future perfect progressive (also called the future perfect continuous) are used to talk about actions that will continue to a future action, state, or time.

FORM Future Perfect and Future Perfect Progressive

■ To form the future perfect, use:

$$\left.\begin{array}{l} \textit{will} \\ \text{simple present of } \textit{be} + \textit{going to} \end{array}\right\} + \textit{have} + \text{past participle of verb.*}$$

* See Appendix 7 for the past participle forms of irregular verbs.

■ To form the future perfect progressive, use:

$$\left.\begin{array}{l} \textit{will} \\ \text{simple present of } \textit{be} + \textit{going to} \end{array}\right\} + \textit{have} + \textit{been} + \text{verb} + \textit{-ing.*}$$

* See Appendix 3 for spelling rules for verb + -ing.

Affirmative Statements

Future Perfect	Future Perfect Progressive
By the year 2020, we **will (we'll) have worked** there for 20 years.	By the year 2020, we **will (we'll) have been working** there for 20 years.

Negative Statements

Future Perfect	Future Perfect Progressive
We **are** not (We**'re not**/We **aren't**) **going to have worked** long enough to retire by then.	We **are** not (We**'re not**/We **aren't**) **going to have been working** long enough to retire by then.

Yes/No Questions and Short Answers

Future Perfect	Future Perfect Progressive
Q: **Will** you **have worked** for a new company by then?	Q: **Will** you **have been working** for a new company by then?
A: Yes, I **will (will have).**	A: Yes, I **will (will have/will have been).**
No, I **won't (won't have).**	No, I **won't (won't have/won't have been).**

Wh- Questions (Predicate)

Future Perfect	Future Perfect Progressive
What companies **will** they **have worked** for by 2020?	How long **will** they **have been working** by then?

Wh- Questions (Subject)

Future Perfect	Future Perfect Progressive
Who **is** (Who**'s**) **going to have worked** there by 2020?	Who **is** (Who**'s**) **going to have been working** there by then?

FUNCTION Future Perfect and Future Perfect Progressive

Future Perfect

■ Use the future perfect to talk about actions and states, single or repeated, that will occur before a future action, state, or time.

> She **will have flown** to Mars by the year 2020. (single action)
>
> We **are going to have taken** many pictures before we **finish.** (repeated action)

■ Use the future perfect with *for* or *all* (*day,* etc.) to talk about actions or states that continue to a future action, state, or time.

> In 2020, they **will have lived** on Mars for only a short time.

■ Time expressions that are used with the future perfect include *by then* (*next Wednesday, 2020,* etc.), *already, just, yet* (in questions and negatives), *ever* (in questions and negatives), *never, still,* and *several times* (*four times,* etc.). (See Appendix 8 for more about time expressions and adverbs of frequency used with the future perfect.)

Future Perfect Progressive

■ Use the future perfect progressive alone or with *for* or *all* (*day,* etc.) to talk about actions that continue to a future action, state, or time.

> They**'ll have been working** hard before the trip begins.
>
> He **will have been living** on Mars for two years when the next spacecraft arrives. (See Appendix 8 for more about time expressions and adverbs of frequency used with the future perfect progressive.)

Future Perfect Progressive versus Future Perfect

■ The future perfect progressive is used to talk about actions that will continue to a future time, state, or action. The future perfect is used to talk about actions that will be completed at an unspecified time before a future action, state, or time.

> They **will have been gathering** the data when the spacecraft arrives. (continuing up to the time the spacecraft arrives)
>
> They **will have gathered** the data when the spacecraft arrives. (completed before the spacecraft arrives)

■ However, when *for* or *all* (*day,* etc.) is used, there is little or no difference between the future perfect progressive and the future perfect.

> By the time the spacecraft gets to Mars, it **will have been traveling** for seven months. = By the time the spacecraft gets to Mars, it **will have traveled** for seven months.

➤ ■ With both the future perfect and the future perfect progressive, the actions may have begun in the past or may begin in the present or future.

> The spacecraft **left** a month ago. By the time it **gets** to Mars, it **will have traveled/been traveling** for seven months. (The action started in the past.)
>
> The spacecraft **is leaving** now. By the time it **gets** to Mars, it **will have traveled/been traveling** for seven months. (The action is starting in the present.)
>
> The spacecraft **will leave** tomorrow. By the time it **gets** to Mars, it **will have traveled/been traveling** for seven months. (The action will start in the future.)

■ Like other progressives, the future perfect progressive is not usually used with verbs with stative meaning. The future perfect is used instead.

> The spacecraft **will have been** in space for many years before it reaches Pluto.
>
> **Not:** The spacecraft ~~will have been being~~ in space for many years before it reaches Pluto.

GRAMMAR HOTSPOT!

■ Remember, use a present tense in time clauses to talk about future actions or states. The future progressive, future perfect, or future perfect progressive can be used in the main clause.

> While I**'m eating** all those great meals, I**'ll be thinking** about you.
>
> **Not:** While I~~'ll be eating~~ all those great meals, I'll be thinking about you.
>
> Before I **leave** the U.S.A., I **will have graduated** from the university.
>
> **Not:** Before I ~~will have left~~ the U.S.A., I **will have graduated** from the university.

GRAMMAR PRACTICE 2: Future Perfect and Future Perfect Progressive

6 Future Perfect with *Will* and *Be Going To*—Form: *The Exploration of Mars*

A. Information about NASA space exploration programs is available on the Internet. NASA's Web sites often answer the public's questions. Use the words in parentheses to complete the statements and questions in the future perfect with *will*. Complete the short answers. Use contractions with subject pronouns and with *not*.

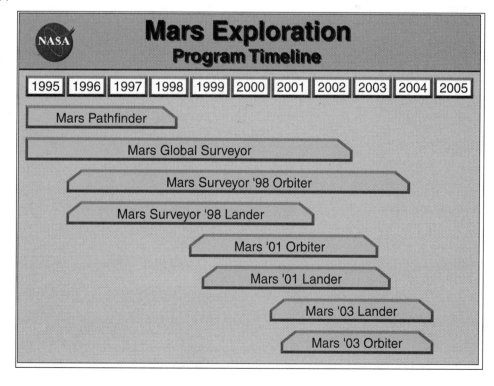

Q: The timeline for the Mars Surveyor Program ends in 2005. ___Will the program have___

___completed___ (the program, complete) its planned missions by then?
    1

A: Yes, ___it will/will have___. We _____ (launch) orbiters and landers to
         2   3

explore Mars three times.

Q: _____ (the orbiters, view) most of Mars by 2005?
        4

A: Yes, _____. Also, the landers _____ (explore) several places
            5   6

on the surface of Mars by sending out rovers—robot-like vehicles.

Q: _____ (the program, send) a human mission to Mars by 2005?
        7

A: No, _____. We _____ (not, get) enough information by
          8   9

then. We _____ (not, develop) all the technology we need. But we
            10

_____ (make) a great deal of progress toward a future human mission.
    11

B. Use the words in parentheses to complete the statements and questions in the
future perfect with *be going to*. Use contractions with subject pronouns and with *not*.

Q: ___Are scientists going to have gotten___ (scientists, get) a lot of new information
                1

by the end of the Mars Surveyor Program?

A: ___Yes, they are/they're going to have___. The landers _____ (analyze)
                2   3

Mars's atmosphere and its rocks and soil. We've designed the experiments care-

fully, so each one _____ (collect) lots of useful data.
                        4

Q: What _____ (the program, achieve) by 2005?
            5

A: By then, we _____ (search) for evidence of past life on Mars.
                    6

We _____ (gain) more knowledge about Mars's climate.
        7

Q: _____ (a spacecraft, bring) rocks from Mars back to Earth?
        8

A: It's possible that a sample return mission _____ (launch) by 2005.
                                                9

Until a spacecraft returns with samples, NASA scientists _____ (not,
                                                            10

achieve) all their Mars exploration goals.

C. The information in **A** and **B** was taken from NASA's Web sites at the time this book
was written. If possible, go to a NASA Web site and get current information about
the Mars exploration program. Use the information to write a one-paragraph
report about what the program will have accomplished by the time it ends. Use the
future perfect with *will* at least three times in your report.

7   Using the Future Perfect with *Will: What Will You Have Done by Then?*

A. Work with a partner. Use the cues and the future perfect with *will* to ask and answer questions about what each of you expects to accomplish in the future. Take turns.

> Example: Student A: What will you have done by ten o'clock tonight?
>
> Student B: By ten o'clock tonight I will have finished my homework.

1. 10 o'clock tonight

2. Saturday

3. the end of next month

4. a year from now

5. five years from now

6. 10 years from now

7. the time you are 60 years old

B. Which one of your partner's expectations seems the most ambitious, that is, like it will take the most effort to achieve? Report this expectation to the class.

> Example: Five years from now, Mae will have gotten a Ph.D. in civil engineering.

8   Using the Future Perfect with *Be Going To: Are You Going to Have Gone to Mars by Then?*

A. Work with a partner. Imagine that a private company, Red Planet Travel Services, plans to develop tourism on Mars and has drawn up a schedule with dates for its plan. Student A looks at the schedule on this page. Student B looks at the schedule on Exercise Page E–3. Ask and answer questions to complete the dates. Use the future perfect with be going to. Take turns.

> Example: Student A: When are the engineers going to have finished designing the reusable rocket?
>
> Student B: They're going to have finished designing it by December 2003.

Red Planet Travel Services

1. January 1999—the company begins taking reservations for tourist trips

2. *December 2003*   —the engineers finish designing the reusable rocket

3. May 2004—the engineers test the first rocket

4. _____—the first unmanned mission gathers data

5. February 2006—the first supply rocket delivers equipment

6. _____—the scientists leave on first human mission

7. June 2010—the construction crew builds hotels

8. _____—the company invites travel agents to try the service

9. February 2012—the travel agents visit Mars

10. _____—the company begins regular trips for tourists

B. Imagine that you work for a company that wants to develop tourism on the moon or on another planet. Your company needs to attract investors. Use your imagination to make up a schedule like the one in **A** for your company. Then use the information in the schedule to write a paragraph to describe the plan for potential investors. Use the future perfect with *be going to*. Include a sentence with *not*.

> Example: Lunar Holidays has already begun taking reservations for trips to the moon. We have planned our company's future carefully. The company isn't going to have begun tourist trips until 2015. By January 2005 our technicians are going to have begun testing. . . .

9 Future Perfect Progressive with *Will* and *Be Going To*—Form: *Terraforming Mars*

A. Some people believe that it will be possible, and perhaps even necessary, to "terraform" Mars, that is, to transform it into an earth-like environment that people can live in. Use the words in parentheses to complete the statements with the future perfect progressive with *will*. Use contractions with subject pronouns and with *not*.

Terraforming Mars is an enormous challenge. But by the time we begin the project in the middle of the twenty-first century, we __'ll have been preparing__ (prepare)

for more than 50 years and will have plenty of information. Small crews of astro-

nauts _____ (travel) to Mars regularly by then. Scientists _____

(search) for evidence of present or past life. This search _____ (not, take)

place) everywhere on Mars—only where life is most likely. By the time people begin

to colonize the planet, astronauts and scientists _____ (stay) on Mars for

long periods, and engineers _____ (build) bases. These groups

_____ (not, bring) many supplies from earth because such supplies won't

be necessary. Instead, they _____ (learn) how to live on Mars with the

resources that are available there.

B. Use the words in parentheses to complete the statements with the future perfect progressive with *be going to*. Use contractions with subject pronouns and with *not*.

By the year 2150, the terraforming project __is going to have been going on__ (go

on) for almost a hundred years. Mars _____ (not, change) rapidly, but

some gradual changes _____ (occur). The colonists _____

(expand) the bases into towns. They _____ (raise) crops in greenhouses.

Special equipment _____ (pump) water to the surface of the planet.
₆

Other equipment _____ (add) nitrogen, oxygen, and water vapor to the
₇

planet's atmosphere.

🔟 Using the Future Perfect Progressive: *By Then, She'll Have Been Studying for a Long Time*

A. Courtney is a student and a future astronaut. Use the information from the time line to complete the sentences. Use the future perfect progressive with *will*.

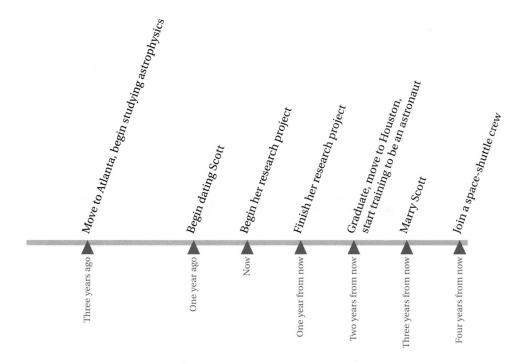

1. Courtney is living in Atlanta now. She will move to Houston in two years. By

    then, _she'll have been living in Atlanta_ for _five years_ .

2. She's studying astrophysics now. She'll graduate in two years. By then,

    _____ for _____.

3. She and Scott are dating now. They'll get married in three years. By then,

    _____ for _____.

4. She's beginning to work on her research project now. She'll finish in one year. By

    then, _____ for _____.

5. She'll start training to be an astronaut in two years. She'll join a space-shuttle

    crew in four years. By then, _____ for _____.

B. Fill in the time line with information and predictions about your life. Include activities beginning in the past, present, and future. Then, write groups of **three** sentences, using the items in **A** as a model. Use the future perfect progressive with *will* in the third sentence of each group.

> Example: I'm studying English now. I'll graduate from the English program in a year. By then, I'll have been studying English for two years.

Now

▮▮ Future Perfect and Future Perfect Progressive in Sentences with Time Clauses: *Mars Direct*

A. Mars Direct is a plan to put humans on Mars relatively soon using technology that is available now. Combine the pairs of sentences into one sentence using the time word given, the future perfect with *will*, and the simple present. In each pair, the action in the first sentence happens first. There are **two** ways to write each sentence.

1. by the time: We will get a lot of knowledge about Mars from unmanned missions.
                    The Mars Direct missions will begin.

> By the time the Mars Direct missions begin, we will have gotten a lot of knowledge about Mars from unmanned missions. OR We will have gotten a lot of knowledge about Mars from unmanned missions by the time the Mars Direct missions begin.

2. before: The project director will choose a crew of four astronauts.
The first spacecraft will go to Mars.

3. before: We will send an unmanned Earth Return Vehicle (ERV) to Mars.
The astronauts will leave earth.

4. by the time: The ERV will be on Mars for 13 months.
The astronauts' rocket will take off from earth.

5. by the time: The ERV's robots will explore the landing site for the astronauts.
The astronauts will reach Mars.

B. Combine the pairs of sentences into one sentence using the time word given, the future perfect progressive with *will*, and the simple present. In each pair, the first sentence happens first. There are **two** ways to write each sentence.

1. by the time: The astronauts will travel for 180 days.
The astronauts will land on Mars.

> *By the time the astronauts land on Mars, they will have been traveling for 180 days.* OR *The astronauts will have been traveling for 180 days by the time they land on Mars.*

2. before: They will exercise intensively to keep their bodies strong.
They will reach their destination.

3. when: The ERV will produce fuel from Martian natural resources.
The astronauts will arrive on Mars.

4. when: The astronauts will explore Mars for a year and a half.
The astronauts will get into the ERV to return to earth.

5. by the time: The four astronauts will live together for two and a half years.
The four astronauts will come back to earth.

12 Using Future Progressive, Future Perfect, and Future Perfect Progressive: *The Exploration of Mars—The Human Factor*

A mission to Mars is going to take 18 months. During that time four astronauts will be living together in a tiny spacecraft with limited supplies. Imagine that you are going to interview an astronaut to find out what he or she will be experiencing on the mission.

A. Use the cues and your own ideas to write *wh-* and *yes/no* questions in the future progressive, future perfect, and future perfect progressive.

1. what kind of food/you/eat ___What kind of food will you be eating?_____

2. how/you/spend/your free time _____?

3. how/you/stay/in touch with your friends on earth _____?

4. your family/worry/about you _____?

5. you/get/lonely/by the time you reach Mars _____?

6. you/quarrel/with the other astronauts/by the time you return _____?

7. you/experience/a lot of stress/by the time you return _____?

8. _____?

9. _____?

B. Work with a partner. Use the questions you wrote in **A** to interview each other.
Take turns playing the part of the astronaut.

    Example: Student A: *What kind of food are you going to be eating?*

                Student B: *I'm going to be eating a lot of dried food.* OR *I'm going
to be eating fish that I raise in tanks on the spacecraft.*

Report your partner's most interesting answers to the class.

Phrasal Verbs; Tag Questions

A. Read the following paragraph.

Many people believe that it's necessary to **put off** a human mission to Mars until we have developed more advanced technology. But some space-science researchers think that better technology isn't necessary and that a Mars exploration mission will be able to **set off** soon. Why will explorers **take on** the challenges of traveling to a cold, distant planet? They'll have the same motives as past explorers: knowledge, fame, and profit. The profit motive might be especially important in encouraging explorers to **put up** the money to be first to reach Mars. Successful explorers will have many possibilities for financial gain: They may be able to **take over** new territory; they'll **set up** bases and perhaps even colonies; they'll **bring back** valuable resources; and they'll **bring out** books, movies, and television programs for fascinated audiences on earth.

B. The **boldfaced** verbs in the reading are phrasal verbs. Phrasal verbs have two words, a verb and a particle. Work with a partner.

1. Look at the phrasal verbs in the reading. Write the verbs next to their meanings.

a. ___bring back___ : return with   e. _____ : accept responsibility for

b. _____ : produce or publish   f. _____ : claim control or ownership of

c. _____ : postpone   g. _____ : start on a journey

d. _____ : invest or pay in advance h. _____ : create or establish

2. Are phrasal verbs with the same verb similar to each other in meaning?

3. What happens to the meaning of a verb when the verb combines with a particle to form a phrasal verb?

4. Can you predict the meaning of a phrasal verb from the meanings of its two words?

GRAMMAR BRIEFING 1: Phrasal Verbs

Phrasal verbs (also called two-word verbs) combine a verb with an adverb. The meaning of the phrasal verb often cannot be predicted from the meanings of its two parts.

FORM Phrasal Verbs

■ Phrasal verbs consist of verb + adverb (called a particle). Phrasal verbs can occur in any tense. The most common particles in phrasal verbs are *up, out, down, off, on,* and *over.* Other particles include *along, back, behind, in, through,* and *together.* (See Appendix 9 for a list of common phrasal verbs.)

■ Some phrasal verbs do not have objects.

> The storm **didn't let up** until late in the day.
>
> **Watch out!** That rock's going to fall!
>
> Our car **has broken down.**
>
> The plane **took off** on time.
>
> They **had gone on** before we got there.
>
> **I'll come over** tomorrow.

■ Some phrasal verbs have objects. When a phrasal verb has a noun as an object, the particle may come before or after the object.

> I'm **picking** Mary **up** soon.   I'm **picking up** Mary soon.
>
> **Check** the place **out.**   **Check out** the place.
>
> **Call** the search **off.**   **Call off** the search.
>
> The fire **burned** the house **down.**   The fire **burned down** the house.
>
> He **took** the company **over.**   He **took over** the company.
>
> She **has taken** extra work **on.**   She **has taken on** extra work.

■ When the object of a phrasal verb is a pronoun, the particle always comes after the object.

> She **called** him **up.**   **Not:** She ~~called up him.~~
>
> I'm **picking** her **up** soon.   **Not:** I'm ~~picking up her soon.~~

FUNCTION Phrasal Verbs

■ The meaning of a phrasal verb is different from the meaning of the verb + the meaning of the particle. Phrasal verbs with the same verb but different particles are different in meaning. Consider the verb *put:*

>   put = place, set, or lay
>
> He **put up** the money for the tickets.   put up = paid
>
> We **will put off** the trip until April.   put off = postpone
>
> They **are putting on** a great party.   put on = host
>
> He **was** constantly **putting** her **down.**   put down = insult

■ A phrasal verb may have more than one meaning. The phrasal verb may have an
   object in one meaning and not in another.

We **will set off** tomorrow.	set off = start a journey
Her red hair **sets** her **off** from the rest of the family.	set off = make different from others
The town **has set off** fireworks on Independence Day for many years.	set off = cause to explode
His lateness **set** her **off**.	set off = make angry

GRAMMAR HOTSPOT!

■ The words used as particles in phrasal verbs can also occur in prepositional
   phrases. In this case, they are prepositions that indicate location or direction. The
   verb + preposition is not a phrasal verb, and it has the meaning of the verb + the
   meaning of the preposition.

> He climbed **up the tree.** (Preposition *up* tells in what direction he climbed.)
>
> They went **out the door.** (Preposition *out* tells where they went.)

■ Sometimes the same combination of words can be either a phrasal verb + object
   or a verb followed by a prepositional phrase.* There are two ways to tell the
   difference:

• The meaning of a phrasal verb is different from the meaning of its two words.

• A phrasal verb object can—or, if a pronoun, must—come before the particle.

They **looked up** a word.	(phrasal verb + object: **look up** = search in
They **looked** a word **up.**	a dictionary; pronoun object must come
They **looked** it **up.**	before particle)
Not: They ~~looked up it.~~	
They **looked up** the mountain.	(verb with prepositional phrase: **look up** =
Not: They ~~looked a mountain up.~~	look in an upward direction; object must
They **looked up** it.	come after preposition)
Not: They ~~looked it up.~~	

* A verb + prepositional phrase is also different from a verb + preposition combination
followed by an object (see Grammar Briefing 2, page 120).

GRAMMAR PRACTICE 1: Phrasal Verbs

1 Identifying Phrasal Verbs: *A Success I*

Underline the phrasal verbs. If the verb has an object, **circle** the object. Including the examples, there are **14** phrasal verbs.

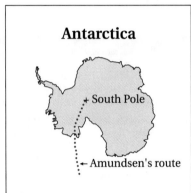

Antarctica

+ South Pole

← Amundsen's route

   In the early twentieth century, the earth's polar regions seemed almost as remote and dangerous as Mars does today. Despite the difficult conditions, a few polar explorers figured out (ways) to reach their destinations and come back safely. One man stands out as an example for future explorers— Roald Amundsen.

   Amundsen was born in Norway in 1872. While he was growing up, he wanted to be a polar explorer. He therefore built up his endurance in extremely cold and difficult conditions. He worked out by skiing long distances. He also learned how to travel and live as the Inuit, the native people of the Arctic, did, so he got along well in bitterly cold climates. Amundsen's strength and adaptability paid off later on. He understood the risks of polar expeditions, especially frostbite, hunger, and exhaustion. So before he took on an expedition, he always prepared for it carefully.

   In 1910, Amundsen took up the goal of being the first to reach the South Pole. He worked out plans for an expedition and set off with a small crew. Then he found something out: a British expedition led by Robert Falcon Scott was also trying to reach the South Pole. Amundsen and Scott were in a race. How did this race turn out?

2 Phrasal Verbs: *A Success II*

Use the appropriate form of the phrasal verbs given above each paragraph to complete the paragraph. (If necessary, look in Appendix 9 for help.)

let up   push on   ~~set in~~   set up

After Amundsen's ship landed in Antarctica in February 1911, he and his crew

worked hard and fast before the dark, icy winter _____*set in*_____. They

_____ supply depots (storage places) and trail markers along the first
2

part of their route. In October, after the Antarctic winter finally _____,
3

Amundsen and four men started south, traveling on skis and sleds pulled by dogs.

Despite fierce blizzards, Amundsen and his men _____.
4

get through   head back   keep up   mark off   set back

Their difficulties didn't _____ their progress _____ for
5

long, so they _____ their spirits _____. On December 14 they
6

reached the South Pole and realized that they had beaten the British!

Amundsen _____ the area with flags. After three days, the
7

Norwegians _____ north. They returned on January 25, 1912, having cov-
8

ered 1,860 miles in 99 days. Amundsen's adaptability, determination, and careful

preparations had _____ them _____.
9

3 Phrasal Verbs; Placement of Noun and Pronoun Objects: *A Successful Failure*

A. Ernest Shakleton was a Briton who had failed to reach the South Pole in 1908
but who had then become a popular hero and made lots of money by telling
stories about his experiences. Use the words in parentheses and appropriate
verb forms to complete the sentences. Place the objects after the particles
where possible.

When Amundsen's expedition succeeded in 1911, Shakleton could no

longer become the first to reach the South Pole, but this didn't

____*keep him back*____. He ____*thought up another scheme*____: he would
1. (keep back / him)   2. (think up / another scheme)

be the first to travel across Antarctica. In 1915 he _____.
3. (put together / an expedition)

However, the expedition's ship became trapped in thick ice. The pressure of the ice

_____. After their ship sank, Shakleton and the crew were
4. (break up / the ship)

left drifting on floating ice packs with very few supplies.

South
Georgia   **Antarctica**

Elephant
Island   + South Pole

Ross Sea

Shakleton _____ and made a plan to reach safety. They still
                5. (think over / their situation)

had a couple of small boats, and they _____ as they walked
                                            6. (pull along / them)

across the ice. After weeks of walking and sailing in the small boats, they reached

Elephant Island, a desolate ice-covered place. Many of the men were too weak

to go on. So Shakleton _____ and went to get help. He
                            7. (leave behind / them)

sailed 800 miles in a small open boat. After he got to the Falkland Islands, near

South America, he attempted several rescues, but each time problems

_____. Finally, eighteen weeks later, he reached Elephant
        8. (drive back / him)

Island. Miraculously the men were all still alive. After Shakleton

_____, he _____ to England. And
        9. (pick up / them)   10. (bring back / them)

he _____, too.
        11. (bring back / another exciting story)

B. Write a one-paragraph story about a rescue. You can tell a story that you know or
make one up. Use at least five phrasal verbs, including some phrasal verbs with
objects. Read your story to the class.

4 Phrasal Verbs—Meaning: *Polar Explorers*

Use the appropriate form of the phrasal verbs given above each set of sentences to
complete the sentences.

bring down: cause something or somebody to fail or lose power

bring in: earn profits or income

~~bring off~~: accomplish something

bring out: produce or publish something

bring on: cause something to appear or happen

1. Because of his careful planning, Amundsen _____*brought*_____ his expedition

    _____*off*_____ successfully.

2. Polar explorers went for long periods without fresh food; their poor diet

    often _____ a disease called scurvy.

3. Several early expeditions to the South Pole were unsuccessful—disease and

    other problems _____ them _____.

4. Although Shakleton didn't succeed in reaching the pole, he _____ a
   book that was a popular success.

5. Shakleton was a marketing genius—his lectures _____ a lot of money.

come back: return

come down: to be continued over time by tradition

come off: happen or occur

come out: result, end up, turn out

come up: appear, arise

6. Sailing and exploring in arctic regions was a Norwegian custom

   that _____ to Amundsen from his ancestors.

7. When men with scurvy ate fresh meat, their health _____.

8. Amundsen was well-prepared, so everything _____ fine in the end.

9. On Shakleton's expedition, a serious problem _____—his ship sank.

10. Amundsen didn't encounter any unexpected difficulties, so his expedition

   _____ on schedule.

5 Particle versus Preposition: *Look This Over*

The **underlined** word is a particle in one sentence and a preposition in the other.
Circle the letter of the sentence that contains the particle and **rewrite** the sentence
with the object following the verb.

1. (a.) When Carla and Bill left the house, they turned <u>off</u> the light.

   b. When Eugene got to the hotel, he turned <u>off</u> the road.

   When Carla and Bill left the house, they turned the light off.

2. a. When the car skidded on ice, it ran <u>off</u> the road.

   b. Everyone in the group needed a map, so Paula ran <u>off</u> some photocopies.

3. a. Judy checked <u>in</u> her purse to make sure that her plane ticket was still there.

   b. Ethan checked <u>in</u> his room key when he left the dormitory at the end of the year.

4. a. When Mark and Terry talked long-distance for hours, they ran <u>up</u> a huge bill.

   b. When the children got out of school, they ran <u>up</u> the street.

5. a. The committee passed <u>over</u> two other candidates and chose Tim for the job.

   b. You passed <u>over</u> the Hudson River when you drove across the bridge.

6. a. After they learned where he was hiding, the police ran <u>down</u> the suspect.

   b. After the center passed the ball, the rest of the players ran <u>down</u> the field.

7. a. As soon as I looked <u>over</u> the ridge, I saw the valley below it.

   b. As soon as I looked <u>over</u> the final exam, I saw that it wasn't difficult.

GRAMMAR BRIEFING 2: Verb-Preposition Combinations; Phrasal Verbs with Prepositions

Verb-preposition combinations combine a verb with a preposition. (Like phrasal verbs, these combinations are sometimes called two-word verbs.) Their meaning often is related to the meaning of the verb. Phrasal verbs can also combine with prepositions. (These combinations are sometimes called three-word verbs.)

FORM Verb-Preposition Combinations

■ Verb-preposition combinations can occur in any tense. Prepositions that commonly combine with verbs include *about, at, for, from, in, of, on, to,* and *with*. (See Appendix 10 for a list of common verb-preposition combinations.)

■ In verb-preposition combinations, the preposition is followed by an object.

> They **confide in** each other.
>
> We **lived on** seaweed.
>
> **Think about** your decision.

■ In some verb-preposition combinations, the verb also can have an object.

>   V   O   Prep   O
> His clothing **didn't protect** him   **from** the rain.
>
> She **searched**   the map   **for**   the road.

FUNCTION Verb-Preposition Combinations

■ The meaning of a verb-preposition combination often can be figured out from the meaning of the verb. The preposition affects the meaning of the verb but usually does not significantly change it. The preposition often does not have its own separate meaning (of direction, location, etc.). Verbs of attitude, sense, speech, and thought are common in these combinations.

> I **agree with** you that the trip was hard.   (attitude)
>
> We**'ve heard about** a great trip.   (sense)
>
> I**'ll talk to** the travel agent before then.   (speech)
>
> We **believed in** the Loch Ness monster.   (thought)

■ A verb-preposition combination + object is a verb + prepositional phrase, like those discussed in the Grammar Hotspot on page 115. The difference is that the verb-preposition combination forms a fixed unit and the preposition in this unit doesn't have its usual meaning.

> They **lived on** seaweed.   (verb-preposition combination + object: **live on** = live by eating)
>
> They **lived on** the mountain.   (verb + prepositional phrase: **live on** = live in a location on)

FORM Phrasal Verbs with Prepositions

- Phrasal verbs can combine with prepositions. (See Appendix 11 for common phrasal verbs with prepositions.)

	Phrasal Verb	Prep	
We	**were running out**	**of**	food when the supplies finally arrived.
They	**have caught up**	**with**	the rest of the group.
She	**had gotten back**	**from**	the hike before we did.
He	**was watching out**	**for**	falling rocks.

GRAMMAR HOTSPOT!

- Verb-preposition combinations are different from phrasal verbs because in verb-preposition combinations:
  - the preposition doesn't significantly change the meaning of a verb;
  - the object always follows the preposition;
  - *up, out, off,* and *down,* which are common in phrasals, are **not** used.

    He **played down** the problems. (phrasal verb meaning "make seem less important")

    He **played** the problems **down.**

    He **played with** the children. (verb-preposition combination; meaning of verb not changed)

    Not: He ~~played the children with~~.

GRAMMAR PRACTICE 2: Verb-Preposition Combinations; Phrasal Verbs with Prepositions

6 **Identifying Verb-Preposition Combinations:** *Looking for Adventure?*

Underline the verb-preposition combinations. For each, **circle** the object of the preposition. Including the example, there are **16** verb-preposition combinations.

When you <u>read about</u> (men like Amundsen and Shakleton,) do you ever wonder

about their motives? Were they simply looking for adventure or was it something

more?

At the end of the nineteenth century, explorers concentrated on the polar regions because most of the earth had been explored. People were eager to know about the poles. So governments and organizations paid for expeditions.

Newspapers wrote about the explorers, so almost everyone had heard of them and thought of them as heroes. People worried about the explorers and waited for their return. When the explorers returned, they talked about their exploits. If, like Shakleton, they were great storytellers, the public paid to listen to them. They could grow rich as well as famous.

Amundsen succeeded; Shakleton failed but became famous. Don't forget about Scott, who also searched for the South Pole. What happened to him?

7 Verb-Preposition Combinations: *Preparing for the Unexpected*

A. Use the appropriate form of the verb-preposition combinations given above each paragraph to complete the paragraph.

   ~~dream of~~   plan for

Both Roald Amundsen and Robert Falcon Scott were experienced explorers who
___dreamed of___ reaching the South Pole. But their personalities were very different,
       1
and they _____ their expeditions in different ways.
                 2

   concentrate on   prepare for   rely on   talk to

   Amundsen _____ practical experience and careful preparation.
                      3
Before he explored an area, he _____ experienced people and got useful
                                        4
information from them. Amundsen _____ the details of an expedition.
                                            5
He always _____ the worst possible conditions, so he was ready for the
                  6
unexpected.

agree with   believe in   hope for   prevent from   worry about

Scott was a British naval officer who _____ tradition and deter-
                                                              7
mination. He didn't _____ details. He expected to have good luck
                                          8
and _____ good weather. Unfortunately, Scott's personal feelings
              9
often _____ him _____ making wise decisions. For example,
                10
he felt that using dogs to pull his sleds was cruel. He _____ people who
                                                                          11
believed that the men should pull the sleds, although this was exhausting.

die from   forget about   succeed in   think of

Amundsen and Scott both _____ reaching the South Pole. People
                                      12
considered Amundsen to be a cold and calculating man and _____ him
                                                                            13
quickly. People _____ Scott as a heroic leader for years after, although he
                      14
and his men _____ exhaustion, cold, and hunger on the way back to their
                      15
ship.

B. When you are traveling to a new place, how do you prepare for the trip? Write **five**
sentences describing your typical preparations. Use verb-preposition combinations
from **A;** you can also use combinations in Appendix 10.

> Example: I like to be well organized, so I worry about details. I talk to friends
> about what to expect.

8   Verb-Preposition Combinations versus Phrasal Verbs: *Do You Know about the Antarctic Region?*

Amundsen is questioning a man who wants to be a member of his expedition. Complete
the man's answers, changing the noun objects in the questions to pronouns. Be careful
to put the pronoun in the correct position.

1. *Q:* I need someone who is knowledgeable. Do you know about the Antarctic
   region?

   A: Yes, I _know about it_ _____.

2. *Q:* You must have great endurance. Have you built up your strength?

   A: Yes, I _'ve built it up_ _____.

3. *Q:* My plans are summarized in these papers. Have you looked over these
   papers?

   A: Yes, I _____.

4. *Q:* These are the maps of the route I plan to follow. Have you looked at these
     maps?

   A: Yes, I _____.

5. *Q:* I need an experienced hunter. Have you tracked down wild animals?

   A: Yes, I _____.

6. *Q:* The men on this trip must be adaptable. Do you learn from your mistakes?

   A: Yes, I _____.

7. *Q:* Our equipment must be tested in advance. Will you try out the equipment?

   A: Yes, I _____.

8. *Q:* We'll eat the same thing every day. Will you live on biscuits and dried meat?

   A: Yes, I _____.

9. *Q:* The trip will be very dangerous. Have you thought about the dangers?

   A: Yes, I _____.

10. *Q:* Are you still determined to come along? Have you thought over your decision?

   A: Yes, I _____.

9 Phrasal Verbs with Prepositions: *Running Up against Difficulties*

Use the appropriate form of the phrasal verb-preposition combinations given above each
paragraph to complete the paragraph. (If necessary, look in Appendix 11 for help.)

   catch up + with   ~~run up + against~~   stand up + to   start out + for

Scott's expedition __ran up against__ difficulties from the beginning. Scott
                         1

_____ the South Pole two weeks after Amundsen because of problems
     2

with his equipment. He had planned to use motorized sleds, but they didn't

_____ Antarctic conditions. Scott never _____ Amundsen.
     3   4

   close in + on   face up + to   keep on + at   miss out + on

Scott and his men began their journey south on November 1, 1911, but bad

weather soon _____ them. Despite the terrible conditions, they
                    5

_____ the tiring job of pulling their sleds to the pole. They finally reached
     6

it on January 17, 1912—only to see the Norwegian flags Amundsen had left there.

With sinking spirits, they _____ the fact that they had been beaten. They
                                 7

had _____ the prize for which they had struggled.
        8

cut down + on   gave up + on   keep up + with   run out + of

On the return journey, Scott's group _____ supplies and luck.
                                                            9

Because they _____ food rations, they became weak and confused. One
                              10

of the men became very sick. He _____ the group for a while but soon
                                              11

this became impossible. The others struggled on to a point only 11 miles from their

next supply depot. Each day they tried to start for it, but blizzards drove them back.

Finally, they _____ their attempts. By the end of March, Scott and his
                              12

men were dead.

10 Using Phrasal Verbs with Prepositions and Verb-Preposition Combinations: *Your Expedition Diary*

We know the story of Scott's expedition because he kept a diary, which was found
with his body. In his final messages, he wrote:

> We took risks——we knew we took them; things have come out against
> us. . . . I do not think we can hope for any better things now. We shall stick it
> out to the end but we are getting weaker of course and the end cannot be
> far. . . . For God's sake, look after our people.

Imagine that you are on an expedition in a remote and dangerous place, for example,
Antarctica or a desert, jungle, or mountain. Write a two-paragraph diary entry. Use at
least four phrasal verb–preposition combinations from exercise 9 and four verb-preposition combinations from exercises 6, 7, and 8.

> Example: Before we started out for the mountaintop, we had prepared for
> bad conditions. Then we ran up against difficulties. First, . . .

Read your paragraphs to the class.

GRAMMAR BRIEFING 3: Tag Questions

A tag question is a statement with a short question ("tag") added at the end. The statement can be in any verb tense
and can use a modal auxiliary verb (see Chapter 14). Tag questions are used to seek agreement or to get information.

FORM Tag Questions

Forming Tag Questions

■ To form tag questions, add to a statement:
   be, do, have, or modal + pronoun.

> You haven't been to Alaska, **have you**?

■ When the statement is affirmative, the tag is usually negative. The negative tag is almost always contracted. When the statement is negative, the tag is affirmative.

<u>**Affirm.**</u>   <u>**Neg.**</u>

You**'re** hungry, **aren't** you?

<u>**Neg.**</u>   <u>**Affirm.**</u>

You**'re not** hungry, **are** you?

■ The pronoun in the tag corresponds to the subject in the statement.

Bob and John are leaving tomorrow, aren't **they**?

Verb Forms in Tags

■ The verb form in the tag usually agrees with the subject of the statement. However, with *I am,* the tag is usually *aren't I.*

She's going with you, **isn't she?**

I am going with you, **aren't I?**

■ If the statement has a modal auxiliary verb and/or other auxiliary verbs, use the first of these auxiliary verbs in the tag.

We **can** still get tickets, **can't** we?

They **won't have returned** by June, **will** they?

You **weren't living** there then, **were** you?

I **hadn't been climbing** at that time, **had** I?

■ If the statement doesn't have auxiliary verbs but has the main verb *be,* use *be* in the tag.

They **are** in Egypt, **aren't** they?

He **was** in the Bahamas last year, **wasn't** he?

■ If the statement has neither an auxiliary verb nor the main verb *be,* use *do* in the tag.

You **go** to the beach every year, **don't** you?

She **doesn't travel** well, **does** she?

Answers to Tag Questions

■ The answer to a tag question can be affirmative or negative. Tag questions can be answered like *yes/no* questions.

Q: You**'re going** with me, **aren't you**?

A: Yes, I am. OR No, I'm not.

■ When the statement is affirmative, the speaker usually expects an affirmative answer. When the statement is negative, the speaker usually expects a negative answer.

Q: You**'ve hidden** it in your backpack, **haven't you**? (positive answer expected)

A: Yes, I have.

Q: He**'s not telling** the truth, **is he**? (negative answer expected)

A: No, he's not.

Other Subjects with Tags

■ With subjects such as *everyone, somebody, anyone,* and *nobody,* use *they* in the tag. With subjects such as *everything, something,* and *nothing,* use *it* in the tag. With negative subjects, such as *no one* and *nothing,* use an affirmative tag.

> **Everyone** is going to be here tomorrow, aren't **they**?
>
> **Something** happened, didn't **it**?
>
> **Nobody** lives there anymore, **do they**?

■ With *this* and *that,* use *it* in the tag. With *these* and *those,* use *they* in the tag.

> **That** isn't right, is **it**?
>
> **Those** are right, aren't **they**?

■ With *there is* and *there are,* use *there* in the tag.

> **There** is a plane leaving soon, isn't **there**?

FUNCTION Tag Questions

■ A tag question is often used just to seek agreement or confirmation. In this use, the tag is spoken with falling intonation. It is not intended as a question, and the listener often just nods or responds with some expression of agreement.

> It**'s** hot today, **isn't it**?

■ A tag question can be used to get information. In this use, the tag is spoken with rising intonation like a *yes/no* question. The listener is likely to indicate yes or no or otherwise give information.

> It**'ll be** hot today, **won't it**?

TALKING the TALK

■ An affirmative statement can be followed by an affirmative tag. This usually suggests sarcasm on the part of the speaker.

> So you **expect** sympathy from me, **do you**? Well, you're not going to get it.

■ Tag questions can also be formed with expressions, including *right, isn't that right, isn't that so,* and *correct.* These expressions can be used with both affirmative and negative statements and all verb tenses. These tag questions are answered like other tag questions.

> He won't be in today, **right**?
>
> She'll be back from her trip by then, **isn't that right**?

GRAMMAR PRACTICE 3: Tag Questions

▮▮ Tag Questions—Form: *Test Anxiety—I'll Be Ready, Won't I?*

Complete the tag questions.

1. Tests cause anxiety, ___*don't they*___?

2. Ms. Moore doesn't give difficult tests, _____?

3. The first test is going to cover Columbus's voyages to America, _____?

4. Christopher Columbus wasn't from Portugal, _____?

5. The other students already know a lot about the topic, _____?

6. You weren't absent from class, _____?

7. There is a lot to learn, _____?

8. We can study together, _____?

9. Kim and Oliver hadn't studied before this week, _____?

10. Those weren't the right answers, _____?

11. Someone will fail the test, _____?

12. Victoria was taking notes, _____?

13. That could be a question on the test, _____?

14. The library has all the information we need, _____?

15. This isn't taking too much time, _____?

16. You and I will have learned everything by tomorrow, _____?

17. I'm driving you crazy with all these questions, _____?

18. I've never failed an exam before, _____?

19. Nobody's perfect, _____?

12 Listening to Tag Questions: *Christopher Columbus*

A. Listen to the questions once, paying attention to the speaker's intonation. Then listen again and decide whether the speaker is seeking agreement or wants information. **Check** the correct choice (✓).

The speaker is sure and is seeking agreement.	The speaker is not sure and wants information.
1. ____✓____	_____
2. _____	_____
3. _____	_____
4. _____	_____
5. _____	_____
6. _____	_____
7. _____	_____
8. _____	_____
9. _____	_____
10. _____	_____
11. _____	_____

B. Read the information about Columbus on Exercise Page E–3. Listen to the questions again and answer each one orally as a class.

Example: "Columbus set out on his first voyage in 1492, didn't he?" Yes, he did.

C. Work with a partner. Go back to exercise 11. Take turns asking and giving the expected answers to the questions. Use falling intonation.

Example: Student A: Tests cause anxiety, don't they?

Student B: Yes, they do.

13   Using Tag Questions: *Columbus Brought Back More Than Gold, Didn't He?*

When Columbus and other Europeans went to the New World (America), they
brought back foods that hadn't been known in the Old World (Europe as well as
Africa and Asia). At the same time, they introduced Old World plants and animals to
the New World.

Work with a partner. Look at the plants and animals mentioned in the questions for
Student A or Student B. Decide whether you think they came from the Old World or
New World. **Circle** the answers that fit your guesses, and then complete the tag questions. Ask your partner the questions. Your partner answers them, using the information
on Exercise Page E–3.

> Example:
> Student A: Bananas grew / (didn't grow) in the New World before the time of
>
> Columbus, _____did they_____?
> Student B: Right. They grew in the Old World first.

Student A:

1. Corn grew / didn't grow in the Old World originally, _____?

2. Honeybees were living / weren't living in the New World when Columbus

   arrived, _____?

3. People in the New World had seen / hadn't seen horses before the Europeans

   came, _____?

4. There were / weren't potatoes in the Old World before 1492, _____?

5. Before the fifteenth century, people in the Old World had / didn't have tomatoes,

   _____?

6. Wheat is / isn't originally from the New World, _____?

Student B:

1. Before Columbus arrived, New World people had / didn't have chickens,

   _____?

2. People in the New World had had / hadn't had chocolate before Columbus's voy-

   ages, _____?

3. Oranges grew / didn't grow in the Old World first, _____?

4. Sugar cane was growing / wasn't growing in the New World when Columbus

    arrived, _____?

5. There was / wasn't tobacco in the New World before 1492, _____?

6. Vanilla is / isn't originally from the Old World, _____?

14 Using Tag Questions: *You're from Spain, Aren't You?*

How well do you know your classmates? Write **five** statements with information about your classmates that you're quite sure is true.

    Example: Luis is from Spain.

Write **five** statements with information that you aren't so sure about.

    Example: Amy has four sisters.

Then go around the classroom, checking the information in your statements by using tag questions. Use falling intonation for the information you're quite sure about:

Luis, you're from Spain, aren't you?

Use rising intonation for the information you aren't so sure about:

Amy, you have four sisters, don't you?

How often were you right?

UNIT WRAP-UP

Error Correction

Correct the errors in the transcript of a radio talk show. Some errors can be corrected in more than one way. Including the example, there are **17** errors.

Host: This is Radio Talk Time. If you have an interesting opinion, I want to

          from
    hear ~~of~~ you. Call up me and tell me your thoughts.

Caller: What do you think about NASA's space program? I've thought it about. It's all

    a lie. Nothing is real, isn't it?

Host: You're joking, don't you?

Caller: No, I'm serious. NASA announced that it be going to send a spacecraft to

    Mars next October. But they don't really send it to Mars. We'll believe that it's

    on Mars, but they'll be fool us.

Host: How they'll do that? When they'll send the spacecraft to Mars, we'll see the pictures that it sends back.

Caller: It's going to be seeming to us that a spacecraft is on Mars. Antarctica looks a lot like Mars, isn't it? By the time they'll launch the fake spacecraft next October, they'll have sent people to Antarctica with video cameras and a fake rover. After they set the cameras up there, they'll be able to send back pictures of the rover. While we're going to be watching the videos on television, we're going to be looking at Antarctica, not Mars. But we won't be knowing that, will we?

Host: I'm sorry, sir. We've run out of time. It's time for the weather forecast. It's snowing tomorrow.

Caller: Wait! Don't hang me up on! I'm right, aren't I?

Task 1: Your Island Vacation

Work with a partner. Imagine that you are going to Getaway Island for a three-day vacation. First, use your imagination and fill in the map with the features of the island, for example, towns, beaches and other natural attractions, hotels and stores, amusement parks and other entertainment places—anything you want to include. Then discuss what you are going to do when you visit there. When you have decided on a plan for your trip, write two paragraphs about it. In the first paragraph, describe what you'll be doing day by day. Use *will, be going to,* and the future progressive. In the second paragraph, summarize what you'll have done by the end of the vacation. Use the future perfect. Show your map and read your paragraphs to the class.

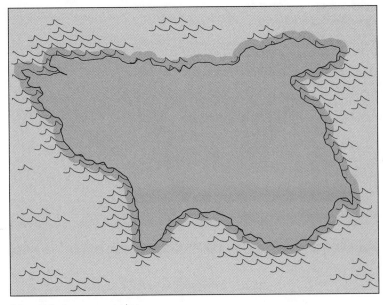

Getaway Island

Task 2: Your Outdoor Vacation

Work in small groups. Plan a trip to a national park in the United States for your group. You can find information about various parks at a library or on the Internet—use National Park Service as the topic for your search. Which park are you going to visit? When will you leave? How long will you stay? How are you going to get there? What activities are you going to do? What equipment and supplies will you need to take? What responsibilities will each member of the group have? Write notes about your plans. Then give an oral report about your plans to the class, referring to your notes as needed. Which trip sounds the most adventurous? Which one sounds the most educational?

Task 3: Ask the Oracle

An oracle is someone who is thought to have knowledge about the future. One member of the class should play the part of the oracle. He or she should look at Exercise Page E–4 and follow the instructions there. The other members of the class should each write **three** questions about their future travels to ask the oracle. Two of the questions should be *yes/no* questions; one should be a tag question. Use a different future form in each question.

> Example: Am I going to go on a trip soon? Will I have gone to Mars by the time I'm fifty? I'm going to spend my honeymoon in Hawaii, aren't I?

Take turns asking your questions for the oracle to answer.

Task 4: Acting Out the Verbs

Work in small groups to write and then perform a skit. Each group chooses one of the lists of phrasal verbs on Exercise Page E–4. The story of your skit is up to you, but it should use all the phrasal verbs in your list and should include actions that will show the meanings of these verbs. Everyone in the group should have a role. Present your skit to the rest of the class.

Unit Four

Noun Phrases

Topic Focus: *Food*

UNIT OBJECTIVES

- **proper and common nouns**
  (*Emily Custer* just opened a *restaurant.*)

- **count and noncount nouns**
  (I can make some *suggestions* if you want *advice* about what to order.)

- **uses of definite and indefinite articles**
  (I didn't like *the* omelet you gave me. Can I have *a* doughnut instead?)

- **numbers, measure phrases, and general quantifiers**
  (I had *two* doughnuts and *a cup of* coffee with *a little* cream and sugar.)

- **adjectives and other noun modifiers**
  (I crave *delicious fresh home-grown* tomatoes.)

- **reflexive, reciprocal, and indefinite pronouns**
  (Andrew made the cake *himself.* Liz and Val helped *each other* with the entrees. *Everything* is ready now.)

- **possessives—determiners, nouns, pronouns, and phrases**
  (This is *my* office. It isn't *Ms. Anderson's* office. *Hers* is down the hall in the corner *of the building.*)

INTRODUCTORY TASKS

Reading and Listening

📼 Read and listen to this passage from a guidebook for international visitors to the United States:

Food Choices

There's one type of American food that people from many countries have become familiar with before they ever visit the United States—fast food. So it's natural that you may consider fast food to be **the typical American food**. And you'll find that **lots of Americans** do eat fast food, often because we want to save time. But as you travel through **the country**, you will also discover **many interesting differences among places and people**. Our food choices and our eating habits reflect our regional, cultural, and individual differences. Also, these choices and habits are always changing, and sometimes **our tendencies** are contradictory.

For example, recently **Americans** have been going out to eat at restaurants more than ever before. Does this mean that we don't have **much interest in home cooking**? Not at all. We've also been buying **lots of new cookbooks**, and quite a few

people are taking up cooking as **a hobby**. Cooking programs on television have become so popular that we even have **a channel devoted to them**. In fact, **some professional chefs** have become big celebrities.

Some Americans don't worry much about **their diets**. But many of us have serious concerns about health and nutrition. We have questions about **the chemicals that might be in our food** and about the safety of new foods created in scientific laboratories. Many of us also worry about the amount of fat in our diets. This doesn't mean that we can resist **our strong desires for fatty foods**. **One person** can't resist a chocolate bar; another can't resist an ice cream cone or **a hot pizza covered with cheese**.

At the end of your visit to the United States, you may not be able to make many general statements about our food except for this one—there's plenty of it!

Comprehension Check

Read each sentence. Circle **T** if the sentence is true or **F** if the sentence is false.

1. The author of the passage believes that Americans eat fast food because it's the typical American cuisine. **T** (**F**)

2. There's a lot of variety in food and eating habits in the United States. **T** **F**

3. Most Americans aren't very interested in cooking. **T** **F**

4. It isn't common for Americans to worry about their diets. **T** **F**

5. Some people who worry about fat in their diets also eat fatty foods. **T** **F**

Think about Grammar

A phrase is a group of related words. One type of phrase is the noun phrase. In the reading, some of the noun phrases are boldfaced. Some of the boldfaced noun phrases are shown in the chart. Look at the chart and then complete parts **A** and **B**.

A. Circle the letter of the correct choice to complete the sentences.

1. A noun phrase always has
   (a.) a noun/b. a noun and a determiner].

2. The words *a* and *the* are articles. Articles are [a. determiners/ b. modifiers].

3. Quantifiers tell the amount or number of a noun. Examples of quantifiers are [a. *many, lots of,* and *some*/b. *our* and *their*].

4. Possessives indicate a noun as belonging to someone or something. Examples of possessives are [a. *many, lots of,* and *some*/ b. *our* and *their*].

5. Quantifiers and possessives are [a. determiners/b. modifiers].

6. Modifiers describe and give more information about nouns. In a noun phrase, modifiers can come [a. only before/b. before and after] the main noun.

Determiner	Modifier(s) before the Main Noun	Main Noun	Modifier after the Main Noun
the	typical American	food	
many	interesting	differences	among places and people
our		tendencies	
		Americans	
lots of	new	cookbooks	
a		channel	devoted to them
some		Americans	
their		diets	
the		chemicals	that might be in our food

B. Work with a partner. In the reading, there are eight boldfaced noun phrases that aren't in the chart. Find them and write them on the chart, putting each element into the appropriate column.

Nouns and Determiners

Introductory Task: *Survey on the Cooking and Eating Habits of Your Class*

A. Work with a partner. Take turns asking each other the questions. Make a check mark before each of your partner's answers.

1. How much time do you spend cooking each day?
   ☐ 0 to 30 minutes   ☐ 30 to 60 minutes   ☐ 60 minutes or more

2. How many meals from fast-food restaurants do you eat each week?
   ☐ no meals   ☐ one or two meals   ☐ three to five meals
   ☐ six or more meals

3. How much ice cream do you eat each week?
   ☐ no ice cream   ☐ very little ice cream   ☐ some ice cream
   ☐ a lot of ice cream

4. How much fruit do you eat each day?
   ☐ no fruit   ☐ very little fruit   ☐ some fruit   ☐ a lot of fruit

5. How many vegetables do you eat each day?
   ☐ no vegetables   ☐ very few vegetables   ☐ some vegetables
   ☐ a lot of vegetables

6. How much coffee do you drink each day?
   ☐ 0 cups of coffee   ☐ one or two cups of coffee
   ☐ three or more cups of coffee

B. Find out about your class as a whole. Write the questions on the blackboard and add up the answers in each category. As a class discuss the results. What can you conclude about the group's habits?

   Example: *We don't spend much time cooking.*

GRAMMAR BRIEFING 1: Types of Nouns and Determiners

Nouns name people, places, and things. There are proper and common nouns. Common nouns can be count or noncount. Determiners usually come before common nouns to introduce, identify, or tell the quantity of the nouns.

FORM AND FUNCTION Types of Nouns

Proper and Common Nouns

Proper Nouns

- Proper nouns name particular people, places, and things. They always start with a capital letter.

    Names of people: **Mrs. Fields, Betty Crocker**

    Names of places: **South America, New Orleans,** the **Missouri River,** the **Ritz Hotel**

    Titles: *Good News Cookbook, The New York Times, Sports Illustrated*

    Days of the week, months, holidays: **Friday, June, Easter**

    Nationalities, languages, religions: **Mexican, Japanese, Islam**

- Because proper nouns refer to particular people, places, and things, identified by their names, they are not usually used with articles or other determiners.

    France is known for its cuisine.

    Asia is known for good seafood.

    We went to **Mount Everest.**

- However, *the* is used with some place names, including some names of countries, regions, geographical features, buildings, and vehicles. (See Appendix 12 for a list of proper nouns with *the*.)

    The United States is in North America.

    The Middle East produces dates.

    We went to **the Rocky Mountains.**

    My favorite restaurant is **the New York Deli.**

    A group of colonists sailed from England on **the** *Mayflower.*

- Proper nouns sometimes act like common nouns. That is, they no longer refer to particular people, places, or things. In such cases, they can be used with determiners.

    There are **three Jasons** in my class. (three students with the name Jason)

    We can meet on **a Friday** next month. (any day that is a Friday)

The is used with family names in the plural form to mean the family with that name.

    The Smiths are our neighbors. (the Smith family)

Common Nouns

- Common nouns are not names of particular persons, places, or things. They do not usually start with a capital letter unless they are the first word in a sentence.

    That **man** is a famous **chef.** (people)

    That **restaurant** is in the **city.** (places)

    We all have **opinions** about the **food** that we like. (things)

Count and Noncount Nouns

- Some common nouns are count nouns; that is, they name people, places, and things that can be counted. Other common nouns are noncount nouns (also called mass nouns or uncountable nouns). Some nouns that are noncount nouns in English are count nouns in some other languages.

> **idea** (count noun)   one idea, three ideas
>
> **advice** (noncount noun)   **Not:** ~~one advice, three advices~~

Count Nouns

- Count nouns can be singular or plural. Verbs are singular or plural depending on the sentence subject.

> A **banana was** in the bowl.   Two **bananas were** in the bowl.

- Regular plural count nouns add -*s*/-*es* to the singular. Irregular plural count nouns differ from the singular in some other way (*man/men, mouse/mice*), have the same form as the singular (*deer/deer, species/species*), or come from other languages and have kept their original plural form (*bacterium/bacteria, criterion/criteria, analysis/analyses*).

> We ate some **bananas.** (regular plural)
>
> We cooked three **fish** for dinner. (irregular plural)

(See Appendix 13 for spelling rules for regular plural count nouns. See Appendix 14 for pronunciation rules for regular plural nouns. See Appendix 15 for common irregular plural count nouns.)

In addition, some count nouns have only a plural form and always take plural verbs.

> A chef's **clothes are** usually white.

- Collective nouns, which are usually count nouns, refer to groups of people or animals. Examples include *audience, committee, crowd, group,* and *team.* Singular forms of verbs and pronouns are usually used with singular collective nouns.

> The **team** of experts **has** finished **its** work.

Noncount Nouns

- Because noncount nouns are not countable, they cannot be plural.* They always take a singular verb.

> Her **advice** is good.   **Not:** Her ~~advices are~~ good.

- Categories of noncount nouns include:

> Names of groups of similar items: **clothing, equipment, food, fruit, furniture, garbage, homework, jewelry, money, traffic**
>
> Liquids: **coffee, milk, soup, tea, water**
>
> Solids: **glass, gold, ice, paper, silver, wood**
>
> Foods: **bread, butter, cheese, spinach, chicken, flour, rice, salt, sugar**
>
> Gases: **air, oxygen, smoke, steam**
>
> Natural phenomena: **cold, fire, electricity, heat, humidity, rain, scenery, weather**
>
> Abstract ideas: **advice, beauty, confidence, education, energy, fun, health, hospitality, information, luck, news,* pride, progress, space, time**

Fields of study: **business, chemistry, engineering, history, mathematics,* nutrition**

Activities: **baseball, chess, cooking, driving, soccer, tennis, traveling, walking**

(See Appendix 16 for common noncount nouns.)

* Some noncount nouns, such as *news* and *mathematics,* end in *s*. These nouns are not plural; they always take a singular verb (e.g., The **news** about the restaurant **is** surprising).

Nouns Used as Count or Noncount Nouns

■ Nouns that refer to abstract things can be used as noncount nouns to indicate a concept in general or used as count nouns to mean an instance of that concept. Such nouns include *art, business, crime, education, freedom, history, justice, law, life, truth.*

> **Education** is important. (education in general)
>
> We are getting **a** good **education.** (an instance of education)

■ Some nouns that refer to concrete things can be used as noncount nouns to indicate the substance or as count nouns to mean a type or a serving of the substance. Such nouns include *aspirin, cake, cheese, chocolate, coffee, food, pastry, tea,* and *wine.*

> All living things need **food.** (substance)   I like many different **foods.** (types)
>
> I like **coffee** in the morning. (substance)   I'd like **a coffee** to go, please. (serving)

FORM AND FUNCTION Determiners

■ Determiners come before common nouns. There are various kinds of determiners: articles, quantifiers, demonstratives, and possessives.

- *A/an* (the indefinite article) and [0] (the zero article) introduce nouns that are unknown or indefinite to the speaker and/or listener. *The* (the definite article) identifies nouns that are known to the speaker and listener. (See Grammar Briefing 2, page 146.)

  > **A** well-known chef won **an** award for his recipe for dessert.
  >
  > [0] Vegetarians don't eat [0] meat.
  >
  > **The** chef received **the** award last week.

- Quantifiers indicate the quantity of the noun. (See Grammar Briefing 3, page 154.)

  > **Many** chefs entered the contest, but only **five** chefs won awards.
  >
  > **Some** restaurants change their menus every month.
  >
  > **Few** restaurants can afford top-notch chefs.

- Demonstratives indicate a noun as close (*this, these*) or far (*that, those*), in terms of physical distance or more abstractly, for example, in terms of time.

  > **Those** chefs over there won awards **this** year.

- Possessives indicate the noun as belonging to someone or something. (See Chapter 9, Grammar Briefing 3, page 174.)

  > **Their** recipes will be printed in a new cookbook.

■ As will be seen in Grammar Briefings 2 and 3, the type of noun (singular count, plural count, noncount) affects the choice of determiners.

GRAMMAR PRACTICE 1: Types of Nouns and Determiners

Proper and Common Nouns: *Into the Melting Pot*

Read the following passage. **Capitalize** the proper nouns. **Underline** the common nouns.

The united states is known as a "melting pot" of cultures, and this term could
apply to its food, too. The food has always blended ingredients and styles from
many different cultures.

When christopher columbus arrived in the fifteenth century, he discovered
foods that were unknown to europeans—including turkey and pumpkins. Most of
us probably don't remember that these foods are native to america, except each fall
on thanksgiving, the holiday celebrating the feast shared by indians and colonists
from england.

As each group of immigrants has come to the united states—from places like
ireland, china, and italy, and, more recently, from countries in southeast asia and
latin america—it has contributed its own foods and style of cooking.

Individuals have expanded our knowledge about cooking, too. An example is a
woman named alice waters, the owner of a famous restaurant in berkeley, california.
She has taught us how to use the freshest herbs, vegetables, and fruit to create
unusual dishes.

2 Count and Noncount Nouns: *Back to the Melting Pot*

Look again at the common nouns you underlined in exercise 1. Some of them are count nouns and some are noncount nouns. **Circle** the noncount nouns.

> Example:
>
>   U   S
>
> The united states is known as a "melting pot" of cultures, and this term
>
> could apply to its food, too.

3 Using Articles with Proper Nouns: *Regional Specialties I*

A. Different regions of the United States have different food specialties. Insert *the* where needed with proper nouns in the following sentences. (If necessary, look in Appendix 12 for help.)

1. When English colonists sailed across *the* Atlantic Ocean to North America on

   Mayflower, they landed in New England, an area that's known for its maple

   syrup, blueberries, lobster, and clams.

2. There are certain foods closely identified with South, especially cornbread.

3. New Orleans, a city in Louisiana, where Mississippi River flows into Gulf of

   Mexico, has its own typical cuisine, which shows influences from France and

   Africa.

4. After they settled in Midwest, immigrants from Germany, Scandinavia, and

   Netherlands continued to prepare the traditional foods of their native countries.

5. Cattle are raised on ranches in Rocky Mountains, so visitors often have steaks

   when they're staying at Brown Palace Hotel in Denver, the capital of Colorado.

6. The food of West Coast, like that of Hawaiian Islands in Pacific, has been influ-

   enced by Asia.

B. Think of a regional specialty that you know about, either from the United States or another country. Write **one** sentence about it. Include the name of the region it comes from.

> Example: In the Mediterranean region, people prepare many excellent
> seafood dishes.

Read your sentence to the class.

4   Proper Nouns Acting as Common Nouns: *Regional Specialties II*

Complete the dialogue by using the indicated article or, if an article is not appropriate, write **NA** for "no article."

A: Let's have a potluck dinner soon. We'll ask everyone to bring a special food from

the region where they grew up.

B: That sounds like fun. We can have it on _____*a*_____ (a, NA) Sunday next
                                              1

month.

A: I think it would be better to have it on _____ (a, NA) Saturday next
                                            2

month.

B: Okay. Let's invite _____ (the, NA) Callahans. They're from
                       3

_____ (the, NA) Boston, and they make great clam chowder.
4

A: Let's invite _____ (the, NA) Tom, too. I talked to him on
               5

_____ (a, NA) Tuesday, and I know he'd like to come. He's a great cook.
6

B: I know several Toms. Which one do you mean?

A: I mean _____ (the, NA) Tom with black hair. He's the guy from
          7

_____ (the, NA) Springfield.
8

B: I'm not sure I know him. Do you mean _____ (the, NA) Springfield,
                                         9

Massachusetts?

A: No, I mean Springfield, Illinois. Say, did you know there's _____ (a,
                                                                10

NA) Springfield in almost every state?

5   Count Nouns versus Noncount Nouns; Plural Count Nouns: *A Good Career Choice*

Complete the dialogue by using the correct form of the nouns under the blanks. (If necessary, look in Appendices 13, 15, and 16 for help.)

Allison: I wanted to get some ____*information*____ about career choices, so I went to see
                                 1. (information)

my advisor. It's always hard for me to make important ____*decisions*____.
                                                        2. (decision)

Magda: Did she have any _____ for you?
                            3. (advice)

Allison: She gave me a lot of helpful _____. Now I'm thinking about
4. (suggestion)

becoming a professional cook.

Magda: I think you can expect to do a lot of hard _____. Do you have
5. (work)

any _____?
6. (experience)

Allison: I've had plenty of restaurant _____, including washing
7. (job)

_____ and polishing _____. But so far I haven't had
8. (dish)   9. (silverware)

any formal _____. The advisor said that cooking has become an
10. (training)

excellent profession for _____. They've made a lot of
11. (woman)

_____ in being accepted as executive chefs.
12. (progress)

Magda: It will be exciting to prepare your creations for lots of _____. But
13. (person)

before you go to cooking school, you'll need to buy some really good

_____ for peeling and chopping _____.
14. (knife)   15. (vegetable)

Allison: Professional kitchens have lots of _____.
16. (machinery)

Magda: But really good restaurants don't use many food-processing

_____. So chefs are on their _____ most of the day.
17. (machine)   18. (foot)

Allison: Yeah, but some of them are real _____!
19. (celebrity)

6 Subject-Verb Agreement: *Culinary Education*

Circle the correct form of the verb.

1. The media [has/**have**] made cooking seem glamorous.

2. The news [is/are] good for people who want to be professional chefs—there are lots of jobs available.

3. What [is/are] the main criterion that cooking schools use to judge applicants?

4. The admissions committee [makes/make] its decisions next week.

5. Mathematics [is/are] important for chefs and restaurant managers.

6. Bacteria [is/are] becoming more dangerous, so it's important to keep kitchens clean.

7. Please be sure that your clothes [is/are] clean.

8. The professor's food cost analyses [has/have] helped restaurants become more profitable.

9. The group [was/were] larger than I expected.

10. Some animal species [is/are] raised for meat, although we often have a different name for the meat.

11. In the future, those deer over there [is/are] going to be on a restaurant menu as "venison."

12. This sheep in the pen [is/are] going to be "mutton."

7 Nouns Used as Count and Noncount Nouns: *Good Food and Good Fortune*

A. Use the appropriate noun phrases given before each dialogue to complete the conversations.

food, a food, foods

Dustin: Let's go out to eat. What kind of _____food_____ do you like best?
                                                    1

Joel: I like many different ethnic _____, but my favorite is Chinese,
                                          2

especially the spicy dishes made with fish.

Dustin: That's _____ that I like, too. There's a great Chinese restaurant
                       3

nearby.

beer, a beer

Waitress: What would you like to drink?

Dustin: Do you have _____?
                            4

Waitress: Yes, we do.

Dustin: I'd like _____.
                       5

business, a business

Joel: Naomi told me that you've gone back to school. What are you studying?

Dustin: I'm studying _____. I'd like to own _____ in the
                            6   7

future.

cake, a cake

Waitress: Are you ready for dessert? The chef made _____. It has
                                                          8

almonds in it.

Joel: No, thanks. I don't really like _____. But I do want fortune
9

cookies.

experience, experiences

Dustin: I like this fortune. It says, "You are destined to have exciting

_____."
10

Joel: Some of the fortunes aren't really fortunes. They're proverbs like "There's

no better teacher than _____."
11

life, lives

Joel: Here's another one: "Learn to treasure even the difficulties of

_____."
12

Dustin: This one's better: "You and your loved ones will find more happiness than

sorrow in your _____."
13

beauty, a beauty

Dustin: This is the last one: "_____ will surround you everywhere you
14

go."

Joel: I want one that says "You will meet _____ and she will love you
15

forever."

B. Work with a partner. Write your own one-sentence fortunes or proverbs. Use
each of the following **four** noncount-count pairs:

education/an education, friendship/a friendship, love/loves,
opportunity/opportunities

Read your sentences to the class.

8 Identifying Determiner Types: *As American as Apple Pie*

Circle all the determiners in the following passage. Mark the articles with an **A** (do *not*
mark the zero article), the quantifiers with a **Q**, the demonstratives with a **D**, and the
possessives with a **P.**

⟨The⟩ United States has always been a nation of immigrants. Many immigrants

created new foods. One example is chop suey, a mixture of some vegetables, some

pork, and soy sauce. Although its name may sound Chinese, this dish was invented in America. And what about our famous "Italian" combination, spaghetti and meat-

balls? Italians have these foods, but the combination is American. And then there's

vichyssoise, a cold soup made of leeks and potatoes, which is served at many fine

French restaurants. What's your opinion? Is this soup originally French? Nowadays,

few people realize that it was created by a chef in New York.

GRAMMAR BRIEFING 2: Definite and Indefinite Articles

The choice of article depends partly on the type of noun. It also depends on the context in which a noun is used. The context includes the language context—the words and sentences used—and also the situation and the speaker's and listener's knowledge.

FORM AND FUNCTION Definite and Indefinite Articles

The Definite Article (*The*)

- *The* is used with all common nouns—noncount, singular count, or plural count.
- *The* is used with a noun when both the speaker and the listener know which person, place, or thing the noun is referring to. The noun does not have to be introduced—for speaker and listener, the noun has a definite reference. This can happen when:
  - the noun has already been mentioned.

    I made some cookies and a cake. **The cookies** were delicious, but **the cake** was horrible.

  - the noun is a part of or is otherwise clearly related to something that has already been mentioned.

    I baked a birthday cake. **The frosting** was a little too sweet. (The frosting is part of the cake that has been mentioned.)

  - the noun is made definite by a modifier.

    The bread on the table is delicious. (The modifier on the table tells which bread.)

  - the noun is unique—there is only one.

    The sun was shining, so they ate outside. (There is only one sun.)

  - the noun is a part of everyday life for both the speaker and the listener.

    I'll feed **the dog.** (The family has one dog and the speaker is referring to it.)

  - the noun is part of the larger social context of the speaker and the listener.

    I saw **the president** on TV. (The speaker is clearly referring to the president of the country.)

  - the noun is part of the immediate situation—speaker and listener can see, hear, or otherwise identify it.

    Could you pass **the butter?** (The listener can probably see the butter.)

The Indefinite Article (*A/An*)

■ *A/an* is used only with singular count nouns. It is used when the speaker and listener don't both know which person, place, or thing the noun is referring to. The context does not make the noun definite, so the noun has to be introduced. This happens when:

- a noun is known to the speaker but unknown to the listener.

  I bought **a cake** to bring to the party. (listener doesn't know what the cake is)

- a noun is known to the listener but unknown to the speaker.

  When did you hire **a new chef?** (speaker doesn't know who the chef is)

- a noun is unknown to both the speaker and the listener.

  I need to buy **a cake** for the party. (neither speaker nor listener knows yet what cake)

■ *A/an* is used in a subject complement, where it classifies the subject but does not refer to a specific person, place, or thing.

  My brother is **a chef.**

■ The indefinite article is *a* before consonant sounds and *an* before vowel sounds.

  a kitchen, **a** hospital, **a** uniform
  an orange, **an** honor, **an** umbrella

The [0] Article

■ The [0] article is used instead of the indefinite article *a/an* with plural count nouns and with noncount nouns.

  The chef used **[0] bananas** in the fruit salad. (plural count noun)
  The chef used **[0] juice** in the punch. (noncount noun)

■ Some words commonly occur with the [0] article, especially in certain phrases with prepositions (e.g., *breakfast, lunch, dinner; go to/be in bed, school, class, college*, etc.; *go by train, bus*, etc.; *at night, before morning*, etc.).

  We ate **[0] dinner,** but we didn't have a snack.
  He eats a lot **at [0] night** but not in the morning.

■ The quantifier *some* is sometimes used instead of the [0] article when the speaker wants to indicate an indefinite quantity of the noun. It is not used when the focus is on the category of the noun, rather than on quantity. (For more on *some*, see Grammar Briefing 3, page 154.)

  After dinner I'd like **[0]/some dessert.** (indefinite quantity)
  I like **[0] dessert.** (focus on category "dessert," not quantity)

Article Use in Generic Statements

■ Subject nouns in generic statements refer to categories or general types of people, places, or things. They don't refer to specific people, places, or things. Generic statements often classify, define, or generalize.

  An orange is a citrus fruit. (classification)
  The orange is a round fruit grown in hot climates. (definition)
  Oranges are a good source of vitamin C. (generalization)

■ Generic statements can often use *the, a/an,* and [0] with little difference in meaning.

    An orange is a citrus fruit.   =   **The orange** is a citrus fruit.   =   **Oranges** are a citrus fruit.

■ [0] is the article most commonly used in generic statements. It is used with plural count nouns and noncount nouns. *A/an* and *the,* used with singular count nouns, are less common.

    Oranges are a good source of vitamin C. ([0] + plural count)

    Fruit is a good source of vitamins. ([0] + noncount)

    An orange is a good source of vitamin C. (indefinite article + singular count)

    The orange is a good source of vitamin C. (definite article + singular count)

■ *A/an* + singular count noun is used only to mean any representative member of a category. It is not used when the focus is on the group or on all members of the category together.

    An orange is a good source of vitamin C. (any representative orange)

    Not: ~~An orange~~ was first brought to the New World by Europeans. (the group of oranges in general)

■ *The* is usually used only with certain nouns—names of animals, plants, mechanical objects, and musical instruments—especially in technical or other formal writing.

    The turkey used to be a wild bird, but now most are domesticated.

    The food processor has helped cooks prepare food more quickly.

    Many restaurants have someone who plays **the piano** to entertain diners.

GRAMMAR PRACTICE 2: Definite and Indefinite Articles

9 Definite and Indefinite Articles: *The Eating Patterns of a North American Family*

▪▪▪ The conversations in Column I took place during a typical week in the life of the Gray family—Mona and Doug and their daughter, Erin. Listen to the conversations once for the main ideas. Listen again and **circle** the correct choice in Column I. Then read the statements in Column II and **circle** the letter of the statement that fits the conversation.

Column I	**Column II**

1. *Erin:* Mom, I've got to hurry! The school bus is coming, and I can't find my lunch box.
 	
   Mona: I haven't seen it. Did you leave it on [(a)/the] table in the living room?
	1. (a.) There's more than one table in the family's living room.
	
	   b. There's one table in the family's living room.

2. *Erin:* Mom, I hope you had time to stop for groceries on your way home from work.
 	
   Mona: They're in the car. You could help me by carrying in [a/the] bag.
	2. a. There's more than one bag of groceries in the car.
	
	   b. There's one bag of groceries in the car.

3. *Doug:* Erin, please don't turn on the television yet. You haven't finished your dinner.
 	
   Erin: Do I have to? I don't really like [0/the] vegetables.
	3. a. Erin doesn't like vegetables in general.
	
	   b. Erin doesn't like tonight's vegetables.

4. *Erin:* Daddy, I'm hungry now. Could I have a
            snack?

   Doug: I guess so. Do you want to eat [a/the] piece
            of leftover pizza?

5. *Mona:* I'm going to be working late tonight. Do you
             think you could cook dinner?

   Doug: Mona, you know I can't cook. Let's eat at
            [a/the] fast-food restaurant in the mall.

6. *Mona:* Erin, try to eat more politely. You've got
             ketchup all over your face.

   Erin: I can't help it, Mom. I like [0/the] French
            fries a lot.

7. *Erin:* Wow! This restaurant is really nice. Dad,
             who's that woman over there?

   Doug: The one in the tall white hat? She's [a/the]
            chef here.

8. *Doug:* Can I have a taste of your dessert? It looks
             like it has a lot of good things in it.

   Mona: It does. I really like [0/the] chocolate.

4. a. There's more than one piece of pizza.

    b. There's one piece of pizza.

5. a. There's more than one fast-food restaurant
        in the mall.

    b. There's one fast-food restaurant in the mall.

6. a. Erin likes French fries in general.

    b. Erin likes these particular French fries.

7. a. The restaurant has more than one chef.

    b. The restaurant has one chef.

8. a. Mona likes chocolate in general.

    b. Mona likes the chocolate in this dessert.

⬛⚪ The Definite Article: *The Story of Their Lives*

Work with a partner. Read the list of reasons for using *the* and the dialogue between
Stuart and his wife, Melissa. Above each **boldfaced** *the* + noun in the dialogue, write
the letter of the reason why the speaker used *the*.

A. The noun has already been mentioned.

B. The noun is part of or is related to something that has already been mentioned.

C. The noun is made definite by a modifier.

D. The noun is unique.

E. The noun is part of Stuart and Melissa's everyday lives or larger social context.

  Stuart: Melissa, I'm glad you're finally home. What's kept you so long?

                                        C
Melissa: I had to work late, so I missed **the bus** that I had planned to take. Then I

           managed to get on a bus, but **the engine** broke down. By the time another

           bus came, it was already dark and **the moon** had come up. Have you

           started cooking dinner?

  Stuart: Not yet. I had a busy day, too. First, I went to a meeting. **The meeting** went

           on for hours. Then I spent the whole afternoon learning how to use a new

           computer. I had some trouble getting used to **the keyboard.** After I got

           home, I wanted to read **the newspaper.** There's an interesting article about

           a city government scandal.

Melissa: What does **the article** say?

Stuart: It's possible that **the mayor** is involved in **the scandal.** She may have to

resign.

Melissa: Let's not worry about that now. We need to think about dinner. We could

make sandwiches, but **the bread** in the cupboard is stale.

Stuart: That's because it's been days since either one of us has had time to go to

the store.

Melissa: This is **the story** of our lives, Stuart. Hand me **the phone,** please. I'm going

to order a pizza.

▊▊ The Indefinite or [0] Article: *Have You Taken Up a New Hobby?*

Read the following sentences. Mark the **boldfaced** nouns with **L** if the noun is not known to the listener; **S** if the noun is not known to the speaker; or **L/S** if the noun is not known to the listener or the speaker.

                                           L/S

1. Let's take **a cooking class.**

2. What's that delicious smell? Are you baking **some cookies?**   *S*

3. I need to buy **a new cookbook.** I'll ask the cooking teacher for recommendations.

4. I saw **a chef** on television this morning.

5. I understand that you've given **a demonstration** on cooking.

6. I hope you can see my new kitchen soon. It has **a professional stove.**

7. Shall we invite **some guests** to dinner this weekend?

8. If you don't want to cook tonight, we could look to see if there's **a delicatessen** on the way home.

9. I heard that you learned to cook at **a restaurant** in Italy.

10. I baked **pastries** while you were gone. Do you want to try them?

12 Definite and Indefinite Articles: *Food Here and There*

Complete the conversations with *a, an, the,* or [0].

In a college dormitory dining hall:

Cindy: Good morning, Angela. Have you already had _____[O]_____ breakfast?
1

Angela: Yeah. I had _____an_____ omelet and _____a_____ doughnut. I
2   3

hated _____the_____ omelet because _____ filling tasted
4   5

strange. _____ food in this dormitory is disgusting.
6

Cindy: I think I'll have _____ doughnut.
7

Angela: I don't want to go to _____ school today. Look at
8

_____ sky. _____ weather is going to be terrible. I
9   10

want to go back to _____ bed.
11

Cindy: Stop complaining. We can go by _____ bus. Do you have plans
12

for tonight?

Angela: Yeah, I do. I'm going to _____ party. Do you want to come along?
13

Cindy: What time does _____ party start?
14

Angela: I'm not sure, but I'll look at _____ invitation.
15

At the party:

Cindy: Calvin, I didn't expect to see you here. I heard that you went on

_____ trip. I'd like to hear about it. Let's have _____
16   17

lunch together sometime.

Calvin: What about tomorrow? We could meet at _____ restaurant, if
18

you're free.

Cindy: Have you been to Liz's Café? _____ sandwiches she serves are
19

delicious.

Calvin: I've seen it. It's close to _____ university, isn't it?
20

Cindy: Right. It's across from _____ library. I'm going to be in
21

_____ class all morning. If _____ teacher lets us out
22   23

on time, I can meet you at _____ café at noon.
24

At lunch the next day:

Calvin: When I was traveling, I found out that this isn't ＿＿＿＿＿＿ only
                                                                              25
        country where fast food is popular. There are ＿＿＿＿＿＿ American
                                                                    26
        fast-food restaurants everywhere now.

Cindy: Do they serve exactly ＿＿＿＿＿＿ same things as they do here?
                                        27

Calvin: Sometimes they do. For example, I went into ＿＿＿＿＿＿ fast-food
                                                                      28
        restaurant in Beijing. I ordered ＿＿＿＿＿＿ hamburger. After I took
                                                  29
        off ＿＿＿＿＿＿ wrapper, I lifted up ＿＿＿＿＿＿ bun and looked
              30   31
        at ＿＿＿＿＿＿ meat. It looked exactly like ＿＿＿＿＿＿ ham-
             32   33
        burger from ＿＿＿＿＿＿ fast-food restaurant in Miami or Omaha. It
                          34
        tasted exactly like one, too.

Cindy: Was that ＿＿＿＿＿＿ most interesting experience you had while you
                          35
        were traveling?

Calvin: I was interested in ＿＿＿＿＿＿ hamburgers at that restaurant in
                                      36
        Beijing because I'm ＿＿＿＿＿＿ international business major, and I'm
                                  37
        interested in working abroad. Someday I may be selling ＿＿＿＿＿＿
                                                                        38
        hamburgers in China.

13   *The, A, [0], Some: Old Recipes*

A. Complete the paragraphs with *a*, *the*, or *some*.

    Nineteenth-century recipes were different from recipes today. For example, an

1844 recipe for pancakes starts: "Make ＿＿＿*a*＿＿＿ thick batter by mixing
                                                1
＿＿＿＿＿＿ flour with ＿＿＿＿＿＿ milk." ＿＿＿＿＿＿ recipe doesn't
        2   3   4
tell you how much flour or milk to use or how to cook ＿＿＿＿＿＿ batter.
                                                              5
    A recipe for soup says: "Find and kill ＿＿＿＿＿＿ squirrel, cut it up, and put
                                                    6
it into ＿＿＿＿＿＿ boiling water. When the soup is nearly done, add
              7
＿＿＿＿＿＿ hickory nuts or ＿＿＿＿＿＿ powdered spices. If you have
        8   9
＿＿＿＿＿＿ young pine tree, add ＿＿＿＿＿＿ top of ＿＿＿＿＿＿ tree."
        10   11   12

B. For each pair, decide which sentence can be completed with either *some* or [0] article and which should be completed with [0]. Then finish each pair by writing *some*/**[0]** or **[0].**

1. a. My hobby is finding _____ old recipes.

   b. Yesterday I found _____ interesting old recipes.

2. a. One of the recipes was for _____ pancakes.

   b. I immediately used it to make _____ pancakes.

3. a. My friend asked me if I was going to cook _____ squirrel soup.

   b. I told her that _____ squirrel soup doesn't appeal to me.

14 Identifying Generic Statements: *Changing Times*

A. In each pair of sentences, one sentence is a generic statement and the other is not. **Circle** the letter of the generic statement.

1. (a.) **A cook** prepares food.

   b. **A cook** talked about the history of cooking on television yesterday.

2. a. **The refrigerator** has made it possible to keep food for long periods of time.

   b. **The refrigerator** is too cold, and everything in it is freezing.

3. a. I stayed up late to read **recipes.**

   b. **Recipes** are useful for inexperienced cooks.

4. a. **A cookbook** is a nice present for someone whose hobby is cooking.

   b. Roxanne gave Duane **a cookbook** for Christmas.

5. a. **The buffalo** ran across the field.

   b. **The buffalo** is the largest land animal in North America.

6. a. **The supermarket** sells food and many other items.

   b. **The supermarket** closes at midnight.

B. Choose two noun phrases from each list. Write **two** sentences using each of the noun phrases you chose. In the first sentence, use the noun phrase to write a generic statement. In the second sentence, use the noun phrase to refer to a specific person or thing.

   Example: *The trumpet is a wind instrument. The trumpet belongs to John.*

1. the trumpet, the guitar, the computer, the automobile, the strawberry, the grasshopper

2. a doctor, an engineer, a poem, a house, a fire, a chair

GRAMMAR BRIEFING 3: Quantifiers

Quantifiers are determiners that tell an amount. Numbers and measure phrases indicate an exact amount; general quantifiers indicate a nonspecific amount.

FORM AND FUNCTION Numbers and Measure Phrases

■ The number *one* is used with singular count nouns; other numbers are used with plural count nouns.

>   I have **one** banana.   He has **two** bananas.

■ Measure phrases, which consist of *a/an* or a number + noun + *of,* are used with count and noncount nouns. Like numbers, they indicate an exact amount. Measure phrases make it possible to count noncount nouns by putting them into units.

>   We ordered **a slice of** cake.   We bought **two pounds of** coffee.

■ The nouns used in measure phrases may refer to:

>   Measures: **a pound of** (meat, etc.), **a kilo of** (cheese, etc.), **a gallon of** (milk, etc.), **a liter of** (juice, etc.), **a cup of** (sugar, etc.), **a tablespoon of** (oil, etc.).

>   Whole units: **a bar of** chocolate/soap, **a loaf of** bread, **a head of** garlic/lettuce, **a bunch of** bananas/carrots/grapes

>   Parts of a whole: **a piece of** paper/bacon/chalk/advice, **a slice of** bread/pie, **a clove of** garlic

>   Containers: **a bag of** chocolates, **a bottle of** juice, **a box of** cereal, **a can of** soup, **a carton of** eggs, **a jar of** jelly, **a package of** cookies, **a tube of** toothpaste

■ Numbers and measure words can be used without nouns when the meaning is clear. Used this way, they are pronouns, not quantifiers.

>   How many apples would you like?   I'd like **one.** (= one apple)

>   How much flour would you like?   I'd like **five pounds.** (= five pounds of flour)

GRAMMAR HOTSPOT!

■ *A pair of, a couple of,* and *both* are used with plural count nouns to mean "two." *A pair of* usually refers to two things that are used or joined together. *A couple of* refers to two separate things, but it can also mean "a small number of." *Both* refers to two of two.

>   He wore **a pair of** sunglasses. (joined)   **Not:** He wore ~~a couple of~~ sunglasses.

>   She bought **a pair of** shoes. (used together)   **Not:** She bought ~~a couple of~~ shoes.

>   They brought **a couple of** apples.   **Not:** They brought ~~a pair of~~ apples.

>   We could go to Joe's Grill or to the Steak House. I like **both** restaurants.

■ *Either* and *neither* are used with singular count nouns. *Either* refers to a choice of one of two. *Neither,* which means "not either," refers to zero of two.

>   You can have **either** chicken or fish. Which one do you want?

>   **Neither** entree comes with pasta. They both come with rice instead.

FORM AND FUNCTION General Quantifiers

■ General quantifiers are used with count and noncount nouns to indicate a non-specific amount.

■ *Each* and *every* are used with singular count nouns. Both mean "the total number or amount," but *each* focuses on the individuals in the group while *every* focuses on the group.

> **Each** dish on the menu has been tested for taste and quality. (focuses on the individual dishes)

> **Every** restaurant in the guide book is good. (focuses on the restaurants as a group)

■ Other quantifiers are used only with plural count nouns, only with noncount nouns, or with both. Quantifiers can express either the positive idea that there is some or enough or the negative idea that there is a small amount or a lack.

Quantifiers used

with plural count nouns	with noncount nouns	with both
Positive*		
		all
		most
many	much	a lot of/lots of
a great many	a great deal of	plenty of
a (large) number of	a/an (large) amount of	
quite a few	quite a little	
several		
		some/any
		enough
a few	a little	
Negative*		
not many	not much	
few	little	
		hardly any
		not any
		no**
		none of

* Note: If a noun itself expresses something negative, a negative quantifier with this noun expresses a favorable situation; a positive quantifier expresses an unfavorable situation.

> Tony had **hardly any worries.** (negative quantifier + negative noun = favorable situation)

> Tony had **many worries.** (positive quantifier + negative noun = unfavorable situation)

** Note: *No* can be used with singular count nouns as well as plural count nouns and noncount nouns.

> (**No patron/patrons** of the restaurant liked the new cuisine.)

■ *Of* is always a part of certain general quantifiers (*a lot of/lots of, a great deal of,* etc.). *Of* can also be part of other general quantifiers (except for *no* and *every*) when they quantify definite nouns or pronouns. (Nouns are definite when they follow *the*, a demonstrative, or a possessive.)

> **Each of the/those/my students** came.   **Not:** Each of students came.
>
> **Each of them** came.

■ All of the quantifiers listed except *no* and *every* can be used without nouns when the meaning is clear. Used this way, they are pronouns, not quantifiers.

> **Each dish** is good.   **Each** is good.
>
> They have **a lot of food.**   They have **a lot.**

■ *Many* and *much* are used to ask questions about quantity (*How many?/How much?*), in negative statements, and in phrases with *too* and *so* in affirmative statements.

> **How many people** are in your party?
>
> We do**n't** have **much milk** in the refrigerator.
>
> There's **too much** sugar in this tea.

In other affirmative statements, *many* and especially *much* are considered formal. *A lot of* tends to be used instead.

■ *Some* is used in affirmative statements and can be used in questions. *Any* often replaces *some* in questions and usually replaces it in negative statements.

> Would you like **any/some** dessert?   No thanks, I don't want **any.**

■ *A few* and *a little* express the positive idea that there is some; *few* and *little* express the negative idea that there is hardly any or not enough.

> There are **a few** really healthy dishes in this restaurant. (positive idea: some healthy dishes)
>
> There are **few** really healthy dishes in a fast-food restaurant. (negative idea: hardly any healthy dishes)
>
> I have **a little** time, so let's eat in a nice restaurant. (positive idea: some time)
>
> I have **little** time. Let's eat fast food. (negative idea: hardly any/not enough time)

GRAMMAR PRACTICE 3: Quantifiers

15 Numbers and Measure Phrases: *A Shopping Diary*

Market research companies collect information about people's buying habits. They ask people to keep "shopping diaries" describing each trip to the supermarket. Use the appropriate numbers and measure phrases given above the paragraphs to complete the sentences in this shopping diary.

a bunch of   a couple of   a gallon of   ~~a head of~~   a jar of   a pair of

I went to the produce department first, and I bought ___*a head of*___ lettuce,
                                                                                    1

_____ grapes, and _____ melons. Then I remembered that the
        2   3

children wanted _____ peanut butter, so I got that. I noticed
                        4

_____ sunglasses that I liked, so I put them into my cart, too. Then I went
        5

to the dairy department and got _____ milk.
                                              6

a carton of   four bars of   half a pound of   one   two loaves of   two tubes of

I also bought _____ eggs there. In the delicatessen, I bought
                      7

_____ cheese. Then I went to the bakery, where I got _____
        8   9

bread. I also got _____ doughnut for the trip home. In another aisle
                          10

I got _____ toothpaste and _____ soap.
            11   12

a bottle of   a cup of   both   either   neither   several slices of

I thought about buying _____ ice cream or chocolate for the children. But
                                13

I decided against _____ items, because _____ one is nutri-
                          14   15

tious. I bought the children _____ juice instead. I remembered that I
                                    16

needed _____ roast beef, so I went back to the delicatessen. While I was
              17

there, I got _____ coffee to drink with the doughnut.
                    18

16 General Quantifiers: *A "Big" Trend*

A. Write the correct quantifiers to complete the passage.

There is a "big" trend in food in the United States—it seems that

_____*many*_____ food portions and packages have become enormous.
  1. (much / many)

_____ Americans notice this trend anymore, but _____
2. (Not much / Not many)   3. (quite a few / quite a little)

international visitors do. A first-time visitor from Europe commented, "They serve

_____ food in _____ restaurants here. _____ meal
4. (a great many / a lot of)   5. (every / most)   6. (Each / All)

that I've had has been big." An Asian visitor added, "The meals are huge. How do

you eat _____ food?"
              7. (so much / so many)

Marketing experts say that the focus on size began _____ time ago in
                                                                                                      8. (several / some)
fast-food restaurants. _____ customers feel that they are getting a better
                                              9. (Most / Much)
deal when they buy a bigger meal. In fast-food restaurants these days,

_____ customers pass up the chance to "up-size" their meals for
10. (hardly any / not much)

_____ more money.
11. (a few / a little)

_____ manufacturers of food products noticed the popular-
12. (A great deal of / A number of)
ity of oversize servings in restaurants. As a result, these companies now make

_____ products in "grand," "jumbo," or "mammoth" sizes. They
13. (many / a large amount of)
have had _____ success with these products. A new-products
              14. (a great many / a great deal of)
consultant says this success is natural. "_____ years ago, there was a
                                                            15. (Several / A little)
trend toward small portions. _____ Americans are rebelling against that
                                          16. (A lot of / Much)
now. They just want to have _____ food."
                                        17. (plenty of / a great many)

B. Compare the food portions discussed in **A** to portions in other places you know
about. What is your opinion of this trend toward big packages and portions?

17 General Quantifiers; General Quantifiers as Pronouns: *More Market Research*

Market researchers also get information by conducting interviews with shoppers as they
leave the store. **Circle** the correct choice. Where both choices are correct, circle both.

Interviewer: Do you mind answering [(a few)/a little] questions about your purchases
                                                    1
                    today? It won't take [(much)/(a lot of)] time.
                                                2

Shopper: I don't mind. I have [some/any] time.
                                          3

Interviewer: Did you have [many/lots of] items on your shopping list?
                                        4

Shopper: I forgot to bring the list, but it only had [a little/a few] items.
                                                                  5

Interviewer: I'll just write that you had [no/any] list. Did you spend [much/a lot of]
                                                    6   7

                    money today?

Shopper: Yeah. I got [much/lots of] things. I hope [some/any] of them are the
8   9

right things. I bought [some/any] ice cream because we don't have
10

[some/much] at home. I got three packages of hot dogs. I always like
11

to have [plenty of/a large amount of] hot dogs.
12

Interviewer: It looks like you bought [quite a little/a lot of] potato chips, too.
13

Shopper: Yes. We had [little/hardly any] at home, and I wanted to be sure we had
14

[any/enough].
15

Interviewer: Did you buy [any/some] fresh vegetables?
16

Shopper: No, as a matter of fact, I got [none/no] at all.
17

Interviewer: Did you buy [any/some] sweets?
18

Shopper: I don't usually buy [any/some] sweets, but I bought [any/some] today.
19   20

Actually, I bought [lots/much]. It was an impulse—I was feeling hungry.
21

Interviewer: Do you have [much/a lot of] experience with shopping?
22

Shopper: I don't have [much/a lot], but I know what I like.
23

18 Few, A Few; Little, A Little: Shopping Behavior

Complete each sentence with *few, a few, little,* or *a little.*

I.

Marketing Expert: Let me give you ____a little____ advice. Don't put impor-
1

tant items just inside the entrance of the store, because

____few____ shoppers notice anything in that area.
2

Also, shoppers, especially women shoppers, don't like to be

crowded when they're making decisions. They don't like

stores with _____ space in the aisles.
3

Supermarket Manager: How many men say that they do most of the food shopping?

Marketing Expert: _____ men say that they do most of the shop-
4

ping. Men rarely say that because in general women do the

food shopping for their families.

II.

Wife: I've got a lot to do today and _____ time to do it. Would you
                                              5

mind going to the grocery store?

Husband: I don't think we need to go to the store yet. We have _____
                                                                    6

cheese and _____ pickles. We can make _____
                        7   8

sandwiches.

Wife: Never mind. I'll go. Do you have any money?

Husband: Sure, I have _____. How much do you need?
                            9

III.

Marketing Expert: Women are usually more patient than men. Men seem to have

_____ patience for shopping. Also, children who go to
        10

the store with their fathers can talk them into buying almost

anything. _____ fathers can refuse their children's
              11

requests.

IV.

Child: Look, Daddy, they have chocolate-covered chocolate chip cookies. Could

we please get some cookies? Pretty please?

Father: Okay, you can get _____, but let's not tell your mother.
                                12

19 Quantifiers With and Without *Of: Focus Groups*

Market researchers also get information by asking people to participate in focus groups.
Complete the sentences by writing *of* or [0].

1. Many _____0_____ companies want to know what products appeal to consumers.

2. A lot _____of_____ food manufacturers use focus groups to do market
   research.

3. Each _____ the members of a focus group has an opportunity to
   respond.

4. Each _____ member of the group gives an opinion about the product.

5. Every _____ product that company introduces has been tested in
   focus groups.

6. Several _____ Jane's friends have participated in focus groups.

7. Market researchers have found that most _____ Americans hate shopping for food.

8. Most _____ them consider food shopping to be work and not fun.

9. I tasted a little _____ yogurt.

10. Only a little _____ the yogurt tasted good.

11. Has any _____ these flavors appealed to you?

12. Have you tried any _____ new flavors that appealed to you?

13. Focus-group testing has indicated that some _____ your advertisements will be successful.

14. Plenty _____ products are introduced in this country every year.

20   Using Quantifiers: *Let's Get Plenty of Steaks*

Work in groups of three. Imagine that you have just arrived in a place where you will be taking a special English language course for two days. The three of you are going to be sharing a kitchen and cooking and eating all your food there. You need to go to the supermarket for the food. Decide which items you are going to buy and how much of each. You must choose five items from the list below and five items not on the list. Write a sentence about each of your choices. In addition, write three sentences about items that you don't want any of. Use a different measure phrase or general quantifier in each sentence.

Example: We'll need half a pound of coffee. We're going to buy several lobsters because we all like them. We won't get any peanut butter.

beans	cheese	eggs	milk	rice
bread	coffee	frozen dinners	oranges	salad dressing
candy	cookies	jam	pasta	spinach
carrots	corn flakes	lettuce	peanut butter	steaks

Read some of your sentences to the class. Which group's choices sound the best? Why?

Modifiers, Pronouns, and Possessives

Introductory Task: *What's Your Reaction?*

A. Check the box before the statement that describes your reaction to the particular food. If your reaction is somewhere in between, check the middle box.

1.

☐ Broccoli is a vitamin-filled green vegetable. It has a pleasant flavor.

☐

☐ Broccoli is an unpleasant vegetable. It has a very strong, bitter flavor.

2.

☐ Chocolate is my favorite candy. I can't resist eating lots of rich, wonderful chocolate.

☐

☐ Chocolate isn't an exciting food. I don't eat much chocolate.

3.
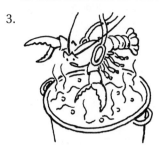

☐ I love to eat lobsters. I really enjoy their delicious, juicy white meat.

☐

☐ I refuse to eat lobsters. I have no desire to put a frightened lobster into boiling water.

4.

☐ Snails make a wonderful meal. I like them cooked with melted butter and
fresh garlic.

☐

☐ I would never eat snails. They're slimy, disgusting garden pests.

B. Work in small groups. First, compare your reactions to the foods in the pictures.
Were they similar or different? Then discuss other foods that you like or dislike very
much. Why do you like or dislike these foods? Find two foods that everyone in the
group likes and two foods that everyone in the group dislikes. As a class, compare
likes and dislikes. Are there any foods that all the groups agreed on?

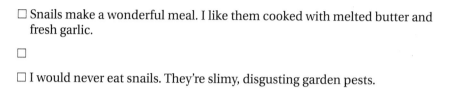

GRAMMAR BRIEFING 1: Modifiers

Modifiers of nouns describe and give more information about nouns. Nouns are modified by adjectives, which
come between the determiner and the noun, and by adjective phrases and adjective clauses, which follow the
noun.

FORM AND FUNCTION Modifiers

Modifiers before Nouns

■ Adjectives are the most common modifiers of nouns. Adjectives describe nouns
by telling their appearance and other qualities.

large yellow banana	**strong black Colombian** coffee
hot apple pie	**long wooden** spoon

■ Participial adjectives end in *-ing* and *-ed,* like the present and past participles.*
With *-ing* adjectives that describe feelings, the person, place, or thing the noun
refers to produces the feeling. With *-ed* adjectives that describe feelings, the person, place, or thing the noun refers to experiences the feeling. (Note: a participial
adjective modifies a noun; present and past participles are parts of the verb.)

What a **boring** woman! No one wants to talk to her. (*-ing:* the woman produces the feeling of boredom)

What a **bored** woman! She doesn't have anything to do. (*-ed:* the woman
experiences the feeling of boredom)

* The adjective has the same form as the participle. When the past participle doesn't end in *-ed,* neither does the adjective (e.g.,
broken, ground).

■ Sometimes a noun can modify another noun. The noun modifier is singular in form.

> The **steak restaurant** is close to our house. (= restaurant for steaks)
>
> Let's use **paper plates.** (= plates made of paper)

■ Compound modifiers often consist of a noun, adjective, or adverb + -*ing* or -*ed* adjective or of a number + noun. A hyphen is usually used between the parts of the modifier.

> **store-bought** cake (noun + -*ed* adjective)
>
> **fun-loving** chef (adverb + -*ing* adjective)
>
> **black-eyed** peas (adjective + -*ed* adjective)
>
> **ten-pound** turkey (number + noun)

■ Intensifiers, such as *really* and *very,* are sometimes used before an adjective to strengthen the meaning of the adjective.

> There's a **really good** restaurant near here.

Order of Modifiers before Nouns

■ When a noun is preceded by more than one adjective, the adjectives tend to occur in a particular order, by category. For example, opinion adjectives (*interesting, boring, ugly, nice,* etc.) tend to come before appearance adjectives (*small, short, long,* etc.). Usually, there are not more than three adjectives before a noun.

Opinion	Appearance (including size, height, length)	Age	Shape	Color	Nationality / Origin	Material	Noun
lovely		new				cotton	apron
	smooth		round	yellow			squash
delicious					Turkish		coffee
	small	old			Wedgwood		plate

However, modifier order can sometimes be varied, especially for emphasis (e.g., *beautiful young woman* is usual, but *young, beautiful woman* is also possible).

■ With two or more adjectives, use a comma between adjectives that seem to modify the noun equally (hint: such adjectives can be separated by *and*). Do not use a comma if the second adjective seems more closely related to the noun.

> **new, untraditional** school (the new and untraditional school)
>
> **new public** school (the school is a public school and it's new)

■ When used, a noun modifier comes before the noun, after any adjectives.

> **vegetable** dish (noun modifier + noun)
>
> delicious **chicken** entree (adjective + noun modifier + noun)

Modifiers after Nouns

■ Adjective phrases and adjective clauses follow the nouns that they modify. They are discussed in Unit 5.

> the chef **interested in Oriental cuisine** (adjective phrase)
>
> the dessert **that the chef made** (adjective clause)

GRAMMAR HOTSPOT!

■ The noun in number + noun modifiers is singular in form.

That's a **ten-year-old wine.**   **Not:** That's a ~~ten-years old wine.~~

We ate a **three-course dinner.**   **Not:** We ate a ~~three-courses dinner.~~

GRAMMAR PRACTICE 1: Modifiers

1 Identifying Modifiers: *Another Look*

Work with a partner. Go back to the introductory task on page 162. Find the modifiers that come before nouns in the sentences, **underline** them, and **circle** the noun that they modify.

Example: Broccoli is a <u>vitamin-filled</u> <u>green</u> (vegetable.) It has a <u>pleasant</u> (flavor.)

2 *-ing* and *-ed* Adjectives—Meaning: *Food and Feelings*

A. Use the adjectives given above each section to complete the sentences.

I. satisfied/satisfying

Waiter: Did you enjoy your dinners?

Customer: Yes, we did. Please give our compliments to the chef. That was a really

<u>   satisfying   </u> meal.
        1

Waiter: I will. The chef likes to have <u>   satisfied   </u> diners.
                                  2

comforted/comforting

II. *Psychologist:* When adults feel stressed, they want _____ foods, often
                                                    3

   the foods they loved as children. When they eat these foods, they

   feel less stressed. They feel like _____ children again.
                                                    4

relaxed/relaxing

III. *Fitness Instructor:* For relaxation, it's better to exercise than to eat. Sports and

   workouts at the gym are _____ activities. And a
                                        5

   _____ person may be able to handle stress without
        6

   frequent visits to the refrigerator.

bored/boring

IV. *Vicky:* I was thinking about boredom and food. Do you think that

   _____ people sometimes eat just because they need
        7

   stimulation?

   Jennie: Yes, I do. Whenever I'm doing a _____ assignment, I have a
                                                    8

   hard time concentrating until I eat chocolate.

tempted/tempting

V. *Meg:*   This bakery has the most _____ pastries I've ever seen. Don't
                                            9

   they look delicious?

   Terry: My feeling is that a _____ person shouldn't resist temptation.
                                    10

   Let's try them!

B. Work with a partner. Write two sentences about each kind of person.

1. amusing people; amused people

   Amusing people tell jokes and funny stories. They're fun to be with.

   Amused people smile and laugh. They're having a good time.

2. annoying people; annoyed people

3. boring people; bored people

4. interesting people; interested people

5. shocking people; shocked people

3 Noun Modifiers: *Food Safety*

Change the words in parentheses to noun modifier + noun and complete the sentence.

1. Handle ___steak knives___ carefully. They're very sharp.
   (knives for steaks)

2. Always wash _____ very thoroughly. Eggs can carry dangerous germs.
   (beaters for eggs)

3. Don't let the _____ stay open too long. Warm food can spoil.
   (door to the refrigerator)

4. Don't let small children play with _____. The children could suffocate.
   (bags made of plastic)

5. Never try to dry a wet newspaper in the _____. It could catch fire.
   (oven powered by microwaves)

6. Accidents can happen. Keep a _____ in the kitchen.
   (extinguisher for fires)

7. Keep your fingers out of the _____. The blades are dangerous.
   (processor for food)

8. Do you think that we really need all this _____?
   (advice about safety)

4 Compound Modifiers: *Long-Lasting Memories*

Complete the second sentence with a compound modifier formed by using the appropriate words from the first sentence.

1. Childhood memories last a long time. They're ___long-lasting___ memories.

2. I was once with my grandmother for a vacation that lasted two months. I was with her for a _____ vacation.

3. My grandmother cooked on a stove that burns wood. It was a _____ stove.

4. When I was young, we ate cookies that were baked at home. They were _____ cookies.

5. The meals that my mother served were cooked well. They were _____ meals.

6. Now I have a child who is eight years old. She's an _____ child.

7. My mother is a woman with gray hair. She's a _____ woman.

8. My mother doesn't cook much anymore because cooking is an activity that can really consume time. It's a _____ activity.

9. But I still have memories of a kitchen that smells sweet. I remember a _____ kitchen.

5 Order of Modifiers: *What Are Your Cravings?*

A. Food cravings are very strong desires for a certain food. Rewrite the modifiers under the blanks in an appropriate order. Include commas when they are indicated.

Hank: What am I craving right now? I'd like a ___really big, thick___ hamburger.
1. (big / , / really / thick)

But I don't crave the _____ hamburgers from fast-food
2. (boring / little)

restaurants.

Rolf: I've been thinking about pizza. I'm going to have a _____
3. (pepperoni / delicious)

pizza as soon as I can. I'm going to get it at a _____
4. (charming / Italian / old / , /)

restaurant in my neighborhood.

Greta: I crave ice cream constantly. At the moment, I want a

_____ scoop of triple-fudge ice cream. I want it in a
5. (round / big / very)

_____ bowl.
6. (china / blue / lovely)

Patty: My favorite snack is _____ chips. I get the ones that come
7. (corn / crunchy / very)

in a _____ bag. And I dip them in a
8. (plastic / large / blue)

_____ sauce.
9. (chili / red / tasty)

Barbara: In the springtime, I get a weird craving for _____
onions.   10. (/ , / green / French / long)

Tanya: I'm trying to lose weight, so I've stopped eating butter. But I dream about

the kind of butter in the _____ box. It has a picture of a
11. (cardboard / , / rectangular / yellow)

_____ woman on it.
12. (Native American / young / beautiful)

B. Write **five** sentences about foods that you crave or like best. In each sentence, use two or three modifiers to describe a noun. Use an intensifier in at least two sentences.

> Example: I crave delicious smooth milk chocolate. I like very strong, black Colombian coffee.

Read your sentences to the class. Do many people have the same cravings?

6 Using Modifiers: *Memories of the Past*

A. Read the following story about Dino, who wanted to open a restaurant that would serve people's favorite foods—the ones they loved eating in their childhood. Use your imagination to rewrite the story and include more description by adding modifiers before nouns. It isn't necessary to add modifiers before all the nouns. Pay attention to modifier order. Include at least two of each of the following: *-ing* or *-ed* adjectives, noun modifiers, and compound modifiers. Change *a* to *an* where necessary.

> Example: First, he talked to an amusing thirty-year-old Greek woman named Helen . . . OR First, he talked to a very short, plump woman named Helen . . .

Dino asked various people to tell him about their memories. First, he talked to a woman named Helen. She told him stories about the meals her grandmother cooked. She described the fish, the vegetables, and the desserts. Then Dino talked to a teacher named Vinnie, who remembered some meals. Vinnie also talked a lot about the house and the garden where he lived and played as a child. After that, Dino heard from Evan, a man who loved music and art. But Evan didn't want to be reminded of his childhood. Finally, Dino met a woman named Cora. Cora had grown up in a family that lived in a city. She had memories of hot dogs and candy. Cora told Dino about the boyfriend she had just broken up with. In the end, Dino realized that his idea wouldn't work—people's feelings about food are too complicated. He decided to write stories instead. He married Cora and wrote her story first.

B.   Read your version of the story to the class.

GRAMMAR BRIEFING 2: Pronouns

Pronouns replace noun phrases that have already been mentioned or that are clear from the context. Pronouns have the same function that nouns do. There are different types of pronouns.

FORM AND FUNCTION Reflexive, Reciprocal, and Indefinite Pronouns; *Other*

Reflexive Pronouns

■ Reflexive pronouns are used instead of object pronouns when an object refers to the same person or thing as the sentence subject. The reflexive pronouns are *myself, yourself, himself, herself, itself, ourselves, yourselves,* and *themselves.*

> **The cook** burned **herself.** (subject and object refer to the same person)
>
> **They** have confidence in **themselves.** (subject and object refer to the same people)

■ Reflexive pronouns are also used to emphasize a noun. In this use, they often come immediately after the noun.

> I **myself** warned him against doing that.
>
> I had a question about the food. The **chef himself** came to my table to answer it. (*chef* is emphasized as it is unexpected for a chef to come to a table)

■ Reflexive pronouns are also used with *by* to mean "alone."

> I was eating **by myself.** (alone)

Reciprocal Pronouns

■ *Each other* and *one another* are reciprocal pronouns. They are used when two or more people or things, named in the subject of the sentence, give and receive the same feelings or actions.

> The chef and the waiter like **each other.** (The chef likes the waiter, and the waiter likes the chef.)
>
> The children really cooperate well with **one another.** (Each of the children cooperates with the other children.)

Indefinite Pronouns

■ Indefinite pronouns are used to talk about unspecified people or things or about people or things in general.

Some	Any	No	Every
someone	anyone	no one	everyone
somebody	anybody	nobody	everybody
something	anything	nothing	everything

Anybody/anyone can learn to make a great soufflé. (all people; people in general)

Everything tastes good when you're hungry. (all things; things in general)

I have all my books and papers, but I know that I'm forgetting **something.** (an unspecified thing)

■ Indefinite pronouns are used as subjects, subject complements, and objects. When used as subjects, they take singular verbs.

Everyone likes the restaurant. **Nobody** is disappointed. (subject)

He must be **someone** important. (subject complement)

The chef is angry about **something.** (object of preposition)

■ In questions, pronouns with *some-* and pronouns with *any-* are used with little difference in meaning. In negative statements, pronouns with *any-* tend to be used. In affirmative statements, pronouns with *some-* mean a certain but unspecified person or thing; pronouns with *any-* mean all, or no particular, persons or things.

Did you see **somebody/anybody** in the kitchen?

I didn't eat **anything** yet today.

He tells his secrets to **someone.** (There is a particular person he tells his secrets to.)

He tells his secrets to **anyone.** (He tells his secrets to whatever people are around.)

■ Indefinite pronouns can be modified. Modifiers, including adjectives, follow the indefinite pronoun.

Anyone who likes unusual food will like that new restaurant.

Tonight the chef is preparing **something new and exciting.**

Other: Form and Function

■ The pronouns *other* and *another* refer back to a noun already mentioned. They indicate an additional one or more of that noun. With *the other* and *the others,* all additional instances of that noun are referred to. With *another* and *others,* only some additional instances are referred to.

One train leaves at two o'clock; **the other** leaves at three o'clock. (implies there are only these two trains)

One train leaves at two o'clock; **another** leaves at three o'clock. (implies there are trains in addition to these two)

TALKING the TALK

■ *One* can be used as an indefinite pronoun to make statements about people in general. The use of *one* is very formal.

> In choosing a meal, **one** should always follow **one's** preferences.

You is often used informally to make the same kind of statements.

> **You** can use **your** fingers to eat most fast food. (you = people in general)

■ *He or she* (*him or her, his or her*) is often used with indefinite pronouns. (In the past, *he* [*him, his*] was usually used, but now use of *he* to mean "anyone/every-one" is seen as excluding females.) Alternatively, *they* is used in place of *he or she*, especially in informal situations. However, avoid *they* in formal writing.

> Anyone can come with us if **he or she** buys/**they** buy a ticket.

> Everyone will pay for **his or her**/**their** own meal.

He or she is also used with noun phrases that require singular forms.

> Each student will be judged by **his or her** participation in class.

GRAMMAR PRACTICE 2: Pronouns

7 Reflexive and Reciprocal Pronouns—Meaning: *Seeing Differences*

Work with a partner. Explain the difference in meaning or emphasis between the sentences in each pair.

1. a. Lewis saw himself in the mirror.

   b. Lewis saw him in the mirror.

   > In (a), *himself* refers to Lewis. Lewis saw Lewis in the mirror. In (b), *him*
   >
   > refers to a man but not to Lewis. Lewis saw another man in the mirror.

2. a. Lucy and Trevor ordered dinner for themselves.

   b. Lucy and Trevor ordered dinner for each other.

3. a. Monica and Howard were writing letters to them.

   b. Monica and Howard were writing letters to each other.

4. a. Eva was talking to her.

   b. Eva was talking to herself.

5. a. Dora served herself dinner.

   b. Dora herself served dinner.

6. a. I myself have gone to Paris.

   b. I've gone to Paris by myself.

7. a. I talked to the President himself.

   b. I talked to the President myself.

8   Reflexive and Reciprocal Pronouns: *Movable Feasts*

Circle the correct pronoun.

1. Today one out of ten meals in the United States is eaten in a car. But when I was
   growing up, [we/ourselves] always sat at the dining room table. My mother put
   all the food on the table, but [she/herself] didn't serve [us/ourselves]. We helped
   [us/ourselves] to the food.

2. Whenever I was sick, my father [myself/himself] served [me/myself] breakfast
   in bed. This was unusual, though.

3. My sister has five-month-old twins, Yolanda and Yvonne. Right now she's busy
   feeding [them/themselves]. When the twins are old enough to feed
   [them/themselves] my sister won't be so busy.

4. Yesterday my children ate in the car. They took turns feeding [themselves/each
   other]. First, Toby put a chicken nugget into Sam's mouth. Then, Sam put a
   chicken nugget into Toby's mouth.

5. *A:* After we pick up our food, let's sit in the car and listen to the radio while we eat.
   B: Let's talk to [ourselves/one another] instead. I want to hear about your trip.

6. Sometimes I like to be alone in my car. I can sing to [me/myself] and no one
   else can hear.

9   Indefinites—Form, Meaning, and Subject-Verb Agreement: *Something for Everyone*

Use combinations of the words below to complete the sentences. In cases where more
than one answer is possible, give any correct answer. In sentences with verbs in parentheses, **circle** the correct verb.

some		one
any	+	body
no		thing
every		

1. The drawer was empty. ____Nothing____ [was/were] in it.

2. I need to answer all my e-mail messages. I haven't written back to

   __anyone / anybody__ for ages.

3. I asked _____ at work how to spell your name, but _____
   knew.

4. Yoko loves Rickie more than _____ she's ever met.

5. Harriet goes running with _____, but I don't know his name.

6. Wally goes running with _____ who happens to be around.

7. *A:* When you go to the store, please get me _____ to eat.

   B: What do you want?

   A: I don't care. _____ that tastes good will be fine.

8. *A:* Do you have all the ingredients for the soup?

   B: Yes, I do. I have _____ I need.

9. *A:* You look worried. [Is/Are] _____ wrong?

   B: No, _____ [is/are] wrong. I don't have any problems.

   _____ [is/are] okay.

10. *A:* _____ [is/are] knocking at the door. Are you expecting

    _____ to visit?

    B: No, _____ [is/are] supposed to be coming now.

11. *A:* Is Sean a vegetarian?

    B: He used to be, but not anymore. Now he pays no attention to what he eats.

    He eats _____.

12. *A:* Is Otis a vegetarian?

    B: Yes, he is. He doesn't eat _____ with meat in it.

10 · Forms of *Other: Sharing*

Complete the sentences by using *another, others, the other,* or *the others*.

1. *A:* Thanks for the cookie. It was delicious.

   B: There are plenty more. Do you want ____*another*____?

2. *C:* I have two cookies. I'm going to eat one. Do you want to eat _____?

3. *A:* I'm like a lot of young single people. I like living by myself. I don't want to

   share my food or space.

   B: I'm used to sharing everything with _____. I grew up in a big family.

   A: So did I. That's why I'm so happy being alone now. I got tired of sharing with

   all _____ in my family.

4. *A:* I brought back the CD you loaned me. Can I trade it for _____?

   B: Sure, but why just borrow one? I have a lot of CDs. If you want to borrow

   _____, you can pick out as many as you'd like.

5. *A:* Would you like something to eat or drink? I know how to make exactly five

things. Tea and coffee are two of them; instant noodles and scrambled eggs

are _____; and, believe it or not, lobster Newburg is

_____.

B: I'm sorry. I heard tea and coffee, but I didn't hear _____. Could

you repeat them?

6. *A:* I like Irene because she has many fine qualities. One is kindness.

_____ is honesty.

B: And _____ is generosity. She gave me her last piece of chocolate

this morning.

GRAMMAR BRIEFING 3: Possessives

Possessives typically indicate belonging. There are four forms: possessive determiners, possessive nouns, possessive pronouns, and possessive phrases with *of*.

FORM AND FUNCTION Possessives

- Possessives indicate ownership or a relationship, such as amount, part to whole, or origin.

  his restaurant, **the Smiths'** house, the desk **of the administrative assistant** (ownership)

  two hours' worth of long-distance service, **a month's** salary (amount)

  the restaurant's kitchen, the leg **of the table,** the lobby **of the Exeter Hotel, her** arm (part of whole)

  the cheeses **of France, Shakespeare's** plays, **our** reason for coming (origin)

- The possessive determiners are *my, your, his, her, its, our, their,* and *one's.* As determiners, these words come before the noun and any modifiers and cannot be used with articles.

  I ate **my** dinner alone last night.   **Not:** I ate ~~the~~ my dinner alone last night.

  Their delicious meals are getting cold while they talk.

- Possessive nouns can be formed from any noun—proper, count, or noncount. Add *'s* to any noun except a plural noun that ends in *s;* add only the apostrophe (') to a plural noun that ends in *s.* Possessive nouns occur in the determiner position, although as nouns they can have determiners of their own.

  Carol's cooking is wonderful.

  The Joneses' party was fun.

  The chef's kitchen is spotless. (one chef)

  The chefs' kitchen is spotless. (more than one chef)

■ The possessive pronouns are *mine, yours, his, hers, ours,* and *theirs*. Possessive pronouns can be used when the context—language or otherwise—makes clear what noun they replace.

> She gave away her banana, but I ate **mine.**

> (Pointing to a homework assignment) Did you do **yours** yet?

■ Possessive phrases are prepositional phrases beginning with *of*. Possessive phrases follow the noun.

> The seat **of the chair** needs to be fixed. (of the chair = the chair's)

■ Possessive nouns and possessive determiners are usually used for people and other animate (living) things. They can be used for inanimate things that perform an action and natural phenomena. Possessive phrases are usually used for inanimate things. They are also used to avoid a long string of words before the main noun.

> **His** watch was broken. (person)

> **The train's** dining car is full. (inanimate thing that performs an action)

> Ocean tides are affected by **the moon's** orbit. (natural phenomenon)

> The color **of the stone** is gray. (inanimate thing)

> The chef **of a well-known five-star restaurant** will give the cooking class. (avoids "a well-known five-star restaurant's chef")

GRAMMAR PRACTICE 3: Possessives

Possessives—Form and Meaning: *Biology + Engineering = Bioengineering*

Work with a partner. **Underline** the possessive forms in the sentences and mark each one with the letter of the meaning it indicates.

a. ownership   **b.** amount   **c.** part to whole   **d.** origin

1. *a*
   The scientist's microscope is on a table in the laboratory.

2. The top of the table is covered with equipment.

3. *A:* How much new equipment did he buy?

   B: He bought ten thousand dollars' worth.

4. The exports of the United States include bioengineered food products.

5. Have you seen bioengineered vegetables on the shelves of a grocery store?

6. Bioengineers discovered the gene after four years' work.

7. Quite a few farmers have tried growing bioengineered potatoes in their fields.

8. The researcher's discovery has increased agricultural production.

12   Possessive Determiners, Possessive Pronouns, and Possessive Nouns: *Technology and Food*

Complete the sentences with the correct possessive form of the pronoun or noun in parentheses.

1. Wait a minute, Richard. You put on _____ my _____ (I) lab coat by mistake.

   _____ Yours _____ (you) is over there.

2. This laboratory has one director. The _____ director's _____ (director) job is to plan the experiments.

3. The company has several directors. The _____ (directors) job is to make decisions about the policies the company will follow.

4. The _____ (company) goal is to develop foods that are easier to grow and process.

5. The _____ (companies) technology has created new types of plants.

6. *A:* Can you help me? I'm looking for the _____ (boss) office.

   B: I'm sorry, this office isn't _____ (she). You want the office with

   _____ (Ms. Tanaka) name on the door. This is _____ (Ms. Harris) office.

   A: It isn't easy to find a _____ (person) office in this building.

   B: You can find _____ (people) office numbers in _____ (we) directory.

7. In this laboratory, the _____ (scientists) work involves changing the characteristics of plants by changing _____ (they) genes.

8. The _____ (scientist) experiment involved changing the characteristics of a plant by putting genes from bacteria into _____ (it) cells.

9. It's possible to insert _____ (animals) genes into plants, too.

10. *A:* Where are Hillary and Richard? Are these salads _____ (they)?

    B: Yes, they are. This is _____ (she) salad, and that one is

    _____ (he).

11. *A:* _____ (you) salads look all right, but you should try some of

_____ (I). It has a bioengineered tomato in it.

B: That's okay. We don't really want _____ (you). _____
(we) are more natural.

C: Actually, I'm interested in that tomato. What's _____ (it) flavor
like? Does it taste like chicken?

13 Possessive Nouns versus Possessive Phrases: *Mother Nature*

Complete the sentences by forming possessive nouns and possessive phrases using the
words in parentheses. In each sentence use the preferred possessive form. Add *the*
where necessary.

1. I was curious about what _____*the engineer's research*_____ involved.
    (engineer / research)

2. What will ___*the benefits of the research*___ be?
    (research / benefits)

3. Will food that has been genetically changed affect

    _____?
    (people / health)

4. Can newly created genes escape from _____ and
behave in unknown ways?   (cells / plants)

5. _____ described the experiments that she is
    (five-year-old biotechnology company / director)
supervising.

6. She believes that, as a result of bioengineering,

    _____ will be able to resist diseases and insects.
    (farmers / crops)

7. Bioengineering has the potential to increase _____.
    (earth / food supply)

8. _____ has made new developments possible.
    (distinguished American organic chemist / work)

9. A mechanical problem has caused _____ to be
delayed.   (plane / departure)

10. While the mechanics look for _____, I have some
time to think about bioengineering.   (problem / cause)

11. Could bioengineers accidentally create something like
    _____?
    (Dr. Frankenstein / monster)

12. Is it possible to put _____ into broccoli?
    (strawberries / genes)

14 **Using Possessives:** *Engineering Mistakes?*

Work with a partner. Find ten unusual things in the drawing and write a sentence about
each of them.

Example: *The tractor's wheels are square.*

UNIT WRAP-UP

Error Correction

Find and correct the errors in the restaurant review. Some errors can be corrected in
more than one way. Including the example, there are **21** errors.

   Last week, I had dinner at Magnificent Food, ~~a~~ newest restaurant in town. I
                                                   the

invited the friend to come with me. The owner of Magnificent Food is the famous

chef. His name is Charles whitney. My friend and I were looking forward to eating

delicious specialties prepared by Mr. Whitney hisself.

   After we arrived at the restaurant, we had to wait, so we ordered a pair of drinks

and began to look at the four-pages menu. When our table was finally ready, we

asked the waiter for some advice about what to order. Although he didn't seem to have a lot of knowledges about the menu, he made any suggestions. We ordered two appetizers; one was smoked fish, and another was mushroom soup. The smoked fish looked beautiful, but it's flavor was strange. A mushroom soup had too many salt in it. The other people in the restaurant got their main courses right away, but we had a long wait for our because of a problem in the kitchen. The waiter didn't know the cause of the problem. When our plates finally came, there was plenty food on them. I had ordered a regional specialty from South. It shouldn't have been a bored dish, but it was—every bite was tasteless. My friends' steak looked very appetizing, but everything on her plate were cold. We decided to go to an excellent small European café across the street for coffee and dessert.

New restaurants often have few problems, so I wasn't expecting perfection at Magnificent Food. But I wasn't expecting to be such a disappointing customer. I hope that this restaurant improves and lives up to its name.

Task 1: A Very Special Dinner Party—Who's Invited?

Work in small groups. Imagine that your group is going to give a very special dinner party. You can invite any seven famous people, living or dead—no one will refuse to come to your party. You can invite people like Elvis Presley, Bill Gates, Hillary Clinton, Michael Jordan, John F. Kennedy, Leonardo Di Caprio, Oprah Winfrey, or anyone you choose. First, think of people you would like to invite and discuss them. Decide on seven guests that you would all like to invite. Then write two or more sentences about each person and the reason the group wants to invite him or her. Pay attention to your use of articles, modifiers, and pronouns in your sentences.

> Example: Leonardo DiCaprio is a talented, handsome actor. We want to
> invite him because he's one of the most well-known movie stars in the world.
> OR Elvis Presley was a great performer. We want to talk to him about his
> music and his personal life.

Read your sentences to the class. Which group's dinner party will be the most interesting? Why?

Task 2: Review a Restaurant

Work with a partner. Imagine that the two of you are restaurant reviewers for a newspaper. First, decide what restaurant you want to review. The restaurant can be a real one or one that you make up, and it can be any kind of restaurant—ethnic, fast food, casual, or elegant. Then write a three-paragraph review. Describe the food (how it looks and tastes), the service (what the waiters or waitresses are like, how well they do their job), and the decor (what the restaurant and its furniture look like). Pay attention to your use of determiners and pronouns. Use at least one of each of the following: a participial adjective, a noun modifier, a compound modifier, a possessive noun, a possessive determiner, and a possessive phrase.

Task 3: Create a Culture

Work in groups of three. The three of you are all members of the same imaginary culture. Discuss and decide the answers to these questions: What does your culture consider to be appropriate food for each meal? How much of each food do people eat at each meal? Is the food eaten in separate courses or all together? Who does the cooking in families? Are there any prohibited foods (foods that you aren't allowed to eat)? What do people eat when they celebrate special occasions? Describe your culture's food and food habits to the class. Pay attention to your use of count and noncount nouns, measure phrases, quantifiers, and modifiers.

> Example: In our culture, most people eat one small meal, one large meal, and several snacks each day. We eat the small meal as soon as we wake up in the morning. We usually have a few dill pickles, a piece of apple pie or some ice cream, and a cup of hot tea. . . . Our most important holiday is on June 21st. On that day, everyone eats young green onions and hard-boiled eggs.

Unit Five

Adjective Clauses and Adjective Phrases

Topic Focus: *Personality*

UNIT OBJECTIVES

■ **adjective clauses**
(The scientist developed a theory *that explains differences among people.*)

■ **relative pronouns (*that, who[m], which, whose*) as subjects and objects in adjective clauses**
(He is the scientist *who developed the theory.* He is the scientist *whom I interviewed.*)

■ ***where* and *when* in adjective clauses**
(The place *where you live* affects you. I'd like to know the year *when you were born.*)

■ **restrictive versus nonrestrictive adjective clauses**
(A man *who wears pink socks every day* is a little unusual. Dudley Dowrong, *who always wears all his clothes backwards,* is an eccentric.)

■ **adjective phrases**
(The woman *covered with tattoos* likes being different.)

INTRODUCTORY TASKS

Reading and Listening

▪▪▪ Read and listen to the radio interview on page 183. Then complete the Comprehension Check.

Comprehension Check

Read each sentence. Circle **T** if the sentence is true or **F** if the sentence is false.

1. Professor Schiller studies people's personalities.   (**T**)   **F**

2. According to Professor Schiller, we are born with the internal factors that help form our personalities.   **T**   **F**

3. *Laterborns* are children born second, third, fourth, and so on.   **T**   **F**

4. Professor Schiller agrees that all brothers and sisters in the same family experience growing up in the same way.   **T**   **F**

5. It is a proven fact that birth order is responsible for personality differences.   **T**   **F**

```
************************************************************
```
Host: Lorrie Kress
Guest: Professor Bruno Schiller
```
************************************************************
```
A: Hello, everyone. I'm Lorrie Kress, and this is "Alive in Our Times." My guest today is a psychologist **who does research on personality**. The information **contained in his new book** is fascinating. I'd like to welcome Professor Bruno Schiller, **whom I admire very much**.

B: Thank you, Lorrie.

A: Professor Schiller, personality is something **that many people want to know more about**. Why is this?

B: I think it's because personalities are complex. Our personality is made up of many different characteristics. For example, a person can be calm or excitable, shy or outgoing, and creative or practical. And understanding ourselves is important. If we understand ourselves, we can make better decisions **about things like jobs**.

A: I agree. But how are personalities formed?

B: Well, Lorrie, psychologists have developed many theories **about this**. Basically, two kinds of factors **working together in our childhood** form our personalities. First, there are internal factors. These are the characteristics **that we are born with**. And second, there are external factors. These factors include our surroundings, our family and friends, and our experiences.

A: My sisters and I, **who had the same parents and the same experiences as children**, have really different personalities now. Why?

B: Actually, there are theories **which might explain the differences among children in the same family**. According to these theories, your personality differences are caused by birth order—by whether you are the oldest, a middle, or the youngest child **in your family**. A firstborn child experiences things differently than a laterborn child does. Only children, **who don't have any brothers or sisters**, are in many ways similar to firstborn children.

A: So, Professor Schiller, what are some characteristics **that birth order might be responsible for**?
B: Well, birth order might determine whether you are creative or practical. It could be responsible for your being a conservative, **who prefers keeping things as they are**, or a liberal, **who is willing to change things**. Also, your birth order might encourage you to become a conformist, **acting as others do**, or a nonconformist, **acting differently than others do**.

A: Can you guess my birth order?

B: Perhaps. Let me ask you a few questions...

Think about Grammar

A. A **clause** is a group of related words that has a subject and a verb. A **phrase** is a group of related words that doesn't have a subject and/or doesn't have a verb. Here are a sentence from the reading and two similar sentences. The three sentences have the same main clause: *The information is fascinating.* Two of the sentences have an adjective phrase; one sentence has an adjective clause.

   a. The information **contained in his new book** is fascinating.
   b. The information **in his new book** is fascinating.
   c. The information **that is contained in his new book** is fascinating.

1. Which sentences have the adjective phrases? _____ _____

2. Which sentence has the adjective clause? _____

   Which word is the subject of the adjective clause? _____

B. Now answer these questions about adjective phrases and clauses.

1. Which word in the main clause *The information is fascinating* does each phrase

   or clause above modify? _____

2. Why are these called **adjective** phrases and clauses? (For a hint, see the definition of adjectives on page G–1.)

C. Work in pairs. Look at the **boldfaced** structures in the reading. Decide which are adjective clauses and which are adjective phrases. Write **AC** for adjective clauses and **AP** for adjective phrases.

   Example: My guest today is a psychologist **who does research on personality.**   AC

Adjective Clauses

Use the following questionnaire to get information to test the birth-order theory of personality development.

A. Work with a partner. Read the questions to your partner. Your partner chooses the answer that describes her or him better and responds in a sentence.

> Example: I'm someone who likes new experiences.

Write **a** or **b** for each answer. Then your partner asks you the questions.

1. Are you someone who a) likes new experiences or b) doesn't like much change?

   _____

2. Do other people see you as a person who a) is a little insecure or b) is

   self-confident? _____

3. Are you someone that a) tries to dress and act as others do or b) tries to dress

   and act differently? _____

4. In your work or studies, are you someone who a) likes to be imaginative and

   creative or who b) likes to be practical and realistic? _____

5. Are you a person who a) enjoys being in a position of power or b) isn't interested

   in having power over others? _____

6. Politically, do you see yourself as someone that a) wants to keep things the same

   or b) wants to change things? _____

7. Are you somebody who a) usually follows rules or b) is willing to bend or break

   rules? _____

When you are both finished, turn to Exercise Page E–4 and follow the instructions there.

B. According to the theory, does your partner have the personality characteristics of a

firstborn or a laterborn child? _____

Is your partner a firstborn or a laterborn child? _____
As a class, count how many people are firstborns **and** according to the theory have the personality characteristics of firstborns. Count how many people are laterborns **and** according to the theory have the personality characteristics of laterborns. Then count how many people the theory does **not** work for. Does the theory work for most of the class members? What is your opinion of the theory?

GRAMMAR BRIEFING 1: Adjective Clauses; Subject and Object Pronouns

An adjective clause (also called a relative clause) is a clause that modifies a noun. An adjective clause identifies, describes, or gives more information about the noun it modifies. The adjective clauses in this chapter are restrictive adjective clauses. (See Chapter 11 for nonrestrictive adjective clauses.)

FORM Adjective Clauses; Subject and Object Pronouns

Adjective Clauses

■ An adjective clause begins with a relative pronoun. Relative pronouns do not change form for masculine or feminine, or for singular or plural. The relative pronoun and the noun it modifies refer to the same person or thing.

> A **scientist who** studies personality has developed a theory. (who = a scientist)

■ A sentence with an adjective clause can be thought of as combining two sentences that have noun phrases referring to the same person or thing.

> A **scientist** has developed a theory. + This **scientist** ~~studies~~ who studies personality.
>
> → A **scientist who** studies personality has developed a theory.

> A scientist has developed a **theory.** + Many people respect **it** that.
>
> → A scientist has developed a **theory that** many people respect.

■ An adjective clause can modify any noun in a sentence. Place the adjective clause after the noun modified, as close as possible to the noun.

> A **scientist** who studies personality has developed a theory.
>
> A scientist has developed a **theory** that explains personality differences.

■ An adjective clause may also modify an indefinite pronoun, for example, *someone, everybody,* or *something*:

> She is **someone** who is creative.

Subject Relative Pronouns: *Who, Which, That*

■ A relative pronoun can be the subject of its clause.

>   S   V   O
> A scientist **who** studies personality has developed a new theory.
>
> (= A scientist has developed a new theory. + A **scientist** studies personality.)

■ The subject relative pronouns are *who, which,* and *that. Who* is used for people; *which* is used for things;* *that* is used for people and for things.

> A **scientist who/that** studies personality has developed a new theory.
>
> The scientist has developed a **theory which/that** explains personality.

■ In adjective clauses with subject relative pronouns, the verb of the clause must agree in number with the noun modified.

> I know **psychologists** who **believe** in that theory.
>
> **Not:** I know psychologists who ~~believes~~ in that theory.

Object Relative Pronouns: *Who, Whom, Which, That,* [0]

■ A relative pronoun can be the object of the verb in its clause.

$$\overset{O}{\text{whom}}\ \overset{S}{\text{I}}\ \overset{V}{\text{admire}}$$

The scientist **whom** I admire does research.

(= The scientist does research. + I admire **the scientist.**)

■ The object relative pronouns are *who, whom, which,* and *that. Who* and *whom* are used for people; *which* is used for things; *that* is used for people and for things.* The object relative pronoun is often omitted (**[0]** = no relative pronoun).

The scientist **who/that/[0]** I admire does research.

I accept the theory **which/that/[0]** the scientist developed.

* *Things* are everything that is not human, including abstractions and most animals.

GRAMMAR HOTSPOT!

■ When using adjective clauses, be careful not to include an extra pronoun. It is as if the relative pronoun replaces another pronoun. So use only the relative pronoun.

The theory was developed by the scientist. + I admire **him.**

→ The theory was developed by the scientist **that** I admire.

Not: The theory was developed by the scientist that I admire him.

■ Subject relative pronouns cannot be omitted.

A scientist **who/that** studies personality has developed a new theory.

Not: A scientist [0] studies personality has developed a new theory.

■ *What* cannot be used as a relative pronoun.

Everything **which/that/[0]** he wrote is false.   **Not:** Everything what he wrote is false.

TALKING the TALK

■ Contractions with subject relative pronouns *who* and *that* are common in speaking and informal writing.

She's someone **who's** creative.

■ The object relative pronoun *whom* is considered more formal than *who, that,* or [0]. In speaking, *who, that,* and [0] are more common than *whom.*

More informal:

She is a teacher **[0]** students admire.

She is a teacher **that** students admire.

She is a teacher **who** students admire.

More formal:

She is a teacher **whom** students admire.

In writing, however, using *who* as an object relative pronoun is generally considered incorrect; *whom* (or *that* or [0]) should be used.

GRAMMAR PRACTICE 1: Adjective Clauses; Subject and Object Pronouns

1 Identifying Adjective Clauses: *Psychologists and Mothers*

In the following passage, **underline** each adjective clause and **circle** the noun or pronoun it modifies. Put a **second line** under the subject of each adjective clause.

Are you a (person) who is shy? Or are you a person who is outgoing? And why are you shy or outgoing? Are these characteristics which were part of your personality when you were born? Or are they characteristics which you developed because of your life experiences? These are questions that psychologists have been trying to answer for a long time. According to modern psychologists, a combination of biological factors and experience shaped your personality. This is something that mothers know, too. Each child that a mother has seems different from the others even as an infant. And as the children grow, the mother can see differences in their experiences. She can see how the experiences that her children have help to shape their characters. Sometimes the theories that psychologists develop express what mothers have known all along!

2 Forming Adjective Clauses; Subject Relative Pronouns: *People and Their Personalities I*

Use the first pair of sentences to add adjective clauses to the second pair of sentences. Use any appropriate subject relative pronoun (*who, which, that*).

1. One businessman is a nonconformist. The other businessman is a conformist.

    The businessman ___who / that is a conformist___ wears a suit and tie to work.

    The businessman ___who / that is a nonconformist___ wears a Mickey Mouse T-shirt and yellow shorts to work.

2. One person is outgoing. The other person is shy.

    The person _____ wants to be the host of a TV talk show.

    The person _____ would prefer to watch the TV talk show.

3. Some people are pessimists. Other people are optimists.

    People _____ buy lottery tickets.

    People _____ buy life insurance.

4. One activity appeals to a lazy or busy person. Another activity appeals to an energetic person.

   The activity _____ is cooking a ten-course dinner.

   The activity _____ is calling a restaurant to have dinner delivered.

5. Some jobs require hostility. Other jobs require friendliness.

   Professional wrestlers have jobs _____.

   Used car salesmen have jobs _____.

3 Forming Adjective Clauses; Object Relative Pronouns: *People and Their Personalities II*

Use the first pair of sentences to add adjective clauses to the second pair of sentences.
Use any appropriate object relative pronoun (*who, whom, which, that,* [0]).

1. We call some people generous. We call other people selfish.

   People __*who / whom / that / [0] we call generous*__ share their chocolate cake with others.

   People __*who / whom / that / [0] we call selfish*__ eat the whole cake themselves.

2. Tiffany considers one boyfriend unromantic. Tiffany considers another boyfriend romantic.

   The boyfriend _____ gave her perfume and jewelry.

   The boyfriend _____ gave her motor oil and power tools.

3. Chris thinks that one roommate is thoughtless. Chris thinks that another roommate is thoughtful.

   The roommate _____ always washes all the dishes.

   The roommate _____ always leaves dirty dishes in the sink.

4. A serious person likes some activities. A fun-loving person likes other activities.

   Thinking about and discussing important problems are activities

   _____.

   Joking and laughing about funny events are activities

   _____.

5. Lion tamers need one characteristic. Bird watchers can have another characteristic.

   Timidity is a characteristic _____.

   Bravery is a characteristic _____.

4 Using *Someone + Who: Who Does It Better?*

Work with a partner. Take turns asking and answering questions about people and their characteristics. Follow the example. Use *someone who* as in the example.

1. Hair stylist: creative or practical?

> Student A: Should a hair stylist be *someone who's* **creative** or *someone who's* **practical?**
>
> Student B: I think a hair stylist should be *someone who's* **creative.**
>
> Student A: Why?
>
> Student B: I want to have a hair style that's new and unusual.
>
> OR:
>
> Student B: A hair stylist should be *someone who's* **practical.**
>
> Student A: Why?
>
> Student B: Hair stylists should think of hair styles that are easy to take care of.

2. Car mechanic: creative or practical?

3. Scientist: conformist or nonconformist?

4. Soccer player: calm or excitable?

5. Mountain climber: adventurous or careful?

6. The leader of a country: optimistic or pessimistic?

5 Combining Sentences to Form Sentences with Adjective Clauses: *Another Theory*

Use the second sentence to form an adjective clause modifying the appropriate noun in the first sentence. Show all relative pronouns (*who, whom, which, that,* [0]) that are possible.

1. Last week I read a book. It was about psychology.

> Last week I read a book which was about psychology.
>
> Last week I read a book that was about psychology.

2. The psychologist studies personality. He is the author.

3. He wrote about a theory. It explains personality type.

4. I talked to a scientist about the book. I know her very well.

5. My friend disagrees with the theory. The psychologist developed it.

6. Another researcher developed a theory. My friend finds it more convincing.

7. According to this theory, some personality characteristics have a source. The source is biological.

8. Chemicals can influence our personalities. The chemicals are in our brains and bodies.

9. These chemicals can affect our response to events. We experience the events.

10. What do you think of this theory? My scientific friend believes it.

6 Relative Pronouns: *Birth Order and Personality*

Fill in the blanks with all the choices (*who, whom, which, that,* [0]) that are possible.

     Are you someone _____who/that_____ was a firstborn child? Or were you a later-
                            1

born in your family? Some psychologists believe that your birth order and the rela-

tionships _____ you had with the others in your family had a lot to do
                2

with the personality _____ you have now.
                 3

     Parents are people _____ young children need. Brothers and sisters
                  4

are people _____ young children don't necessarily need and sometimes
            5

wish they didn't have. Children _____ are born first enjoy having all of
                6

their parents' attention. This attention is something _____ they want to
                   7

keep. Children _____ are born later also want to get attention. Each later-
          8

born wants to create a situation _____ is new and different and hopes to
              9

be the child _____ the parents notice most.
         10

     As a result of their early experiences, firstborns may become adults

_____ are conservative and prefer to keep things as they are. Firstborns
    11

also tend to be natural leaders _____ are more self-confident than later-
           12

borns. Because of their place in the family, laterborns may become adults

_____ are liberal and open to new experiences. They tend to be imagina-
    13

tive and adventurous. Of course, you may know laterborns _____ you
             14

consider to be self-confident leaders. And you probably know firstborns

_____ you regard as creative adventurers. This is because there are many
    15

factors _____ can be important in forming personality. Do you think that
      16

your birth order is a factor _____ explains a part of the personality
         17

_____ you have now?
    18

7 Writing Sentences: *Describing Personalities*

A. Work with a partner. Choose **one** of the people in the photos on page 192. (Keep
your choice a secret from other class members.) Discuss the person you have chosen: Who is she? What do you think her personality is like? What are her talents,
likes, dislikes, and interests? In your discussion, use sentences with adjective clauses.

Example: She looks like someone who's shy. OR She's a woman who enjoys sports and is very adventurous. OR I think she's probably the kind of person that children like.

B. Write a description of the person you chose, but **don't** include anything about her appearance. Use at least five adjective clauses.

C. Read your description to the class. Can the class guess which person you are describing?

GRAMMAR BRIEFING 2: Relative Pronouns as Objects of Prepositions; Possessive Relative Pronouns

A relative pronoun also can be the object of a preposition in its clause or can be a possessive form.

FORM Relative Pronouns as Objects of Prepositions; Possessive Relative Pronouns

Relative Pronouns as Objects of Prepositions: *Whom, Who, Which, That,* [0]

■ A relative pronoun can be the object of a preposition in its clause.

           O of Prep   Prep

    She is a scientist **whom** we agree **with**.

    (= She is a scientist. + We agree **with her.**)

■ When the relative pronoun is the object of a preposition in its clause, use the same forms as for the objects of verbs: *whom* and *who* for people; *which* for things; *that* for people and for things.

    She is a scientist **who/whom/that/[0]** we agree **with**.

    She has developed a theory **which/that/[0]** we are interested **in**.

■ The preposition may be placed at the end or at the beginning of an adjective clause. If the preposition is at the beginning of the clause, *whom* or *which* must be used. Do not use *who* or *that*. Do not omit the object relative pronoun ([0]).

                Prep   0 of Prep
She is a scientist **with whom** we agree.

                   Prep 0 of Prep
She has developed a theory **in which** we are interested.

Possessive Relative Pronoun: *Whose*

■ The relative pronoun *whose* is a possessive like *my, her, his,* etc., and must be followed by a noun.

    I spoke to the scientist **whose article** we read.

    (= I spoke to the scientist. + We read **her article**.)

■ *Whose* + noun may be the subject of an adjective clause or the object of the verb or of a preposition in an adjective clause.

                  S   V
    I heard the scientist **whose work** is attracting so much interest.

                0   S   V
    I met the scientist **whose work** I admire.

          Obj of P   Prep
    She is the scientist **whose work** I was telling you about.

■ *Whose* usually refers to people but can also refer to things.

    The psychologist developed a theory **whose** validity has not yet been proven .

TALKING the TALK

■ Prepositions at the beginning of an adjective clause are considered formal. They are common in written English but are less common in spoken English.

More informal:

    The professor is someone [0] I agree **with.**

    The professor is someone **that** I agree **with.**

    The professor is someone **who[m]** I agree **with.**

More formal:

    The professor is someone **with whom** I agree.

GRAMMAR PRACTICE 2: Relative Pronouns as Objects of Prepositions; Possessive Relative Pronouns

8   Combining Sentences; Clauses with Prepositions: *Finding the Right Job I*

Combine these pairs of sentences using the second sentence as an adjective clause.
Show all possible patterns.

1. The teacher explained personality types. We met with her.

    The teacher with whom we met explained personality types.

    The teacher whom we met with explained personality types.

> *The teacher who we met with explained personality types.*
> *The teacher that we met with explained personality types.*
> *The teacher [O] we met with explained personality types.*

2. The psychologist discussed careers. We listened to him.

3. I learned about some jobs. I am suited for them.

🔾 Combining Sentences; Clauses with *Whose: Finding the Right Job II*

Combine these pairs of sentences using the second sentence as an adjective clause
with *whose.*

1. The teacher explained personality characteristics. We heard her lecture.

   > *The teacher whose lecture we heard explained personality types.*

2. She talked about people. Their personalities are well suited for the work they do.

3. She gave us the names of some psychologists. Their specialty is personality
   testing.

4. The psychologist was friendly. I went to his office.

5. I took a personality test. He explained its results to me.

6. I am an outgoing person. My personality is practical.

7. I am also a serious student. My interests are international.

8. I want to travel to many countries. I will enjoy meeting their people.

9. In today's newspaper I read about a job. I meet its requirements exactly.

10. I called several companies. I read their job ads in the newspaper.

11. The manager said she will interview me. I really want to work for her company.

🔟 Relative Pronouns as Objects of Prepositions; Possessive Relative Pronouns: *Your Preferences and Your Personality*

Fill in the blanks, using *whom, who, which, that, whose,* and [0]. Show all the possible
completions.

Psychology is a subject __which, that, [O]__ many people are interested in. And
                                    1

there are many people for _____ psychology can be useful. They include
                                 2

people trying to choose the job _____ they are best suited for. By using
                                        3

psychology to understand their personality types, they can make choices

with _____ they will be satisfied.
           4

Psychologists often use a test to determine a person's personality type. A psy-

chologist _____ name was Carl Jung developed the theory
                 5

on _____ this kind of test is based. Jung said that people's preferences
       6

show their characteristics. So the way in _____ a personality test
                                                    7

determines your type is by asking you about your preferences. A personality test

may ask you about the kinds of people _____ you feel comfortable with.

8

Do you like to be with a few people with _____ you have close friendships

9

or with many people to _____ you aren't so close? A test may also ask if

10

you are someone _____ preference is for dealing with facts or with theo-

11

ries. It may ask about how you make decisions. Is logical reasoning something

on _____ you depend or do you usually follow your feelings? Finally, a

12

test may ask about how you organize your life. Are you someone _____

13

life is carefully planned or is your life flexible and open to change?

When you are trying to understand your type, there are two important

points _____ you should be aware of. First, in some cases there may not

14

be one preference with _____ you strongly identify. Second, there are no

15

"good" or "bad" preferences. People are different, and these differences are useful.

Understanding and accepting the different types of people _____ you

16

study or work with can help you get along with them.

If you find a job _____ you are excited about, it will probably be

17

one _____ you will succeed in.

18

▮▮ Adjective Clauses with Prepositions: *What Are Your Interests?*

You have just been hired by MYMIX, a large multinational corporation. They want to
know more about your interests so they can decide which department to place you in.
Answer the questions, using the cues in parentheses and using the example as a model.

MYMIX CORPORATION
PERSONNEL DEPARTMENT
1. Which corporation are you most enthusiastic about? ([0] . . . about)
The corporation [0] I am most enthusiastic about is MYMIX.
2. What kind of work are you interested in? (which . . . in)
3. What free-time activities are you involved in? ([0] . . . in)
4. Which school subject have you excelled in? (that . . . in)

5. Which person are you most grateful to? (to whom . . .)

6. Which famous person do you most identify with? ([0] . . . with)

7. Which world problem are you most concerned about? (about . . . which)

8. What kind of job are you best suited for? ([0] . . . for)

▐12▌ Completing Sentences with Adjective Clauses: *An Alien Invasion?*

Last night you had a terrifying experience that left you unable to do your homework or even speak. As a result, you need to write a letter to your teacher explaining what happened. Complete the following with adjective clauses. Include one clause with *whose* and at least one with a preposition.

Dear _____,

    I'm very sorry that I haven't done my homework, but I hope you will

excuse me. Last night I was kidnapped by extra-terrestrial aliens. I

don't know which planet they were from, but there were three types of

creatures.

1. The first type were human-like aliens
   <u>who had dark bulging eyes and huge hairless heads</u>.

2. The second type were aliens _____.

3. The third type were aliens _____.

4. They all wore clothes _____.

5. The aliens spoke English to me, but among themselves they

   spoke a language _____.

6. They took me onto a spaceship _____.

7. On the spaceship, they told me they were interested in talking

   to humans _____.

8. They asked me questions _____.

9. While I was on their spaceship, I could hear

   music _____.

10. The aliens were eating special extra-terrestrial food

    _____.

11. They didn't give me any of the food, but when they

    had finished questioning me, they gave me a drink

    _____.

    Early this morning the aliens finally brought me back home. I

    know I have a creative imagination, but this is not science fic-

    tion!

Your student,

_____

11

More about Adjective Clauses; Adjective Phrases

Introductory Task: *Time and Place*

A. Read this excerpt from Professor Bruno Schiller's book *Personality and Culture:*

> Childhood is the **time when** your personality was formed. So the **place where** you grew up had an influence on you. Your culture was an important factor in shaping your personality and behavior. For example, in some cultures, children are encouraged to conform and to fit in with others. In other cultures, children are allowed or even encouraged to be nonconformists, at least in some ways. . . .
>
> Of course, behavior that is conformist or usual in one culture may be considered nonconformist or unusual in another culture. . . .

B. Work in small groups. Think about ways of behaving or dressing that would be usual in some countries or times but unusual in other countries or times. Think of three examples. For each, write **two** sentences, using *place where* or *time when.*

> Example: Japan is a place where people eat raw fish. Poland is a place where people don't usually eat raw fish.
>
> The eighteenth century was a time when men wore powdered wigs. The twentieth century was a time when men didn't usually wear powdered wigs.

Discuss your sentences with the class.

GRAMMAR BRIEFING 1: Adjective Clauses with *Where* and *When*

Adjective clauses about places and times can be introduced by the relative adverbs *where* and *when,* as well as by an object relative pronoun.

FORM Adjective Clauses with *Where* and *When*

Adjective Clauses with *Where*

■ *Where* can begin an adjective clause that modifies the noun *place* or a noun that refers to a place—*country, city, building, house, room, street,* and so on.

> Your friend wants to know the name of the city **where** you were born.

■ Instead of *where,* the adjective clause can have an object relative pronoun and a preposition.

> Your friend wants to know the name of the city **in which** you were born. OR
> Your friend wants to know the name of the city **which/that/[0]** you were born **in**.

Adjective Clauses with *When*

■ *When* can begin an adjective clause that modifies the noun *time* or a noun that refers to a period of time—*century, year, day, night,* and so on.

> Your friend wants to know the day **when** you were born.

■ Instead of *when,* the adjective clause can have an object relative pronoun. A preposition is often omitted with relative pronouns other than *which.*

> Your friend wants to know the day **on which** you were born/
> **which** you were born **on**. OR Your friend wants to know the day
> **that/[0]** you were born (on).

GRAMMAR HOTSPOT!

■ Do not use a preposition with *where* or *when.*

> Your friend wants to know when you were born.
>
> **Not:** Your friend wants to know when you were born ~~on~~.

■ Do not use question word order with *where* and *when* used to introduce adjective clauses.

> *Wh-* question: Where **is your house?**
>
> Adjective clause: Please describe the place where **your house is.**
>
> **Not:**   Please describe the place where ~~is your house~~.

GRAMMAR PRACTICE I: Adjective Clauses with *Where* and *When*

1 Adjective Clauses of Time and Place: *Your Childhood*

A. A researcher who is studying personality formation wants to know about the surroundings of your childhood. Describe them, using a different pattern for each
answer. Use [0] if no word goes in the blank.

Example: __My elementary school__ was a place __in which__ I felt bored

__[0]__ .

1. _____ was a place _____ I felt bored _____ .

2. _____ was a place _____ I felt safe _____ .

3. _____ was a place _____ I felt confused _____ .

4. _____ was a place _____ I felt excited _____ .

5. _____ was a place _____ I felt frightened _____ .

B. The researcher also wants to know about the experiences of your childhood.
Describe them, following the example, and using a different pattern for each answer.
You can use any time expression (*moment, hour, day, week, year,* etc.). Use a preposi-
tion only if necessary.

Example: A time when I felt adventurous was

__the day on which I first traveled overseas__ .

1. A time when I felt adventurous was _____ .

2. A time when I felt sad was _____ .

3. A time when I felt enthusiastic was _____ .

4. A time when I felt happy was _____ .

5. A time when I felt generous was _____ .

2 Adjective Clauses with *Where: Your Life Now I*

You have a friend who lives far away and wants to know about your surroundings. Write
six sentences about the location or appearance of the places in your life. Use *where* and
one of the following pairs of cues in each sentence.

Example: The pool where I swim is in the student recreation center.
(location) OR The pool where I swim has blue stripes on the bottom.
(appearance)

city/town : live	library : study	field : play soccer
house/apartment/dormitory : live	grocery store : buy food	pool : swim
school/college : study	post office : mail letters	place : work
cafeteria : eat lunch	theater : see movies	place : ?

3 Adjective Clauses with *When: Your Life Now II*

Your friend also wants to know what your days are usually like. Write sentences about your days, using *a time when* and each of the following prompts.

1. dawn

      Example: <u>Dawn is a time when I'm usually asleep.</u>

2. morning _____

3. afternoon _____

4. evening _____

5. night _____

6. the weekend _____

GRAMMAR BRIEFING 2: Restrictive versus Nonrestrictive Adjective Clauses

There are two types of adjective clauses. Restrictive adjective clauses, covered in Chapter 10 and Grammar Briefing 1, page 199, identify the noun or pronoun modified. Nonrestrictive adjective clauses provide additional information about a noun or pronoun.

FORM Nonrestrictive Adjective Clauses

■ In nonrestrictive adjective clauses, use *who, which, whom, whose, where,* and *when.* Do not use the relative pronoun *that.* Do not omit the object relative pronoun.

> Professor Schiller, **who** teaches psychology, wrote a book.
>
> His book, **which** we read, is about personality and culture.
>
> Albert Einstein, **about whom** we learned, was a creative physicist.
>
> Glenn Gould, **whose** music I admire, was an eccentric pianist.
>
> In Holland, **where** my friend lives, people often eat raw fish.

■ Always put commas around a nonrestrictive clause. The commas stand for pauses in speaking.

> Professor Schiller, (pause) who is a psychologist, (pause) studies personality.

(With restrictive clauses, commas are **not** used. Do not pause before or after a restrictive clause.)

FUNCTION Restrictive versus Nonrestrictive Adjective Clauses

Restrictive Adjective Clauses

■ Restrictive adjective clauses identify the noun or pronoun modified by telling which one(s) or what kind of person(s) or thing(s) it is. They give information the listener needs in order to know who or what the noun or pronoun refers to.

> Artists **who/that are creative** attract a lot of attention. (Certain artists attract attention—artists who are creative; *who are creative* tells which artists attract attention.)

> My daughter **who/that is six** already shows signs of being a nonconformist. (The speaker has more than one daughter; *who is six* identifies which daughter the speaker is referring to.)

■ If a restrictive adjective clause is omitted, the basic meaning of the sentence is changed.

> Artists who are creative attract a lot of attention. ≠ Artists attract a lot of attention.

Nonrestrictive Adjective Clauses

■ Nonrestrictive adjective clauses add information about the noun or pronoun modified but are not needed to identify it.

> Artists, **who are creative,** attract a lot of attention. (Artists in general attract attention; *who are creative* adds information about artists in general.)

> My daughter, **who is six,** already shows signs of being a nonconformist. (The speaker presumably has only one daughter; *who is six* adds information about the daughter.)

■ If a nonrestrictive adjective clause is omitted, the basic meaning of the sentence is not changed.

> Artists, who are creative, attract a lot of attention. = Artists attract a lot of attention. (And they are creative.)

■ Nouns are already identified and therefore followed by nonrestrictive, rather than restrictive, adjective clauses when:

- they are proper nouns (names of people, places, or things).

> **Professor Schiller,** who teaches psychology, has written an important book.

- they are in some other way unique.

> **My mother,** who valued creativity, encouraged me to be an artist.

- the previous context has identified them.

> Last week I read **a book** about personality. **The book,** which explained conformity, was fascinating.

GRAMMAR HOTSPOT!

■ Remember! In nonrestrictive clauses do not use *that* and do not delete object relative pronouns.

> Professor Schiller, **whom** I respect, is a psychologist and author.

> **Not:**   Professor Schiller, ~~that I respect~~, is a psychologist and author.

> **Not:**   Professor Schiller, ~~I respect~~, is a psychologist and author.

GRAMMAR PRACTICE 2: Restrictive versus Nonrestrictive Adjective Clauses

4 Distinguishing Restrictive and Nonrestrictive Clauses: *Look Again*

Return to the passage on page 183 and look again at the **boldfaced** adjective clauses.
Which are restrictive adjective clauses and which are nonrestrictive adjective clauses?
Underline the nonrestrictive clauses.

5 Sentence Combining, Nonrestrictive Clauses: *Famous Eccentrics*

Eccentricity is a type of nonconformity: Eccentrics are highly individualistic people who
act or dress in unusual and original ways. Read the groups of paired sentences. Use the
second sentence in each pair to write a nonrestrictive clause modifying the appropriate
noun in the first sentence. Be sure to include commas.

1. a. Emily Dickinson was a great American poet.
      Dickinson lived in the nineteenth century.

   Emily Dickinson, who lived in the nineteenth century, was a great American poet.

   b. Dickinson never went out of her room.
      She always wore white.
   c. Her poems became famous only after her death.
      She hid them in little boxes.

2. a. The telephone was perfected in 1876 by Alexander Graham Bell.
      He was a Scottish-American inventor.
   b. Bell also tried to teach his dog how to talk.
      Bell experimented in the area of human speech.
   c. The windows of his house were covered at night to keep out moonlight.
      He was fearful of moonlight.

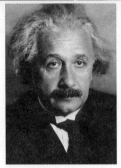

3. a. The most famous Canadian classical pianist was Glenn Gould.
   Gould's recordings are widely admired.
   b. The pianist often sang along as he performed.
   He soaked his hands in very hot water before playing.
   c. Gould often wore woolen overcoats, mittens, scarves, and hats in midsummer.
   Cold air drafts were terrifying to him.

4. a. Benjamin Franklin was a famous statesman and inventor in the eighteenth century.
   In that century the United States became an independent country.
   b. Franklin's habit was to take "air baths."
   He believed they were good for his health.
   c. "Air bathing" might be considered odd today.
   It meant sitting naked in front of an open window and breathing deeply.

5. a. Albert Einstein was the most creative physicist of the twentieth century.
   Many people considered Einstein an eccentric.
   b. In his later years, his home was in Princeton.
   There he was known for being absent-minded.
   c. Einstein often went without socks and forgot to comb his hair.
   It stuck out in all directions.

6 Restrictive versus Nonrestrictive Clauses: *What Do the Messages Mean?*

Professor Schiller is out of town at a conference. Several messages have been left on his answering machine. Listen to them twice. Then **circle** the letter of each correct choice.

1. Walter probably has
   a. more than one brother.
   b. only one brother.

2. Jamal probably has
   a. more than one brother.
   b. only one brother.

3. At Vivian's store,
   a. all the compact discs Professor Schiller ordered have arrived.
   b. only some of the compact discs Professor Schiller ordered have arrived.

4. At Isabel's store,
   a. all the compact discs Professor Schiller ordered have arrived.
   b. only some of the compact discs Professor Schiller ordered have arrived.

5. In David's class
   a. all the students definitely passed.
   b. some students might not have passed.

6. In Lynn's class
   a. all the students definitely passed.
   b. some students might not have passed.

7. Amanda implies that
   a. all of her friends are nonconformists.
   b. only some of her friends are nonconformists.

8. Donald implies that
   a. all of his friends are nonconformists.
   b. only some of his friends are nonconformists.

9. Although *Susan* is a proper noun, the adjective clauses that modify it are
   a. nonrestrictive clauses, giving additional information.
   b. restrictive clauses, needed to identify the noun.

7 Nonrestrictive and Restrictive Clauses—Pronouns and Punctuation: *Eccentricity and Eccentrics*

> Henry David Thoreau, who was a nineteenth-century American author, wrote in *Walden*, "If a man does not keep pace with his companions, perhaps it is because he hears a different drummer. Let him step to the music which he hears. . . ."

Complete the following passage with *who, whom, which, that, whose, when, where,* or *[0]*, and add commas where they are needed. If more than one relative pronoun or adverb is possible, give any correct form.

(1) Eccentricity is a trait _____ ___which___ is difficult to define, but most of us probably can identify an eccentric when we meet one. (2) We can be both fascinated and threatened by a person _____ ___who___ behaves strangely. (3) Some eccentrics __,__ ___who___ behave in a way ___that___ is only slightly nonconformist __,__ might be described as minor eccentrics. (4) This category of eccentrics might include, for example, someone _____ ___who___ wears pink socks every day or ___whose___ hobby is collecting candy wrappers. (5) But there are also people ___who___ behave flamboyantly or bizarrely; they are major eccentrics.

Britain seems to have many major eccentrics. (6) For example, there is a man _____ ___who___ calls himself Chief Shiloh and always dresses in a Native American costume. (7) And there is John Slater __,__ ___who___ has walked the length of Britain barefoot and in pajamas. (8) His home __,__ ___which___ fills with sea water regularly, _____ is a cave on the coast of Scotland.

(9) There are Americans __,__ ___who___ qualify as major eccentrics, too. (10) One example is Al Joyner __,__ ___who___ rides around the town of Virginia Beach on his invention—a machine __,__ ___which___ is half bicycle, half rocking horse. (11) The horse half __,__ ___which___ Al calls Disco __,__ is brightly decorated with reflectors and wears a pearl necklace. (12) There have been some famous American eccentrics, too; for example, Howard Hughes __,__ ___who___ was a handsome billionaire. (13) Hughes __,__

_____*whom*_____ people first knew as a designer of airplanes and an adventurous

pilot ,_____ became a movie producer. (14) Later on, he began to dress in filthy

rags and moved to a hotel in Las Vegas ,___ *where*___ he lived in isola-

tion until 1976 _____ *when*_____ he died.

[Adapted from Dr. David Weeks and Jamie James, *Eccentrics: A Study of Sanity and Strangeness.* Villard, New York, 1995.]

8 Writing Sentences with Nonrestrictive Clauses: *World Record Holders*

A. The following entries from *The Guinness Book of Records* describe the unusual record performances of six individuals. For each entry, write **two** different sentences, each containing a nonrestrictive adjective clause. Include some sentences with *whose*, *when*, and *where*. It is not necessary to include all the information given in each entry in your sentences. Punctuate carefully.

1. **Bubble blowing.** David Stein of New York City created a 50-foot-long bubble on June 6, 1988. He made the bubble using a bubble wand, dishwashing liquid, and water.

   > The person with the record for bubble blowing is David Stein, who made a 50-foot-long bubble in 1988.
   >
   > On June 6, 1988, when he created a 50-foot-long bubble, David Stein set the world record for bubble blowing. OR
   >
   > David Stein, whose home is in New York City, made a record-setting bubble of dishwashing liquid and water.

2. **Cherry stem tying.** Al Gliniecki of Pensacola, Florida, tied 833 cherry stems into knots with his tongue in one hour on April 24, 1992.

3. **Gum wrapper chain.** The longest gum wrapper chain measured 12,105 feet and was made by Gary Duschl of Waterdown, Ontario, Canada, between 1965 and 1994.

4. **Motionlessness.** Antonio Gomes dos Santos of Zare, Portugal, stood motionless for 15 hours, 2 minutes, 55 seconds on July 30, 1988, at the Amoreiras Shopping Center, Lisbon, Portugal.

5. **Longest fingernails.** As of February 25, 1995, Shridhar Chilal (born 1937, Pune, Maharashtra, India) had the longest fingernails. The nails on the fingers of his left hand measured a total of 226 inches. He last cut his nails in 1952.

6. **Most tattoos.** Tom Leppard of the Isle of Skye, Scotland, has the most tattoos. He has chosen a leopard-skin design, with all the skin between the spots tattooed yellow. Tattoos cover about 99.2 percent of is body.

B. Is Al, who ties cherry stems with his tongue, more eccentric than Tom, who covers himself with tattoos? As a class, discuss the record-holders and rank them according to how eccentric they are. Why do you think these people do these things?

C. Do you know anyone you would describe as an eccentric? Do you know about any famous eccentrics? Write a paragraph describing an eccentric, either one you know personally or one who is famous. Use at least three restrictive and two nonrestrictive adjective clauses.

GRAMMAR BRIEFING 3: Adjective Phrases

An adjective phrase, like an adjective clause, modifies a noun. Unlike an adjective clause, an adjective phrase doesn't have a subject and/or doesn't have a verb. Adjective phrases can be formed from adjective clauses that have subject relative pronouns.

FORM Adjective Phrases

Adjective Phrase Formation

■ Formation from an adjective clause with *be*

To change an adjective clause with *be* to an adjective phrase, delete the subject relative pronoun and the form of *be*.

Adjective Clause		Adjective Phrase
The book ~~which is~~ by Professor Schiller is fascinating.	→	The book by Professor Schiller is fascinating.*
The book ~~which was~~ written by Professor Schiller is fascinating.	→	The book written by Professor Schiller is fascinating.
Those men ~~that were~~ wearing earrings shocked my grandmother.	→	Those men wearing earrings shocked my grandmother.
Anyone ~~who is~~ angry at society might become a rebel.	→	Anyone angry at society might become a rebel.

* Adjective phrases that begin with a preposition are prepositional phrases.

■ Formation from an adjective clause with a verb other than *be*
   To change an adjective clause without *be* to an adjective phrase, delete the subject relative pronoun and change the verb to its present participle (*-ing*) form.

Adjective Clause		**Adjective Phrase**
People <u>who live in big cities</u> often see nonconformists.	→	People <u>living in big cities</u> often see nonconformists.
A person <u>who lived in San Francisco</u> often saw beatniks and hippies.	→	A person <u>living in San Francisco</u> often saw beatniks and hippies.
Punk music <u>which contains rude words</u> offends some people.	→	Punk music <u>containing rude words</u> offends some people.

Restrictive and Nonrestrictive Adjective Phrases

■ If an adjective clause is restrictive, the corresponding adjective phrase is restrictive. Do not use commas. If an adjective clause is nonrestrictive, the corresponding adjective phrase is nonrestrictive. Use commas.

Restrictive	**Nonrestrictive**
The man ~~who is~~ <u>covered with tattoos</u> likes being different (adjective clause)	Tom Leppard, ~~who is~~ <u>covered with tattoos</u>, likes being different. (adjective clause)
→ The man <u>covered with tattoos</u> likes being different. (adjective phrase)	→ Tom Leppard, <u>covered with tattoos</u>, likes being different. (adjective phrase)

GRAMMAR PRACTICE 3: Adjective Phrases

9 Forming Adjective Phrases from Adjective Clauses: *Rebels I: The Beat Generation*

Rebellion is another type of nonconformity: Rebels, who are often young people, reject authority and society's rules. Change the **underlined** adjective clauses to adjective phrases.

In the 1950s, people began gathering in a San Francisco neighborhood

~~which is~~ <u>known as North Beach</u>. They were young, rebellious people
   1

<u>who were looking for freedom from society</u>. These people,
   2

<u>who were named "beatniks" or "Beats,"</u> wanted to experience life fully.
   3

The 1950s were a time of conformity in the United States. The beatniks

thought of conformists as "squares." The beatniks' lifestyle,

which included their clothes and homes, was not at all "square." The clothing
                    4

that was worn by beatniks was usually black, and men often wore beards and san-
         5

dals. Beatniks typically lived in crowded apartments

which were called "pads." They went to poetry readings and listened to
        6

"cool" jazz.

The rebellious philosophy of people who were in the Beat Generation
                                                         7

was expressed by its poets and novelists. In 1956 Allen Ginsberg published

Howl!, a poem which was full of anger and shocking images. At about the
                      8

same time, *On the Road* was published. *On the Road* is Jack Kerouac's famous novel

which describes Beat life. For Kerouac the term "beat" was related to "beatitude,"
        9

which means a kind of spiritual joy. Looking for this joy in life is an important
                 10

theme which is in his work and in the philosophy of the Beats.
         11

🔟 Forming Adjective Clauses from Adjective Phrases: *Rebels II: The Love Generation*

Change the **underlined** adjective phrases to adjective clauses.

                                                           who were
In the 1960s a new generation of nonconformists ⋏ called

"hippies," gathered in San Francisco. The hippies, too, were young
     1

people rebelling against conformity and authority. They were protesters
         2

against war and injustice.
         3

The hippies, <u>wanting to "drop out" of society</u>, had a different lifestyle. Their
4

clothing was "psychedelic," <u>meaning bright, colorful, and fantastic</u>. The men had
5

long hair and necklaces <u>made of beads</u>. Their music was electric rock,
6

<u>played by groups like the Jefferson Airplane and the Grateful Dead</u>.
7

The hippies' style and ideas, <u>disturbing to many in the older generation</u>, had a
8

wide influence. Many young people <u>eager for peace and freedom</u> joined the Love
9

Generation.

▮▮ Combining Sentences, Forming Adjective Phrases: *Rebels III: The Punks*

Combine the sentences. Use the second sentence as an adjective phrase. Use commas
with nonrestrictive phrases.

1. The first punks were rebellious young people. They were drawn to rock music.

   The first punks were rebellious young people drawn to rock music.

2. In the 1970s and 1980s, some frustrated young people decided to become punks.
   These young people felt angry at the conformist society that surrounded them.

3. Punk rock was the music played by punks. They tried to express their anger in a
   harsh and original way.

4. The names of punk bands expressed their point of view. The bands included
   Animal Things, the Subhumans, the Misfits, and the Germs.

5. Sid Vicious and Johnny Rotten are angry-sounding names. The names were
   taken by two punk musicians.

6. The words were often very rude and hostile. They were in the songs the punks sang.

7. Punks got attention for their outrageous style. This style included spiked hair, ripped clothing, and dog collars.

UNIT WRAP-UP

Error Correction

Find and correct the errors in adjective clauses and phrases. Some errors can be corrected in more than one way. Including the example, there are **14** errors.

                                                     who

Do you know that there are people ~~which~~ think your blood type reveals your

personality? They believe in the blood type theory of personality.

According to this theory, that hasn't been proven scientifically, there is a relation-

ship between blood type and personality. People who believes in the blood type theory

think you can use it to discover your natural talents and tendencies. They think it's

something what can help you find the right job or the right boyfriend or girlfriend.

What are the positive characteristics that a Type O person has them? According

to *You Are Your Blood Type,* in which the theory is explained, Type O people are goal-

oriented realists. Ronald Reagan, whom was the president of the United States, and

Queen Elizabeth are two leaders with Type O blood.

A person who his blood type is A usually has a good sense of order. He keeps the place where he lives in very neat. A Type A is also a person that tends to be idealistic,

hard-working, and sensitive.

People who having Type B are the most likely to be nonconformists. They are

people who's nature is to be creative and flexible. Some jobs, that Type B people are

suited for, are artist, designer, and golfer.

Type AB is the rarest blood type. It was the blood type of John F. Kennedy whom

many Americans admired. The book describes Type AB people as natural leaders

with characteristics that including logical thinking and honesty.

> —Nomi Toshitaka, *You Are Your Blood Type: The Biochemical Key to Unlocking the Secrets of Your Personality.* 1988, New York: Pocket Books.

Task 1: The Category Game

A. Work in teams of two or three. Decide on a category for each group of words. Then express the category in a sentence containing an adjective clause.

1. creative, outgoing, shy, eccentric, careful

    They're all personality characteristics which people can have.

2. the sun, an egg yolk, a school bus, a lemon, a dandelion

    They're all things that are yellow.

3. an X-ray technician, a nurse, a physical therapist, a surgeon, a dietitian

4. hot chocolate, gasoline, alcohol, blood, syrup

5. flood, flavor, flexible, flower, fleet

6. ears, chopsticks, dice, stereo speakers, ice skates

7. a kidnapper, a murderer, a thief, an arsonist, a drug smuggler

8. birthday, wedding, anniversary, holiday, graduation

9. a court, an arena, a course, a field, a stadium

10. a house, a bottle, a box, a skull, a refrigerator

11. an announcer, a lecturer, a singer, an adviser, a violinist

12. a blanket, a stove, the sun, love, a bath

13. fish, frogs, humans, ducks, polar bears

B. Now each team thinks of three groups of five words that somehow fit into categories like those in **A.** The team reads its lists to the other teams. The other teams try to be the first to guess the category. Each guess must be in the form of a question containing an adjective clause.

> Example: Are they all things that are yellow?
> Keep score. The winner is the team that guesses the most categories correctly.

Task 2: Writing Definitions—A Creativity Challenge

Imagine that the following nonsense words are real English nouns for people, places, times, and things, including activities and feelings. Think of a possible meaning for each word and write your definition for it. Each definition should include two or three adjective clauses and phrases, both restrictive and nonrestrictive. Try to use all types of adjective clauses and phrases. You can be as creative as you wish.

> Example: A bowpam is a furry animal which lives in Australia, where it eats only the leaves of the rose bushes growing in people's gardens. OR Bluther is the feeling that you have at those times when you expect that the teacher is going to call on you and that you won't know the answer to the question she asks.

1. bowpam
2. bluther
3. gyrgot
4. ploshkin
5. morokoves
6. quingle
7. alberdy
8. termunters
9. zenvidix
10. insorlene
11. strolth
12. exmiants

Task 3: Families and Personalities

In his book, American author Ian Frazier tells about growing up in a family of five children and the personality differences among the children:

> From a certain point of view, we were five towheaded children, a set in graduated sizes. Sandy-Davy-Suzy-Fritz-Maggie. . . . But from another point of view, we kids were random people who happened to be related. Our similarities could be seen on the surface, but our differences were unknown, possibly enormous, and not, we suspected, the ones our parents used to distinguish us. We struggled and fought and threw tantrums and misbehaved to find out what the true differences might be. Now when I talk to my brother and sisters about those years, it is as if each of us grew up in a different family.
> —Ian Frazier, *Family.* 1994, Farrar Straus & Giroux: New York. p. 252

Think about Frazier's experience and your own. Do you think children in the same family are likely to be similar or likely to be different? Do you think that you and your brothers and/or sisters have different memories about your childhood?

Write one or two paragraphs describing similarities and/or differences among the children in your family and how you think these came about. Or, if you are an only child, write about the effect of growing up without brothers or sisters. Try to use at least five adjective clauses and phrases.

Unit Six

Gerunds and Infinitives

Topic Focus: *Entertainment*

UNIT OBJECTIVES

- **gerunds**
  (***Singing*** is her profession.)

- **infinitives**
  (It's fun ***to watch*** television.)

- **verbs taking gerunds, infinitives, or both**
  (Jeff ***enjoys*** listening to music. He ***wants*** to go to the concert. He ***remembered*** reading about it. He ***remembered*** to get the tickets.)

- **performers of actions in gerunds and infinitives**
  (Kirsten didn't understand ***their*** liking horror movies. She asked ***them*** to tell her the reason.)

- **progressive infinitives**
  (They had hoped ***to be making*** their own movies by now.)

- **perfect gerunds and infinitives**
  (They appreciate ***having seen*** his movies. They're fortunate ***to have met*** the star of the movie.)

A Popular Export?

The United States's biggest export is its popular culture. Popular culture includes forms of entertainment that appeal to large numbers of people—for example, television programs, movies, and popular music. These American entertainment products have never been more popular internationally than they are now, but they also cause controversy. Here are some opinions expressed by people in various countries:

A: "I like **to listen** to American music because there are so many different styles. **Listening** to it gives me the opportunity **to experience** the cultural diversity of the United States. I'm studying English in order **to understand** the songs better."

B: "We need **to protect** our language and culture. We can do this by **not showing** so many American television programs and movies. Our goal is **to preserve** our cultural traditions."

C: "I dislike **having** so much American entertainment in this country and throughout the world. It's the same everywhere, so it's causing cultural differences among countries **to disappear**. It's important for the world **not to lose** cultural diversity."

D: "I like **watching** Hollywood movies. The movie-makers are good at **telling** enjoyable stories that appeal to lots of different people. American movies have been popular internationally since the 1920s. I don't think we've lost our cultural identity as a result of **watching** them."

E: "My everyday life is pretty boring. **To escape** is a pleasure for me. So my favorite free-time activity is **watching** action-adventure movies. I can dream of **being** a hero."

F: "It's easy **to blame** American television programs and movies for **bringing** violence to this country. But the United States isn't the only source of the violent images we see."

Comprehension Check

Read each sentence. Circle **T** if the sentence is true or **F** if the sentence is false.

1. Music, movies, and television are forms of popular culture.   (T)   F

2. The speakers all have similar reactions to American entertainment.   T   F

3. Speaker A is learning English for the purpose of understanding the songs better.   T   F

4. Speaker B believes that showing fewer American television programs and movies is a way to protect her country's language and culture.   T   F

5. Speaker F blames American television programs and movies for all the violent images in his country.   T   F

Think about Grammar

A. The **boldfaced** words in the passage are gerunds (the base form of a verb + *-ing*) and infinitives (*to* + the base form of a verb). Look at the passage and **underline** the gerunds and **circle** the infinitives.

B. Gerunds and infinitives are similar in many ways but differ in others. Complete the following sentences based on the passage by writing *Gerunds, Infinitives,* or *Both gerunds and infinitives.*

1. _____Both gerunds and infinitives_____ can be the subject of a sentence.

2. _____ can come after verbs.

3. _____ can come after adjectives.

4. _____ can come after prepositions.

5. _____ can come after a noun.

6. _____ can be followed by a noun.

7. _____ can be negative.

Gerunds and Infinitives

chapter

12

Introductory Task: *Entertainment Tonight*

A. Work in groups of three. Imagine that tonight you are going to watch television and listen to the radio together. You can watch only two television programs and can listen to only two radio programs, and you can watch or listen to only one program at a time. First, each of you should look at the schedule and choose the two television and two radio programs you prefer—one for each time.

	TV Channel I	TV Channel II	FM Radio Music I	FM Radio Music II
8:00 – 8:30	"Wildlife Wonders" (*nature program*)	"An Alien Presence" (*science-fiction drama*)	"Hot and Cool" (*jazz*)	"The Best Classic Oldies" (*rock and roll, 1952–1987*)
8:30 – 9:00	"Sports Highlights" (*football, basketball, figure skating, etc.*)	"Buddies" (*situation comedy*)	"Latin Tempos" (*salsa stars and hits*)	"Movies and Musicals" (*soundtracks and Broadway show tunes*)
9:00 – 9:30	"Bulletproof" (*police drama*)	"Washington Affairs" (*news, political commentary*)	"Cowboy Round-up" (*country-western*)	"Soul Sounds" (*rhythm and blues*)
9:30 – 10:00	"Animatronic Killers vs. the Punctuator" (*animated action*)	"M.D." (*hospital drama*)	"Here's the Rap" (*hip-hop*)	"On the Beat" (*pop/rock hits*)

Now discuss your preferences and come to a decision about the four programs you will watch and listen to. In your discussion, include the following structures:

want, don't want, and *would like* + *to watch / to listen to* (use these to talk about specific programs);

enjoy, don't enjoy, like, and *dislike* + *watching / listening to* (use these to talk about kinds of programs).

Example: Student A: "I would like to watch 'An Alien Presence' at eight o'clock." Student B: "I don't enjoy watching science-fiction programs. I want to listen to the rock and roll program then."

B. Tell the class the programs your group has chosen. Use *decide* or *agree* + *to watch / listen to.*

Example: "We decided to listen to the jazz program at eight o'clock."

GRAMMAR BRIEFING 1: Overview of Gerunds and Infinitives; Gerunds

Gerunds and infinitives are formed from verbs. They function as nouns, although infinitives can also have other functions (see Grammar Briefing 2) and only gerunds can be objects of prepositions.

FORM AND FUNCTION Gerunds and Infinitives

Form

■ To form gerunds, use the base form of the verb + -*ing*.*

> I enjoy **dancing.**

* See Appendix 3 for spelling rules for the -*ing* form of the verb.

■ To form negative gerunds, use *not* + the gerund.

> They talked about **not dancing.**

■ To form infinitives, use *to* + the base form of the verb.

> I want **to dance.**

■ To form negative infinitives, use *not* + the infinitive.

> He decided **not to dance.**

■ Gerunds and infinitives can occur alone or as part of phrases.

> We like **singing.**   We like **to sing.**
>
> We like **playing the piano.**   We like **to play the piano.**

Function

■ Gerunds and infinitives can function as nouns—as subjects, subject comple-ments, and objects of verbs. As subjects, they take singular verbs.

> **Singing songs with friends** is fun. (subject)   **To sing songs with friends** is fun. (subject)
>
> My hobby is **singing.** (subject complement)   My hobby is **to sing.** (subject complement)
>
> I like **singing.** (object)   I like **to sing.** (object)

■ Some verbs can be followed by either gerunds or infinitives with little difference in meaning.* These verbs include *begin, continue, hate, like, love, prefer,* and *start.*

> Let's start working soon. = Let's start to work soon.

* See the following section for verbs followed only by gerunds; see Grammar Briefing 2 for verbs followed only by infinitives; see Chapter 13 for verbs followed by both with a difference in meaning.

FORM AND FUNCTION Gerunds

■ Gerunds are often used as the subjects of sentences.

> **Going to concerts** can be exciting.

■ Gerunds can be the objects of phrasal verbs (e.g., *give up, put off, take on*). Gerunds can also be the objects of prepositions, verb-preposition combinations (e.g., *depend on, look into, talk about*), and *be* + adjective + preposition combi-nations (e.g., *be accustomed to, be happy about, be interested in*).*

He **put off getting** the tickets, so they didn't have good seats. (phrasal verb + gerund)

I**'m thinking about buying** tickets for the concert. (verb-preposition combination +gerund)

They**'re interested in seeing** that concert. (*be* + adjective + preposition + gerund)

* See Appendix 9 for a list of common phrasal verbs. See Appendix 10 for a list of common verb-preposition combinations. See Appendix 17 for a list of common adjective + preposition combinations that are followed by gerunds.

■ Verbs that take gerunds but not infinitives as objects include:

appreciate	discuss	finish	miss	recommend
avoid	dislike	keep	postpone	resent
delay	enjoy	mention	quit	suggest
deny	excuse	mind	recall	understand

We **missed seeing** Madonna in concert.

(For a more complete list of verbs followed only by gerunds, see Appendix 18.)

■ *By* + gerund is used to express how something is done.

You get tickets **by calling** the theater.

They celebrated **by going out** to dinner.

■ *Go* + gerund is used in certain expressions related to recreational activities. Gerunds used in this way include *bicycling, camping, dancing, fishing, hiking, jogging, running, sailing, shopping, sightseeing, skating, skiing,* and *swimming.*

We **went dancing** last night.

■ Gerunds are used with other common expressions, including:

be busy	spend/waste + expression of time/ money
can't help	sit/stand/lie + place
find/catch + noun/pronoun	it's no use / it's not worth
have fun (a good time, a hard / difficult time, trouble / problems / difficulty)	

She**'s busy talking.**

We **caught them talking.**

You**'ll spend the whole night talking.**

We **stood there talking.**

GRAMMAR HOTSPOT!

■ Be careful not to confuse gerunds with the present participle used in verbs in the progressive tenses.

My hobby is **singing.** (gerund *singing* as subject complement)

Susan **is singing** in the rain. (present progressive of verb *sing*)

GRAMMAR PRACTICE 1: Overview of Gerunds and Infinitives; Gerunds

1   Using Verbs That Take Both Gerunds and Infinitives: *What's Your Opinion?*

A. Work with a partner. People all over the world have experienced American popular culture, including television and music. How do you think they react to American television and music? Write **four** sentences with gerunds and infinitives using the following verbs: *like, love, prefer, hate, begin, continue.* Include negatives.

> Example: People like watching American programs because they like to see something new and different. OR In many countries people don't like having so many American programs on television. They prefer to watch local programs.

B. Read your sentences to the class. As a class, discuss your different opinions about this topic.

2   Gerund versus Present Participle: *Culture Shock?*

In the following text, **underline** the gerunds and present participles. Mark the gerunds **G** and the present participles **PP.**

                             PP
    I'm an American student, and I'm <u>taking</u> my first trip outside the United States.

                  G
Before I started <u>traveling</u>, I'd been looking forward to experiencing a completely

different culture. But not all the experiences that I'm having are new and different.

For example, at the moment, I'm listening to the radio. Willie Nelson is singing,

"On the road again. . . . The life I love is making music with my friends." I don't mind

listening to country-western music at home, but hearing it in this country seems

very strange. Watching television here is a surprise, too—many of the programs

come from the United States. I'm experiencing a weird kind of culture shock!

3 Gerunds as Objects of Prepositions: *The Roots of Rock and Roll*

A. Complete the sentences with an appropriate preposition and a gerund formed from the word in parentheses. (If necessary, look in Appendices 10 and 17 for help with prepositions.)

In the 1950s, television and Elvis Presley were responsible _____for_____
                                                                      1

(make) ___making___ rock and roll popular. Elvis's voice had a special quality,

and he was known ___about/for___ (move) ___moving___ in a unique way while
                        2

he sang and played the guitar. Although some people disapproved _____of_____
                                                                          3

(watch) ___watching___ him perform, Elvis succeeded ___in___ (attract)
                                                             4

___attracting___ huge audiences.

How did Elvis create his style of rock and roll? He was enthusiastic

___about___ (listen to) ___listening to___ rhythm and blues, a form developed by
      5

black American musicians. He was interested ___in___ (play)
                                                   6

___playing___ like rhythm and blues musicians did. Another influence was

country-western music—the traditional music of the South, which Elvis was used

___to___ (hear) ___hear___. Both rhythm and blues music and
      7

country-western music were good _____at_____ (express) _expressi_____ com-

mon experiences and feelings. Here are examples of lyrics from country-western

songs: "I'll keep ___lovin____ (love) _____ you until the end of time."

"Don't you ever get tired ____of____ (hurt) ___hurting___ me?"

B. Work with a partner. First, add an appropriate preposition to complete the following *be* + adjective + preposition and verb-preposition combinations. Make sure that each combination can be followed by a gerund. (If necessary, look in Appendices 10 and 17.)

1. be accustomed _____to_____   5. be interested ___in_____

2. be afraid _____of_____   6. dream _____of_____

3. be enthusiastic ___about____   7. get tired _____of_____

4. be good _____at_____   8. look forward ___to_____

Then ask each other questions with *What is something that you* + the combinations + the gerund *doing*.

Example: Student A: *What is something that you are accustomed to doing?*
Student B: *I'm accustomed to getting up early. What about you?*

4 Gerunds as Objects of Verbs: *Matching by Preferences*

A. When American students start college, they often live in dormitories with roommates. In order to find roommates who get along well, colleges ask students to describe themselves. Write **six** sentences about your preferences in studying, taking care of your room, watching television, and listening to music. In each sentence, use at least one of the following verbs followed by a gerund: *avoid, can't imagine, detest, dislike, enjoy, feel like, finish, keep, like, mind, miss, postpone, prefer.*

Example: *I usually postpone studying until late at night. I'm not very tidy, and I don't mind living in a messy room. I don't feel like watching TV very often, except for science-fiction dramas. I've never missed seeing an episode of "Star Trek." I detest listening to rock music. I prefer playing my CDs of Broadway show tunes.*

B. Read your sentences to the class. Try to decide which students would get along best as roommates. (Hint: Colleges have discovered that music preferences matter the most.)

5 By + Gerund: *Entertainment Challenges*

A. Work with a partner. Think of at least two ways to answer each of the following questions. Use *by* + gerund in your answers.

1. How can you play the guitar without using your hands?

   You can play the guitar by plucking the strings with your teeth or toes.
   You can do it by asking someone else to play it for you.

2. How can you find out when a TV program will be on if you don't have a schedule?

3. How can you operate a CD player without touching it with your fingers?

4. How can you get into a concert if all the tickets have already been sold?

5. How can you become more physically fit while watching TV?

B. As a class compare answers. For each question, choose your favorite solution.

6 Gerunds with *Go* and Other Expressions: *Popular Culture in Two Generations*

Use the words in parentheses and the expressions given above each paragraph to complete the sentences. Use each expression once.

be busy   ~~go~~   ~~having a hard time~~   sits home   spends too much time   wastes his money

Parent: I'm ___having a hard time living___ (live) with my teenage son these days. He

used to ___go bicycling___ (bicycle) with his friends, but now he

spends too much ~~time~~ fine in listening ___ (listen to) loud, aggressive music. He ___wastes his money for him___

(buy) CDs by bands with names like Mötley Crüe. And he ___sits home___

(go) to Megadeth and Metallica concerts when he should ___be busy doing___

(do) his homework.

can't help   catch me   go   have a good time   have problems   it's no use

Son: My parents _____ (understand) my interest in heavy metal

music, and ___it no use___ used to explained (explain) it to them. They ___caught me listen to___

(listen to) music that was popular before I was born. My mom and dad

___went dancing___ (dance) sometimes. My mom's favorite dance tune is "Let's

Twist Again" by Chubby Checker. I guess they _____ (like) it, but

you'll never ___have a good time to play___ (play) any of their old record albums.

B. Write **four** sentences about your past and present entertainment and recreational activities. Use gerunds and the following expressions: *have fun, have a good time, spend time, go.*

Example: I have fun playing cards with my friends. OR When I was young, I often went fishing with my father.

7 Using Gerunds: *The Music That We Keep Listening To*

A. A researcher, Robert M. Sapolsky, wondered why some people like listening to new kinds of music but others don't. He conducted a survey and concluded that age is the explanation—if you are over 35 when a style of popular music is introduced, you probably will never choose to listen to it. Most people continue listening to styles of music that they first heard when they were 20 or younger.

Work in a small group. Use the words and expressions given to talk about your own music preferences and those of people who are older or younger than you. Decide whether you agree or disagree with the researcher's conclusions.

Example: I'm interested in trying new music, but my parents keep listening to music that was popular when they were young.

Verb: *appreciate, avoid, enjoy, (dis)like, don't mind, keep, miss, understand, quit*

Verb-Preposition: *care about, (dis)approve of, talk about, insist on*

Be + Adjective + Preposition: *be accustomed to, be fond of, be interested in, be enthusiastic about, be used to*

Other Expressions: *can't help, have trouble, have problems, spend . . . time, it's no use*

B. Use the words and expressions given above to write sentences with gerunds.

1. Write three sentences about music preferences that you have in common with other members of your family or with friends.

     Example: My mother and I both enjoy playing old Beatles records.

2. Write three sentences about differences of opinion about music that you have with other members of your family or with friends.

     Example: I dislike hearing the music that my teenage children like, but it's no use complaining about it.

GRAMMAR BRIEFING 2: Infinitives

Infinitives are not as nounlike as gerunds: They are not often used in subject position and cannot be objects of prepositions. They have adverb and adjective functions as well as noun functions.

FORM AND FUNCTION Infinitives

■ Infinitives can occur in subject position. However, more often *it* is put in the subject position and the infinitive is put after the predicate. The meaning is the same.

     To dance professionally is her dream. = **It** is her dream **to dance professionally.**

     To advertise your products is important. = **It** is important **to advertise your products.**

■ Unlike gerunds, infinitives **cannot** be objects of prepositions.

     I'm thinking **about buying tickets.   Not:** I'm thinking about ~~to buy tickets~~.

■ Verbs that take infinitives but not gerunds are listed below.* Verbs that take infinitives fall into three groups.

   • Verb + Infinitive
     Some verbs are followed directly by an infinitive. These verbs include:

agree	decide	learn	seem
appear	hope	offer	tend
can afford	intend	plan	wait

     He **agreed to sing.**

- Verb + Noun Phrase + Infinitive

  Some verbs are followed by a noun phrase and then an infinitive. These verbs include:

cause	hire	persuade	trust
convince	invite	remind	warn
force	order	tell	

  She **convinced John/him to sing.**

(See Chapter 13, Grammar Briefing 1, page 235, for verbs that follow this pattern but also take gerunds.)

- Verbs (+ Noun Phrase) + Infinitive

  Some verbs can be followed directly by an infinitive or can have a noun phrase before the infinitive. These verbs include:

ask	choose	need	would like
beg	expect	want	

  She **asked to sing.**   She **asked John to sing.**

* See Appendix 19 for more complete lists of these groups of verbs.

■ Certain adjectives can be followed by infinitives. Many of these adjectives describe feelings or attitudes. They include:

afraid	careful	eager	lucky	relieved	stunned
amazed	content	fortunate	pleased	reluctant	willing
anxious	delighted	glad	prepared	sad	
ashamed	determined	happy	proud	shocked	
astonished	disappointed	hesitant	ready	sorry	

They were **happy to sing.**

■ Infinitives can be used with *in order* to express purpose. In this use, infinitives are functioning as adverbs. *In order* can be omitted, with no difference in meaning.

Why did you come here? I came here (**in order**) **to sing.**

■ Infinitives are also used with *too* and *enough*.

- *Too* comes before an adjective or adverb. *Too* often implies a negative feeling or situation.

  The children are **too old to get in for half price.**

- *Enough* comes after an adjective or adverb but usually comes before a noun. *Enough* often implies a positive feeling or situation.

  The children are **young enough to get in for half price.**

  I have **enough money to buy tickets for everyone.**

■ Infinitives can modify nouns, functioning as adjectives.

I heard about an easy new **way to learn languages.**

GRAMMAR HOTSPOT!

■ Use the infinitive, not *for* + gerund, to indicate purpose. *For* + noun phrase can sometimes be used to express purpose, but *for* + gerund cannot.

> We're here **(in order) to do business.**   **Not:** We're here ~~for doing~~ business.
>
> They're here **for business.**

■ *To* is part of some verb-preposition and *be* + adjective + preposition combinations, for example, *look forward to, be used/accustomed to,* and *be opposed to.* This *to* is a preposition, not part of an infinitive, and is followed by a gerund.

> We **were used to singing** in a choir.   **Not:** We were used to ~~sing~~ in a choir.
>
> We **are looking forward to dancing.**   **Not:** We are looking forward to ~~dance~~.

TALKING the TALK

■ Infinitives can sometimes be shortened to *to* when the meaning is clear.

> Have you ever sung with a band? No, I am too lazy **to.** (to = to sing with a band)
>
> I've never visited Russia, but I'd like **to.** (to = to visit Russia)

GRAMMAR PRACTICE 2: Infinitives

8   It + Infinitive, Infinitive as Subject: *Is It Your Dream to Be a Rock Star?*

Restate each sentence in **two** ways using an infinitive.

1. Becoming a rock star isn't easy.

   To become a rock star isn't easy.
   It isn't easy to become a rock star.

2. Becoming a successful rock musician takes hard work and creativity.

3. Developing a unique style is necessary.

4. Being able to compose music is essential.

5. Writing expressive song lyrics is important.

6. Creating artistic videos is a great challenge.

9   Verb + Infinitive Patterns: *Our Band*

Complete the sentences with *her,* [0], or *her* / [0].

1. a. We agreed _____[0]_____ to play in the band.

   b. We invited _____her_____ to play in the band.

   c. We wanted __her / [0]__ to play in the band.

   d. We hoped _____ to play in the band.

2. a. I told _____ to practice often.

   b. I expected _____ to practice often.

   c. I planned _____ to practice often.

   d. I persuaded _____ to practice often.

3. a. Simon offered _____ to sing the new song.

   b. Simon taught _____ to sing the new song.

   c. Simon would like _____ to sing the new song.

   d. Simon chose _____ to sing the new song.

4. a. We decided _____ to record the song.

   b. We asked _____ to record the song.

   c. We convinced _____ to record the song.

   d. We needed _____ to record the song.

10 Verb + Infinitive Patterns: *The Music Channel*

Music channels on television broadcast a variety of programs, including interviews of performers. In the following interview, complete the sentences with an infinitive or an appropriate pronoun and infinitive.

A: Lucie, welcome to the show. Your latest video seems __*to be*__ (be) very
                                                                    1

popular with our viewers all over the world. I want __*you to know*__ (know) how
                                                            2

happy I am that you are here tonight.

B: I would like _____ (thank) you for inviting me.
                        3

A: First of all, I want _____ (know) more about your background.
                               4

B: Well, my mother is a classical pianist, and she taught _____ (play) the
                                                                    5

piano. And I learned _____ (write) songs by being around my father,
                            6

who's a poet. Although my parents expected _____ (continue) with
                                                    7

classical music, I chose _____ (not, do) it because I had become fasci-
                              8

nated by music styles from other parts of the world. I needed _____
                                                                      9

(develop) my own style. My parents were a little disappointed at first, but I

persuaded _____ (let) me travel so that I could bring diverse styles
                10

into my music.

A: This year you received the music association's award as the best new solo

artist. When you decided _____ (become) a musician, did you
                                    11

expect _____ (be) so successful so soon?
              12

B: Of course, I hoped _____ (be) successful. I've also worked very hard,
                                    13

so when the music association chose _____ (receive) the award,
                                                            14

I was thrilled.

A: Do you intend _____ (continue) your concert tours?
                          15

B: Right now I plan _____ (not, perform) for a year because I want to
                              16

experiment with new forms of music.

A: As one of your greatest fans, I would like _____ (know) how much I'm
                                                                17

looking forward to hearing your new music.

▌▌▌ Using Verbs with Infinitives: *I Want (You) to Tell What's Going On*

A. Work with a partner. Look at these scenes from four common types of television
shows. Discuss what the characters might be doing. Use your imagination. Then
write about three of the scenes. For each description, use at least three of the verbs
given followed by infinitives.

1. Police Drama   2. Situation Comedy

    warn, want, tell, offer, attempt, ask   would like, tell, refuse, persuade, pretend, beg

Example: The police officer is warning her not
to go into the house. She wants to know what happened. . . .

3. Cooking Program

4. Hospital Drama

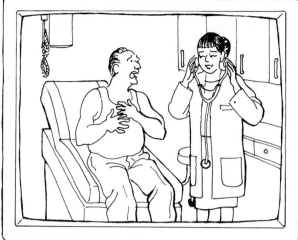

would like, teach, learn, invite, hope, ask

trust, tell, seem, need, expect, agree

B. Tell the class your description of one of the scenes.

12 Adjectives Followed by Infinitives: *Television versus Reality*

A. Work in small groups. What kind of image does American television give of the United States? How well does this image fit reality? Neysa, who is twenty, is going to visit the United States for the first time. The image she has is based largely on American TV programs. Write sentences to answer the following questions.

1. What is she anxious to do?

   She's anxious to meet a lifeguard on a beach in California.

2. What is she reluctant to do? _____

3. What is she determined to do? _____

4. What is she willing to do? _____

5. What is she afraid to do? _____

6. What is she eager to do? _____

B. What were Neysa's reactions when she visited the United States? Working in your groups, complete the sentences with infinitive phrases.

> Example: *She was surprised to see small houses.*

1. She was surprised _____.

2. She was shocked _____.

3. She was not surprised _____.

4. She was disappointed _____.

5. She was relieved _____.

6. She was pleased _____.

13 Infinitive of Purpose: *Why Do We Do It?*

A. People watch different kinds of television programs for different reasons. Work with a partner. Think of a reason that people watch each of the following kinds of programs. Write sentences with *in order* + an infinitive or an infinitive.

1. situation comedies	4. game shows	7. talk shows
2. sports events	5. science-fiction dramas	8. hospital dramas
3. news programs	6. cartoons	9. soap operas

> Example: *People watch situation comedies in order to laugh.* OR *We watch situation comedies to relax.* OR *I watch situation comedies to see my favorite actors.*

B. Discuss your reasons with the class. What is the main reason that people watch each kind of program? What are the main reasons that people watch TV in general?

14 Infinitives with *Too* and *Enough*: *Changing Channels*

A. Using the words in parentheses, write sentences with *too* or *enough*, as appropriate, and an infinitive.

The Sports Show

Dan: Casey, I'd like your prediction on tonight's game. Will the Blues win?

Casey: The Blues are __good enough to beat__ (good, beat) any team. But they may
                                      1

be _____ (weak, win) tonight. Harris has been injured. He doesn't
              2

have _____ (strength, play) many minutes.
              3

Dan: I've heard that Mihalic may join the Blues soon. Is he very talented?

Casey: Yes, he's _____ (talented, be) a top player. But it's _____
                          4   5

and... (soon, know) if he'll live up to his talent. It would be great to have him, though.

I hope he can join _____ (soon, help) the Blues this season.
                                         6

Police Drama

Captain: Have you talked to the victim's wife?

Detective: Not yet. She's _____ (upset, talk about) what happened.
                                              1

Captain: Do you have a suspect?

Detective: Yeah, but I hope that it isn't _____ (late, catch) him. He stole a
                                                                      2

lot of money. He has _____ (money, live on) for a long time.
                                              3

Captain: Then we need to find him soon. I hope you're _____ (smart,
                                                                                                          4

figure out) how to do it.

B. Work in small groups. Think about the many different kinds of television programs, and discuss the following questions. Give reasons for your answers. Include some sentences that use *too* and *enough* with infinitives.

1. Which kinds of programs are five-year-old children old enough to watch? Which programs are they too young to watch?

> Example: Five-year-old children shouldn't watch police dramas. They're too violent for them to watch.

2. Which kinds of programs are twelve-year-old children old enough to watch? Which programs are they too young to watch?

15   Infinitives as Adjectives: *The Value of Television*

Television has both positive and negative aspects. Think of some positive aspects of television and different television programs. Write **four** sentences with each of the following nouns + infinitive phrases: *ability, chance, opportunity, way.*

> Example: Television gives people a chance to learn about new and different things. OR Watching "Moneyline" is a good way to get information about business.

16   *To* as a Preposition versus *To* as Part of an Infinitive: *Children and Television*

Use the words in parentheses to complete the sentences with a gerund or the base form of the verb.

In the United States, there are several parents' organizations that are dedicated

to ____improving____ (improve) television for children. These organizations were
     1

determined to ____force____ (force) the television networks to establish a new
                 2

rating system. Once parents are accustomed to _____ (use) the rating
                                                        3

system, they can block the violent television programs that they aren't willing to

_____ (allow) their children to watch. But certain parents are opposed
        4

to _____ (allow) their young children to watch any television, including
       5

educational programs. Some of these parents are concerned that their children will

want to _____ (watch) too much television. They also believe that tele-
             6

vision encourages children to become consumers. Children not only look forward

to _____ (see) the programs, but they are also eager to _____
       7   8

(buy) the toys and other products that are associated with them.

17   Using Infinitives; Infinitives Shortened to *To*: *Your Own Talk Show*

A. Imagine that you are the host of a television talk show. Your next guest will be a
person who is well known in the world of entertainment—for example, a television
or music star. Decide who the guest will be. What do you want to ask her or him?
Complete the following *yes/no* questions.

1. Can you afford __to buy a Rolls-Royce_____?

2. Have you ever wanted _____?

3. Are you afraid _____?

4. Do you feel fortunate _____?

5. Are you too _____?

6. Do you have enough _____?

7. Have you had an opportunity _____?

8. Would you like _____?

B. Work with a partner. Ask your partner the questions you wrote in **A.** Your partner plays the part of the star and uses his or her imagination to answer the questions. The answers should include some infinitives shortened to *to*.

> Example: Student A: *Can you afford to buy a Rolls-Royce?* Student B: *Yes, I can afford to.* OR *Yes, I can afford to, but I don't want to.*

Then reverse roles. Present your interviews to the class.

More about Gerunds and Infinitives

Introductory Task: *A Crime Movie*

A. Work with a partner. The sentences describe what happened in a crime movie. In each sentence, look at the **boldfaced** verb and infinitive or gerund. Decide which happened first—the action expressed by the verb or the action expressed by the infinitive or gerund. Mark the action that happened first with **1** and mark the action that happened second with **2** (e.g., in 1., planning comes first, then stealing). If both actions happened at the same time, mark both with **1.**

1. A group of thieves **planned   to steal** some jewels from a museum in Greece.

2. A burglar alarm was connected to the floor of the museum, so they **decided to enter** from the roof.

3. A witness ran to the police station and **reported seeing** someone on the roof.

4. The thieves, who didn't know that they had been seen, **kept lifting** jewels out of the building.

5. They **wanted to finish** the job.

6. They **intended to sell** the jewels to a man in Amsterdam.

7. The police caught them several days later, but they **denied stealing** anything.

8. While they were in jail, the thieves got into an argument, and finally, one of them **admitted stealing** the jewels.

B. Complete the sentences with the term *gerund* or the term *infinitive.*

1. The action expressed by the _____ tends to occur after the action expressed by the verb.

2. The action expressed by the _____ tends to occur before or at the same time as the action expressed by the verb.

GRAMMAR BRIEFING 1: Gerunds versus Infinitives

Some verbs can be followed only by gerunds; others only by infinitives. Still others can be followed by both, sometimes with a difference in meaning. These patterns are partly explained by a difference between gerunds and infinitives: Gerunds tend to express actions that are happening or have happened. Infinitives tend to express actions that will happen or could happen.

FUNCTION Gerunds versus Infinitives

Verbs That Take Only Gerunds or Only Infinitives

■ Gerunds often follow verbs that indicate that an action is happening or has happened (e.g., *enjoy*). The action expressed by the verb comes at the same time or after the action expressed by the gerund. Infinitives often follow verbs that indicate that an action will or could happen (e.g., *hope*). The action expressed by the verb comes before the action expressed by the infinitive.

> We **enjoy going** to concerts. (You can enjoy only things you are doing or have done—not things you haven't done yet.)

> We **hope to go** to the concert. (You can hope only for things that could happen—not for things that have already happened.)

Verbs That Take Both Gerunds and Infinitives

■ Some verbs that can be followed by a noun phrase + infinitive can also be followed by a gerund. The gerund means the action in general; the noun phrase + infinitive means the action for the person or people indicated. These include *advise, allow, encourage, permit, require,* and *urge.*

> They **advised tap dancing** for exercise.

> They **advised me to tap dance** for exercise.

■ While some verbs can take gerunds or infinitives with no difference in meaning (see Chapter 12, Grammar Briefing 1, page 218), other verbs can take both but with a difference in meaning. These verbs include *remember, forget, regret, stop, try,* and *get.*

• *Remember* or *forget* + gerund indicates that the subject does or doesn't have a memory of an action that has already happened. The remembering or forgetting comes after the action of the gerund. (*Forget* + gerund is often used with *never.*)

> I'll never **forget singing** in the choir. (I sang in the past, and I will not forget in the future.)

> I'll always **remember singing** in the choir. (I sang in the past, and I will remember in the future.)

Remember or *forget* + infinitive indicates that the subject does or doesn't think to perform an action. The action could happen—and does or doesn't. The remembering or forgetting comes before the action of the infinitive.

> I **forgot to go** to choir practice last night. (Last night I forgot about going to choir practice, so then I didn't go.)

> I **remembered to go** to choir practice last night. (Last night I remembered about going to choir practice, so then I went.)

- *Regret* + gerund indicates a feeling of sorrow about an action that has already happened.

> I **regret singing** in the choir. (In the past I sang in the choir, and now I am sorry.)

Regret + infinitive is usually used with a verb such as *inform* or *tell* to indicate a feeling of sorrow about bad news that will now be told.

> I **regret to inform** you that you didn't win the contest. (I'm sorry about what I'm going to tell you: you didn't win.)

- *Stop* + gerund indicates that an action happened in the past but then stopped.

> She **stopped smoking.** (She used to smoke but then she stopped.)

Stop + infinitive indicates stopping in order to then do an action. (*Stop* + infinitive can be used with or without *in order.*)

> She **stopped (in order) to smoke.** (She stopped whatever she was doing so she could then smoke.)

- *Try* + gerund implies that the attempted action occurred. The action may or may not have been successful in achieving the desired goal.

> He **tried screaming for help,** but nobody heard him. OR He **tried screaming for help,** and the police came running over. (The action of screaming actually happened.)

Try + infinitive often implies that the attempted action did not occur at all.

> He **tried to scream for help,** but the words didn't come out. (The action of screaming didn't happen.)

- *Get* can be used with the gerunds *moving* and *going* to mean "start."

> I'm going to **get going on this work** right away.

Get + infinitive is used to mean "have permission" or "have a privilege."

> I **get to leave the office early** if I finish the work.

Get + noun phrase + infinitive is used to mean "cause or convince someone to do something."

> We **got the boss to give us the afternoon off.**

GRAMMAR PRACTICE 1: Gerunds versus Infinitives

▌ Verbs Taking Only Gerunds or Only Infinitives: *Creating the American Dream*

Somewhere, over the rainbow, skies are blue,
And the dreams that you dare to dream really do come true.
                                                 —*The Wizard of Oz,* 1939

A. Use the words in parentheses to complete the sentences with an infinitive or gerund. (Think about whether the action comes before, at the same time, or after the action of the verb.)

Many of the first Hollywood movie makers came to the United States in the late

1800s and early 1900s. Like the other immigrants of the time, they aspired

___to assimilate___ (assimilate)—that is, to adapt to their new land. They were strug-
         1

gling _____ (become) successful, and they hoped _____
           2   3

(create) a new life for themselves. The early movie makers were able to make the

kinds of movies that audiences, which included many immigrant and working-class

families, appreciated _____ (see). On the movie screen, they created a
                              4

vision of the America that they wanted _____ (live) in, one in which they
                                               5

could shape their destinies. The movie makers also understood that people who

need _____ (work) hard in order to survive enjoy _____
         6   7

(escape) from their everyday lives. They created fantasies so that people could sit in

a movie theater and imagine _____ (be) in another place or time. People
                                    8

everywhere kept _____ (go) to Hollywood movies to experience the
                      9

dreams. And when they finished _____ (watch), they believed that it
                                        10

might be possible to make the dreams become reality.

B. Work with a partner. Write **three** answers to each question. In each answer include an infinitive phrase or gerund phrase and one of these verbs: *appreciate, can imagine, enjoy, hope, need, want.*

1. People watch movies for many different reasons. What are some reasons that they watch them?

   Example: *They enjoy escaping from reality.*

2. Choose one of the following types of movies: action-adventure movies, animated movies, comedies, crime movies, disaster movies, horror movies, musicals, romances, science fiction, thrillers, and Westerns. Why do people like watching that type of movie?

> Example: *comedies*—They enjoy seeing other people in embarrassing situations that we're all familiar with.

2 Verbs Taking Gerunds and Infinitives: *Entertainment and More*

A. Use the words in parentheses in gerund or infinitive form to complete the sentences.

1. Seeing movies allows you ___to experience___ (experience) other cultures.

2. Some people advise _____ (go) to movies for education as well as entertainment.

3. Teachers sometimes encourage their students _____ (watch) movies to improve their listening skills.

4. However, teachers almost never permit you _____ (miss) class in order to go to a movie.

5. Getting information from a movie doesn't require _____ (understand) all the words.

6. Most theaters don't allow _____ (talk) during movies, so please wait until later to ask questions.

7. There are some very good old movies that I advise you _____ (rent) at the video store.

8. For example, I urge you _____ (see) *Breaking Away*. It's funny, and you can get a sense of life in an American college town in the 1970s.

B. Work alone and then with a partner. Think of two movies you would advise your partner to see. For each movie write **two** sentences, giving your advice and the reason for it. Use *advise* (or *encourage* or *urge*) with an infinitive.

> Example: I advise you to see 2001: A Space Odyssey. It has great special effects and you can imagine being in another world.

Tell your partner what you have written.

C. Decide on two movies that you and your partner both like. Give advice to the class about them. Use *advise* with a gerund.

> Example: We advise seeing Casablanca. It has romance and suspense.

3 *Remember, Forget, Stop,* and *Try: Slapstick Comedy*

A. Stan Laurel and Oliver (Ollie) Hardy were a famous slapstick comedy team. In their movies, there are lots of silly mistakes, collisions, falls, and arguments. Listen to the descriptions of typical slapstick situations involving Stan and Ollie. Then listen again and **circle** the correct answers.

1. Did Ollie put his hat on his head? (Yes) / No
2. Did Stan take the cake off the seat of the car? Yes / No
3. Did Stan leave the roller skate at the top of the stairs? Yes / No
4. Did Ollie turn on the water? Yes / No
5. Did Stan leave the ladder leaning against the house? Yes / No
6. Did Ollie and Stan start the car? Yes / No
7. Did Ollie and Stan put up the sail? Yes / No
8. Did Ollie go out with Stan then? Yes / No
9. Did Stan go out with his wife then? Yes / No

B. Listen again. This time you will hear an explanation of what happened. Check your answers in **A.**

4 Verbs That Take Both Gerunds and Infinitives: *The Hughes Brothers*

Rollo and Lucky Hughes's neighbor Mrs. Gray is an elderly widow. She deposited $5,000 in the bank, but the bank made a mistake and didn't credit her account. Now she can't pay her bills and is desperate. Rollo and Lucky have decided to rob the bank to get her money back. Use the words in parentheses to complete the sentences with gerunds or infinitives.

Scene I: Rollo and Lucky's home

Rollo: Let's get _____going_____ (go). Did you remember _____to put_____ (put) gas
                            1   2

in the car?

Lucky: Yeah, I did. I was going to wash the car, too, but I forgot _____ (do) it.
                                                                                          3

Rollo: That's not important now. Where's my comb? It was here earlier. I remember

_____ (see) it on the table.
           4

Lucky: Have you tried _____ (look) in the bathroom?
                                    5

Rollo: I've looked everywhere. We'll stop _____ (buy) one on the way to
                                                            6

the bank.

Lucky: Your hair looks okay. Why do you need a comb?

Rollo: Don't you remember? I'm going to get the bank teller _____ (give)
                                                                              7

us the money by having a comb in my pocket and pretending it's a gun.

Scene II: At the bank

Rollo: Would you please get _____ (move), Lucky? What's the problem?
                                        8

Lucky: I'm really nervous. I can't stop _____ (shake).
                                                    9

Rollo: Don't worry. Just remember _____ (hand) the note to the teller. . . .
                                                10

(Lucky hands the teller a note that says, "Give us $5,000 and nobody will

get hurt.")

Teller: I recognize you. You're Lucky Hughes! You were in my class in high school.

I'll never forget _____ (go) to school with you.
                            11

Scene III: In a courtroom

Judge: Before I sentence you, you get _____ (make) a statement. Do you
                                                12

have anything to say?

Lucky: We meant well, Your Honor. We were trying _____ (help) Mrs.
                                                                    13

Gray. We regret _____ (rob) the bank.
                            14

Judge: You didn't rob the bank—you just tried to. However, attempted robbery is

itself a serious crime. I regret _____ (tell) you that you're going
                                          15

to jail.

5 Using Gerunds and Infinitives: *Your Movie Script*

A. Work in groups of three. Write a short script for a scene from any kind of movie (e.g., action-adventure, comedy, disaster, horror, romance, science fiction). There should be a role for each person in the group. In your script, use at least three of these verbs followed by a gerund or by an infinitive: *forget, remember, stop,* and *try.* Also, use at least two verbs that are followed only by gerunds and at least two that are followed only by infinitives. You can choose from the following list or use any other appropriate verbs: *admit, agree, deny, dislike, enjoy, finish, hope, intend, keep, need,* and *plan.*

B. Perform your movie scene for the class.

GRAMMAR BRIEFING 2: Performers of Gerunds and Infinitives; Progressive Infinitives; Perfect Gerunds and Infinitives

Like other actions, the actions expressed by gerunds and infinitives are performed by someone. The performer is sometimes understood from the sentence but sometimes needs to be expressed. Infinitives can be used in the progressive form. Both gerunds and infinitives can be used in the perfect form.

FUNCTION Performers of Action in Gerunds and Infinitives

Performer of Gerund Action

■ Sometimes the action of the gerund is understood as performed by the subject of the sentence or by people in general.

> I hate losing my keys. (The sentence subject, I, performs the action of losing keys.)
>
> Doctors recommend exercising. (People in general perform the action of exercising.)
>
> Swimming is a lot of fun. (Swimming is fun for people in general.)

■ Sometimes a specific performer of the gerund action needs to be indicated. This performer is indicated with a possessive noun or a possessive determiner.

> I really appreciate **Tim's/his** writing that letter for me. (Tim performs the action of writing.)
>
> **John's/His** leaving early really annoys me. (John performs the action of leaving.)

Performer of Infinitive Action

■ The action of the infinitive often is understood as performed by the subject of the sentence.

> Barbara plans to cook dinner for you. (Barbara performs the action of cooking.)
>
> Phil is always eager to please people. (Phil performs the action of pleasing.)

■ With verbs of the pattern verb + noun phrase + infinitive, the noun following the verb is usually understood as performing the action of the infinitive.

> I convinced **John** to go to the party. (John performs the action of going.)

■ Sometimes a specific performer needs to be indicated. This performer is indicated by *for* + noun or object pronoun.

> I'll wait **for Jack/him** to come home. (Jack performs the action of coming home.)
>
> I'd be happy **for Jack/him** to come along. (Jack performs the action of coming along.)

TALKING the TALK

■ In speech, the performer of the gerund action is often indicated by a nonpossessive noun or an object pronoun instead of the possessive form.

> I really appreciate **Don/him** doing that for me.

FORM AND FUNCTION Progressive Infinitives; Perfect Gerunds and Infinitives

Form

■ Infinitives can occur in the progressive form. Gerunds, which themselves end in *-ing*, cannot. Both gerunds and infinitives can occur in the perfect form.

	Gerund	**Infinitive**
Progressive Form		*to be* + verb + *-ing*
		to be singing
Perfect Form	*having* + past participle	*to have* + past participle
	having sung	**to have sung**

Function

■ Use the progressive form of infinitives to indicate an activity in progress or the ongoing nature of an activity.

> She had hoped **to be working** in a better job by now. (Working is an ongoing activity.)

■ Use the perfect form of gerunds or infinitives to indicate that an activity is in the past in relation to the time of the verb.

> We appreciate **having heard** her sing. (The hearing happened before the appreciation.) (Compare: We appreciate hearing her sing. The hearing can be at the same time as the appreciation and can even happen in the future.)
>
> We're fortunate to **have heard her sing.** (The hearing happened in the past.) (Compare: We're fortunate to hear her sing. The hearing happens now or in the future.)

GRAMMAR HOTSPOT!

■ Certain types of verbs cannot be followed by gerunds or infinitives; they must be followed by other forms.

- Sensory verbs such as *feel, hear, listen to, look at, notice, observe, see, smell,* and *watch* are followed either by the base form of the verb or by the *-ing* form. Do not use a possessive before the *-ing* form.

  We **watched** John/him **perform.**

  We **watched** John/him **performing.   Not:** We watched ~~John's/his~~ performing.

- Like *get* (see Grammar Briefing 1, page 236), *have, let,* and *make* are causative verbs. However, instead of being followed by a noun phrase + infinitive, these verbs are followed by a noun phrase + the base form of the verb.

  We **got him to sing.**

  We **had/let/made him sing. Not:** We had/let/made him ~~to sing~~.

GRAMMAR PRACTICE 2: Performers of Gerunds and Infinitives; Progressive Infinitives; Perfect Gerunds and Infinitives

⑥ Performers of Gerunds: *Indiana's Adventures*

A. *Raiders of the Lost Ark* and the other Indiana Jones movies are among the most popular adventure movies ever made. Combine the sentences. Replace the **boldfaced** word in the second sentence with a gerund phrase based on the first sentence. In combining, change the first sentence in any way needed. Include a possessive form for the performer of the gerund where needed.

1. Indiana went to find the lost Ark of the Covenant. Indiana was excited about **this.**

   Indiana was excited about going to find the lost Ark of the Covenant.

2. Indiana found his former girlfriend Marion in Nepal. Marion didn't appreciate **this.**

   Marion didn't appreciate Indiana's / his finding her in Nepal.

3. Marion shot a man who was aiming at Indiana. Indiana was pleased by **this.**

4. Marion disappeared in Cairo. Indiana was upset about **this.**

5. Indiana found her in a tent where she had been tied up. Indiana was happy about **this.**

6. He didn't untie her. She resented **this.**

7. Indiana dropped into a pit full of poisonous snakes. Indiana hated **this.**

8. The villains pushed Marion into the pit, too. Marion was terrified by **this.**

9. Indiana found the lost ark. **This** made the villains very angry.

10. They captured Marion. **This** infuriated Indiana.

11. Indiana told her not to look at the evil spirits coming from the ark. Indiana saved Marion's life by **this.**

B. Work with a partner. Use the sentences you wrote in **A** to tell your partner about *Raiders of the Lost Ark.* Use nonpossessive forms.

> Example: Marion didn't appreciate Indiana [or him] finding her in Nepal.

C. Work with a partner. Write **three** sentences about situations in a movie that you've both seen. Use gerund phrases and use possessive forms for performers of gerunds.

> Example: Rhett didn't appreciate Scarlett's loving another man.

7 Performers of Infinitives: *Remaking King Kong*

A. Use the information in the first sentence to complete the second sentence. Use *for* with a noun phrase when necessary.

1. The director asked Adam, "Will you act in the movie?"

   The director asked ___Adam to act in the movie.___

2. Adam asked the director, "Can I play the leading role?"

   Adam asked ___to play the leading role.___

3. The director said to Adam, "If you'll play the leading role, I'll be happy." The

   director will be happy _____.

4. Adam said, "If I play the leading role, I'll be happy." Adam will be happy

   _____.

5. Then the director talked to Adam for a long time, and finally Adam said, "Okay. I'll wear a gorilla costume." The director persuaded

   _____.

6. Then the director said to Adam, "You're going to climb to the top of the Empire State Building." The director intended

   _____.

7. Adam said, "No problem. I'll climb to the top of the building." Adam wasn't

   afraid _____.

8. Adam's girlfriend Suki said to him, "Adam, please don't climb to the top!" Suki

   was afraid _____.

9. Adam said, "I'm going to win an Academy Award." Adam intended

   _____.

10. Suki said to Adam, "In that case, you can do it!" Suki was willing

    _____.

B. Imagine that you're going to direct a movie in which your classmates play roles. Write **six** sentences about your plans. Include at least two sentences with *for* + noun or pronoun. Use structures that take infinitives—*expect, intend, persuade, want, would like*, or other verbs and *be* + *eager, happy, pleased*, or other adjectives.

> Example: I want to make a science-fiction movie. I'm eager for Lena to play the part of an alien. I'm going to ask her to pilot the alien space ship.

8 Progressive Infinitives; Perfect Gerunds and Infinitives—Form: *What Do You Say When the Dream Comes True?*

The following are possible acceptance speeches by Academy Award winners.

A. Use the words in parentheses to complete the sentences with progressive infinitives.

Best Actor: I hadn't expected ___to be standing___ (stand) here tonight. The entertainment industry has given me many opportunities. I'm happy

_____ (work) in such a wonderful industry. Thank you,
   2
everyone.

Best Actress: I'd prefer _____ (not, cry) right now, but this is such an
   3
important event in my life. Everyone seems _____ (wait)
   4
for me to say something. And I had hoped _____ (make) a
   5
memorable speech at this moment. But I can't say more than thank

you with all my heart.

Best Director: Do I deserve _____ (hold) this golden statue? Yes, I do!
   6

B. Use the words in parentheses to complete the sentences with perfect infinitives and perfect gerunds.

Best Supporting Actress: First, I want to thank my director. I appreciate

___having had___ (have) the opportunity to work with him.
   1
I'm also fortunate ___to have had___ (have) the help of many
   2
other people. I'll never forget _____ (win) this award.
   3

Best Supporting Actor: This is a great honor, and I'm pleased _____
   4
(receive) it. I'm delighted _____ (work) with the
   5
rest of the cast. And I don't deny _____ (be)
   6
lucky. I was lucky _____ (be) in the right place
   7
at the right time with the right people.

C. Imagine that you have just received an Academy Award for acting in or directing a movie. Write a one-paragraph acceptance speech. Use at least two of each of the following: progressive infinitives, perfect gerunds, and perfect infinitives. Use any appropriate verbs, adjectives, or *be* + adjective + preposition combinations (e.g., *admit, deny, deserve, expect, forget, hope, remember, seem, delighted, fortunate, happy, pleased, be glad about,* or *be proud of*).

Read your speech to the class.

🙂 Progressive and Perfect Gerunds and Infinitives—Function: *Movie Makers—The Next Generation*

The following sentences are from statements that film studies students made about their backgrounds and activities. Complete the sentences by using the words in parentheses to form gerunds and infinitives. Where possible, use progressive and perfect forms.

James: When I was ten, I saw *Psycho,* by Alfred Hitchcock, for the first time. I'll

always appreciate ___having seen___ (see) that movie then because it made
                         1

a big impression on me. Even now, whenever I see *Psycho* I'm shocked by

___seeing___ (see) the shower scene.
    2

In high school, I studied drama. Now I feel fortunate ___to have studied___
                                                           3

(study) drama. This year I'm studying film-making. I'm pleased

___to be studying___ (study) film-making. Someday, I want ___to make___
        4   5

(make) a thriller like Hitchcock's thrillers.

Usha: Before I came here, I lived in India. I feel fortunate _____ (live)
                                                                  6

in India because it has a great film-making tradition. Now I'm living in

New York. I feel fortunate _____ (live) in New York. But I hope
                               7

_____ (return) to India someday.
    8

Now I'm studying script writing. I'm glad _____ (learn)
                                               9

about script writing. Before I started film school, I studied art. Now I don't

regret _____ (study) art. By making movies, I can combine
           10

painting with storytelling.

Danielle: When I was very young, I took photographs for the first time. After they

were developed, I was proud of _____ (take) them, and photog-
                                    11

raphy became very important to me. Even now, whenever I take pho-

tographs, I have a good time _____ (take) them.
                                12

Years ago, I saw *Ran* by Akira Kurosawa. When I decided to study film,

I knew that a reason was my _____ (see) *Ran*. I wanted to learn
                                    13

_____ (use) photography like Kurosawa did.
        14

Roberto: I'm working hard in film school. I didn't expect _____ (work) so
                                                                    15

hard this semester. I finished the script for my first movie recently. Writing

it took a long time, so afterward I was relieved _____ (finish) it.
                                                        16

This semester we're filming it as a class project. We're happy

_____ (film) it, but it's a big project.
        17

⒑ Sensory Verbs, Causative Verbs, and Verbs Followed by Infinitives: *The Wizard of Oz*

The following is a summary of *The Wizard of Oz*, a movie classic from 1939. (The summary is in the simple present—a tense often used in telling stories.) Use the words in parentheses to complete the sentences. In some cases, more than one form is correct.

At the beginning of the movie, we hear Dorothy ___*singing/sing*___ (sing)
                                                        1

"Somewhere Over the Rainbow." She is at home in Kansas with her little dog, Toto. A

tornado strikes, and Dorothy and Toto are carried over the rainbow into the land of

the Munchkins. Dorothy watches the little Munchkins _____ (dance).
                                                            2

Soon Dorothy wants _____ (go) back to Kansas. The Good Witch gives
                        3

her a pair of red slippers and tells her _____ (follow) a yellow brick road
                                                         4

to the Emerald City, where she will find the Wizard of Oz, who will help her. Soon

after she starts down the road, Dorothy finds the Scarecrow, who gets her

_____ (take) him with her so that he can ask the Wizard _____
          5   6

(give) him a brain. Next, they discover the Tin Man, who has Dorothy

_____ (oil) him. Dorothy lets the Tin Man _____ (come) along,
          7   8

because he hopes _____ (get) a heart. They meet the Cowardly Lion and
                              9

allow him _____ (come). He wants to get the Wizard _____
                    10   11

(give) him courage. After the Wizard finally lets them _____ (enter) the
                                                                      12

Emerald City, they tell him why they are there. The Wizard makes them

_____ (go) to the castle of the Wicked Witch. When the Witch sets fire to
          13

the Scarecrow, Dorothy throws water at the flames. The water kills the witch—we

hear her _____ (scream) and see her _____ (melt). Later the
                  14   15

Good Witch reappears. She tells Dorothy and her friends that they always had what

they were looking for, but that they had to find it out for themselves. She has

Dorothy _____ (click) the heels of her slippers three times, and Dorothy
                 16

and Toto are back in Kansas.

UNIT WRAP-UP

Error Correction

Correct the errors in the passage. Including the example, there are **13** errors.

Going to Graceland

Every year, thousands of people from all over the world travel to Memphis,

       to visit
Tennessee, ~~for visiting~~ Graceland, Elvis Presley's home. I've never been to

Graceland, but I want going there. I look forward to do it someday because Elvis has

a very important place in the history of American popular culture. I wasn't enough

old to see Elvis when he was alive, but I'll never forget to hear "Love Me Tender" for the first time. I've watched his movies, and I've talked to people who saw his per-

forming in the 1950s. They're fortunate to see him then. I would like to have seen his

stage performances because sometimes I have problems to understand why he

shocked people so much.

I think that Elvis was an example of the American dream—a poor boy who

became successful by using his talent and energy. When he was young, he dreamed

to be rich. But later his success was difficult for him deal with. He was very gener-

ous, and he often went to the store for buying Cadillacs and other expensive gifts

for people. Being so generous caused him to have financial problems, though. He

started taking too many pills, and he became famous for to eat lots of fried food.

Now we are used to think of Elvis as a troubled person who lost control of his life—

an American tragedy. But I prefer to keep remembering his musical achievements.

Wrap-up Tasks

Task 1: A Game Show Pre-Test

A. Work in a small group. Imagine that you work for a cable-television channel, English Language Learning Network. You produce a game show called "Grammar Challenge." Many people would like to be contestants on "Grammar Challenge." In order to select the best contestants, you have decided to test their ability to use gerunds and infinitives. Write a fill-in-the-blanks test with twelve items.

Example:

1. I tried _____ (scream) for help, but no one heard me.

2. That car is too expensive for me _____ (buy).

B. After your teacher has checked your test, make copies of it for the other students in the class. After they have completed it, check their answers.

Task 2: A Fan Letter

Write a letter to an actor or singer whom you admire. Include at least six of the following: a verb followed by a gerund, a verb + preposition followed by a gerund, a verb followed by an infinitive, an adjective followed by an infinitive, a noun modified by an infinitive, an infinitive of purpose, *by* + a gerund, *too* + infinitive, and *enough* + infinitive.

Example:

Dear Bob,

I'm writing to express my admiration for your singing. I had a chance to hear your latest album recently, and I want you to know how much I liked listening to it. . . .

Task 3: The Popularity of American Entertainment—What's Your Opinion?

A. Work in small groups. Read the following statement:

American entertainment products—especially music, television programs, and movies—will continue to be popular and successful internationally well into the twenty-first century.

Decide whether you agree or disagree with the statement and why. In your discussion, use some of the words listed in sentences with gerunds and infinitives.

Example: I agree. People prefer to watch American movies, and they will continue watching them. OR I disagree. People are going to become more enthusiastic about seeing movies from other countries, and they're going to stop watching so many American movies.

Verbs: *appreciate, (dis)approve of, avoid, continue, enjoy, keep, like, love, need, prefer, refuse, start, stop, try, would like*

Expressions: *be worth, have fun, spend time*

***Be* + Adjective + Preposition:** *(in)capable of, concerned about, critical of, enthusiastic about, interested in, responsible for*

B. Write a paragraph explaining why you agree or disagree with the statement. Use at least **six** sentences with gerunds and infinitives.

Unit Seven

Modals

Topic Focus: *Courtship and Marriage*

UNIT OBJECTIVES

- **ability modals**
  (A typical four-year-old *can* talk.)

- **belief modals**
  (If you have "M.D." after your name, you *must* be a doctor.)

- **social modals**
  (What *should* I wear to my friend's wedding?)

- **perfect modals**
  (Things *might have* gone better for you.)

- **belief modals in the past**
  (Love *must have* been dangerous for Romeo and Juliet.)

- **social modals in the past**
  (You *should have* gotten married by now.)

- **progressive and perfect progressive modals**
  (Nora *should be working* in the library. Kelly *could have been daydreaming.*)

INTRODUCTORY TASKS

Reading and Listening

`·-·` Read and listen to this dialogue from a cultural anthropology class.

Read and listen to this dialogue from a cultural anthropology class.

Teacher: Before class ends, I want to remind you that the mid-term exam is next week. You **should** read the information that I've written on the blackboard about it. **Can** everyone see the blackboard?

Student A: **Is** the exam **going to** be difficult?

Teacher: It **shouldn't be** too difficult. Students who have come to every class and done all the reading **should** do well on it. Of course, you **must** review the material. A review is always necessary. And I have a suggestion: You **might** work together in study groups.

Student B: **May** I ask one more question? **Could** you repeat the definition of "courtship"?

Teacher: Of course. Courtship is part of the process of choosing a mate, that is, a husband or wife. Courtship refers to social activities between males and females that **might** lead to marriage. Dating **can** be a part of courtship, as it often is in this country, but it doesn't **have to** be—courtship customs are different in different cultures. And the ways of choosing a mate differ, too. There are various possibilities. For example, the individuals themselves **may** find their mates. Or their family members **could** be the ones who find suitable mates for them. Or they **might** ask a matchmaker, or go-between, to identify potential mates. But even if families or matchmakers arrange an introduction, this doesn't necessarily mean that the individuals **must** marry one another. In most cases, the individuals **are allowed to** make the final decision.

Student C: In this culture, most people think that a decision to marry **ought to** be based on romantic love—that you **shouldn't** marry someone unless you're strongly attracted to them. How important is romantic love as a basis for choosing a mate in other cultures?

Teacher: Well, cultural anthropologists who have done research on this topic believe that romantic love **must** be nearly universal. That is, they're certain that it occurs almost everywhere. But they have found it isn't universally important as a basis for marriage. In many cultures, family considerations are more important. I know you're interested in this topic, so we **will** discuss it more next week, but we've run out of time. You **may** go now.

Comprehension Check

Read each sentence. Circle **T** if the sentence is true or **F** if the sentence is false.

1. The study of courtship and marriage customs is a part of the field of cultural anthropology.   (T)   F

2. Courtship always leads to marriage.   T   F

3. Dating is a courtship custom that occurs in only some cultures.   T   F

4. According to the teacher, in most cases individuals make the final
   decision about their marriage partner.   **T**   **F**

5. Romantic love is the basis for marriage in most cultures.   **T**   **F**

Think about Grammar

The **boldfaced** words in the reading passage are modals and modal-like expressions. Modals have various functions: They are used to express ability, to express belief, and to do other things like give advice or permission and to make requests or suggestions. Most modals can be used for more than one of these functions.

A. Work with a partner. Look at the following pairs of sentences from the reading. In one sentence in each pair, the modal is a belief modal. It expresses the speaker's degree of certainty about something—that is, the speaker's feelings about whether something is certain, likely, or just possible. In each pair, **circle** the letter of the sentence that contains a belief modal.

1. a. You **should** read the information that I've written on the blackboard.

   (b.) Students who have come to every class and done all the reading **should** do
       well on the exam.

2. a. **Can** everyone see the blackboard?

   b. Dating **can** be a part of courtship.

3. a. **Could** you repeat the definition of "courtship"?

   b. Their family members **could** be the ones who find suitable mates for them.

4. a. Individuals themselves **may** find their mates.

   b. You **may** go now.

5. a. Courtship refers to social activities that **might** lead to marriage.

   b. You **might** work together in study groups.

6. a. You **must** review the material.

   b. Cultural anthropologists believe that romantic love **must** be nearly universal.

B. The modals in the sentences that don't contain belief modals have other functions. In which sentence(s) is the modal used to:

1. give advice or make a suggestion to someone? ___1 a. should___ _____

2. express ability to do something? _____

3. to give permission to do something? _____

4. make a request for someone to do something? _____

5. express the necessity to do something? _____

Modals

Introductory Task: *How Certain Is She?*

Work with a partner. Read each group of statements made by Andrea and then answer the questions.

1. a. Theresa **is** married. She introduced me to her husband.

    b. Dale **might be** married. It's possible that he is, but I really don't know.

    c. Brian **must be** married. He wears a wedding ring.

    d. Dana **could be** married. Maybe she is, and maybe she isn't.

Which **boldfaced** verb or modal + verb combination(s) did Andrea use when she was

      fully certain about the situation? _____is_____

      very certain about the situation? _____

      not very certain about the situation? _____ _____

2. a. Tamika **might not be** married. It's possible that she isn't, but I don't have any way of knowing for sure.

    b. Elliot **must not be** married. I've seen him at movies and restaurants with several different women.

    c. Sheila **isn't** married. I know for a fact that she is single.

    d. Marco **couldn't be** married. He's only sixteen, and he lives with his parents.

Which **boldfaced** verb or modal + verb combination(s) did Andrea use when she was

      fully certain about the situation? _____

      very certain about the situation? _____ _____

      not very certain about the situation? _____

3. All the sentences in item 1 are affirmative. All the sentences in item 2 are negative. One modal expresses a different degree of certainty in negative sentences than it does in affirmative sentences. Circle the modal:

      could   might   must

GRAMMAR BRIEFING 1: Overview of Modals; Ability Modals

One-word modals (e.g., *can*) and phrasal modals (e.g., *be able to*) are auxiliary verbs. Modals express ideas related to certainty, necessity, and ability.

FORM AND FUNCTION Modals

Form

■ The one-word modals are *can, could, may, might, shall, should, will, would,* and *must.*

■ One-word modals are like other auxiliary verbs (i.e., *have, be*) in their position in statements and questions. However, unlike other auxiliaries, they don't change form and are followed by the base form of the verb.

- In affirmative statements, use: modal + base form of verb.

    I **can** speak English.

    He **should** call her.

- In negative statements, use: modal + *not* + base form of the verb.

    I **could not** go. I **couldn't** go.

    She **cannot*** go. She **can't** go.

    You **may not*** smoke here.   **Not:** You mayn't smoke here.

* *Can + not* is usually written as one word. *May not* is not contracted.

- In questions, use: modal + subject + base form of verb, for *yes/no* questions; *wh-* word + modal (+ subject) + base form of verb, for *wh-* questions

    Should they come? (*yes/no* question)

    What **can** he do? (*wh-* question about the predicate)

    Who **might** come? (*wh-* question about the subject)

■ Phrasal modals begin with *be* or *have* and end with *to.* They include *be able to, be allowed to, be going to, be supposed to, be to, have to,* and *have got to.* The *be* and *have* change form.* Phrasal modals with *have* include *do* in questions and negatives.

    She **is able to** speak English.

    We **weren't supposed to** be home yet.

    Do you **have to** go home now?

* *Have got to* has no future or past form, but it does change form in the present: *She **has got to** do her homework.*

■ Several other forms act like modals. These include *ought to* and *had better.*

    They **ought to** return the books that they borrowed.

    She **had better** not be late.

Ought to is usually not used in negative statements or in questions. *Had better* is usually not used in questions. In speaking, *had better* is usually contracted to *'d better.* Its negative form is *had better not.*

■ One-word modals do not occur with other one-word modals, but they can occur with phrasal modals. Phrasal modals can also occur with other phrasal modals.

    I **may be able to** go. (modal + phrasal modal)

    You **have to be able to** swim in order to go. (phrasal modal + phrasal modal)

Function

- Modals express ability, different degrees of certainty, and different degrees of necessity. Most modals have more than one meaning.

  He **could** swim well. (past ability)

  The phone **could** be busy. (present certainty—weak degree)

- Different modals often express similar meanings. Phrasal modals are often similar in meaning to one-word modals—for example: *can* and *be able to; will* and *be going to; must* and *have to, have got to; may* and *be allowed to.*

TALKING the TALK

- In speech, *have/has to, have/has got to,* and *ought to* are often pronounced "hafta, hasta," " 've gotta, 's gotta," and "oughta."

FORM AND FUNCTION Modals of Ability

- *Can, could,* and *be able to* express ability to do something. *Can* expresses ability in the present or in general. *Could* expresses ability in the past. *Be able to* expresses ability in the present, past, or future.

  I **can** hear the television in the other room. (present ability)

  He **could** speak Spanish as a child, but he **couldn't** speak English. (past ability)

  We**'ll be able to** use the new computers once we've taken the course. (future ability)

- *Be able to* is used to express ability with the present perfect.

  I**'ve been able to** swim since I was six.   **Not:** I ~~could~~ swim since I was six.

- *Be able to,* not *could,* is used to express ability connected to a single event. If, however, the event is expressed in a negative statement, either form can be used.

  Last night, the police **were able to** catch the thief.   **Not:** Last night, the police ~~could~~ catch the thief.

  Last night, the police **weren't able to** catch the thief. = Last night, the police **couldn't** catch the thief.

GRAMMAR PRACTICE 1: Overview of Modals; Ability Modals

1 One-Word Modals, Phrasal Modals, and Modal-like Expressions—Form: *A Student-Teacher Conference*

Complete the sentences using the correct form of the words in parentheses. Use contractions with *not* where possible.

S: I'm sorry that I __couldn't come__ (could / not / come) to class last Friday.
            1

I _____ (have to / stay) home because I was sick. _____
        2   3

(I / may / ask) you some questions?

T: Yes, of course.

S: When _____ (we / have to / turn in) our term papers?
              4

T: Everyone _____ (be supposed to / turn in) their papers before the
                  5

final exam. Students _____ (can / give) them to me earlier, but
                            6

they _____ (may / not / turn them in) after the exam.
            7

S: _____ (we / be allowed to / choose) any topic related to courtship?
      8

T: Yes, you are, but you _____ (ought to / think about) it carefully. Your
                                9

paper _____ (have got to / include) examples to illustrate your ideas,
            10

but it _____ (must / not / be) too long, so choose a topic that's not too
          11

broad. But don't pick a topic that you _____ (can / not / find) enough
                                              12

information about.

S: I'm interested in personality characteristics that attract people when they're

choosing a mate.

T: You _____ (might / be able to / find) some interesting information on
          13

that in the library.

S: I'll go look now, since I _____ (have to / not / go) to class yet. Thanks
                                14

very much.

2 Present, Future, and Past Ability: *Developing Survival Skills*

A. Complete the sentences with an appropriate form of *be able to*. Where *can* or *could* is possible, write it as well. Use negatives where indicated. Use contractions with *not*.

I. What quality is most important to people when they are choosing a mate? According to social scientists, the answer is an agreeable personality. People want someone that they __*can / are able to*__ get along with well. There might be a spe-
1

cial reason for this. Children __*can't / aren't able to*__ (not) survive without a great
2

deal of attention. Of course, a mother may _____ take care of her
3

children on her own. But children might have an easier time when they grow up

with two parents who _____ get along well and cooperate in raising
4

them.

II. Eli is a four-year-old child. His parents are very proud of his rapid development.

For example, when he was 18 months old, he _____ speak in com-
5

plete sentences. When he was three, although he _____ (not) write
6

yet, he _____ read simple books. He _____ do sim-
7   8

ple arithmetic problems for several months now.

Eli's parents _____ take turns looking after him since he was
9

born. Last Monday, for example, his father stayed home with him, and his mother

_____ finish an important project at her office. Yesterday, his father
10

_____ (not) stay home, but his mother stayed with him. She took Eli
11

to the library, and he _____ find some good books to read.
12

Tomorrow his mother might _____ take him to her office. Even
13

though Eli is a very capable child, he _____ (not) take care of him-
14

self until he is much older. At some point, he _____ survive on his
15

own, but until then he will need his parents' care and cooperation.

B. Read the following statements. For each one, write a sentence that gives an example of the statement. Use *can, can't, could,* or *couldn't* where possible. Use a form of *be able to* otherwise.

1. Ten years ago I was able to do things that I'm not able to do now.
     I could learn to speak foreign languages easily.

2. Ten years ago I wasn't able to do things that I'm able to do now.

3. Ten years from now I'll be able to do things that I'm not able to do now.

4. There are things that I might be able to do soon.

5. I have many useful abilities now.

GRAMMAR BRIEFING 2: Belief Modals

Belief modals express different degrees of certainty on the part of a speaker. Modals used to express degrees of certainty about the present and future include *must, have to, have got to, will, be going to, should, ought to, may, might,* and *could.* (For modals that express degrees of certainty about the past, see Chapter 15, Grammar Briefing 1, page 278.)

FORM AND FUNCTION Belief Modals

Degrees of Certainty about the Present

■ Modals that express degrees of certainty about the present include *must, have to, have got to, should, ought to, may, might, can* (in its negative form, *cannot*), and *could.* If speakers are fully certain, they do not use a modal (e.g., *He is here.*). Modals in affirmative sentences express degrees of certainty about what is true. Modals in negative sentences express degrees of certainty about what isn't true.

Degree of Certainty	Modal—Affirmative Sentence	Modal—Negative Sentence
strongly certain	**must, have to, have got to**	**must not (mustn't), could not (couldn't), cannot (can't)**
↓	**should, ought to**	**should not (shouldn't)**
not very certain	**may, might, could**	**may not, might not (mightn't)**

■ *Must, have to,* and *have got to* are used when the speaker is convinced that the situation is almost certainly true: In the speaker's mind there is no other logical possibility.

> He **must** be here. His books are on his desk.

In their belief use, these modals usually do not occur in questions.

■ *Should* and *ought to* are used when the speaker feels that there are other possibilities but that this possibility is by far the most likely.

> He **should** be home. He's usually home at this time.

Should and *ought to* are generally not used to express a possibility that is undesirable.

> The food here is probably bad.   **Not:** The food here ~~should be~~ bad.

■ *May, might,* and *could* are used when the speaker feels this possibility isn't necessarily more likely than others.

> He **might** be home. I really don't know.

■ *Could not* and *cannot,* unlike *could,* express a very strong degree of certainty. Often *could not* and *cannot* are used to express great surprise, especially about something that is unpleasant.

> He **couldn't** be in Colombia. I saw him yesterday. (strong certainty)
>
> The food **can't** be gone! The party just started. (surprise about something unpleasant)

■ *Have to, have got to,* and *ought to* are not used to express degrees of certainty in negative sentences.

> He **shouldn't** be home yet.   **Not:** He ~~ought not to~~ be home yet.
>
> They **must not** be here yet.   **Not:** They ~~don't have to~~ be here yet.

■ Adverbs and adjectives are sometimes used to express meanings similar to those expressed by belief modals. Adverbs used this way include *certainly, probably, possibly,* and *maybe.* Adjectives include *certain, probable, likely,* and *(im)possible.*

> The dinner is **probably** ready by now. = The dinner should be ready by now.

> It is **possible** that we will be late. = We might be late.

Degrees of Certainty about the Future

■ Modals that express degrees of certainty about the future include *will, be going to, should, ought to, may, might,* and *could.* Speakers use these modals to express how likely they think their predictions are.

Degree of Certainty	Modal—Affirmative Sentence	Modal—Negative Sentence
strongly certain	**will, be going to**	**will not (won't), not be going to**
↓	**should, ought to**	**should not (shouldn't)**
not very certain	**may, might, could**	**may not, might not (mightn't)**

■ *Will* and *be going to* express certainty about the situation or event predicted. However, these forms are often used with an adverb such as *probably* that weakens the prediction.

> He **will probably** come to the party.

■ *Could* and *ought to* are not used in negative sentences.

> We **may not/might not** come tomorrow. **Not:** We ~~could not~~ come tomorrow.

■ *Will* is usually used in questions about the future. *May* is not used in such questions.

> **Will** he be here tomorrow?   **Not:** ~~May~~ he be here tomorrow?

GRAMMAR HOTSPOT!

■ Notice! *Must, have to,* and *have got to* are not used for degrees of certainty about the future. They are used for degrees of certainty about the present.

> He'**ll** (probably) be here tomorrow.   **Not:** He ~~must~~ be here tomorrow.

GRAMMAR PRACTICE 2: Belief Modals

3   Belief Modals—Degrees of Certainty about the Present: *Making Guesses*

Rob responded to this ad: "I'm looking for a suitable match for my well-educated sister. Information available by e-mail upon request...." He has received a reply, but the e-mail system is not working correctly, and information is missing. Read Rob's thoughts about the message. Use information in the message to complete the sentences with *must, have to, have got to, should, ought to, may, might,* and *could.* For each completion, write all the forms that you think express the intended meaning. Use *not* where necessary. Use contractions with *not* where possible.

Here's some information about my sister, Nicola Kumar, M.D., who . . .

In her work, she cares for both adults and children . . .

She was born on May 19, 19 . . .

In addition to water sports, she enjoys . . .

You can reach her at home most evenings by calling (604)-447-3914.

She is usually at home after 7 P.M. . . .

It ___*shouldn't*___ be difficult to figure out more about Nicola. There are
         1

clues in the message. For example, there's an M.D. after her name. She

___*must / has to/ has got to*___ be a doctor. It's the only logical possibility.
               2

But what kind of doctor is she? She _____ be just a children's doctor.
                                           3

There are lots of possibilities, though. She _____ be a surgeon. Or
                                                    4

she _____ be an eye doctor, or. . . .
         5

I wonder how old she is. People don't finish medical school before at least their

late 20s. So she _____ be older than 25, but she _____ be older
                    6   7

than 30.

Based on the e-mail, it looks like she _____ enjoy swimming and
                                              8

sailing—my favorite sports—although I can't be 100% sure. Apart from that,

we _____ have a lot in common—I hope so—or we _____ have
        9   10

a lot in common—that would be too bad.

Her telephone area code is the same as mine. This area code is now used only

for my city, so she _____ live very far away. It's 8:30 now. Based on the
                       11

e-mail, she _____ be at home now. I think I'll try calling her.
                12

4   Belief Modals—Degrees of Certainty about the Present: *Singles Seeking Mates*

One way to find a mate is to advertise in a newspaper. Work with a partner. Read
the following ads and the questions that follow them. Discuss possible answers, using
belief modals.

> Example: *Pat's a medical professional. Pat may be a dentist.* OR *Pat*
> *doesn't want to meet anyone who has a pet. Pat mustn't like pets.*

Then write sentences to answer the questions. In each sentence use one of the following modals: *must, have to, have got to, may, might, can* or *could.* Include at least two negative sentences about each person.

MEDICAL PROFESSIONAL

In my free time, I read *Sports Illustrated*, *Car and Driver*, *Gourmet*, and *Fine Cooking*. I'm very tall, and play a team sport.

I drive a red Japanese car, wear red clothing, often have quiet dinners at home, and avoid going to restaurants.

Please don't respond if you have a pet. My name is Pat.

1. What's Pat's profession?

    a.   *Pat may be a dentist.* _____

    b. _____

2. What sport does Pat play? _____

3. What brand of car does Pat drive? _____

4. What are some of Pat's likes, dislikes, and interests?

    a. _____

    b. _____

    c. _____

5. What is Pat's personality like? _____

6. Is Pat a man or a woman? _____

SCIENTIST

(I've published a book,
Distant Galaxies, and many
articles in *Sky and
Telescope*.)

In my free time, I read
detective stories, *Travel*, and
Art and Architecture. I play a
racquet sport.

I listen to music by Bach
and Mozart and have
visited museums in many
countries.

I'm interested in meeting
a vegetarian who is willing
to walk or take public
transportation everywhere
we go. No rock and roll fans
please! My name is Chris.

---

1. What's Chris's profession? _____

2. What sport does Chris play? _____

3. Does Chris have a car? _____

4. What are some of Chris's likes, dislikes, and interests?

    a. _____

    b. _____

    c. _____

5. What is Chris's personality like? _____

6. Is Chris a man or a woman? _____

5 Belief Modals—Degrees of Certainty about the Future: *Finding Mr. or Ms. Right*

A. Complete the sentences using the information in parentheses. Use *be going to, will, ought to, should, could, may,* and *might.* In each blank write all the possible forms. Use *not* where necessary. Use contractions with *not* where possible.

Liz: Helen, you've studied recent courtship trends. What are your predictions?

Will we see changes in the methods Americans use to find mates?

Helen: Things have been changing. And they ___will / are going to___ (very certainly)

1

continue to change. These changes ___mightn't / may not___ (possibly not)

2

happen everywhere in the country, though.

Liz: What kinds of changes do you expect to see?

Helen: In the past, many Americans just waited to meet a suitable person. This

method _____ (probably not) be the most common way to find
₃ — rendered as below

method _____ (probably not) be the most common way to find

mates in the future. Many people are just too busy to meet suitable mates by

chance. This situation _____ (certainly not) change soon.

Liz: Advertising on the Internet _____ (possibly) become a more

popular way of finding a mate.

Helen: Yes. But advertising _____ (possibly not) become as popular as

another strategy that has been used in many cultures—going to a match-

maker. In the future, we _____ (probably) see more people using

professional matchmakers. With matchmakers, people _____

(very certainly) have a better chance of finding Mr. or Ms. Right.

B. What are your predictions about the ways people will find mates in the future?
Complete the following sentences using modals that express your degree of certainty. Include *not* in some sentences. Use *probably* with *will* or *be going to* where
appropriate to weaken your predictions. Add **two** sentences of your own. As a
class, compare predictions.

1. Many young single people ___will probably___ live far from their families in the
   future.

2. There _____ be many people advertising for mates in newspapers.

3. Advertising for a mate on the Internet _____ become more common.

4. It _____ become more common for people to use matchmakers.

5. Using family connections to find a mate _____ become less
   common.

6. Compared to now, it _____ be more difficult for men to find mates.

7. Compared to now, it _____ be easier for women to find mates.

8. _____

9. _____

🌀 Belief Modals: *Matchmakers in Action*

Rose and Vera are matchmakers. They are trying to find a suitable mate for Lola. **Circle the correct form; if both forms are correct, circle both.**

Rose: Lola is talented and intelligent. It [___ought not to /(shouldn't)___] be difficult to

find suitable men for her.

Vera: Yes, but Lola is very demanding. It [(is going to)/(will)] take a lot of searching

to find just the right man.

Rose: Lola is studying engineering. Eddie's an engineer. They [___should / must___]

get along well if they meet.

Vera: Rose, look at Eddie's picture. He [___must / has to___] be at least sixty years old.

I think he [___might / should___] be too old for her.

Rose: What about Chad? He's a handsome twenty-five-year old. Oh, but he's a

vegetarian, and Lola loves steaks. He [___mayn't / mightn't___] be right for

her. . . . Say—Sky's a young, steak-eating engineer. He [___could / may___]

have all the qualities that Lola wants. He travels occasionally, so he

[___couldn't / may not___] be home now, but I'm going to call him.

Vera: And what about Lola? [___May / Will___] she check with us soon?

Rose: Let me call her. . . . There's no answer. She [___mustn't / doesn't have to___]

be home now. And she [___may not / could not___] check with us until

next week. . . . But when she does and she hears about Sky, she

[___has to / is going to___] be very happy.

GRAMMAR BRIEFING 3: Social Modals

Some social modals relate to things like permission, requests, and offers. Others relate to things like suggestions, advice, obligations, and prohibitions. Different social modals express different degrees of formality, politeness, and authority. Social modals used in talking about the present and future include *can, could, may, might, will, would, shall, be supposed to, be to, should, ought to, had better, must, have to,* and *have got to.* (For social modals used to talk about the past, see Chapter 15, Grammar Briefing 2, page 284.)

FORM AND FUNCTION Social Modals

Permission, Requests, and Offers

■ Modals that are used for permission, requests, and/or offers include *can, could, may, will,* and *would.* In each case, several modals can be used. The choice of modal is influenced by the formality of the situation and the relationship between the speaker and listener. Some modals are considered more formal and/or more polite.

> Student to teacher: **Could** you (please) explain this example?
>
> Student to student: **Can** you (please) lend me your pen?

However, in most situations speakers can use any of the possible modals. And politeness is also expressed by tone of voice and the use of words like *please.*

■   **Permission**

More formal   **may**
↓   **could**
Less formal   **can**

• *May, could,* and *can* are used to ask for permission.

Request for Permission	Possible Response
Can I use your phone?	Sure, you **can.** It's on the table.

• *May* is considered quite formal. It is often used in public announcements.
• *Could* is not used to give permission.

> Passengers in rows 1–10 **may** board now.
> **Not:** Passengers in rows 1–10 ~~could~~ board now.

■   **Requests**

More formal   **would, could**
↓
Less formal   **will, can**

• *Would, could, will,* and *can* are used to ask someone to do something.

Request	Possible Response
Will you open the door for me?	Of course I **will.**

• *Would* and *could* are usually not used in responses.

■   **Offers**

More formal   **shall**
                may
                could
↓   **will**
Les formal   **can**

• *Shall, may, could,* and *can* are used to make an offer in a question. *Can* and *will* are used to make an offer in a statement.

Offer	Possible response
May I help you?	Yes, thank you.
I'll help you in a few minutes.	OK. Thanks.

• *Shall* is only used with *I* or *we* and is not very common.

■ Responses to requests for permission, to requests, and to offers made as questions can take the form of answers to *yes/no* questions. However, affirmative responses are often made friendlier by using expressions such as *certainly, of course,* and *sure.* Negative responses are often softened by using expressions like *I'm sorry, but . . . , I'm afraid (that) . . . ,* and *I'm afraid not.*

> A: Could you tell me what time it is?
>
> B: **Certainly.** It's 3:30.
>
> A: Could you tell me what time it is?
>
> B: No, I can't. **I'm afraid** I don't have a watch.

Suggestions, Expectations, Advice, and Necessity

■ Modals can be used in telling listeners what to do. Different modals express different strengths. Depending on the modal, the speaker may be stating a necessity or just a suggestion:

> You **have to** go now. (strong—necessity)
>
> You **could** go now. (weak—suggestion)

	One-Word Modals	Phrasal Modals; Modal-like Expressions
Suggestion	**shall**	
		could, might
Advice/opinion	**should**	**ought to**
Expectation		**be supposed to, be to**
Warning		**had better**
Necessity/obligation	**must**	**have to, have got to**
Lack of necessity		**not have to**
Prohibition	**must not (mustn't), cannot (can't)**	**not be allowed to**

■ *Shall* is used to make friendly suggestions about possible actions or activities. *Shall* is not very common. It is used only in questions with *I* or *we.*

> **Shall** we go now?

■ *Could* and *might* are the modals generally used to make suggestions. However, in questions or negative statements, *should* tends to be used.

> A: What **should** I do about Allison?
>
> B: You **might** try to talk to her. If that doesn't work, you **could** just ignore her.

■ *Should* and *ought to* are used to give advice and to state opinions. (Remember: *Ought to* is usually not used in negatives or in questions.)

> You **ought to** go home if you aren't feeling well. (advice)
>
> The city **should** fix the holes in this road. (opinion)

■ *Be supposed to* and *be to* are used to express expectations, for example, about correct behavior. The expectations are sometimes based on rules or instructions.

> You**'re to** take two teaspoons of the medicine twice a day.
>
> The doors **aren't supposed to** open until 9:00.

To express expectations about the past, use these modals with past forms of *be.*

> They **were supposed to** be back last week.

- *Had better* is used to give warnings. Its use implies there will be negative consequences if the warning isn't followed.

  You**'d better** not be late for dinner.

  You**'d better** hand in that paper now. The teacher won't accept late papers.

- *Must, have to,* and *have got to* are used to express necessity or obligation. The necessity or obligation may be based on rules, laws, or requirements. *Must* is considered stronger or more formal than the others: It is used more often in announcements and documents, and less often in speech.

  You **must** be 18 to vote. (law)

  You **must** send in your transcript if you want to apply. (procedure, rule)

  He **has to** work this weekend. (The boss told him, it's his turn, or he just feels he should.)

  In questions *have to* is generally used. *Have got to* cannot be used. Although *must* can be used, it often has the special function of making a complaint. Only *have to* has a past form (*had to*).

  Do you **have to** work this weekend? **Not:** ~~Have you got to~~ work this weekend?

  Must you play your music so loud? (complaint)

- *Have got to* does not have a negative form. The negatives of *have to* and *must* have different meanings. *Don't/Doesn't have to* is used to say that something is not necessary. *Must not* is used to say that something is prohibited. Prohibition can also be expressed by *cannot* and *not be allowed to.*

  You **don't have to** eat in the cafeteria, but you can if you want to.

  You **must not** eat or drink on the bus.

  We **can't** smoke in this building.

TALKING the TALK

- *Should* and *ought to* are usually used by someone who has the authority to give advice. When a person doesn't have this authority, *should* and *ought to* can sound impolite. Instead, *could* and *might* are used to offer suggestions.

  Teacher: For homework, you **should** study for the test. Is there anything you'd like me to do to help you prepare for it?

  Student: You **could** give us a study guide.

GRAMMAR PRACTICE 3: Social Modals

7 Permission, Requests, and Offers: *Match the Modal to the Situation*

Work with a partner. Write questions to ask in the following situations. For each situation use an appropriate modal and the information given. There are no wrong answers, but some choices might be more appropriate than others. Use each modal once.

can   could   may

1. a. You're on an airplane that has several empty seats. You want to move to a window seat.

      You: ___Could I move to a window seat_____?
    Flight attendant: Of course.

  b. You're sitting with your sister in her kitchen. You want to get a drink of water.

      You: _____?
    Your sister: Sure.

  c. You're at a formal party at the home of an older woman whom you don't know well. You want to look at her garden.

      You: _____?
    The hostess: Certainly.

will   would

2. a. You're in class. Your math professor has just explained a problem. You ask her to go over that problem again.

      You: _____?
    The professor: Certainly.

  b. You're in class. You ask a friend to lend you his calculator for a few minutes.

      You: _____?
    Your classmate: Sure.

can   could   may

3. a. You are studying at home with a good friend. You offer to get him a cup of coffee.

      You: _____?
    Your friend: Yeah, thanks.

  b. You are in an office at the school where you are a student. The secretary has some letters ready to mail. You offer to mail them for her.

      You: _____?
    The secretary: Thanks.

  c. You are walking across the campus of the school where you are a student. You see a professor who is much older than you struggling with the heavy books he's carrying. You offer to carry them for him.

      You: _____?
    The professor: Yes, thank you.

8 Permission, Requests, and Offers—Form: *Another Matchmaker*

Ken has decided to ask a matchmaker to search for a wife for him. **Circle** the correct form.

Secretary: Good morning, sir. [__(May) / Will__] I help you?
                                   1

Ken: Yes, thank you. I have an appointment with Ms. Mota.

Secretary: [__Might / Would__] you have a seat, please? Ms. Mota [__shall / will__] be
                        2   3

with you in a few minutes. [__May / Will__] you fill out this form while
                                        4

you're waiting?

Ken: Certainly, I [__will / would__]. I'm sorry, I don't have a pen.
                                5

[__Could / Would__] I borrow one, please?
                6

Secretary: Of course. You [__could / can__] use this one.
                                          7

Ms. Mota: I [__may / will__] help you now.
                        8

Ken: Thank you. [__May / Will__] I introduce myself? I'm Ken Tanaka.
                                9

Ms. Mota: You're a very polite young man. I'm sure we'll find you a bride very soon.

9   Making and Responding to Requests and Offers: *You Want to Ask Nicely*

Work with a partner. Take turns making polite requests and offers in the following situations. Make affirmative responses friendlier and soften negative responses.

1. You're in a store. You want to pay with a credit card.

   Student A: Could I pay with a credit card?
   Student B: Yes, of course, you can. OR I'm sorry, but we don't accept credit cards.

2. Class has just ended. You want to make an appointment with your professor.

3. You're at a party at a friend's house. You want to help him serve the food.

4. You're at home. Your brother's boss calls, but your brother isn't home. You want to take a message.

5. You're in a restaurant. You want to move to a quieter table.

6. You're riding in a car with your friend. You want to turn on the radio.

Now think of four more situations in which people need to make polite requests or offers. With your partner practice these requests and offers and the responses.

10 Suggestions, Expectations, Advice, and Necessity: *Wedding Customs*

A. Hiro, who is a Japanese visitor to the United States, has been invited to the wedding of an American couple he knows. He's never been to an American wedding, so he's asking his friend Laura for advice. The sentences in the brackets tell you the meanings that Hiro and Laura are expressing. Use the expressions given to complete the sentences. Use each expression once. Use contractions where possible.

> be supposed to   ~~should~~   should not   ought to

Hiro: What _____*should*_____ I wear to the wedding? [What's your
                        1

opinion?]

Laura: Well, that depends on the kind of wedding it is. You _____ wear
                                                                      2

clothes that are too casual. [This is my advice.] You _____ find out
                                                              3

if it's a formal wedding. [This is my advice.] Men _____ wear dark
                                                          4

suits to formal weddings. [It's expected of them.]

> be supposed to   have to   might   not be supposed to   should

Hiro: What kind of gift _____ I give the bride and groom? [What's your
                                5

advice?]

Laura: There are lots of possibilities. You _____ give them something
                                                    6

special from Japan. [This is a suggestion.] In the past, guests

_____ take the gift to the wedding. [It wasn't considered to be
            7

correct behavior.] They _____ send it to the bride's house before
                                     8

the wedding. [It was considered to be correct behavior.] Nowadays, it's OK

to take your present to the wedding. In the past, wedding guests

_____ follow a lot of etiquette rules that people don't necessarily
            9

follow anymore. [It was a necessity.]

   have got to   have to   might   ought to

Hiro: In Japan, the guests make speeches or sing songs for the bride and groom at

the reception. _____ I _____ make a speech? [Is it an
                            10

obligation for me?]

Laura: No, you don't. The only thing that you _____ do is to go up to the
                                                           11

bride and groom at some point to give them your best wishes. [It's an obliga-

tion.] You _____ wait to see what the other guests do. [This is my
                    12

advice.] They may offer toasts, or short speeches, to the bride. If they do, you

_____ offer one, too. [This is a suggestion.]
            13

   had better not   have to   must   must not   not have to

Hiro: I'm worried about being able to do everything properly. You

_____ come with me to the wedding. [It's a necessity.]
            14

Laura: Oh no, Hiro. You _____ take uninvited guests to a wedding. [It
                                    15

isn't allowed.] But don't worry. You _____ know much about the
                                                16

customs. [It isn't a necessity.] Oh, but there is something. It's customary for

a bride to wear a blue band called a garter around her leg. At the end of

the wedding, she tosses it, and the single men try to catch it. You

_____ catch it. [This is a warning.] If you do, you'll be the next
            17

to marry.

Hiro: Thanks for warning me! But I'm still worried.

Laura: _____ you worry so much, Hiro? [This is a complaint.] Just have
                    18

a good time!

B. Work with a partner—if possible, one who knows about wedding customs in a culture that you're not familiar with. You should imagine that you've been invited to a wedding in that culture and ask for advice, suggestions, and about expectations for clothing, gifts, behavior, and customs. Use *should, ought to, could, might,* and *be supposed to.* Then reverse roles.

▐▐ Opinion, Obligation, Lack of Necessity, and Prohibition: *The Roles of Marriage Partners*

A. A group of international students are discussing a list of tasks and their ideas about who should do these tasks—the husband and/or the wife.

> Earning the money to support the family
>
> Housework (e.g., doing dishes, doing laundry, making beds, cleaning, taking out the garbage)
>
> Cooking
>
> Repairs and maintenance (e.g., doing household repairs, taking care of the car, gardening and mowing the lawn)
>
> Managing the money (e.g., making a budget, paying bills, deciding about major purchases)
>
> Shopping (e.g., grocery shopping, going to the post office, etc., clothes shopping)
>
> Decorating the house and arranging the furniture

I. Complete the sentences using *should* or *ought to.* If both are possible, write both. Use contractions with *not* where possible.

Discussion
Leader: Please look at the list and give me your opinions. Which

things ___should a husband___ (a husband) do? Which things
       ₁

_____ (a wife) do?
         2

Dana: I think a marriage _____ be a partnership with both people
                            3

doing everything.

Lesley: Well, there's one thing a husband probably _____ (not) do—
                                                      4

decorate the house.

Nate: I agree and think there's one more thing. A husband _____
                                                              5

(not) shop for his wife's clothes!

II. Complete the sentences using *have to, have got to,* and *must.* Use contractions with *not* where possible. Write all correct forms.

Discussion
Leader: What about obligations? _____Does_____ the wife __have to__ do
                                       1

certain things on the list?

Lee: No, I don't think so. These are all things that couples

      ___*have to / have got to / must*___ talk about and share the responsibility
                      2

for. The important thing is that if you promise to do something, you

      _____ (not) forget to do it. Of course, if people are very rich,
             3

they _____ (not) do the cooking and cleaning themselves,
               4

because they can pay someone else. But in general, one person

      _____ (not) make a decision without discussing it with the
          5

other one.

Discussion

Leader: Does everyone agree? _____ a couple _____ share
                         6

in these responsibilities?

Kiko: I think that a wife _____ manage all the money. It's her
                   7

responsibility. She can tell her husband how she's managing it, but she

      _____ tell him.
         8

Adel: In my culture, a woman _____ (not) drive a car—it isn't
                   9

allowed. So a husband _____ take care of the car and do a lot
                10

of the shopping.

Kelly: In my culture, things have changed. In the past, a husband

usually _____ earn the money to support the family because
         11

women didn't have many work opportunities. Now a

lot of women _____ share that responsibility because one
           12

salary isn't enough.

B. Work in small groups. Use the list in **A** as the basis for a discussion. One student should act as the discussion leader and ask the others to give answers to the following questions.

1. In your opinion, are there certain things on the list that a husband or wife should or shouldn't do?

2. Are there certain things on the list that a husband or a wife has an obligation to do? Are there things that aren't necessary for a husband or a wife to do? Are there things that either of them must not do?

3. What other responsibilities and obligations do husbands and wives have?

4. Should couples discuss their expectations and opinions about responsibilities and obligations before they marry?

12 Using Ability, Belief, and Social Modals: *Points of View*

A. As a class, discuss the following statements. Do you agree with either one? Do you have a different point of view?

1. "Marriage partners should find each other on their own. They ought to make a decision to marry based on their romantic love for each other. I can't imagine letting my family influence my choice of a partner. They can't understand my situation—or what I need in a partner—as well as I do."

2. "My family should be involved in finding a suitable partner for me. My decision to marry is going to be influenced more by family considerations than by romantic love. My family can understand me better than anyone else. They will suggest possible partners with whom I will be able to get along well. Romantic love may develop later."

B. Write a paragraph explaining your point of view about finding and deciding on a marriage partner. Use at least two of each of the following types of modals: ability (e.g., *be able to, can*), belief (e.g., *could, will, may, might, must*), and social (e.g., *be supposed to, must, have to, should*).

More about Modals

15

Introductory Task: *Giving Advice*

A. You are Addy Viser, the writer of a newspaper advice column. You have received the following letter.

> Dear Addy Viser,
>
> I'm twenty-five years old. A year ago I fell in love with a woman named Irene. Irene and I wanted to get married, but when my parents found out, they didn't approve because they've never gotten along with her family. My friends thought that I should follow my heart and marry Irene. But I listened to my family's advice and decided not to marry her. Irene married another man yesterday. Now I realize that I can never love anyone else as much as I love Irene, and I feel regretful. **I should have listened** to my friends instead of my family. Do you agree?
>
> Regretful

Read the following possible responses to "Regretful." Check the one that you think is best.

_____ Yes, you **should have listened** to your friends. You **shouldn't have let** your parents' opinion influence you. You **ought to have done** what was right for you.

_____ No, you **shouldn't have followed** your friends' advice. Marriages between people whose families don't get along can be very difficult. Besides, you say that Irene married another man. She **couldn't have loved** you as much as you loved her.

_____ You **should have gotten** advice from a professional counselor. With a counselor's help, you **might have worked** things out with your family. Things **could have turned** out more happily for you.

B. As a class, discuss your responses. Does anyone have other ideas about what "Regretful" should have done in this situation? Use *should have* and *shouldn't have* to give your opinion.

> Example: *"Regretful" should have asked a sympathetic aunt or grandmother to talk to his parents.*

GRAMMAR BRIEFING 1: Perfect Modals; Belief Modals in the Past

The perfect forms of modals are used in talking about the past. Belief modals that express degrees of certainty about what happened in the past include *must have, have to have, should have, ought to have, may have, might have,* and *could have.*

FORM AND FUNCTION Perfect Modals

Form

■ The perfect form of modals consists of: modal + *have* + past participle.

> She **should have arrived** an hour ago.

■ In negative statements, include *not* between *have* and the past participle.

> She **must not (mustn't) have gone** home.

In questions, use: modal + subject + *have* + past participle, for *yes/no* questions; *wh-* word + modal (+ subject) + *have* + past participle, for *wh-* questions.

> **Should** they **have called?** (*yes/no* question)
>
> Who **should** they **have called?** (*wh-* question about the predicate)
>
> Who **should have called?** (*wh-* question about the subject)

Function

■ Modals in the perfect form make it possible to use belief and social modals in talking about past time.*

> She must speak Spanish fluently now; in fact, she **might have spoken** it as a child. (belief modal)
>
> You should look for a new job now; I think you **should have looked** years ago. (social modal)

* As discussed in Chapter 14, phrasal modals that begin with *be* or *have* express past time with the past form of *be* or *have* (*was/were able to, had to, was/were supposed to,* etc.). Remember that *have got to* does not have a past form.

FUNCTION Belief Modals in the Past

■ Modals in the perfect form express different degrees of certainty about events and situations in the past.

Degree of Certainty	Modal—Affirmative Sentence	Modal—Negative Sentence
strongly certain	must have, have to have, have got to have	could not have (couldn't have), cannot have (can't have), must not have (mustn't have)
	should have, ought to have	should not have (shouldn't have)
not very certain	may have, might have, could have	may not have, might not have (mightn't have)

■ The degrees of certainty these modals express are similar to those they express when used to talk about the present (see Chapter 14, Grammar Briefing 2, page 260). For example:

> The thief **must have** escaped through a window. All the doors are locked. (strong certainty)

> The thief **could have** escaped through a window. Or he **could have** sneaked out the back door. (weak certainty—possibility)

> The thief **couldn't have** escaped. The police had completely surrounded the area. (strong certainty)

Notice that, like *couldn't* and *can't*, *couldn't have* and *can't have* express strong certainty.

■ All past belief modals are in the perfect form, including the two phrasal modals that begin with *have* (*have to have* and *have got to have*). (The form *had to* is for the social modal use of *have to*; see Grammar Briefing 2.) *Have got to have* is not often used. *Have to have* is less common than *must have*.

> The life of the typical American pioneer **must have / has to have** been exciting but very difficult.

TALKING the TALK

■ In speech, *have* in the modal perfects is often pronounced "of" or "a." In writing use *have*.

> We **should have** tried harder. = "We **should-of / shoulda** tried harder."

> He **couldn't have** gone there. = "He **couldn't-of / couldn'ta** gone there."

GRAMMAR PRACTICE 1: Perfect Modals; Belief Modals in the Past

1 Perfect Modals—Form: *The Dangers of Romantic Love*

Use the words in parentheses to complete the sentences. Use contractions with *not* where possible.

Maria: Romantic love can lead to tragedy. Do you remember the story of Romeo and

Juliet? They ___had to keep___ (have to / keep) their love a secret because
               1

their families were enemies. Juliet _____ (be supposed to / marry)
                                            2

Count Paris.

Stella: But their story _____ (have to / not / end) tragically.
                              3

Maria: _____ (Juliet / should / obey) her father?
            4

Stella: No, but Romeo and Juliet _____ (should / be) smarter.
                                         5

Maria: How?

Stella: First of all, Romeo _____ (should / not / kill) himself.

                       6

Maria: But Romeo thought that Juliet had died. He _____ (could / not /

                                                   7

know) that she wasn't really dead.

Stella: He _____ (might / try) to find out for sure. He _____

                    8   9

(ought to / rescue) her.

Maria: What _____ (Juliet / should / do) when she discovered that

                        10

Romeo was dead? Without him, she _____ (be able to / not / go

                                                     11

on) living.

Stella: She _____ (have to have / love) him very much. But Juliet was only

                    12

thirteen. She _____ (might / meet) someone else.

                        13

Maria: I don't think so, Stella. Remember, she had to marry Count Paris.

Stella: Poor Juliet! She really was in a bad situation, wasn't she?

2   Perfect Modals: *A Communication Problem?*

Frank is the host of a radio program, "Speaking Frankly." People call him for advice about relationships. Listen to the dialogue once for the main ideas. Then listen again and complete the sentences with the words that you hear. You will hear contracted forms, but you should write full forms.

Frank: Hello! You're on the air. What's your relationship problem?

Elise: Hi, Frank. This is Elise from California. I had a problem with my boyfriend

the other night, and I want to know what I _should have_ done about it.

                                           1

We were driving to our friends' new house, and we got lost. We finally found

the house, but it _should not have_ taken us three hours to do it.

                              2

Frank: Let me guess. Your boyfriend _____ been driving. He

                                           3

_____ asked someone for directions, but he didn't do it.

                4

Elise: Right! How did you know? There were several times when he

_____ stopped to ask someone, but he didn't.

                5

Frank: Elise, try to think of the situation from your boyfriend's point of view.

Imagine that he had stopped to ask someone. You _____ thought
                                                          6

that he wasn't fully in control of the situation.

Elise: He wasn't fully in control of the situation. He _____ asked some-
                                                                   7

one.

Frank: You _____ found the house any faster that way. That person
                        8

_____ known where it was but _____ tried to be helpful
            9   10

and given wrong directions.

Elise: When we finally found the house, our friends had gone out without us. They

_____ wanted to keep waiting. I guess I _____ com-
            11   12

plained, but I did.

Frank: You _____ been upset. But your boyfriend probably
                        13

_____ done anything differently. A lot of men just have a very hard
            14

time asking for directions.

Elise: I understand that now. Thanks, Frank.

3   Belief Modals in the Past—Function: *The Mystery of a Long-Term Marriage*

A. Don's elderly parents live in a small town far from Don. On June 8, he called the captain of the town's police department. Complete the following dialogue with *must have, have to have, have got to have, should have, ought to have, may have, might have,* and *could have.* For each completion, write all the modals that work best in the context. Use *not* where necessary. Use contractions with *not* where possible.

Don: I'm very worried about my parents, Captain. Something strange

<u>must have / has to have / has got to have</u> happened to them. There isn't
                           1

any other explanation for the situation. I tried calling them at noon. They

<u>shouldn't have</u> been out then. They almost always have lunch together
        2

at home at noon. But no one answered.

Captain: I wouldn't worry. There are lots of possibilities. They _____
                                                                             3

gone for a drive.

Don: I called the neighbors. They said that my parents' car is in the driveway.

Captain: In that case, they _____ have gone for a drive in their car. Did
4

the neighbors go inside the house to look around?

Don: No. The door was locked. And they couldn't see inside—my parents

_____ left the curtains closed.
5

Captain: Did the neighbors see anything in the mailbox?

Don: They didn't say, but there probably wasn't any mail. At least, there

_____ been mail, because it usually isn't delivered until later.
6

Also, the neighbors told me that my mother missed the meeting at the

Senior Center this morning.

Captain: There are possible explanations for that. She _____ remem-
7

bered about the meeting.

Don: My mother writes notes to remind herself of things. My parents have dis-

appeared.

Captain: They _____ disappeared. That's highly unlikely. But since you're
8

so worried, I'll go over and take a look.

Don: Thank you. They _____ left a key under the doormat. They usu-
9

ally do.

B. The police captain didn't find Don's parents, but he did find evidence. He thought
about possibilities and drew conclusions. Write sentences using *must have, have to
have, have got to have, could have, may have,* and *might have.* You can write any sentence that fits with the information. Use *not* where necessary.

1. Everything was very orderly in the house.

   He thought: ___They must not have left in a hurry.___

2. Then he found a note that said, "Call travel agency again."

   He thought: ___They may have gone on a trip.___

3. He found an invitation on the desk: "Susie and Jack are to be married in June.
   Please join us for their wedding in Omaha if you can."

   He thought: _____

4. He found a note written by Don's mother that said, "Decline wedding invitation?"

   He thought: _____

5. He saw a brochure from the travel agent, "Antarctic Adventures for Seniors."

   He thought: _____

6. All their warm clothes were still in the closets, and it's winter in Antarctica in June.

   He thought: _____

7. He found a box labeled "Beach Umbrellas." It was empty.

8. He thought: _____

9. He found a receipt on the desk for two tickets to Honolulu on June 8 at 5 A.M.

   He thought: _____

10. He found a note that said, "Don't forget to tell Don about our fiftieth wedding anniversary trip."

    He thought: _____
    The captain called Don. What did he tell him?

4 Using Belief Modals in the Past: *Married Couples*

1.   2.   3.

Work with a partner. Look at the couples in the photographs. What are your impressions of their marriages and lives? Use belief modals in the past to describe their life together before the photo was taken.

> Example: They must have been married for a long time. They might not have had an easy life. They may have had to work very hard.

GRAMMAR BRIEFING 2: Social Modals in the Past

Social modals used in the past include *could have, might have, be supposed to, be to, should have, ought to have, had better have,* and *have to.* These modals are used to talk about what was advisable in the past. They express suggestions, expectations, obligations, and so forth. (Requests for permission, requests, and offers aren't made in past time.)

FORM AND FUNCTION Social Modals in the Past

- The social modals used to talk about the past express degrees of strength similar to those expressed by the social modals used to talk about the present. Using these modals often suggests that something advisable did not happen.

Meaning	One-Word Modals	Other Modals
Suggestion	could have, might have	
Advice/opinion	should have	ought to have
Expectation		be supposed to, be to
Warning		had better have
Necessity		have to
Lack of necessity		not have to
Prohibition	could not (couldn't)	not be allowed to

- As discussed, *be supposed to, be to, have to,* and *not be allowed to* occur with the past forms of *be* and *have.*

   We **were supposed to** read Chapter 14 last week.

- *Could have* and *might have* suggest possibilities that did not occur. *Could have,* which is used more, often implies that an opportunity was lost. Both modals often imply a complaint or criticism.

   He **could have played** basketball in the Olympics, but he broke his leg. (lost opportunity)

   You're late. You **might have called.** (implied complaint)

- *Should have* and *ought to have* are often used to say that something was a good idea but didn't happen or (with the negative of *should*) was a bad idea and did happen.* Both modals imply criticism or regret.

   You **ought to have gone** home as soon as you felt sick. (Going home was a good idea, but you didn't go home—implied criticism.)

   I **shouldn't have stayed** up so late last night. (Staying up late was a bad idea, but I stayed up late—implied regret.)

* Remember, *ought to* is usually not used in the negative or in questions.

- *Be to* and *be supposed to* are used to talk about something that was expected or planned but didn't happen.

   You're late. You **were (supposed) to** be here at nine o'clock.

- *Had better have* is used to give warnings about past actions.

   You**'d better** not **have left** all the lights on downstairs.

- *Had to* is used to express past necessity. *Didn't have to* expresses a lack of necessity. Prohibition in the past is expressed by *couldn't* or *not be allowed to.*

   He **had to** work this weekend, but he **didn't have to** finish the project.

   As children, we **couldn't / weren't allowed to** watch TV until our homework was done.

GRAMMAR HOTSPOT!

■ *Must have* is only a belief modal. Unlike *must,* it cannot express necessity or prohibition.

Necessity:

Yesterday I had to take my brother to the airport.

Not: Yesterday I ~~must have taken~~ my brother to the airport.

Prohibition:

He couldn't take more than two bags.

Not: He ~~must not have taken~~ more than two bags.

GRAMMAR PRACTICE 2: Social Modals in the Past

5   Social Modals in the Past: *Nana's Rules*

A. Rachel is talking to her grandmother, Nana. The material in brackets tells you what they are thinking. Complete each sentence with all the modals appropriate to expressing their thoughts. Use *could have, might have, should have, ought to have, be supposed to, be to, had better have, have to, could,* and *be allowed to.* Use *not* where necessary. Use contractions where possible.

Nana: Rachel, you're thirty-five years old, and you're not married yet. You

     <u>should have / ought to have</u> found Mr. Right by now. [This was a good
                 1

idea, but you haven't done it.]

Rachel: I've tried, Nana. For example, I met a man named Owen at a party. I went

up to him and introduced myself.

Nana: You __shouldn't have__ talked to him first. [It was a bad idea, but you did it.]
            2

You _____ waited for him to introduce himself. [This was a good
                     3

idea, but you didn't do it.]

Rachel: Owen _____ call me the next day. [This was what we planned
                                4

and what I expected.] But he didn't. So I called him.

Nana: You _____ have called him. [This was a bad idea, but you did it.]
                   5

You _____ waited longer. [This is one suggestion.] Or you
                     6

_____ just forgotten about him. [This is another suggestion.]
              7

There are plenty of other nice men.

Rachel: Anyway, I invited him to meet me for dinner. He said that he couldn't

because he _____ work. [It was a necessity.] But that night I saw
                          8

him in a restaurant with someone who certainly wasn't his boss. He

_____ work. [It wasn't a necessity.] He _____ told me
              9   10

the truth. [This was a possibility but it didn't occur, and I'm complaining.]

But then I met Eric.

Nana: Rachel, you _____ invited him out, too. [This is a warning.]
                              11

Rachel: I did. He was shy, so I _____ take the initiative. [It was a neces-
                                          12

sity.] But things didn't work out with him, either.

Nana: Rachel, you _____ found Mr. Right by now, but you didn't follow
                              13

the rules. [You lost the opportunity.] When I was young, women

_____ take the initiative with men. [It was prohibited.] We
              14

_____ speak to a man first or invite him out. [It was prohibited.]
              15

But this was good. We _____ worry about getting involved with
                                16

men who weren't interested. [It wasn't a necessity.] Also, men like to take

the lead. If you follow the old rules, Mr. Right will come to you. I

_____ explained all this to you earlier! [This was a good idea, but
              17

I didn't do it.]

B. In many cultures, dating rules have changed. Write **two** sentences about things that weren't permitted in the past in a culture that you know about. Use *could not* or *not be allowed to*.

> Example: Women weren't allowed to go out with men without a chaperone.

6 Using Social Modals in the Past: *Communication Problems?*

You're Addy Viser. Work with a partner. Read and discuss the following two letters, which people have written to your newspaper advice column. In your opinion, did they do the right thing or should they have done things differently? Write your responses. Use *could have, might have, ought to have,* and *should have* in your sentences. Include some sentences with *not.*

> 1. Dear Addy Viser,
>
>   My wife and I recently celebrated our fifth anniversary. As a surprise for my wife, I got tickets to a Dar Williams concert, because I thought that was her favorite singer. I kept our destination a secret until we got to the concert. After we sat down, she told me that the singer she likes is Lucinda Williams. The evening wasn't perfect, because my wife was disappointed. I didn't feel so good, either.
>
>   Peter

Example:

> Dear Peter, Your wife ought to have appreciated the special effort you made to surprise her. . . . OR You shouldn't have bought tickets before making sure of the name of your wife's favorite singer. . . .

> 2. Dear Addy Viser,
>
>   My boyfriend asked me to look after his houseplants for a month while he was gone. I agreed to do it, although I wasn't really sure what to do. I drove ten miles to his house every day to water them, and I put lots of fertilizer on them. I don't know why, but the plants are nearly dead now. My boyfriend came back yesterday. He didn't thank me for looking after the plants, and he hasn't been as cheerful as he usually is.
>
>   Barbara

7 **Belief and Social Modals in the Past:** *Which Words Should Addy Viser Have Used?*

Circle the correct choice. If both are correct, circle both.

Dear Addy Viser,

I met a woman named Rachel last month and called her the next Saturday afternoon for a date that night. She said that she couldn't go out with me because she (1) [had to help/must have helped] her grandmother. The next week I called her office and left a message for her to call me. I know that she (2)[had to get/must have gotten] the message because her secretary told me she put it on her desk. I (3)[didn't have to work/mustn't have worked] that weekend, so I waited at home for her to call, but she never did. (4) [Ought I to/Should I] have called her again?

Wondering

Dear Wondering,

Yes, you (5) [ought to/should] have called Rachel again. You know she (6) [has to/must] have gotten the message, but you don't know why she didn't respond. Maybe she's decided to follow the old social rules. In the past, women (7) [had to/must have] let men take the lead. They (8) [couldn't telephone/mustn't have telephoned] a man to tell him they wanted to go out. And maybe she wanted to keep your interest by not seeming too eager.

P.S. You (9) [oughtn't to/shouldn't] have waited until Saturday afternoon to call for a date on Saturday night. You (10) [might/could] have asked her for a date for the following Saturday instead. Next time, don't call later than Wednesday!

GRAMMAR BRIEFING 3: Progressive Modals and Perfect Progressive Modals

Progressive modals are used in talking about actions in progress in the present and future. Perfect progressive modals are used in talking about actions in progress in the past.

FORM AND FUNCTION Progressive and Perfect Progressive Modals

Form

■ The progressive form of modals consists of: modal + *be* + verb + *-ing*.

> You **must be joking.**

■ The perfect progressive form of modals consists of: modal + *have* + *been* + verb + *-ing*.

> You **must have been joking.**

■ In negative statements, include *not* after the modal.

> He **couldn't be thinking** seriously about this.
> He **couldn't have been thinking** seriously about this.

Function

- Modals in the progressive form are used instead of modal + base form of verb to emphasize action in progress in the present or future.

    She **must be working** now.

    We **might be working** on the project all next year.

- Modals in the perfect progressive form are used instead of perfect modals to emphasize action in progress in the past.

    He **must not have been paying** attention while the boss was talking.

    He **shouldn't have been sitting** by the pool when everyone else was working.

GRAMMAR PRACTICE 3: Progressive Modals and Perfect Progressive Modals

8 Progressive and Perfect Progressive Modals—Form: *The Symptoms of Romantic Love*

A. Social scientists define "romantic love" as an intense attraction and longing to be with the loved one. People who are experiencing romantic love talk and think about each other constantly. Complete the sentences in the following conversations with the words in parentheses. If possible, put the modals into the progressive or perfect progressive form. (Remember that some verbs can't be used in the progressive.) Use contractions with *not* where possible.

Before class:

Lisa: Hey, Tony! How are things going with Maria?

Tony: I haven't talked to her yet today. I called her this morning, but she didn't

answer. She __mustn't have been__ (must / not / be) home. She
                    1

__could have been jogging__ (could / jog). Or she _____ (might / ride)
              2   3

her bike. Right now, though, she _____ (must / do) her homework.
                                              4

She _____ (could / sit) in the library. Or she _____
          5   6

(might / be) in the computer lab.

Lisa: Are you two going out tonight?

Tony: Yeah, we are. At seven she and I _____ (be going to / eat) dinner.
                                                  7

And by nine we _____ (will / dance) to our favorite song.
                    8

After class:

Anita: Something seems to be wrong with Tony. _____ (he / could / get)
9

sick?

Lisa: No, I don't think so. Why?

Anita: When the teacher asked him a question, he couldn't answer it. He

_____ (ought to / know) the answer. She had just explained the
10

problem. He _____ (could / not / pay) attention.
11

Lisa: Well, he _____ (should / not / daydream), but he couldn't help it.
12

He's in love with Maria.

Anita: That explains everything!

B. Imagine that you know Tony and Maria. What would you think in the following situations? Write the number of sentences indicated. Use appropriate modals (e.g., *must, might, could, should,* and *ought to*) in the progressive or perfect progressive form. Include *not* in at least three sentences.

1. Maria has a class in room 203 from 11 to 12 every day. You saw Tony standing outside room 203 at 11:55 yesterday. (1 sentence)

    Tony must have been waiting for Maria.

2. You telephoned both Tony and Maria last night, but their lines were busy. (1 sentence)

3. You saw Tony in a flower shop this morning. Tomorrow is Mother's Day. (2 sentences)

4. You're in class with Tony. The teacher is lecturing, and Tony is staring out the window. (3 sentences)

5. Tony has two exams tomorrow. You see him writing a love letter to Maria. (2 sentences)

9 Using Perfect, Progressive, and Perfect Progressive Modals: *What Was Your Problem?*

A. Write a letter to Addy Viser's advice column. Describe a problem, either a real one or one you make up, that you had with another person, for example, a friend, coworker, husband, or wife. Ask for advice. In your letter, use at least two modals in the past (e.g., *I shouldn't have told her about my old girlfriend.*), at least one modal in the progressive form (e.g., *She might be thinking about ending our relationship.*), and at least one modal in the past progressive form (e.g., *She must have been talking to another man last night.*).

B. Work with a partner. Exchange letters. Write responses giving advice and suggestions about handling the problems. Use some modals in the past. Include at least one modal in the progressive form and at least one modal in the past progressive form.

UNIT WRAP-UP

Error Correction

Find and correct the errors in modals and modal-like expressions. Some errors can be corrected in more than one way. Including the example, there are 12 errors.

must have heard

By now, you ~~must hear~~ of Ms. Monish, the marriage counselor whose advice column appears in hundreds of newspapers. Every day thousands of people write to Ms. Monish. They ask her, "May you give me some advice?" or "I was confused. What should I have done?" When people tell her they are considering divorce, she responds, "Surely, you must joke. You shouldn't get a divorce. You are able to work out your marriage problems in the future." Recently, she criticized a divorced woman by telling her, "You mustn't have divorced your husband. You should have try harder." Sometimes she writes, "A man's way of communicating can be different from a woman's. You ought to try to understand your husband better."

Because so many people read Ms. Monish's column and follow her advice, I wanted to know more about her background and qualifications. I finally could interview her one day. But when I talked to her, I mustn't find out much because she refused to answer my questions about her past. In order to learn more, I must ask other people. One of her friends told me that Ms. Monish has been married and divorced twice. When I heard this, I thought, "Ms. Monish has to have had marriage problems of her own in the past. She mustn't have worked those problems out very well." Her friend told me, "Ms. Monish's first marriage mustn't break up. And her second marriage hadn't got to, either. She couldn't communicate well with her husbands, and now she regrets it. But she must of learned a lot from her experiences."

Task 1: Describing Yourself and Your Ideal Spouse

Imagine that you have gone to a matchmaker to find your ideal husband or wife. The matchmaker needs some information from you. Write short paragraphs to answer the questions in 1, and write a longer paragraph to answer the questions in 2.

1. What abilities do you or don't you have now? What abilities do you expect to have in the future? (Use *can* and *be able to*.)

   Example: I can't cook very well, but I can wash dishes. . . . Two years from now I'll be able to program computers.

2. What abilities does your ideal mate have? (Use *can* and *be able to*.) What qualities are possible, necessary, or not necessary in your ideal mate? (Use *can, might, could, should, ought to, must, have to*, and *have got to*.)

   Example: My ideal husband is someone who can cook very well. . . . He doesn't have to be handsome, but he must have a sense of humor. . . .

Task 2: Join the Politeness Patrol

A. Work with a partner. As members of the "Politeness Patrol," your task is to change impolite (i.e., abrupt or inappropriate) requests, offers, and responses into polite ones, using modals and other polite expressions.

1. a. *Young student:* Hey, there. I need change for a dollar. Give me some.

   Older stranger: Here.

   b. *Young student:* Excuse me. Could you please give me change for a dollar?

   Older stranger: Certainly I can.

2. a. *Man, asking for a date:* Want to go to a movie?

   Woman: No way. I'm busy.

   b. *Man, asking for a date:* _____

   Woman: _____

3. a. *Student:* I'm going to carry your books for you.

   Teacher: Do it.

   b. *Student:* _____

   Teacher: _____

4. a. *Guest:* Those apples look good. You're going to let me have one.

   Host: Take it.

   b. *Guest:* _____

   Host: _____

B. Now think of typical situations where people ask permission, make requests, or make offers (e.g., asking permission to use someone's phone). Write two "impolite" dialogues like those in **A.** Then write the same dialogues in a polite version, using modals and other polite expressions. Present both versions to the class. Use the tone of your voice to make the impolite dialogues sound very impolite and the polite dialogues sound very polite.

Task 3: Dilemmas

A. Work in groups of three. Discuss the following difficult situations. Use belief and social modals in the past—for example, *may (not) have* and *should (not) have*. Use belief modals to make predictions about the future—for example, *might (not)* and *will (not)*. Then decide what actions are possible, advisable or not advisable, and necessary or not necessary for Pauline and Carol to take. Use social modals—for example, *could, should (not), must (not),* and *(not) have to.*

1. *Pauline:* I have a good friend named Marcia, who has been married for a year to a man named Bruce. Last Friday night I went to a movie alone. While I was in the theater, I noticed that Bruce was sitting in the row ahead of me. (I'm sure that Bruce didn't see me.) I was very surprised to see that he was at the movie with a woman that I didn't recognize. I haven't told Marcia about this. I've been worrying about it, and I'm not sure what to do.

2. *Carol:* Six months ago, Michael asked me to marry him, and I accepted his proposal because he is a very kind and responsible man. Everyone in my family likes Michael very much. Three hundred people have been invited to our wedding, which is scheduled to take place in two weeks. Last week I ran into Austin. I had fallen in love with Austin in high school, but we hadn't seen each other for a long time because we went to colleges in different cities. He was disappointed to hear about my marriage plans. Now all of my old feelings for Austin are coming back.

B. On your own, choose **one** of the two situations. Write a paragraph about it and the actions you think are possible, advisable, or necessary for Pauline or Carol to take. Use any appropriate modals and perfect modals, including at least five of the following: *could (have), may (have), might (have), have to (have), must (have), should (have),* and *ought to (have).*

Unit Eight

Passives

Topic Focus: *World of Sports*

UNIT OBJECTIVES

- **passive sentences in different tenses**
  (Medals *are awarded* in every Olympics. A Canadian *was awarded* the first Olympic medal for snowboarding.)
- **passive sentences versus active sentences**
  (The ball was hit by Hank Aaron. Hank Aaron hit the ball.)
- **passive sentences with and without agents**
  (Sports are played *by professional and amateur athletes.* Sports are played in many different places.)
- **get passives**
  (Professional athletes *get paid* large salaries.)
- **passive causatives**
  (The team *had new astroturf put in* the stadium.)

INTRODUCTORY TASKS

Reading and Listening

Read and listen to this passage.

The World of Sports

Sports **are being played** by increasing numbers of athletes. Moreover, great strides **have been made** by athletes in recent years. In the past, years often went by before new records **were set**. But now records **are being broken** at an ever faster pace by ever stronger and more focused athletes. Some old records **haven't been broken** yet but likely **will be broken** in the not-too-distant future.

Sports have become a huge entertainment industry. Sports events **are attended** by millions of devoted fans. Many more fans **can be found** in front of their televisions on the days that their teams play. Some fans spend a lot of time and money following their favorite teams and athletes.

Sports **are played** in facilities that are architectural and engineering wonders. Large, modern arenas and stadiums have opened in many cities, new ones **are being built,** and more **will be constructed** in the future.

Millions of dollars are **being spent** on sports every year. Modern stadiums are expensive, and large salaries **are paid** to top professional athletes. Who will pay these costs? Many people believe that too much money **is being spent** on new stadiums and that such large salaries **shouldn't be paid** to professional athletes. **Can** fans **be expected** to support the costs? Tickets for some sports events have become so expensive that many fans can't afford them. **Will** these fans **be forgotten** by the sports industry as it goes after larger profits elsewhere? Corporate sponsors are purchasing box seats and season tickets that are too expensive for the average fan.

What is the future of sports? Can the sports industry continue to pay high salaries and build expensive new stadiums? Some experts predict that the costs will become greater than the profits. This may cause problems for one of the world's top entertainment industries.

Comprehension Check

Read each sentence. Circle **T** if the sentence is true or **F** if the sentence is false.

1. Many athletic records have been broken.   (**T**)   **F**

2. Most professional athletes receive large salaries.   **T**   **F**

3. Everyone agrees that money should be spent on new stadiums.   **T**   **F**

4. Fans can always afford tickets to sports events.   **T**   **F**

5. The sports industry may face problems in the future.   **T**   **F**

Think about Grammar

A. Look at the following active and passive sentences and complete the statements.

> Active sentence: Increasing numbers of athletes play sports.
>
> Passive sentence: Sports are played by increasing numbers of athletes.

1. The subject of the active sentence is the words _____. The object of

   the active sentence is the word _____.

2. The object of the active sentence becomes the _____ of the passive

   sentence. The subject of the active sentence appears in the passive sentence fol-

   lowing the word _____.

3. In an active sentence, the subject is the **performer** of the action of the verb and

   the object is the **receiver** of the action of the verb. In a passive sentence, in con-

   trast, the _____ is the receiver of the action of the verb, and the per-

   former follows the word _____.

B. In the reading passage, the sentences with **boldfaced** verbs are passive.
Find a passive:

1. in the simple present   _are attended_

2. in the present progressive   _____

3. in the simple past   _____

4. in the future   _____

5. in the present perfect   _____

6. in the negative   _____

7. with a modal   _____

chapter 16

Passive Overview

A. Fill in each blank with the letter of the sport that completes the sentence. See how many answers you can get right! Compare answers with your classmates.

a. American football
b. Baseball
c. Basketball
d. Bowling

e. Golf
f. Ice hockey
g. Lacrosse
h. Snowboarding

i. Soccer
j. Swimming
k. Volleyball

1. ____b____ **is** often **called** "America's national pastime."

2. _____ **was developed** from rugby and soccer.

3. _____ **was invented** in Scotland.

4. _____ **couldn't have been invented** in a warm climate.

5. _____ **is being played** professionally in more countries than any other sport.

6. _____ **hadn't** yet **been invented** in the 1950s but became popular by the 1980s.

7. _____ **may be considered** one of the earliest sports.

8. _____ **has been played** since 1895, with points being scored when a ball **is hit** over the net and **isn't returned** by the other team.

9. _____ **was being played** by Native Americans before Europeans came to America.

10. _____ **was created** in December 1891 as an indoor winter sport.

11. _____ **will** probably **not be included** in the Olympics even though professional competitions **have been held** for years.

Check your answers on Exercise Page E–5.

B. Work with a partner. Take turns asking and answering the following questions.

1. Which sports **are being played** at this time of the year?

2. Which sports **are played** by teams?

3. Which sports **are** usually **considered** individual sports?

4. Which sports **are watched** by many people?

5. Which sports **have been televised?**

6. Which sports **were invented** recently?

GRAMMAR BRIEFING 1: Form of Passive Sentences

Passive sentences are formed using *be* plus the past participle of the main verb. Passive sentences can be formed with verbs in any tense. Only transitive verbs can be used.

FORM Passive Sentences

■ To form passive sentences, use: a form of *be* + past participle of main verb.*

> Some football games **are played** on Monday nights.
>
> The house on the corner **was designed** by a well-known architect.

* See Appendix 7 for the past participles of irregular verbs.

Passive Sentences versus Active Sentences

■ Passive sentences differ in form from active sentences in three ways:

- Passive sentences use *be* + the past participle of the main verb.
- The object of an active sentence becomes the subject of a passive sentence.
- The subject of an active sentence, if included in the passive sentence, occurs in a prepositional phrase beginning with *by*.

>   subject   verb   object
> Active sentence: The committee **sends out** notices each Tuesday.

>   subject   verb   prepositional phrase
> Passive sentence: Notices **are sent out** (by the committee) each Tuesday.

Passive Sentences with Verbs in Different Tenses

■ Passive sentences can have verbs in any tense.* For example:

Simple present	The grass **is watered** (every evening).
Simple past	The grass **was watered.**
Future	The grass **will / is going to be watered.**
Present progressive	The grass **is being watered.**
Past progressive	The grass **was being watered.**
Present perfect	The grass **has been watered.**
Past perfect	The grass **had been watered.**

* Although possible, passives are less common with tenses not shown (e.g., present perfect progressive). The reason is that a verb with many auxiliaries can sound awkward (e.g., *has been being watered*).

■ Passive sentences can also include modals.

> The new plans **might be discussed** at today's meeting.
>
> The new plans **might have been discussed** at yesterday's meeting.

■ To form negative passive sentences, place *not* after the first auxiliary.

> The grass **isn't watered** very often.
>
> The plans **might not have been discussed** at the meeting.

■ To form questions with passives, use:

- first auxiliary + subject + (other auxiliaries +) past participle of main verb, for yes/no questions;
- (wh- word +) first auxiliary + (subject +) (other auxiliaries +) past participle of main verb, for *wh-* questions.

> **Is** today's game **being broadcast** by CBS? (*yes/no* question)
>
> **Why have** we **been told** so many lies? (*wh-* question about predicate)
>
> **Who was chosen** for the team? (*wh-* question about subject)

Verb Types and Passive Sentences

■ Passive sentences can be formed only with transitive verbs—that is, verbs that take objects in active sentences. (Remember, the subject of a passive sentence corresponds to the object in an active sentence.) Passive sentences are not formed with intransitive verbs, which do not have objects. (Common intransitive verbs include *appear, arrive, be, belong, collide, come, cry, die, disappear, emerge, fall, go, happen, look, occur, rain, seem, sleep, snow, stand, stay,* and *walk.*)

> A truck **hit** my car. (Transitive verb, active sentence—*my car* is an object.)
>
> My car **was hit** by a truck. (Transitive verb, passive sentence—*my car* is a subject.)
>
> The two vehicles **collided.** (Intransitive verb, active sentence—*collided* isn't followed by an object; no passive sentence is possible.)

Notice that transitive phrasal verbs can be used to form passives. (For phrasal verbs, see Chapter 7, Grammar Briefing 1, page 114.)

> At the last moment the meeting **was called off.**

■ Some transitive verbs are not used in passive sentences. These verbs include *cost, fit, have, lack, measure* (in stative meaning), *resemble, suit,* and *weigh* (in stative meaning).

> The tickets **cost** fifty dollars.   **Not:** ~~Fifty dollars was cost (by the tickets).~~

■ Some transitive verbs take a direct object and an indirect object (e.g., *give, tell*). Either object can be subject of a passive sentence.

> IO   DO   DO   IO
> My parents told **me that story.** (OR My parents told **that story** to me.) (Active sentence)
>
> Subject
> **That story** was told (to) **me** by my parents. (Passive sentence)
>
> Subject
> **I** was told that story by my parents. (Passive sentence)

■ A few verbs occur only in passive sentences. The most common of these is *be born.*

> Cecilia **was born** in Centralia.

GRAMMAR HOTSPOT!

■ Remember! Verbs like *happen* and *seem* are not transitive and are not used in passive sentences.

> An accident **happened.**   **Not:** An accident ~~was happened.~~
>
> They **seemed** happy.   **Not:** They ~~were seemed happy.~~

GRAMMAR PRACTICE 1: Form of Passive Sentences

1 Forming Passive Sentences: *Names for Sports Facilities*

Underline the objects in the active sentences. Remember to underline the entire noun phrase. Complete the passive sentence. Do not include the *by* phrase.

1. Today sports teams can earn a lot of money from the places where sports are played.

   Today ___*a lot of money can be earned*___ from the places where sports are played.

2. Teams often name sports facilities for sponsors, companies that pay in return for publicity.

   _____ for sponsors, companies that pay in return for publicity.

3. In the past, teams didn't name sports facilities for sponsors.

   In the past, _____ for sponsors.

4. Teams named sports facilities for famous players and coaches.

   _____ for famous players and coaches.

5. Why do teams name sports facilities for sponsors?

   Why _____ for sponsors?

6. Sponsors pay large fees to the teams in return for the use of the sponsors' names.

   _____ to the teams in return for the use of the sponsors' names.

7. Teams have named sports facilities for airline sponsors.

   _____ for airline sponsors.

8. Will teams name all sports facilities for sponsors in the future?

   _____ for sponsors in the future?

9. According to many people, teams shouldn't name sports facilities for sponsors.

   According to many people, _____ for sponsors.

10. However, the large fees that sponsors pay lower the total cost of a sports facility.

    However, _____ by the large fees that sponsors pay.

2 Passive Sentences with Verbs in Different Tenses—Form: *The Places Where Sports Are Played*

Use the words in parentheses to complete the passive sentences. Use appropriate verb tenses. Use contractions with negatives.

Eric: This is Eric Wilson on San Diego's number one sports radio station. Kevin

White, sportscaster for KXYZ TV in Denver, is with me today. With its five

professional sport teams, Denver __is considered__ (consider) one of the
                                              1

most sports-crazed cities in the U.S. Exciting changes are happening now in

the places where sports _____ (play) in Denver. Kevin, let's start
                                      2

with Mile High Stadium, where Broncos football and Colorado Rapids soc-

cer _____ (play). When _____ (it, build)?
            3   4

Kevin: In 1948, but it _____ (not, call) Mile High then. The original name
                                  5

was Bears Stadium, and it _____ (use) for baseball, but since 1960
                                      6

Broncos football _____ (play) there. Over the years, Mile High
                              7

_____ (call) the loudest outdoor stadium in North America
        8

because Broncos fans are so devoted.

Eric: What is the future of Mile High? After all, it's getting pretty old.

Kevin: You're right. Plans for a new stadium _____ (finalize) now.
                                                              9

Eric: Where _____ (the new stadium/build)?
                      10

Kevin: The city will build the new stadium on the same site. But, first, the fate of

McNichols Arena _____ (must, decide), too.
                            11

Eric: What is McNichols Arena?

Kevin: It's home to Nuggets basketball and Avalanche ice hockey. The architects for

the Broncos' new stadium believe that McNichols _____ (should,
                                                                12

demolish) right away to make way for the stadium. City officials believe that

McNichols _____ (can, use) for special events until a new arena,
                  13

the Pepsi Center, _____ (complete).
                          14

Eric: _____ (The Pepsi Center, finance) with tax money?
              15

Kevin: No, it _____ (finance) privately with some of the money coming
               16

from Pepsi.

Eric: What about Coors Field, where the Colorado Rockies play?

Kevin: Coors Field, which opened in 1995, _____ (design) to combine
                                                           17

modern comfort with old-time atmosphere. True to their reputation, Denver

fans have come in record numbers, and attendance records

_____ (broke) at Coors Field several times since it opened.
            18

Eric: That's about all the time we have. Thanks, Kevin, for being with us today.

3 Passive Sentences—Questions and Answers: *Stadiums*

Work with a partner. Complete the chart about the Astrodome by asking your partner
questions with passives using the words on page 304. When no *wh-* word is given, ask a
yes/no question. Your partner should use the information on Exercise Page E–5 to answer
with passive sentences. Then your partner asks you questions to complete the chart
about the Skydome. You should answer using the information on Exercise Page E–5.

Example: Student A: Where was the Astrodome built?
Student B: The Astrodome was built in Houston, Texas.

The Astrodome	The Skydome
Location: _Houston, Texas_	Location: _____
Year opened: _____	Year opened: _____
Uses: _____	Uses: _____
Playing surface: _____	Playing surface: _____
Other facts: _____	Other facts: _____
_____	_____

The Astrodome

1. where/build
2. when/open
3. what/use/for
4. games/play/on grass
5. can/roof/open
6. separate fields/use/for baseball and football
7. why/call/"The Original"

The Skydome

1. where/build
2. when/open
3. what/use/for
4. games/play/on grass
5. can/roof/open
6. how/turf/fasten

4   Transitive and Intransitive Verbs: *Player Salaries*

Label the **boldfaced** verbs with a *T* for transitive or an *I* for intransitive. Then go back and **circle** all transitive verbs that are used in the passive.

(1) Professional athletes **are paid** (T) some of the highest salaries in the world.

(2) In addition to their salaries, many of these athletes **have** income from endorse-ments. (3) They **allow** their names to be used to promote products, and they **are featured** in advertisements. (4) These athletes **work** hard, but are they worth what they **receive?**

(5) How **are** their total earnings **determined?** (6) One factor is popularity: to some extent, the earnings of professional athletes **reflect** the popularity of their sports. (7) More **is earned** by football players than by hockey players or baseball players. (8) But basketball players **appear** to be the top earners in sports year after year. (9) Eleven of the top forty earners in 1997 **were** basketball players.

(10) What **do** high salaries **cost** the teams? (11) According to one financial ana-lyst, many sports teams **are falling** into debt and may not be able to afford high salaries in the future. (12) Fan support **hasn't diminished** yet, and fans still **come** in record numbers, but as tickets become more expensive, this may change.

(13) What will **happen** in the future? (14) The trend toward high salaries

seems unlikely to change any time soon unless the money to pay these salaries

can't be found.

5 Active versus Passive Sentences: *Tiger and The Masters*

A. Use the words in parentheses to complete the sentences. Make the sentences passive where possible. Otherwise, make the sentences active. Use appropriate verb tenses.

The Masters Tournament, one of the most important golf tournaments,

_____is held_____ (hold) every spring. For a golfer, winning the Masters
     1

_____ (be) a dream come true.
     2

As an infant, Tiger Woods _____ (like) watching his father practice
           3

hitting golf balls into a net in the garage, so he _____ (give) a miniature
          4

putter (a type of golf club) when he _____ (be) a few months old. This
         5

putter _____ (become) his favorite toy. Something unusual
    6

_____ (occur) when Tiger was still less than a year old. Tiger
   7

_____ (stand up) by himself and began hitting golf balls into the net, just
   8

like his father. His parents were thrilled. As he got older, Tiger _____
                  9

(encourage) to learn to play the game, and he _____ (give) support
          10

through the long hours of practice and exhausting tournaments. On April 13, 1997,

every golfer's dream _____ (come) true for Tiger Woods. At just 21 years,
        11

Tiger Woods _____ (win) the Masters.
     12

Tiger's success has had an astounding impact on interest in golf. Since his win

at the Masters, many young players _____ (motivate) to start playing golf;
        13

many more _____ (can, expect) to take up the game in the future. Perhaps
    14

before long, the Masters _____ (win) by one of these young players.
     15

B. Work with a partner. Write **eight** sentences on a sport you know about. You can describe the sport, the players, and/or special events in the sport. Use one of the following verbs in each sentence. Make passive sentences where possible.

call	hit	kick	learn	occur	resemble	run
score	seem	send	stay	throw	weigh	win

Example: In American football, the football is often thrown by the quarter-back to another player.

6 Direct and Indirect Objects as Subjects of Passive Sentences: *Winner's Circle*

Change the active sentences to passive sentences using the direct object as the subject of the passive sentence. If an indirect object is given, write a second passive sentence with the indirect object as the subject. Include *by* phrases.

The Stanley Cup

1. The National Hockey League gives the Stanley Cup to the top North American team.

   The Stanley Cup is given to the top North American team by the National Hockey League.

   The top North American team is given the Stanley Cup by the National Hockey League.

2. In 1893, Lord Stanley of Preston first presented the Stanley Cup to the top team.

3. That year, the Montreal AAA won the Stanley Cup.

4. Sometimes when a team wins, over the course of the year the team sends the Stanley Cup to each player.

The America's Cup

1. The Royal Yacht Squadron presented the America's Cup to the New York Yacht Club in 1857.

2. The United States won the America's Cup 25 consecutive times over a 132-year period.

3. In 1983, the United States, which lost the race, passed the America's Cup to the Royal Perth Yacht Club of Australia.

4. In 1987, the United States regained the America's Cup.

5. In 1996, the New York Yacht Club awarded the America's Cup to New Zealand.

GRAMMAR BRIEFING 2: Function of Passive Sentences

Passive sentences usually have the same basic meaning as active sentences, but they present information in a different way. Active sentences are much more common than passive sentences. Passive sentences without *by* are more common than passive sentences with *by*.

FUNCTION Passive Sentences

■ Passive and active sentences present information in a different way. The subject of an active sentence is usually the agent of the verb—that is, it performs the action of the verb. The subject of a passive sentence usually receives or undergoes the action of the verb.

> agent   verb   receiver of action
> Active: **Janitors** had cleaned the school from top to bottom.

> receiver of action   verb   agent
> Passive: **The school** had been cleaned from top to bottom by janitors.

■ Sometimes an agent gives information that isn't needed in a sentence. But every sentence must have a subject. In passive sentences, the object of the active sentence becomes the subject, so speakers can omit the agent.

> The school had been cleaned from top to bottom.

> (Compare this sentence to the active sentence and to the passive version with *by* above. Schools are usually cleaned by janitors, so this information isn't needed.)

■ There are various reasons for omitting an agent—that is, for using a passive without a *by* phrase instead of an active sentence:

• The agent is unknown, unimportant, or unnecessary because of the context.

> The Olympics were started in Greece. (unknown)

> The stadium lights were turned on. (unimportant)

> The third-graders are being taught to write in script. (unnecessary—teaching is done by teachers.)

• The agent is a general subject (*people,* impersonal *you* or *they, someone, everyone,* etc.).

> Wars have been fought since the dawn of humanity. (i.e., by people)

> Hats may not be worn indoors. (i.e., by anyone)

• In some cases the speaker may not want to mention, or even indicate, an agent.

> A mistake **was made,** but let's forget it. (*Someone made a mistake* would indicate an unspecified agent.)

■ The topic of a sentence—the person or thing the sentence is about—is generally in subject position. With the passive, it is possible to treat the receiver of the action as the topic and put it in subject position. In such cases the agent is often new information. If so, it is included in a *by* phrase at the end of the sentence. The end of the sentence is often a place for new information.

> A: How is your daughter doing these days?
> B: Oh, she's really happy. She was accepted by the Springfield Academy, which was the school she really wanted to go to. (The daughter, in subject position, is the topic. Springfield Academy is new information included in a *by* phrase at the end, along with further explanation.)

■ Passives are used more in writing than in speech. They are common in news reports and, especially, scientific and other academic writing, where agents are often less important than processes and results.

Samples of the eggs which **have been deposited are taken,** and the larvae which emerge from the eggs **are grown** in sterile bottles. The chromosomes of fully grown larvae **are** then **examined.** (The flies that deposit the eggs and the scientists who take the sample, grow the larvae, and examine the chromosomes are not important. The process and results are important.)

GRAMMAR PRACTICE 2: Function of Passive Sentences

7 Meaning of Passive Sentences: *Can This Game Be Won by the Cougars?*

▪▪▪ Listen to the passage. Then listen again and put a check mark next to the sentence that gives the information that is in the passage.

1. _____ a. Carson expects to lead his team.

   ___✓___ b. People expect Carson to lead his team.

2. _____ a. Other players have been giving Carson the ball.

   _____ b. Carson has been giving other players the ball.

3. _____ a. Peterson is playing in the second half.

   _____ b. Young is playing in the second half.

4. _____ a. Thomas hit the ball.

   _____ b. Sanchez hit the ball.

5. _____ a. Phillips tripped Sanchez.

   _____ b. Sanchez tripped Phillips.

6. _____ a. The players have to talk to the coach.

   _____ b. The coach has to talk to the players.

7. _____ a. Phillips hurt someone in the last play.

   _____ b. Someone hurt Phillips in the last play.

8. _____ a. Stanley Brown is the coach.

   _____ b. Stanley Brown is a player.

8 Receivers in Active and Passive Sentences: *Babe Didrikson Zaharias*

Underline the receiver of the action of the verbs in boldface. **Circle** the performer of the action, if it is given.

(1) In 1950, (an Associated Press poll) **named** Babe Didrikson Zaharias the greatest female athlete of the first half of the twentieth century. (2) Although her name was Mildred, she **was called** Babe by (almost everyone) because, like the famous baseball player Babe Ruth, she **displayed** a talent for hitting home runs. (3) Babe's athletic talent **was** clearly **displayed** in every sport that she tried, including golf, baseball, basketball, bowling, track and field, swimming, tennis, and figure skating. (4) She **was named** woman athlete of the year six times—in 1931, 1945, 1946, 1947, 1950, and 1954. (5) Although she **won** two gold medals in the 1932 Olympics in track and field, she **is remembered** most for her career as a professional golfer and for inspiring other women athletes. (6) She **lost** the fight against cancer and died in 1956 at the age of 42.

9 Omitting the *By* Phrase: *Catch a Wave*

Circle the verbs in the following passive sentences. (Some sentences have more than one verb.) **Cross out** *by* phrases that aren't important or necessary.

1. Some sports, like surfing, (are done) by individuals, not teams.
2. Surfing can be done by surfers with or without a surfboard.
3. The sport was popularized by Duke Kahanamoku in the early twentieth century.
4. Kahanamoku, an Olympic swimmer, was recognized by people as an accomplished surfer when surfing exhibitions were included by some organizers as part of swimming competitions.
5. Surfing is now practiced by people worldwide, partly because formal training isn't needed by surfers.
6. Recently, more and more women have been seen on surfboards by other surfers.
7. Women's interest in the sport is being fueled by Lisa Andersen, a champion surfer.
8. Women are inspired by Andersen's skill on the waves, and they are encouraged by her accomplishments.

🔟 The *By Phrase*: *Individual Sports*

Make passive sentences with the information given. Include the agent in a *by* phrase only
if the agent is important or necessary information. Use appropriate tenses.

Snowboarding

Agent	Action	Receiver	Other Information
1. people	often describe	snowboarding	as surfing on snow
2. Jake Burton and Tom Sims	start	the first snowboard companies	in the late 1970s
3. organizers	first include	snowboarding	in Olympic competition in 1998

1. Snowboarding is often described as surfing on snow.

2. The first snowboard companies were started by Jake Burton and Tom Sims in the late 1970s.

Horse Racing

Agent	Action	Receiver	Other Information
4. people	not always win	important sports events	
5. sportswriter Pat O'Brien	name	the racehorse Secretariat	"the greatest athlete ever"
6. others	call	Secretariat	"the horse of the century"

Marathon Running

Agent	Action	Receiver	Other Information
7. officials	measure	a marathon	at 42 km, 195 m
8. athletes	originally run	this distance	in the 1908 Olympic Games
9. African runners	dominate	the sport	recently

Cycling

Agent	Action	Receiver	Other Information
10. the French	hold	the first road race	in 1869
11. millions of people	watch	the Tour de France	every year
12. Henri Desgranges	organize	the first Tour de France	in 1903

⬚⬚ Continuing the Topic: *Right Name, Wrong Person*

Passive sentences are sometimes used to put the topic of a sentence in subject position. In each item, decide whether **a** or **b** better follows the line above and put a check mark next to your answer.

1. What would it be like to have the same name as a famous athlete? Ask Chicago dentist Michael Jordan.

   ____✓____ a. He has often been confused with the famous basketball player.

   _____ b. People have confused him with the famous basketball player.

2. Once he ordered a bike from a toy store. When he went to pick up the bike,

   _____ a. he was met by fans who wanted an autograph on their basketballs.

   _____ b. fans who wanted an autograph on their basketballs met him.

3. They were disappointed at not meeting the basketball player.

   _____ a. But the dentist was asked to sign the basketballs anyway.

   _____ b. But they asked the dentist to sign the basketballs anyway.

4. He signed the basketballs, "Best wishes, Michael Jordan."

   _____ a. Then the bike was taken home.

   _____ b. Then he took the bike home.

5. Another time, he and his wife made reservations at a restaurant. When they arrived,

   _____ a. they were told that they didn't have reservations.

   _____ b. someone told them that they didn't have reservations.

6. The hostess had thought that Dr. Jordan was kidding about his name.

   _____ a. For this reason, the reservations had been canceled by her.

   _____ b. For this reason, she had canceled the reservations.

7. Dr. Jordan seems to have a sense of humor about his name.

   _____ a. People have given him a lot of attention because of it.

   _____ b. He has been given a lot of attention because of it.

12 Passives in Academic Writing: *Arthroscopic Surgery for Sports Injuries*

A. Read the passage on arthroscopic surgery. Find the sentences that have one or
more passives and **underline** the verbs. Then go back and work with a partner to
answer the following questions.

1. How many sentences in the passage have one or more passives? ____7____

2. How many times is the passive used?

3. In how many of the passives is an agent included in a *by* phrase?

4. Why is the *by* phrase omitted in the passive sentences?

5. Why is the passive used so often in the passage?

Arthroscopic Surgery

Athletic injuries occur in all sports, and injuries to joints, especially the knee,
are common. Surgery for these injuries has become simpler because of the
advances in arthroscopic surgery. One of the most common procedures in sports
medicine today, arthroscopic surgery <u>was developed</u> in 1972 and <u>is performed</u> with
an arthroscope. Using an arthroscope, an orthopedic surgeon can examine, diag-
nose, and treat joint problems that used to require extensive surgery and long recovery periods.

An arthroscope is a thin tool containing a fiber optic light, a magnifying lens,
and a video camera. In arthroscopic surgery, a small incision or cut is made and the
arthroscope is inserted into the incision. Sterile fluid may be injected into the joint
space to enlarge the space, so the tissues can be examined more easily. Repairs are
made to the injury through another small incision. Usually, because the incisions
are so small, stitches are not required and surgical tape can be used to close them.

When injuries are treated with arthroscopic surgery, they heal faster, so little
time is needed for recovery. Although the joint should not be subjected to vigorous
activity for several days following arthroscopic surgery, normal activity can be
resumed within a reasonable amount of time.

B. Write a paragraph on a scientific or other academic topic of your choice which
explains a process or procedure like the one in **A.** Possibilities include biological,
chemical, mechanical, mental, physical, social processes, or any other process you
know or can find out about. Use at least five passive sentences in your paragraph.
Use more than **one** tense and at least one negative. Make sure to use the passive
appropriately.

More about Passives

A. Sports fans do some strange things to support their teams and bring them good luck. Write a check mark next to each statement that you think is true.

_____✓_____ 1. Fans **got** their faces **painted** red, white, and blue to support the United States soccer team.

_____ 2. A barrel (with very little underneath it) **has been worn** by one football fan to every game for many years no matter how cold the weather is.

_____ 3. A couple with World Cup tickets **got married** in the stadium an hour before the game started.

_____ 4. A fan **has gotten** his house **painted** orange and blue, the colors of his team.

_____ 5. A fan **got** his hair **cut** and **colored** to look like a soccer ball.

_____ 6. A fan **had** a designer soccer-ball dress **made** for the World Cup.

_____ 7. Stuffed animals **get taken** to games for good luck.

_____ 8. A baby **was named** Elway, after football quarterback John Elway.

_____ 9. Rubber rats **were thrown** on the ice at hockey games until the practice **was banned** for safety reasons.

_____ 10. A fan **won't have** his lucky shirt **washed** and wears it to all the games.

Compare answers as a class. Then turn to Exercise Page E–5 for the answers.

B. Read the sentences that follow, and then complete them.

1. Three of the sentences in **A** are passive sentences like those in Chapter 16, with

   be + past participle. Two examples of these passives are _____has been worn_____

   and _____.

2. Two of the sentences in **A** are passive sentences that are not formed with *be*.

   These passives are formed with the verb _____ + past

   participle. An example is _____.

3. Five of the sentences in **A** are passive causatives. They are different because they

   include an object. Passive causatives are formed with the verbs

   _____ or _____ + object + past participle.

   Examples with the two different verbs are _____ and

   _____.

GRAMMAR BRIEFING 1: *Get* Passives; Passive Causatives

Get can be used instead of *be* in passive sentences. *Get* and *have* are used with past participles to form passive causatives.

FORM AND FUNCTION *Get* Passives

- In conversation and informal writing, *get* can often be used instead of *be* to form passives.

    The baseball player **got traded** to another team. (= The baseball player was traded to another team.)

- Like passives with *be*, *get* passives can have verbs in any tense and can include modals.

    Your application **might have gotten misplaced.**

- In the simple present and simple past, questions and negatives are formed with *do*.

    When **did** your bike **get stolen?**

    Those notices **didn't get sent out** yesterday.

- Not all passives with *be* can be replaced by *get* passives.

    We **have been told** lies.   **Not:** We ~~have gotten told~~ lies.

    Protective clothing **must be worn** here.   **Not:** Protective clothing ~~must get worn~~ here.

Get works best in passives where something happens to the subject of the sentence—where there is an emphasis on process and change.

    Sorry. The rest of the cake **got eaten.** (emphasis is on the change in the cake—it's gone)

TALKING the TALK

- Remember! *Get* is more informal than *be* in passive sentences in both speaking and writing. *Be* can always be used.

    The mayor **got** reelected. (informal—e.g., conversation, informal letter)

    The mayor **was reelected.** (more formal—e.g., TV or newspaper story, as well as conversation, informal letter)

GRAMMAR HOTSPOT!

■ *-ed* adjectives following *be* or *get* can look like passives. These structures are sometimes called "stative passives." Unlike true passives, they express states, rather than actions, and cannot have a *by* phrase. Since there is no performer of an action, there is no corresponding active sentence. (*Be* is used when the state stays the same; *get* is used when the state changes.)

> We **got** (very) **tired** (while hiking).
>
> We **were** (very) **tired** (after hiking).

Notice that, like other adjectives, *tired* can take the intensifier *very* or other adverbs.

■ Some sentences can be interpreted as either real passives or stative passives (verb + adjective).

> Example: *The door was broken* could be either of the following:
>
> *be* + adjective: The door was (completely) broken. (state)
>
> passive: The door was broken (by John). (action)

FORM AND FUNCTION Passive Causatives

■ To form passive causatives, use: *get* or *have* + object + past participle.

> Emily **gets** her hair **done** twice a week.

■ Passive causatives can occur in any tense, with modals, and in negative statements and questions.

> **Are** you **going to have** your house **painted** this year?
>
> Yes, we **haven't had** it **painted** since we moved in.

■ Causatives express the idea that someone "causes" someone else to perform a service. With causatives, a sentence can be about the person receiving the service and about the service rather than the person performing the service or just the service.

> Passive causative: **I'm getting** a new phone **put in.** (receiver + service)
>
> Active: The telephone company is putting in a new phone (for me). (performer + service)
>
> Passive: A new phone is being put in (for me). (service)

■ Because the focus is not on the performer of the service, the *by* phrase is often omitted.

> They **got** their uniforms **cleaned** (by the laundry service) before the game.

GRAMMAR PRACTICE 1: *Get* Passives; Passive Causatives

1   *Get* Passives: *Bad Things Can Happen to Good Players!*

Complete the sentences with the words in parentheses. Use the *get* passive in appropriate tenses.

Playing professional sports is the ambition of many young athletes. These youngsters dream of one day being as famous as Michael Jordan, and they hope that they ___will get paid___ (pay) a salary like his. But playing professional sports isn't
                    1
easy and can be dangerous.

Professional athletes often _____ (hurt). Over the years, many base-
                                              2
ball players _____ (hit) by baseballs. Few football players
                          3

_____ (not, injure) at some point in their careers. Basketball players
        4

_____ (knock down) while playing, too. Even figure skaters
        5

_____ (can, injure). During a recent competition, a well-known figure
        6
skater _____ (drop) on the ice by her partner.
                  7

Behavior on and off the field can also lead to problems and to lost playing time.

Players _____ (may, suspend) for bad behavior during games and as a
                  8
result may have to sit out for several games. Hockey players are notorious for fight-

ing. They often _____ (kicked out) of the game. Unfortunately, these days
                              9

more and more professional athletes _____ (arrest) for their behavior off
                                                  10
the field.

Finally, a professional athlete's career is often short. When players' performance

begins to decline, players _____ (trade) to other teams. Sometimes they
                                      11
simply _____ (not, hire) for the next season.
                  12

None of this stops young athletes from dreaming of being a top athlete and ask-

ing the question, _____ (I, choose) to play on a professional team?
                              13

2   Get Passives: *Lucky Larry and Poor Pete*

Work with a partner. Look at the chart about Lucky Larry and Poor Pete. Read sentence 1 about Lucky Larry to your partner. Ask your partner a *yes/no* question about Poor Pete based on this sentence and using the same tense. Your partner should use the information about Poor Pete to answer. After sentence 4 your partner reads about Poor Pete and asks you questions about Lucky Larry. Answer with the information given.

Example: Lucky Larry got hired by the top team in his league. Did Poor Pete get hired by the top team in his league?
No, he didn't. He got hired by the worst team in the league.

Lucky Larry	Poor Pete
1. Lucky Larry got hired by the top team in his league.	1. (hire) by the worst team in his league.
2. Lucky Larry got promoted to head coach.	2. (demote) to assistant coach
3. Lucky Larry got offered a great salary.	3. (not, pay) very much money
4. Lucky Larry is going to get paid a bonus.	4. (charge) for his parking space
5. (praise) for his team's success	5. Poor Pete has gotten blamed for his team's failure.
6. (invite) to many social events	6. Poor Pete gets ignored by his friends.
7. (marry) a wonderful woman	7. Poor Pete is getting divorced.
8. (choose) coach of the year	8. Poor Pete will get fired at the end of the year.

3 True Passives versus Stative Passives: *Fan Superstitions*

A. Read the passages. Label the **boldfaced** verbs with a *P* if they are true passives or an
S if they are stative passives. (Remember, stative passives can take the intensifier *very*.)

The Sock Monkey

Brett Morris lost his beloved sock monkey when he was ten, but he never forgot

it. (1) So, when Brett, who is now thirty, **was given** another sock monkey by a friend,
                                                                    P

he **was delighted.** While watching a football game involving his favorite team, Brett
   S

put the sock monkey in front of the TV. (2) Brett **is devoted** to his team, and when

his team won, he and his friends decided the sock monkey was responsible. (3) Now,

they make sure that the sock monkey **gets put** in front of the TV before every game!

Pulled-up Socks

Cleveland Indian baseball fans believe pulled-up socks make their team win.

(1) This practice **got started** because player Jim Thome wears his socks this way in

games. On Thome's birthday, the other players on the team wore their socks pulled

up in his honor, and the Indians won the game. (2) Fans **were excited.** (3) Now they

believe that pulling up their socks will help the team win, so at Indians games many

fans **can be seen** wearing pulled-up socks.

B. Write about a superstition you know. It can be a sports superstition or any other
superstition. Use at least one true passive and one stative passive.

4 Passive Causatives: *Supporting the Team*

A. The Cougars basketball team is very good, but the players are very lazy. As a result, people do things to support the team. Match the agents in List A with their actions in List B. Then write **five** sentences with passive causatives, using *get* or *have*, telling how the agents support the team. Use *the players* as the subject of each sentence.

List A   **List B**

1. an athletic trainer   _____   a. make their travel arrangements

2. a gourmet chef   _____   b. wash their uniforms

3. the coach   _____   c. cut their hair

4. a travel agent   _____   d. make up their plays

5. a laundry service   _____   e. cook their meals

6. a hairstylist   ___1___   f. tape their ankles

> Example: The players get their ankles taped by an athletic trainer.

B. Mismatch the agents in List A with the actions in List B. Then write **three** sentences with a passive causative that tell how the agents don't support the team. Use *the players* as the subject of each sentence.

> Example: The players don't get their ankles taped by a gourmet chef.

C. Work with a partner. Ask and answer questions about personal services you have done by someone else. Use passive causatives with *get* or *have* in the questions and answers.

> Example: Do you get your hair cut by a hairdresser? Yes, I have my hair cut every two months.

5 Using Passive Sentences: *The Games We Play*

A. Read the paragraph. **Underline** passives with *be*, and **circle** *get* passives.

Baseball is played on a field by two teams. A point (or "run") is scored when a

batter-runner safely touches all four bases. Sometimes a runner can run to only one

base at a time, but when the ball gets hit out of the ballpark, the player who hit it is

allowed to run home (the last base) and score.

B. Write a paragraph like the one in **A** about a game that you know how to play (a sport, a card game, a board game, etc.). Focus on the actions or the receivers of the actions, not on the agents. Use at least two passive sentences with *be* and one passive sentence with *get*.

UNIT WRAP-UP

Error Correction

Find and correct the errors in the following passage. Some errors can be corrected in more than one way. Including the example, there are **10** errors.

are given / have been given

There are many nicknames in sports. Some athletes ~~given~~ interesting nicknames

as a result of their actions in games. One such athlete was "Wrong-Way" Riegels,

who played in the 1929 Rose Bowl. The Rose Bowl is an important college football

game that is play on January 1st every year. In the 1929 game, the football was

dropped by a player from Georgia Tech, and Roy Riegels from the University of

California picked it up and began to run. It was seemed that Riegels would score

easily. But for some reason, he got confused and ran 65 yards the wrong way. By the

time he got turn around by a teammate, the other team had also run down the field,

and Riegels got tackled on the one-yard line on the wrong end of the field. Because

of Riegels' run down the field, his team was lost the game 8–7, and he was nick-

named "Wrong-Way" Riegels.

Sometimes the play, not the player, gets the nickname. A famous soccer goal

knows by its nickname, the "Hand of God" goal. This goal was scored by

Argentinean superstar Diego Maradona against the English in the 1986 World Cup.

When the ball kicked over the heads of the English defense, both Maradona and the

English goalkeeper, Peter Shilton, jumped for it. Maradona was appeared to have hit

the ball into the goal with his head, but Shilton protested that Maradona had been

hit it with his hand. The goal was permitted to stand, and the game was won by

Argentina, 2–1. When the television replays proved Shilton correct, Maradona was

declared that the goal had been "a little bit Maradona, a little bit the hand of God."

Task 1: The History of . . .

Find out about the history of a sport from the Internet, an encyclopedia, books, or magazines, and write a paragraph about it. Find out such things as when, where, and by whom it was invented; where it is played; and the future of the sport. Use at least five passives in several tenses, including one negative passive and one passive with a modal. Use both *be* and *get* passives.

> Example: The inventor of golf isn't known, but the game was probably developed in Scotland. It is played on specially designed courses . . .

Task 2: "Get" the Answer

A. Work with a partner. Write **10** interview questions. Include a *get* passive in **five** of the questions and a passive causative (with *get* or *have*) in the other **five**. If you want, you can use some or all of the following expressions.

> *Get* passives: get hired for an unusual job, get invited somewhere special, get charged for something you didn't buy, get offered something for free, get chosen for an award
>
> Passive causatives: get/have special clothing made for you, get/have your hair cut in a style you hated, get/have your picture taken with someone famous
>
> Example: Have you ever gotten hired for an unusual job?

B. Interview someone other than your partner, using the questions you wrote. When the person answers *yes* to a question, ask for details. Report these answers to the class.

Task 3: Guess That Sport

One student thinks of a game or a sport. The other students ask *yes/no* questions about the game or sport, using the passive when possible. The first person who guesses the game or sport gets to think of the next game or sport.

> Example: Is this game played professionally in the United States? Is a ball used in this game?

Task 4: Pros and Cons

A. Read the following statement: Athletes should be paid large salaries.
The class divides into two groups. Regardless of their personal opinions, students in
Group A must support the statement and those in Group B must oppose it. To prepare for a debate, as a group write at least **five** reasons for your position with examples to support them. Use passive sentences when possible.

> Example: The careers of athletes are often shortened by injuries, so they
> need to make a lot of money before they retire. OR Other careers can be
> started after a sports career is ended, so short careers aren't a reason for
> large salaries.

B. Debate the statement. One member of Group A reads a supporting reason and has one minute to add examples and information. Then one member of Group B has one minute to respond to Group A's reason. A different member of Group B then reads one of Group B's reasons for opposition and has one minute to add examples and information. A second member of Group A has one minute to respond. No member of either group may speak a second time until all group members have spoken once.

C. Write a paragraph presenting your opinion about the statement. Give as many reasons and examples as you can. Use at least five passive sentences.

Unit Nine

Conditionals

Topic Focus—*Natural Disasters*

UNIT OBJECTIVES

- **factual conditionals and future conditionals**
  (*If* the temperature *falls* below 32° F, water *freezes. If* it *continues* to rain, there *will be* a flood.)

- **present unreal conditionals**
  (*If* I *were* you, I *would watch* the weather forecast.)

- **past unreal conditionals**
  (*If* an earthquake *hadn't occurred,* the building *wouldn't have collapsed.*)

- **conditionals involving different times**
  (*If* it *hadn't rained* last night, the ground *would be* dry now.)

- **inverted conditionals**
  (*Had* they *heard* the warning, they *could have escaped.*)

- **sentences with *hope* and *wish***
  (I *hope* the storm *will stop* soon. I *wish* the storm *would stop* soon.)

- **alternatives to *if***
  (*Provided that* you go to the basement, you will survive the tornado.)

- **implied conditions**
  (*With a map,* you can find your way to the emergency shelter.)

INTRODUCTORY TASKS

Reading and Listening

Read and listen to the passage about the forces of nature on page 325.

<u>If you were viewing the earth from a satellite now, you would see a beautiful and peaceful-looking planet</u>. But the peaceful appearance of earth from space is misleading. Within earth's atmosphere and beneath its surface, powerful, often violent, forces are constantly at work. **These natural forces can cause a catastrophe if conditions are right. If it's a late afternoon in the early summer, a tornado is probably forming somewhere in the American Midwest. If it's late summer, a hurricane is likely to be moving toward a coastline.** At any particular moment, an earthquake may be occurring somewhere on earth and a volcano may be preparing to erupt.

These events—severe weather, earthquakes, and volcanoes—are part of the cycles of nature and the forces that shaped the earth. **The earth would be a very different place if these events hadn't occurred. For example, the Hawaiian islands wouldn't exist if volcanoes hadn't erupted in the middle of the Pacific Ocean.** Severe natural events continue to have beneficial effects for life on earth; for example, both volcanoes and floods increase the fertility of the soil for farming. **These natural events are hazardous if they negatively affect people and their property. They are not hazardous if people aren't affected. If a volcano erupts underneath an ocean, it probably won't be a disaster at all.** But **if a small earthquake occurs beneath a densely populated city, it can cause tragedy on a large scale.**

More and more people are being affected by violent natural events these days

because the population is increasing in areas where such events are most likely to occur. Our ability to predict some natural events—hurricanes and blizzards, for example—is relatively good, so that we have time to escape or prepare for them. But others occur without warning. **If earthquakes could be predicted, many lives could be saved.** Despite our modern scientific knowledge, humans are no match for the most violent forces of nature. **If we can learn more about prediction of natural events, then perhaps we'll be able to prevent catastrophes.**

[Adapted from Frazier, Kendrick. *The Violent Face of Nature: Severe Phenomena and Natural Disasters.* New York: Morrow, 1979.]

Comprehension Check

Read each sentence. Circle **T** if the sentence is true or **F** if the sentence is false.

1. The author of the passage believes that you are viewing the earth from a satellite now. **T** **(F)**

2. It's possible for tornadoes to form in the American Midwest in the early summer. **T** **F**

3. The Hawaiian islands exist because volcanoes erupted in the middle of the Pacific Ocean. **T** **F**

4. Natural events are always hazardous for people and their property. **T** **F**

5. Earthquakes can't be predicted. **T** **F**

Think about Grammar

The **boldfaced** sentences in the passage are conditional sentences. These sentences contain a condition clause, sometimes called an *if* clause, which expresses a condition, and a result clause, which expresses the result of the condition. Look again at the conditional sentences in the reading. For each one **underline** the condition clause once and the result clause twice.

Conditionals

Introductory Task: *Hazardous Conditions*

A. Work with a partner. Fill in each blank in the first column with the letter of the most logical completion in the second column.

If Clauses	**Result Clauses**
1. If we have a thunderstorm, ___*g*___	a. a blizzard warning will be issued.
2. If the land can't absorb rain quickly enough, _____	b. a flood might occur.
3. If you see a funnel-shaped column of rapidly spinning wind, _____	c. the result is a drought.
4. If the winds of a tropical storm reach 74 miles (120 km) per hour, _____	d. a major earthquake is probably occurring.
5. If a severe snowstorm driven by high winds is expected, _____	e. the storm is officially classified as a hurricane.
6. If there is a long period with no rainfall, _____	f. it's probably a tornado.
7. If the ground is moving violently, _____	g. we will experience hard rain with noise and flashes of lightening.
8. If a volcano erupts, _____	h. lava, ash, and steam come out of the ground.

B. The sentences in **A** describe various natural events. Discuss them as a class. Which ones have you experienced? In which places do or might they occur? Then use a sentence with an *if* clause to tell your classmates about a natural event they might experience if they *go* to a particular place. Use the simple present in the *if* clause, and use *will* or *might* in the result clause.

Example: Thunderstorms are frequent in the summer here. If you stay here in the summer, you will experience a thunderstorm. OR Major earthquakes have occurred in California. If you go to California, you might experience a major earthquake.

GRAMMAR BRIEFING 1: Overview of Conditionals; Factual Conditionals; Future Conditionals

Conditional sentences contain a condition clause and a result clause. Factual conditionals express general truths, habits, and logical possibilities. Future conditionals express conditions and results in a future time.

FORM AND FUNCTION Overview of Conditionals

- Conditional sentences contain two clauses. The condition clause is also called an *if* clause, because *if* is the word most often used to show that a clause states a condition (see Chapter 19, Grammar Briefing 3, page 356, for other words used). The result clause is a main clause. The *if* clause can come before or after the result clause, with no difference in meaning. Use a comma between clauses when the *if* clause is first.

If clause	Result clause
If the sun shines,	water evaporates more quickly.

Result Clause	*If* Clause
Water evaporates more quickly	if the sun shines.

- *Then* can be used to emphasize that a clause states a result. However, it is often omitted. (*Then* is never used if the result clause is first.)

  If you go, **then** I'll go, too. (= If you go, I'll go, too.)

- A negative can be used in the *if* clause, in the result clause, or in both clauses.

  If it does**n't** rain, the flowers will die.

  If it rains, the flowers **won't** die.

  If it **doesn't** rain, we **won't** have enough water next summer.

- Conditional sentences show a relationship between a condition and a result of the condition. The *if* clause expresses the condition; the result clause expresses the result of the condition.

If Clause	Result Clause
If tomorrow is a nice day,	we'll go to the beach.

  (Tomorrow being nice is the condition for our going to the beach. Our going to the beach will be the result of this condition occurring.)

- There are four main types of conditional sentences: factual conditionals, future conditionals, present unreal conditionals (see Grammar Briefing 2), and past unreal conditionals (see Grammar Briefing 3).

FORM AND FUNCTION Factual Conditionals; Future Conditionals

Factual Conditionals

- Factual conditionals are often formed with present or past tense verbs in both clauses. The verbs may be simple and/or progressive.

  If I **have** money, I **spend** it. (simple present, simple present)

  If people **needed** help, he **was** always there to help them. (simple past, simple past)

  If the water's **boiling,** it**'s** hot enough. (present progressive, simple present)

  If he **was talking** on the phone, he **wasn't working.** (past progressive, past progressive)

■ Modals and imperatives can be used in the result clause. Modals can also be used in the *if* clause.

> If I **have** enough money with me, I **can lend** you some. (modal)
>
> If you **need** $20, **take** it from my wallet. (imperative)
>
> If he **can spend** the day in the garden, he is happy. (modal in *if* clause)

■ Factual conditionals can express general truths, habits, or logical possibilities. The habits and logical possibilities may be in the present or past.

- General truths: If it's five o'clock in New York, it's two o'clock in California.

  (Note: Factual conditionals that express general truths usually use the simple present.)

- Habits: If I cook, he washes the dishes.

  (Note: Factual conditionals that express habits usually use the simple tenses.)

- Logical possibilities: If you're having trouble breathing, there must be mold in the air.

  (Note: Modals are especially common in conditionals that express logical possibilities.)

- In factual conditionals that express general truths or habits, *when(ever)* can usually replace *if* with little change in meaning.

  > **When(ever)** it's five o'clock in New York, it's two o'clock in California. (= If it's five o'clock in New York, it's two o'clock in California.)

Future Conditionals

■ Future conditionals are generally formed with a present form of the verb in the *if* clause and *will* or *be going to* in the result clause. (*Will* is more common than *be going to*.)

> If it **is raining** tomorrow, we **will/are going to** cancel the picnic.

■ Other modals, imperatives, and the future perfect can also be used in the result clause.

> If it **rains** tomorrow, we **may/could/should cancel** the picnic. (modal)
>
> If it **rains** tomorrow, **call off** the picnic. (imperative)
>
> If it **rains** tomorrow, we **will have worked** all night for nothing. (future perfect)

■ Future conditionals express what will happen in the future if certain conditions occur. Future conditionals therefore are often used to make predictions. Other common uses include expressing plans, offers, suggestions, requests, refusals, orders, and threats.

> If you study for the test, you'll do well. (prediction)
>
> If you go to Chicago next week, you can see the Cubs play. (suggestion)
>
> If you go to Chicago next week, I'll take you to the airport. (offer)
>
> If you don't behave, I'll tell your parents. (threat)

GRAMMAR PRACTICE 1: Overview of Conditionals; Factual Conditionals; Future Conditionals

▌ Factual Conditionals with Present Tense Verbs—Form: *The Nature of a Tornado*

A. Combine the sentences in brackets to form one sentence with an *if* clause and a result clause. Use the sentences in the order they are given. Decide which sentence in brackets should become which clause. Use *then* where possible. Punctuate carefully.

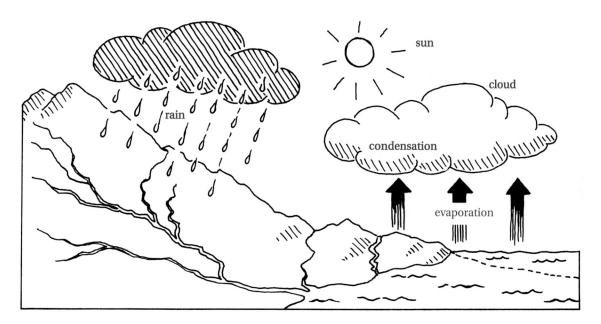

Storms occur as a result of natural processes involving the sun, air, water, and gravity. The sun heats the earth and the air around it.
[Air rises. It is heated.]

1.   _Air rises if it is heated._ _____

The sun heats the water on earth, too.
The sun shines on water. [The water evaporates.]

2.   _If the sun shines on water, then the water evaporates._ _____

This means that the water goes into the air as vapor. As warm air carries water vapor upward, the air becomes cooler.
[The air cools. The water vapor in it condenses.]

3.   _____

That is, the vapor becomes tiny drops of water and forms clouds. The drops may join other drops.
[The drops become too heavy for the cloud to hold. They fall to earth.]

4.   _____

The temperature determines the form in which the drops fall to earth.
[The drops fall as rain. The temperature isn't below the freezing point.]

5. ——

Thunderstorms occur under certain conditions.
[A mass of warm, moist air rises very rapidly. A thunderstorm can occur.]

6. ——

Tornadoes are funnel-shaped windstorms that occur only under one condition.
[A tornado can't occur. There is no thunderstorm.]

7. ——

The area including Texas, Oklahoma, and Kansas is known as "Tornado Alley"
because tornadoes are most frequent there.
[A thunderstorm is moving across Tornado Alley at this moment. A tornado might be forming.]

8. ——

Tornadoes can be extremely destructive.
[A house is hit by a tornado. The house might explode.]

9. ——

B. Look at the sentences you wrote in **A.** In which sentence is it **not possible** to use

when in place of *if?* _____

2 Factual Conditionals with Past Tense Verbs—Form: *The Making of a Television Meteorologist (Weather Scientist)*

A. In his book *Weathering the Storm*, Gary England describes his experiences growing up in Oklahoma. Use the words given to write factual conditionals with past tense verbs. Write the words in the order that they are given. Decide which group of words should become the *if* clause and which should become the result clause. Punctuate carefully.

Before the 1950s, people often had no warning of approaching tornadoes.

1. __If people didn't have warning, disasters occurred.__
   (people/not/have/warning) (disasters/occur)

   As a child, England learned to be cautious about severe weather.

2. _____
   (he/play/outside/when a thunderstorm approached) (he/race/into the house)

   In those days, weather radar and television didn't exist yet.

3. _____
   (people/see/threatening clouds or tornadoes) (they/report/them to the sheriff)

   The sheriff would then sound a warning siren.

4. _____
   (everyone in England's family/run/into the cellar) (they/hear/the siren)

   In the 1950s TV weather forecasts began, and England could sometimes watch them.

5. _____
   (the weatherman/predict/a snowstorm) (he/look forward/to it)

   He spent all his time waiting for the storm.

6. _____
   (he/be/disappointed) (the storm/not/begin/before he went to sleep)

   As soon as he woke up, he looked out the window, hoping that it was snowing.

7. _____
   (it/snow) (he/be/very excited)

B. Write **three** sentences about what you often did in storms or other weather situations when you were a child. Use a progressive in at least one sentence.

> Example: If there was a blizzard, I went sledding. OR I built a snowman if it was snowing.

3 Factual Conditionals with Modals and Imperatives: *Advice about Thunderstorms and Tornadoes*

Work with a partner. Student A looks at this page, and Student B looks at Exercise Page E–5. Student A uses factual conditionals to ask for advice.

> Example: What should I do if I'm inside when a thunderstorm occurs?

Student B answers with factual conditionals that include *should* or an imperative.

> Example: If you're inside when a thunderstorm occurs, you should stay inside. OR If you're inside when a thunderstorm occurs, stay inside.

Then Student B turns to this page and asks for advice and Student A turns to Exercise Page E–5 and answers.

Student A

1. You're inside when a thunderstorm occurs.
2. You're using a computer when a thunderstorm starts.
3. You're outside when a thunderstorm occurs.
4. The weather service issues a "flash flood watch."
5. The weather service issues a "flash flood warning."
6. You're in a car in a mountain canyon and a flood is coming toward you.

Student B

1. You live in an area where tornadoes are common.
2. The weather service issues a "tornado watch."
3. The weather service issues a "tornado warning."
4. You're outside and you see a tornado nearby.
5. You're in a car and a tornado is coming toward you.

4 Future Conditionals—Form and Function: *The Hurricanes of the Future*

A. Use the words in parentheses to complete the future conditionals. Use *will* or *be going to*.

1. The weather everywhere on earth __will/is going to change__ (change) if global

   temperatures __continue__ (continue) to rise.

2. If the climate _____ (become) warmer, the water in the Atlantic

   _____ (get) warmer.

3. If the water in the Atlantic _____ (become) warmer, hurricanes

   _____ (increase) in number and intensity.

4. Also, hurricanes _____ (affect) more people if the population along

   the coastlines _____ (continue) to grow.

5. But people _____ (not/be) injured by hurricanes if they

_____ (take) precautions.

6. If meteorologists' forecasts

_____ (be) accurate, during

the next hurricane season seven hurri-

canes _____ (form) over the

Atlantic.

7. To find out how the National Hurricane

Center follows hurricanes, visit its web

site. If a hurricane _____

(form) at that time, you _____

(be able to see) satellite images of it on
your computer screen.

B. Use your own ideas to complete the following sentences. In each sentence use *will*
or another modal or an imperative. The content of the sentence should be appropriate for the function in parentheses.

1. If forecasts about future climate changes are correct,

_____there will be more hurricanes_____. (prediction)

2. If a hurricane is coming toward the place where you live,

_____. (order)

3. If you go inland to a safe place before a hurricane,

_____. (prediction)

4. If you need any help cleaning up after the hurricane,

_____. (offer)

5. If you want to learn more about hurricanes and other storms,

_____. (suggestion)

GRAMMAR BRIEFING 2: Present Unreal Conditionals

Present unreal conditionals are used to talk about conditions that are not true in the present and about the imagined results of these conditions.

FORM AND FUNCTION Present Unreal Conditionals

Present Unreal Conditionals

■ Present unreal conditionals have a past form of the verb in the *if* clause and *would/could/might* + base form of verb in the result clause. *Were* is used for all persons of *be* in the *if* clause.

> If we **had** a car, we **could drive** to the mall.

> If I **were working** more hours on my job, I **couldn't finish** my school work.

• *Could* can also be used in the *if* clause.

> If she **could sing,** she **would take** voice lessons.

• A progressive is also possible in the result clause (i.e., *would/could/might* + *be* + verb + *-ing*).

> If I **were living** in Paris, I **would be studying** art.

■ The *if* clause of a present unreal conditional expresses a condition that is not true at the present time. The condition might be highly unlikely or impossible. The result clause tells what would happen if this untrue condition were true. It expresses the imagined result of an imagined condition.

> If I were the teacher, I'd give a lot less homework. (The speaker is not the teacher. The imagined result of this imagined condition is less homework.)

> If you were here, we could talk more. (The listener is not there. But the imagined result of the listener's being there would be the listener and speaker talking more.)

■ Present unreal conditionals can be used to talk about the future. They are different from future conditionals in that they are about what is impossible or unlikely in the future.

> If you were coming tonight, we could go to a movie. (The listener probably or definitely is not coming.)

> If wars were never fought again, the world would be a far better place.

■ Present unreal conditionals with *if I were you* are used to give advice.

> **If I were you,** I would be more careful. (= You should be more careful.)

■ *Could* or *might* is used instead of *would* to indicate that, if the unreal condition were true, the unreal result would be only possible, not certain. *Could* can also be used to express ability.

> If I had money, I **might/could** travel around the world. (possibility)

> If I had money, I **would travel** around the world. (definite plan)

> If I were a mathematician, I **could** solve that problem. (ability)

GRAMMAR HOTSPOT!

■ Remember! In unreal conditionals, unlike in factual conditionals, past forms do not express past time. They express the idea that something in the present or future is not real.

> If he **knew** the answer, he would say something. (Unreal conditional: He doesn't know the answer now.)

> If/When he **knew** the answer, he said something. (Factual conditional: He sometimes knew the answer in the past.)

TALKING the TALK

■ In informal spoken English, *was* is sometimes used instead of *were* with first and third person singular forms in unreal present conditionals. This use is not considered acceptable in formal English.

> If your cat **was** more comfortable, it would be asleep. (informal spoken)

GRAMMAR PRACTICE 2: Present Unreal Conditionals

5 Present Unreal Conditionals—Form: *Natural Hazards in the U. S. Pacific Region*

Complete the present unreal conditionals, using the words in parentheses. Use *would* in the result clause. Use progressives where appropriate.

1. Mt. Rainier is a volcano near Seattle, Washington. If it _____erupted_____ (erupt)

   without warning, many people _____would be_____ (be) in danger.

2. Mt. Rainier isn't expected to erupt soon. I _____ (not, feel) worried if

   I _____ (be) near it.

3. Mount St. Helens, another volcano in Washington, is potentially active, so scien-

   tists monitor it. People who live around it _____ (be) concerned

   about their safety if scientists _____ (not, monitor) it continuously.

4. If Mount St. Helens _____ (erupt) at this moment, lava (melted rock)

   and mud _____ (flow) down its sides, and gases and ash

   _____ (shoot) into the air.

5. Tectonic plates are the thick plates of solid rock that rest on the melted rock of

   earth's mantle. If two tectonic plates _____ (not, meet) along the San

   Andreas Fault in California, earthquakes _____ (not, be) so common

   in that region.

6. I don't live near the San Andreas Fault. But I _____ (want) to take pre-

   cautions against earthquakes if my home _____ (be) close to it.

7. Tsunami are waves caused by volcanoes or earthquakes near or under the sea. If

   a giant tsunami _____ (strike) Hawaii, it _____ (cause) sig-

   nificant damage.

8. Tsunami, earthquakes, and volcanoes are hazards in Hawaii. If you

   _____ (vacation) in Hawaii now, _____ you

   _____ (think about) the hazards?

6 Present Unreal Conditionals—Meaning: *Visiting Hawaii's Volcanoes*

Work with a partner. Read each sentence and mark the sentences that follow it **T**
(true) or **F** (false).

1. If Mt. Kilauea in Hawaii Volcanoes
   National Park weren't erupting, I
   wouldn't be so interested in visiting
   the park.

   ____F____ Mr. Kilauea isn't erupting.

   ____T____ I'm interested in visiting the
   park.

2. If it were dangerous to observe the lava
   flows, the park rangers wouldn't let visitors do it.

   _____ It isn't dangerous to observe
   the lava flows.

   _____ The park rangers let visitors
   do it.

3. If flowing lava weren't so hot, you could
   touch it.

   _____ Flowing lava isn't very hot.

   _____ You can touch it.

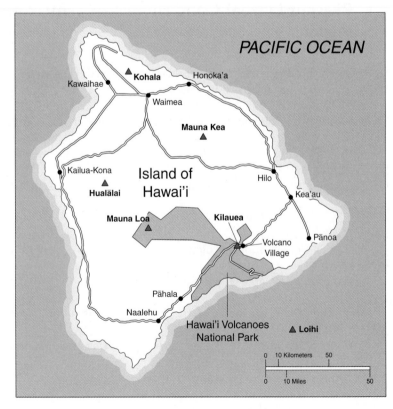

4. The flowing lava would appear to be red if it were night.

_____ The flowing lava doesn't appear to be red.

_____ It's night.

5. I'd drive around the island if I had time.

_____ I want to drive around the island.

_____ I have time to drive around the island.

6. If there weren't a "hot spot" in the earth's crust underneath Hawaii, volcanoes couldn't form new islands there.

_____ There is a "hot spot" in the earth's crust underneath Hawaii.

_____ It's possible for volcanoes to form new islands there.

7 Factual versus Unreal Conditionals: *Earthquakes*

Complete the factual conditionals and unreal conditionals with the correct form of the verbs in parentheses. Use *would* in the result clause of the unreal conditionals.

1. The earth's crust moves. If it ___didn't move___ (not, move), earthquakes

   ___wouldn't occur___ (not, occur).

2. Seismographs are instruments used to record the movements of the earth's

   crust. If an earthquake ___occurs___ (occur), a seismograph

   ___records___ (record) its strength.

3. Seismologists study the movements of the earth's crust. I'm not a seismologist.

   But I _____ (know) a lot about earthquakes if I _____ (be)
   a seismologist.

4. Seismologists use the Richter Scale (0–9.0) to measure the intensity of earth-

   quakes. Earthquakes _____ (be) classified as "moderate" if they

   _____ (measure) 5–5.9 on the Richter Scale.

5. Many very minor earthquakes occur every day. If someone _____

   (pay) you a dollar for every earthquake, you _____ (earn) about
   $9,000 per day.

6. People build earthquake-resistant structures in areas where earthquakes are fre-

   quent. Earthquakes _____ (cause) less damage if people

   _____ (build) these structures.

7. Earthquakes are a hazard in California, so people build earthquake-resistant

   structures there. If they _____ (not, build) these structures, earth-

   quakes _____ (cause) more damage.

8 Present Unreal Conditionals with *Would* and *Could: Daring Scientists*

Use the pairs of factual statements to write present unreal conditionals. Use *would* or
could in the result clause, as appropriate. Use *could* in the *if* clause where appropriate.

1. Natural processes aren't always predictable. They are hazardous to people.

   If natural processes were always predictable, they wouldn't be hazardous to people.

2. We can't control nature. We can't prevent natural disasters.

   If we could control nature, we could prevent natural disasters.

3. Some scientists take risks. People can be warned about approaching dangers.

   _____

4. Volcanologists go to the tops of active volcanoes. They can install equipment to
   monitor changes in them.

   _____

5. Meteorologists need to know more about how tornadoes form. "Tornado
   chasers" try to place scientific instruments inside tornadoes.

   _____

6. Meteorologists can't get enough information about hurricanes from radar and
   satellites. "Hurricane hunters" have to fly airplanes directly through hurricanes.

   _____

9 Present Unreal Conditionals for Advice: *Avoiding Risk*

Work with a partner. Decide what advice you'd give each other in the following situations. Begin each sentence with *If I were you,...*

1. We just had a big storm that blew a power line down next to my house.

   If I were you, I wouldn't touch the power line. OR *If I were you, I'd call the power
   company.*

2. I'm in Hawaii. I want to hike to the top of a volcano, but I don't know whether it's
   safe or not.

3. I'm on vacation in California. I don't know what to do in case of an earthquake.

4. I'm at home, and there's hardly anything to eat in the refrigerator. It's snowing very hard outside.

5. I'm outside playing soccer. Dark clouds are moving in, and I can see lightning.

6. I'm driving my car. It's raining hard, and the windshield wipers aren't working.

7. I want to move to a place where natural disasters are rare.

⏺ Using Present Unreal Conditionals: *The World Would Be Different If . . .*

A. Use the following statements and your own ideas to write present unreal conditionals. Include at least two conditionals with *could* or *might* in the result clauses.

1. There are thunderstorms.

> *If there were no thunderstorms, parts of the earth might be very dry.* OR *I could spend more time playing soccer if there were no thunderstorms.*

2. Tornadoes can touch the ground.

3. Big hurricanes don't strike the coast once a month.

4. There are weather forecasts on the radio and television.

5. The weather isn't nice every day.

6. Earthquakes can't be predicted.

B. As a class compare sentences.

GRAMMAR BRIEFING 3: Past Unreal Conditionals

Past unreal conditionals are used to talk about conditions that were not true in the past and the imagined results of those conditions.

FORM AND FUNCTION Past Unreal Conditionals

Past Unreal Conditionals

■ Past unreal conditionals have a past perfect form of the verb in the *if* clause and *would/could/might* + *have* + past participle of the verb in the result clause.

> If I **had been** here, I **would have been** more careful.

> If they **had studied,** they **could have passed** the exam.

■ The *if* clause of a past unreal conditional expresses a condition that was not true in the past. The result clause tells what would have happened if the untrue condition had been true. It expresses the imagined result of an imagined condition in the past. *Could* and *might* instead of *would* express possibility, rather than certainty; *could* also expresses ability.

> If Lou **had come** earlier, you **could have met** him. (Lou didn't come earlier, and you didn't meet him. But, if the untrue condition—Lou coming earlier—had occurred, the unreal result—your meeting him—would have been possible.)

■ Note a difference from present unreal conditionals, related to past versus present time: In present unreal conditionals, the condition and result are sometimes highly unlikely but possible. In past conditionals, the condition (and therefore the result) is never possible.

> If you were coming tonight, we could go to a movie. (present conditional—highly unlikely but possible)
>
> If you had come last night, we could have gone to a movie. (past conditional—impossible; you didn't come last night)

GRAMMAR HOTSPOT!

■ Although some native speakers use *would* in both clauses of a past unreal conditional, it is generally considered incorrect to use *would* in the *if* clause.

> **If** you **had said** something, I **would have done** something.
>
> **Not:** If you ~~would have~~ said something, I would have done something.

TALKING the TALK

■ In speech, *would have* is often pronounced "'d of" or "'d a." In writing, use *would have*.

> If I had known the test was so hard, I would have studied more for it. = "If I'd known the test was so hard, I'd of / I'd a studied more for it."

GRAMMAR PRACTICE 3: Past Unreal Conditionals

11 Past Unreal Conditionals—Form: *The Dust Bowl*

A. Use the words in parentheses to complete the past unreal conditionals. Use *would*, *might*, or *could* in the result clause to express the indicated meaning. In cases where two forms are possible, write both forms.

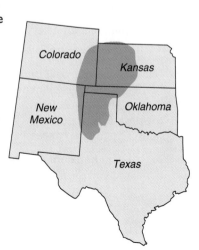

In the 1930s an environmental disaster occurred in the southwestern Great

Plains. This area became known as the Dust Bowl. In the 1920s there was great

demand for wheat. If the price for wheat ___hadn't been___ (not, be) so high, thou-
                                              1

sands of people ___wouldn't have moved___ (not, move) to the Great Plains to start
                      [certainty]

farms. In the 1920s abundant rain fell in the region. If the rainfall ___hadn't been___
                                                                          2

(not, be) unusually good, people ___might/could have known___ (know) that the
                                        [possibility]

Dust Bowl area wasn't suitable for intensive farming.

A terrible drought began in 1931. This drought _____ (not, have)
                                                 3 [certainty]

such serious consequences if the farmers _____ (manage) the land more

carefully. If the farmers _____ (not, plow up) the natural grass to grow
                            4

wheat, the soil _____ (hold) moisture better. If the farmers
                  [certainty]

_____ (plant) trees around their farms, they _____ (protect)
       5   [ability]

the soil from the wind.

Terrible windstorms began in 1932. These storms stripped the land and were

dangerous to people's health. You _____ (get) "dust pneumonia" if you
                                    6 [possibility]

_____ (live) in the Dust Bowl. The dust blew all the way to the East Coast.

If you _____ (be) in New York City on May 21, 1934, you _____
          7   [ability]

(see) huge clouds of dust in the air. If the continent _____ (be) on fire, the
                                                          8

effect _____ (be) similar.
         [certainty]

The farms in the Dust Bowl were ruined. In the 1930s, the United States experi-

enced economic depression. If economic conditions _____ (be) better,
                                                      9

the situation in the Dust Bowl _____ (not, be) so tragic. Thousands of
                                  [certainty]

farmers migrated to California. If the government _____ (not, give) jobs
                                                     10

to many who stayed, they _____ (starve). Finally, in the late 1930s rain
                           [possibility]

began to fall again.

B. If you had been alive during the 1930s, your life would have been different than it is
now. Complete the following sentences with your own ideas. Use each of the following once: *would, could,* and *might.*

1. If I had been born in 1900, _____.

2. If my family had lived on a farm in the 1920s, _____.

3. _____ if I had lived in New York in the 1930s.

▐12▌ Past Unreal Conditionals—Meaning: *Johnstown, Pennsylvania, 1889*

▐···▌   Listen to the following description. You will hear each item twice. Decide whether the statement given expresses a meaning that is similar to the meaning of the item that you heard. If it expresses a similar meaning, mark it with an **S**; if it doesn't, mark it with a **D**.

1. ___*S*___ The fish didn't escape because wire screens were installed in front of the lake's natural outlets.

2. _____ The screens didn't become filled with dirt and plants, so the water could go through them.

3. _____ The water wasn't able to go through the screens, so it created a lot of pressure on the dam.

4. _____ The dam was strong because they repaired it properly.

5. _____ It didn't rain very hard in the spring of 1889, so the lake didn't overfill.

6. _____ People in Johnstown had been warned about the danger of flood often, so they didn't pay attention to the warning they got on May 31, 1889.

7. _____ People jumped onto the pile in front of the bridge, so they had a chance to survive.

8. _____ The pile didn't burst into flames, so hundreds of lives were saved.

9. _____ The deadliest flood in American history wasn't avoided because people didn't pay attention to the warnings.

▐13▌ Past Unreal Conditionals: *They Haven't All Been Disasters*

Severe natural events can have beneficial consequences. Use the information given to write past unreal conditionals.

1. Before a system of dams was built on the Nile River, it flooded annually. As a result, the soil was fertile.

    If the Nile River hadn't flooded annually, the soil wouldn't have been fertile.

2. Volcanoes erupted in the middle of the Pacific. As a result, the Hawaiian Islands were formed.

3. Valuable minerals from deep in the earth were brought to the surface because volcanoes erupted in many places in the world.

4. Many of the earth's mountain ranges were born because earthquakes occurred.

5. Earthquakes shook the western coast of Mexico long ago. As a result, the Baja California peninsula was created.

6. Nature was forceful. As a result, the earth became so rich, varied, and beautiful.

14   **Using Past Unreal Conditionals:** *My Life Might Have Been Different If . . .*

A.   Write **three** factual statements about important events or situations in your life in the past. Then write a past unreal conditional sentence about each statement.

> Example: When I was six years old, my family got a piano. If my family hadn't gotten a piano, I wouldn't have been able to take music lessons.

B.   Write **three** factual statements about things that you didn't do or that didn't happen to you. Then write a past unreal conditional sentence about each statement.

> Example: I didn't fail the entrance examination. If I had failed the entrance examination, I would have had to take it again.

More about Conditionals

Introductory Task: *Incoming!*

A. Read the following script for a scene in a disaster movie.

Scientist: Mr. President, we've just spotted an asteroid speeding toward earth! It's more than five miles in diameter. <u>Provided that</u> our calculations are correct, it will strike the earth one week from today.

President: Let's not panic. Over 70 percent of the earth is ocean. As long as it hits the ocean, it probably won't injure anyone. If it doesn't hit a city, it shouldn't cause a big problem, right?

Scientist: I'm afraid that isn't right, sir. We can't predict where this asteroid will hit. But we know that it's going to cause a catastrophe. In the event that it strikes the ocean, the impact will send huge clouds of water vapor into the atmosphere. The clouds will keep the sunlight from reaching earth for many months. If the asteroid hits land, the impact will fill the atmosphere with clouds of dust and ash. The planet will be dark and cold, and it will be impossible to raise any crops. Unless we can prevent this asteroid from hitting the earth, we're going to end up like the dinosaurs. The human species will become extinct.

President: I hope you have a suggestion.

Scientist: I suggest that we send a crew of astronauts to the asteroid immediately. Providing that the astronauts can land on it, they should be able to set off explosions that will change its orbit. If they can change its orbit, it won't collide with earth!

B. Work with a partner. Forms other than *if* can signal conditionals. Read the script again. Find and **underline** the expressions that could be replaced by *if* or *if . . . not*. Write the expressions on the spaces below.

Same meaning as *if:*

___provided that___, _____ _____ _____,

_____ _____ _____ _____,

_____ _____

Same meaning as *if . . . not:*

_____

GRAMMAR BRIEFING 1: Other Forms in Conditionals

The condition clause and result clause of a conditional can be in different times. *Were to* and *should (happen to)* can be used in conditional sentences about the future. In inverted conditionals, *were, should,* and *had* come before the subject and *if* is omitted. *If so* and *if not* are shortened forms of *if* clauses.

FORM AND FUNCTION Other Forms in Conditionals

Conditionals with Conditions and Results in Different Times

■ Although most of the conditionals in Chapter 18 have condition and result in the same time (past, present, or future), conditionals can mix times. That is, conditions in one time can relate to results in another time. Such conditionals are sometimes called "mixed conditionals."

> If it **snowed** there last week, there **should** still **be** plenty of snow. (factual conditional—past time condition, present time result)

> If I **had studied** something practical, I **could be making** more money now. (unreal conditional—past time condition, present time result)

> If I **were** better at languages, it **wouldn't have taken** me so long to learn French. (unreal conditional—general condition, past time result)

Should (Happen To) and *Were To*

■ In conditionals about the future, *should (happen to)* and *were to* can often be used in the *if* clause.

> If he **should come over** tonight, we'll/we'd go to a movie.*

> If he **were to come over** tonight, we'd go to a movie.*

■ Conditions with *should (happen to)* and *were to* tend to be weaker than those in future conditionals. For example, compared to *If he comes over tonight, we'll go to a movie,* the sentences with *should* and *were to* imply he is less likely to come over.

* Either *will* or *would* can be used with *should (happen to),* but only *would* can be used with *were to.*

Inverted Conditionals

■ Inverted conditionals can be formed when the *if* clause of a conditional includes *were, should,* or *had.* The *if* is omitted, and *were, should,* or *had* is moved before the subject. Inverted conditionals have the same meaning but are more formal.

> **Were I** unhappy, I would tell you. = **If I were** unhappy, I would tell you.

> **Should he call,** let me know. = **If he should call,** let me know.

> **Had I known** his phone number, I would have called him. = **If I had known** his phone number, I would have called him.

■ Contractions are not used in negative inverted conditionals. *Not* follows the subject.

> **Had I not finished** my work, I wouldn't have gone home. = **If I hadn't finished** my work, I wouldn't have gone home.

Conditionals with *If So* or *If Not*

■ Sometimes a condition is clear from a previous sentence. When this happens, it is not necessary to repeat the entire condition. Instead, the short form *if so* or, for negative conditions, *if not* can be used.

> I should pass all my courses this semester. **If so,** I'll graduate in June. (*If so* = If I pass all my courses)

> I should pass all my courses this semester. **If not,** I'll enroll in summer school. (*If not* = If I don't pass all my courses this semester)

GRAMMAR PRACTICE 1: Other Forms in Conditionals

1 Conditionals with Conditions and Results in Different Times: *Has an Asteroid Impact Happened Before? Could It Happen Again?*

A. Use the words in parentheses and the cues under the blanks to complete the sentences in the interview. Use *would* where needed.

Q: Are asteroids and comets really a potential danger to life on earth?

A: I think they are. Most scientists believe that the collision of an asteroid with

the earth 65 million years ago was responsible for the extinction of the

dinosaurs. They ___wouldn't believe___ (not, believe) this if evidence of the
                     1. [unreal present]

collision ___hadn't been found___ (not, found).
              [unreal past]

Q: What evidence has been found?

A: An element called iridium is very rare on earth but is common in asteroids and

comets. If there _____ (be) a high level of iridium in a layer of earth,
                    2. [factual present]

it _____ (come) from a source outside earth's atmosphere. Very high
   [factual past]

levels have been found in the layer that was on earth's surface 65 million years

ago. There _____ (be) very little iridium in that layer if an asteroid
           3. [unreal present]

_____ (not, collide) with earth.
[unreal past]

Q: If an asteroid _____ (strike) the earth 65 million years ago, there

4. [factual past]

_____ (should, be) a crater on earth today. Has the crater been found?

[factual present]

A: Yes, it has. There is a 200-kilometer crater off the coast of Mexico, and the

impact of an asteroid about 65 million years ago is the only logical explanation.

If an asteroid _____ (not, strike) the earth, a crater of that type and

5. [unreal past]

size _____ (not, be) there today.

[unreal present]

Q: Sixty-five million years is a long time ago. Why should we worry now?

A: An asteroid exploded over a wilderness area in Siberia in 1908. Many people

_____ (not, consider) asteroids to be such a threat if this explosion

6. [unreal present]

_____ (not, happen). And Comet

[unreal past]

Shoemaker-Levy 9 collided with Jupiter

in 1994. If you _____

7. [unreal past]

(observe) that collision through a

telescope, you _____

[unreal present]

(not, question) the possibility of

a collision with a comet. If Comet

Shoemaker-Levy 9 _____

8. [unreal past]

(strike) earth instead, we _____

[unreal present]

(not, be) around to talk about it.

B. Use your imagination to complete the sentences so they have past conditions and present results.

1. If a huge asteroid hadn't hit the earth 65 million years ago, _____.

2. If the dinosaurs hadn't become extinct, _____.

3. The earth would be very different now _____.

▣ *Should (Happen To)* and *Were To: Remote Possibilities*

A. Use the conditions and results given to write pairs of sentences about the future. Use *should happen to* in the first sentence and *were to* in the second sentence.

1. Condition: A big asteroid crashes into the ocean. Result: Colossal waves wipe out everything on the coastal lands.

   If a big asteroid should happen to crash into the ocean, colossal waves will wipe out everything on the coastal lands.

   If a big asteroid were to crash into the ocean, colossal waves would wipe out everything on the coastal lands.

2. Condition: A big asteroid strikes in the middle of a continent. Result: Huge clouds of dust and vapor block out the sun's light.

3. Condition: Astronomers detect an asteroid approaching earth. Result: We probably have time to do something about it.

4. Condition: We spot an asteroid on a collision course with earth. Result: Nuclear technology is used to try to change its course.

B. What will or would you do under the following conditions? Write sentences using *should* or *were to.* Then add two more unlikely conditions of your own and write sentences about them.

1. Someone spots an asteroid coming toward earth.

2. The teacher cancels class tomorrow.

3. You win a million dollars in a lottery.

4. You discover a way to prevent earthquakes.

5. _____

6. _____

▣ Inverted Conditionals—Form: *Informing the President*

In each item, if possible rewrite the conditional as an inverted conditional. If inverting the conditional isn't possible, write **NC.**

1. Mr. President, many natural disasters of the distant past had extraterrestrial origins. If I were in your position, I would want to know about possible dangers.

   Were I in your position, I would want to know about the possible dangers.

2. If you have time, I'll tell you about them now.

   NC

3. The earth has been hit by asteroids many times. If we hadn't found their craters, we wouldn't be so certain about this.

4. Asteroids are still a threat. If a large asteroid should hit land, there will be a global catastrophe.

5. When a very small asteroid exploded above Siberia in 1908, many trees were destroyed. If the region had been populated, the explosion would have had serious consequences.

6. Comets are faster and less predictable than asteroids. If they weren't so fast and unpredictable, we wouldn't need to be concerned about them.

7. If a comet should approach earth, we would have little time to do anything about it.

8. Then there is the possibility of gamma ray bursts. If certain stars explode, they release energy in the form of gamma rays.

9. If a large burst of gamma rays were heading toward earth, our chances of survival wouldn't be good.

10. If the government could spend more money on discovering and monitoring asteroids, comets, and gamma ray bursts, everyone would feel safer.

4   *If So* and *If Not: Operation Spacewatch*

A. Read the following passage. If a condition clause can be replaced with *if so* or *if not*, cross it out and write *if so* or *if not* above it. If the clause can't be replaced, write **NC.**

In 1998 an astronomer announced that a newly discovered asteroid, XF11,

                                                    NC
might come very close to earth in 2028. (1)If an asteroid the size of XF11 hit earth, it

would explode with great force. After the announcement, people began to worry

about asteroids. Possibly other, undiscovered, asteroids were heading toward earth.

                              If so,
(2)~~If other asteroids were heading toward earth,~~ we might be in great danger.

Operation Spacewatch is a team of astronomers who look for undiscovered

asteroids. (3)If they discover a large asteroid close to earth, they track its orbit. They

estimate that only about 10% of the near-earth asteroids have been discovered. It's

possible that more money will be devoted to the project. (4)If more money isn't

devoted to the project, it may take decades to discover the rest of the asteroids.

Most astronomers believe that most dangerous asteroids will be discovered

long before they come close to earth. It's likely that we'll have plenty of time to take

action. (5)If we have plenty of time, we can develop technology to deal with the

threat. (6)If we don't have plenty of time, we'll have to use the technology we have.

The best technology available now is rockets and nuclear explosives. (7)If we sent a

rocket with explosives to a threatening asteroid, we could set off an explosion on or

near it. Probably such an explosion will change its orbit. (8)If the explosion changes

its orbit, the asteroid will miss the earth. (9)If the explosion doesn't change its orbit,

we'll need to try another strategy.

B. Use *if so* and *if not* and your own ideas to write **two** sentences to follow each of the given sentences.

1. It may rain tomorrow.

    If so, we'll have the party indoors. If not, we'll be able to play baseball.

2. The weather could be unusually warm next summer.

3. I'll probably finish my homework by ten o'clock.

4. I might have some free time this weekend.

GRAMMAR BRIEFING 2: Sentences with *Wish* or *Hope*

Sentences with *hope* and sentences with *wish* express different kinds of desires. Sentences with *hope*, like factual and future conditionals, are about what is possible. Sentences with *wish*, like unreal conditionals, are about what is not likely or not possible. The verb *hope* or *wish* is in the main clause, followed by a noun clause that can begin with *that*. (For more on noun clauses, see Unit 10).

FORM AND FUNCTION Sentences with *Hope* or *Wish*

Sentences with *Hope*

■ The tense of the verb in the clause following *hope* corresponds to the time the hope is about.

    I **hope** (that) he **caught** his train. (hope about past: past time verb)

    I **hope** (that) he**'s enjoying** himself. (hope about present: present time verb)

    I **hope** (that) you**'ll join** us for dinner. (hope about future: future time verb)

■ Sentences with *hope* express a desire for situations that are possible.

    I **hope** (that) I **can come** to the picnic. (The speaker wants to go to the picnic and might be able to go.)

Sentences with *Wish* about the Present or Future

■ In wishes about the present, *wish* is followed by a past form of the verb. *Could* + base form of the verb can also be used. As in present unreal conditionals, *were* is used for all persons of *be*.

> He **wishes** (that) he **had** more money.
>
> He **wishes** (that) he **could** come with us now.
>
> We **wish** (that) he **were spending** more time with us.

■ In wishes about the future, *wish* is followed by *would* or *could* + base form of the verb. *Were going to* + base form of the verb or *were* + verb + *-ing* can also be used.

> They wish he **would/could** come tomorrow.
>
> They wish he **were going to be** here for the wedding.
>
> I wish I **were taking** a trip this summer. (Remember that when the progressive is used for the future, it can only be used for actions that can be planned. [**Not:** I wish the sun ~~were shining~~ tomorrow.])

■ Sentences with *wish* express a desire for a situation that the speaker believes is unlikely or impossible. They sometimes express a complaint or a regret.

> He wishes he could earn more money. (It is not likely or not possible that he can earn more money. [Compare: *He hopes he can earn more money.* It is possible for him to earn more money.])
>
> I wish my neighbor would stop playing the piano. (complaint)
>
> I wish I could go to the museum with you. (regret)

Sentences with *Wish* about the Past

■ In wishes about the past, *wish* is followed by the past perfect form of the verb.

> We **wish** you **had been** there.
>
> I wish I**'d gone** to Omar's party last night.
>
> I wish I **could have helped** you.

■ Sentences with *wish* about the past express a desire for a situation that didn't occur. They often express regrets.

> I wish I had gotten there on time. (I didn't get there on time.)
>
> I wish that I had traveled a lot when I was young. (I didn't travel a lot when I was young.)

GRAMMAR PRACTICE 2: Sentences with *Wish* or *Hope*

5   *Wish* and *Hope* about the Present and Future: *Making News*

Television reporters often go to the scenes of natural disasters to interview people.
Complete the sentences by using the information given. Where more than one form
is possible, use any appropriate form.

Hurricane on the Gulf Coast of Texas

Reporter: The hurricane is approaching your home. How do you feel about this?

Resident: Well, of course, I wish that the hurricane

_____weren't approaching_____ my home. But it's possible that my
                          1

house won't be badly damaged.

Reporter: I hope that your house ___won't be badly damaged.___ The emergency
                                              2

management officials are going to ask everyone to go to an emergency

shelter soon.

Resident: I wish they ___weren't going to / wouldn't ask___ everyone to go. I'm not
                                        3

ready.

Reporter: It seems that the eye of the hurricane, with the strongest winds around it,

will come ashore here.

Resident: That doesn't sound good. I wish that the eye of the hurricane

_____ ashore here.
                    4

Reporter: Unfortunately, we can't control hurricanes.

Resident: Right now I wish that we _____ them. But
                                                        5

maybe I'll be able to come back home soon.

Reporter: I hope that you _____ back home soon.
                                              6

Good luck!

Flood in Ohio

Reporter: As a result of heavy rain, the river has overflowed its banks, causing seri-

ous flooding. Is the water level going down now?

Resident: No, it isn't. I wish that it _____ now, because
                                                          7

the first floor of my house is covered with water.

Reporter: Do you have flood insurance?

Resident: No, I don't. I wish that I _____ flood insur-
                                                   8

ance. But that's not my only problem. My cat is lost. Maybe she's in a safe

place, though.

Reporter: I hope that your cat _____ in a safe place. . . .
                                                9

It's possible that the president will make government disaster aid

available.

Resident: That's good news. I hope that the president

_____ aid available, so we can clean up and
                    10

repair the damage.

Reporter: Unfortunately, floods happen often along this river. Of course, we wish

that they _____ so often. But whenever they
                         11

happen, we'll be here to give you the news.

Blizzard in Baltimore

Reporter: This evening I'm talking to people about the blizzard that's headed

toward Baltimore. It's going to snow very hard.

Snowplow
Operator: I wish it _____ very hard. Because
                               12

of this storm, I can't spend the evening with my family.

Reporter: Big storms can really disrupt family life. Notice how crowded this super-

market is.

Shopper: I wish it _____ so crowded.

                         13

Reporter: Let's find out how your son feels about the storm.

   Child: I'm looking forward to it. But it isn't snowing now. I wish it

            _____.

                       14

Reporter: The storm won't start until later this evening.

   Child: I wish the storm _____ soon. If we get a lot of

                              15

            snow, school will be canceled.

Reporter: I see. The blizzard won't be a disaster for the children of Baltimore!

6 *Wish* and *Hope* about the Past: *Talking about the News*

Complete the sentences by using the correct forms of the words in parentheses to
express wishes or hopes about the past.

Vicky: Did you watch television last night?

  Joe: No, I didn't, because I had to work. I wish I __had had__ (have) a chance

                                                         1

          to watch television last night. I hope I __didn't miss__ (not, miss) anything

                                                    2

          important.

Vicky: You missed some news program about natural disasters. I wish I

          _____ (know) how they were going to present the stories. If I had

              3

          known, I wouldn't have watched.

  Joe: What do you mean? How did they present the stories?

Vicky: The reporters kept making the situations as dramatic as possible. I wish they

          _____ (not, keep) asking people to talk about their feelings. First,

              4

          they interviewed a man in Texas. I hope his house _____ (not, be)

                                                                    5

          destroyed by the hurricane. Then they interviewed a woman in Ohio. She

          was really upset because her house was flooded and she'd lost her cat. She

          probably wishes she _____ (not, have to) talk about her problems

                                  6

          on national television.

Joe: I hope the poor woman _____ (find) her cat.
                                       7

Vicky: Then they talked to people about a blizzard that hadn't even started yet. Of

course, I hope the blizzard _____ (not, cause) serious problems,
                                        8

but the report was really silly. I wish you _____ (could, see) it. Why
                                                      9

do you think reporters try to make the weather news so dramatic?

Joe: They know that if the weather news is dramatic, more people will watch

television.

▊ 7 ▊ Using *Wish* and *Hope: Nature and Your Life*

A. Write answers to the following questions. Begin each sentence with *I wish* or *I hope.*

1. What is a natural event that you wish you could have watched or experienced?

    Example: I wish I could have watched Comet Shoemaker-Levy 9 hit Jupiter.

2. What are two other interesting experiences of any kind that you wish you had had in the past?

3. What is a natural event that you experienced that you wish you hadn't experienced?

4. What is something that you wish had happened yesterday?

5. What do you wish were different about the weather in the place where you live?

6. Where do you wish you could live?

7. What do you wish you were doing now?

8. What do you wish you were going to do tomorrow?

9. What do you wish you were doing next summer?

10. What is something that you hope happened yesterday?

11. What is a natural event that you hope isn't happening anywhere in the world now?

12. What natural event do you hope will happen in your area soon?

B. Work with a partner. Ask your partner the questions in **A.** Then report **two** of your partner's answers to the class.

    Example: Adel hopes that we'll have a blizzard soon.

GRAMMAR BRIEFING 3: *Alternatives to If; Implied Conditions*

Forms other than *if* can signal conditionals. Conditions are sometimes implied instead of being stated.

FORM AND FUNCTION Alternatives to *If;* Implied Conditions

Alternatives to *If*

■ Forms other than *if* that can signal conditionals include *in the event (that), providing/provided (that), as long as, whether or not, even if, only if,* and *unless.* Some of these are basically equivalent to *if* in meaning; others are not.

- Expressions that are equivalent to *if* include *in the event (that), providing/provided (that),* and *as long as. In the event (that)* is more formal than *if.* Like *if,* it can be used in all types of conditionals. *Providing/provided (that)* is more formal than *as long as;* these expressions tend to be used in factual and future conditionals.

     In the event (that) sales hadn't increased, we would have reconsidered our advertising campaign.

     Providing/provided (that) he is allowed to speak first, he is willing to come to the meeting.

     As long as he's going to be there, I'll be there, too.

- *Whether (. . .) or not* and *even if* are used when the condition does not affect the result. In other words, they indicate that the condition does not matter.

     Whether he comes **or not,** I'll be there. (The result of my being there will occur in any case.)

     He wouldn't sell his house **even if** you offered him a million dollars. (The condition of $1 million won't affect the result of his not selling the house.)

- *Only if* is used when there is one particular condition that will cause the result.

     I will pass my exams **only if** I study. (No other condition will lead to the result of my passing the exams.)

- *Unless* is used to express the one condition that will not cause the result. (*Unless* is often similar to "if . . . not.")

     I will fail my exams **unless** I study. (= If I don't study, I will fail my exams.)

Implied Conditions

■ A condition is sometimes implied instead of being stated. Expressions that signal implied conditions include *with, without, or (else),* and *otherwise.*

     With proper identification, you can board the airplane. (= If you have proper identification, you can board the airplane.)

     Without proper identification, you can't board the airplane. (= If you don't have proper identification, you can't board the airplane.)

     He will come, **or (else)** I won't stay. (= If he doesn't come, I won't stay.)

     He will come. **Otherwise,** I won't stay. (= If he doesn't come, I won't stay.)

GRAMMAR HOTSPOT!

- Be careful! When *only if* comes at the beginning of a sentence, the subject and verb in the main clause are inverted.

    Only if it rains **will** we cancel the picnic.

    Only if she asks **do I help** her with her homework.

- Don't confuse *only if* with *if only*, which is similar to *if* but stronger.

    If only you'd participated more, you would have gotten a good grade. (= *If you'd participated more, you would have gotten a good grade,* but expresses more regret.)

    Only if you had participated more would you have gotten a good grade. (= *If you had participated more but under no other condition . . .*)

  If only can be used alone to express a wish (*If only I'd met you years ago!*).

GRAMMAR PRACTICE 3: Alternatives to *If;* Implied Conditions

8 Alternatives to *If*—Meaning: *Disaster Updates*

`···` Listen to the announcements once for the main ideas. Then listen again and **circle** the letter of the correct restatement of the meaning of the sentence that you heard.

1. Ice storm in New England

    a. If the weather forecast is accurate, it will take at least a week to restore power to most areas.

    b. If the weather forecast isn't accurate, it will take at least a week to restore power to most areas.

2. Hurricane over the Atlantic

    a. The hurricane's coming ashore doesn't matter—it will bring high winds and heavy rainfall to coastal areas.

    b. The hurricane will bring high winds and heavy rainfall to coastal areas if it comes ashore.

3. National Forest Service fire management policy in wilderness areas

    a. If a fire is caused by lightning, the forest service allows it to burn.

    b. The cause of a fire doesn't matter—the forest service doesn't allow it to burn.

4. Volcano activity in the Pacific Northwest

    a. A volcano's being active doesn't matter—seismologists continue to monitor it in any case.

    b. The one condition under which the seismologists continue to monitor a volcano is if it is active.

5. Flood in Illinois

   a. The one condition under which you need to boil drinking water is if you are a resident of the Tri-City area.

   b. Your being a resident of the Tri-City area or another nearby area doesn't matter—you need to boil drinking water.

6. Heat wave in Chicago

   a. City officials' opening a shelter for the elderly won't make any difference—the Red Cross will open one in any case.

   b. If city officials don't open a shelter for the elderly, the Red Cross will open one.

7. Drought in Texas

   a. If doesn't rain soon, the crops will be lost.

   b. Rain won't make any difference to the crops—they will be lost in any case.

8. Tornado in South Dakota

   a. The one condition under which the six people might have survived is if they heard the warning.

   b. If the six people had heard the warning, they might have survived.

9 Alternatives to *If*—Form and Meaning: *Responding in Disasters*

Use the expressions given to write conditional sentences that express the meaning of the underlined information. Use negatives if needed. Put the condition clauses at the beginning of the sentences. Use each expression once.

~~even if~~   ~~only if~~   provided that   ~~unless~~   ~~whether or not~~

1. I'm worried about how our neighbors are getting along in the storm. <u>You may come with me, or you may not. It doesn't make any difference to me. I'm going to check on the neighbors.</u>

   a. ___Whether you come with me or not, I'm going to check on the neighbors.___

   b. ___Even if you don't come with me, I'm going to check on the neighbors.___

2. It isn't a good idea for me to go out into this storm alone. But <u>you may come with me. Under that condition, I'll go to check on the neighbors.</u>

   a. ___Only if you come with me will I go to check on the neighbors.___

   b. ___Unless you come with me, I won't go to check on the neighbors.___

   c. _____

as long as   even if   in the event that   providing that   whether or not

3. Because of the heat wave, it isn't safe for Mrs. Rivera to stay in her hot apart-
   ment. Maybe Mrs. Rivera wants to go to the shelter, and maybe she doesn't. It
   doesn't matter. Lorenzo is going to take her there.

   a. _____

   b. _____

4. It's possible that Mr. Hall has an air-conditioner. Under that condition, he
   doesn't need to go to the shelter.

   a. _____

   b. _____

   c. _____

even if   in the event that   only if   unless   whether or not

5. The Red Cross offers special first aid courses for professional rescuers.
   It's possible that Perry has taken the special first aid course. Under that
   condition, he is qualified to be a professional rescuer.

   a. _____

   b. _____

   c. _____

6. Perhaps you've taken a first aid course before, and perhaps you haven't. It
   doesn't matter. You must complete the special course in order to be certified as
   a professional rescuer.

   a. _____

   b. _____

10 Implied Conditions: *Being Prepared*

A. Write sentences that state the conditions that are implied in the sentences given.

1. You must have a disaster plan, or else you might not be prepared to protect
   yourself.

   If you don't have a disaster plan, you might not be prepared to protect yourself.

2. Without a battery-operated radio, you won't be able to get information from
   local emergency officials.

3. You should have a flashlight. Otherwise, you may be helpless in the dark.

4. You'd better keep a supply of fresh batteries, or your radio and flashlight could
   be useless.

5. You should store fresh water in advance. Otherwise, you might not have water to
   drink.

6. With sufficient fresh water, you can survive for a long time.

B. Use the sentences and expressions given to write sentences with implied conditions. If more than one verb form is possible, use any appropriate form.

1. If we don't ask what kinds of disasters might occur in this area, we won't know what conditions to prepare for. (otherwise)

   We are going to (had better/have to/must/should) ask what kinds of disasters might occur in this area. Otherwise, we won't know what conditions to prepare for.

2. If we don't have electricity, we'll have difficulty keeping our fresh food from spoiling. (without)

3. If we have enough dried and canned food, we can get along until we can go to the store. (with)

4. If Kate doesn't leave now, she won't get home before the storm begins. (or)

5. If you have snow tires, you can drive home in a blizzard. (with)

6. If you don't turn on the radio, you won't know the weather forecast. (otherwise)

7. If we don't stop talking about preparing for disasters, I'm going to get very nervous. (or else)

▮▮ Using Alternatives to *If* and Implied Conditions: *Assembling Your Disaster Supply Kit*

A. Work in groups of three. Imagine that you are on a ship that is caught in a hurricane. The ship is sinking fast, but with one of its lifeboats, you can get to a tiny uninhabited island. You may be stranded on the island for weeks before help arrives. You will have to survive with only the contents of your Disaster Supply Kit. The kit already contains the following: fresh water, canned and dried food, a battery-operated radio, a flashlight, and batteries. In addition, you can put **eight** items from the following list into the kit. Discuss the items in order to decide on the eight that you think are most necessary. For each item that you suggest, use an alternative to *if* or an implied condition to explain your reason.

Alternatives to *if*: in the event (that), providing/provided (that), as long as, whether or not, even if, only if, unless
Implied Conditions: with, without, or (else), otherwise

> Example: *We ought to take the first aid kit. In the event that someone gets hurt, we'll be able to treat the injury.* OR *We have to take the pillows. Without a pillow, I can't sleep at all.*

Write a list of the **eight** items your group agreed on.

blankets	pillows
a box of matches	plastic cups, plates, forks and spoons
a can opener	a sharp knife
a deck of playing cards	a small gas stove with one canister of gas
a first aid kit	soap
a first aid manual	a tent
fish hooks	towels
paper and a pencil	twenty yards of nylon string

B. Write **two** sentences about each item that you've decided to include. Use an alternative to *if* or an implied conditional in the second sentence.

> Example: *We decided to take the tent. Unless we take it, we might have no way to stay dry.*

As a class, compare your choices.

UNIT WRAP-UP

Error Correction

Find and correct the errors in the following passage. Some errors can be corrected in more than one way. Including the example, there are **10** errors.

In 1811–12 the small town of New Madrid, Missouri, was the center of some of the biggest earthquakes ever recorded in the United States. ~~When~~ *If* the area had been densely populated then, the earthquakes would have caused great devastation. The shock waves from the earthquakes traveled for hundreds of miles. Had you lived in Boston, you could of felt them. The area around New Madrid is still a dangerous earthquake zone. If the area wasn't so dangerous, people who live there might not take earthquake predictions so seriously.

In 1989 it was reported that Iben Browning, a business consultant, made this announcement: "If my calculations are correct there is a 50 percent chance of a destructive earthquake striking New Madrid on December 3, 1990." Because many people believed that Browning had predicted previous earthquakes, hundreds of news reporters went to New Madrid. One reporter said, "If an earthquake will occur, it will be the best-recorded event in Missouri history. If even nothing happens, people's reaction to the prediction will make an interesting news story." New Madrid experienced an "earthquake hysteria." Thousands of people bought disaster supplies, many residents decided to spend the week elsewhere, and the schools closed.

December 3 came and went. No earthquake occurred. Many people blamed the reporters for the hysteria. A physicist said, "Browning had not accurately predicted previous earthquakes. The reporters would have found this out if they would have investigated. Only if there is a scientific basis for a prediction, people should take it seriously. Browning based his prediction on studies of ocean tides, but in fact high tides do not cause earthquakes. If it was possible for tides to cause earthquakes, scientific evidence would have been found long ago. Earthquakes cannot be predicted. If only we could predict them!" Red Cross officials were glad that the prediction raised awareness about earthquakes, but wished the hysteria wouldn't have happened. A government official said, "At least we will be better prepared if an earthquake should come."

Task 1: The Chain Reactions Game

Play this game as a class. Use your imagination to describe the possible results of the following past unreal conditions. One student gives a result for the first condition. Then the next student changes that result into a condition and gives a result for it. Continue until everyone has contributed a sentence to the chain of events.

> Example: Student A: If it had snowed yesterday, I wouldn't have come to
> class.
>
> Student B: If I hadn't come to class, I would have spent the day
> at home.
>
> Student C: If I had spent the day at home, I might have baked a
> cake.
>
> Student D: If I had baked a cake, . . .

1. If it had snowed yesterday, . . .
2. If I had lived at the time of the dinosaurs, . . .
3. If everyone in our class had gone to Hawaii last month, . . .

To continue the game, think of your own conditions to start the chain of events.

Task 2: A Guide to Disaster Preparation

Work in small groups. Each group should choose a natural disaster, for example, hurricanes or earthquakes. Write a one-page guide to inform your classmates about how to prepare for the disaster and advise them about where to go and what to do if it occurs or is about to occur. (For information for the guide, try the library or the Internet.) Use at least **eight** of the following expressions: *if, in the event that, providing that, as long as, even if, only if, unless, with, without, or (else),* and *otherwise.*

> Example: If you live in an area with earthquakes, remove all heavy objects from high shelves. Otherwise, the objects might fall during an earthquake and injure someone. In the event that an earthquake should occur, do not go outside.

Task 3: A Disaster Movie

Work in groups of three. Write a script for a dramatic scene in a movie about a volcano eruption, a tornado, a possible asteroid or comet impact, or any other natural disaster. Use each of the following at least once: *hope, wish,* conditionals with *if so* or *if not,* future conditionals, present unreal conditionals, and past unreal conditionals.

> Example: Sabrina: The volcano may erupt soon. If so, we're in real trouble.
>
> Hiro: If the helicopter can land here, it might be able to rescue us. . . .

The scene should include a part for each member of the group. Present your scene to the class.

Unit Ten

Noun Clauses

UNIT OBJECTIVES

■ **noun clauses with *that*, with *wh-* words, and with *if/whether***
(Many readers think ***that fiction should be very different from real life.*** Readers of a mystery aren't sure ***who committed the crime.*** Readers wonder ***whether they can solve the mystery.***)

■ **quoted speech and reported speech**
(Brent said, ***"I'm in love with Katie."*** Brent said ***that he was in love with Katie.***)

■ **reported questions, commands, and requests**
(We asked ***what kinds of books people liked best.*** Mrs. Blair told us ***to write a paper.*** She asked us ***to work in groups.***)

■ **noun clauses after verbs or adjectives of urgency**
(It is important ***that a child have books to read.***)

INTRODUCTORY TASKS

Reading and Listening

Read and listen to this passage.

In almost any bookstore, you'll see large Fiction/Literature section. You'll probably also see **that many works of fiction (i.e., books that tell a story)* are in other sections instead.** These sections have labels such as Romance, Mystery, Science Fiction, Horror, and Westerns. You might wonder **whether the books in these sections are different from those in the Fiction/Literature section** and, if so, **how they are different.**

The answer is **that these books belong to genres** (pronounced JAHN-ruhz), types of fiction that follow certain formulas, or rules. If you pick up an unfamiliar book from the Fiction/Literature section, you won't know **what kind of story it tells.** But if you pick up a book from the Romance section, you can be pretty sure **that it's about a young woman who falls in love.** The reason is **that books in the romance genre almost always follow a certain formula.**

That genre fiction is popular is something no one would question. Booksellers say **that two-thirds of all books sold are genre fiction.** In fact, another name for genre fiction is "popular fiction."

However, experts on literature wonder **why genre fiction is so popular.** Experts also wonder **whether books that are based on formulas can be considered literature** in the sense that, say, Shakespeare's plays are literature.

The first question might not be very hard to answer. A careful look at genre fiction shows **that it's like real life but much better.** The hero, man or woman,** of a work of genre fiction has an important goal–whether it's to save the world from creatures from outer space, find out who the murderer is before he strikes again, or marry the handsome millionaire. Readers are afraid **that the hero will fail.** When they close the book for the last time, they are relieved and gratified **that the hero has succeeded.** They care about **what happens to the hero** because they can identify with the hero and his or her goal. The second question might be harder to answer. See **if you can come up with an answer as you read the unit.**

*Book-length works of fiction are also called "novels."

**Female heroes are also called "heroines."

Comprehension Check

Read each sentence. Circle **T** if the sentence is true or **F** if the sentence is false.

1. Before readers even begin reading a book that is genre fiction, they often have some idea of the kind of story it tells.   (T)   F

2. Works of genre fiction are very popular.   T   F

3. Experts think that books like romances and mysteries cannot be considered fiction.   T   F

4. Experts are not sure that genre fiction can be considered literature.   T   F

5. Readers feel that genre fiction stories are exactly like their own lives.   T   F

Think about Grammar

A. The **boldfaced** words in the passage are noun clauses. Look at the passage and circle the words that introduce the noun clauses. List these words. (If a word is repeated, just list it once.)

_____

B. Look at the pair of sentences from the reading and complete the statements that follow.

a. In almost any bookstore you'll see <u>a large Fiction/Literature section.</u>

b. You'll probably also see <u>that many works of fiction are in other sections instead.</u>

The underlined groups of words in sentences (a) and (b) are different in form but similar in function. The underlined group of words in (b) is a noun clause.

1. The underlined group of words in (b) is different in form from that in (a) because

   it is introduced by the word _____ and because it includes a subject

   and a _____ and is therefore a _____ rather than a phrase.

2. The underlined group of words in (b) is similar to that in (a) because it functions

   as a _____ and, more specifically, as an _____ of *see.*

C. Look in the reading for an example of each of the following:

1. a noun clause that is an object _____

2. a noun clause that is an object of a preposition _____

3. a noun clause that is a subject _____

4. a noun clause that is a subject complement _____

5. a noun clause that follows an adjective _____

chapter

20

Noun Clauses

Introductory Task: *Judging a Book by Its Cover*

A. Look at the four book covers. What kinds of stories do these books tell? Complete the sentences about each book by filling in the letter of the most appropriate noun clause from the list of sentences on page 367.

1. I think ____c____.

2. She is telling him _____.

3. The reader will keep turning the pages

   to find out _____.

1. I think _____.

2. She is telling him _____.

3. The reader will keep turning the pages

   to find out _____.

1. I think _____.

2. She is telling him _____.

3. The reader will keep turning the pages

   to find out _____.

1. I think _____.

2. She is telling him _____.

3. The reader will keep turning the pages

   to find out _____.

1. I think: (a) that this book is a horror story; (b) that this book is a mystery; (c) that this book is a romance; (d) that this book is science fiction.

2. She is telling him: (e) that they must report what they've seen to the commander of the Space Fleet; (f) that she knows that he prefers someone from his own social class; (g) that, if he knows anything about the crime, he'd better talk now; (h) that he can't make her into a monster like him.

3. The reader will keep turning the pages to find out: (i) whether the man and woman will discover their true feelings for each other; (j) whether the person who is really guilty will be caught; (k) whether people will learn the truth before their world is taken over; (l) whether the unnatural evil that has lasted for centuries will be destroyed.

B. Compare answers in a group. What other ideas do you have about these books from their covers? Which one of these books do you think that you'd like to read? Why? Discuss these questions. Use *I think that* . . . and *I think that I'd read* . . . , *because* . . .

> Example: I think that she becomes a prisoner in his castle. . . . I think that I'd read the horror story because I like to feel scared.

GRAMMAR BRIEFING 1: Noun Clauses

Noun clauses are clauses that function like nouns.

FORM AND FUNCTION Noun Clauses

■ Like all clauses, a noun clause has a subject and a verb. A noun clause begins with *that*, a *wh-* word, or *if* or *whether*. These words link a noun clause to the main clause of the sentence.

Main Clause	Noun Clause
He says	**that he isn't feeling well.**
She wondered	**where we were going.**
They don't know	**if/whether they will come.**

■ Noun clauses usually function like nouns. That is, they can be subjects, subject complements, objects of verbs, and objects of prepositions. As subjects, they take singular verbs.

What she said isn't true. (subject)

Her opinion was **that the grass needed water.** (subject complement)

I wonder **whether she will tell me the truth this time.** (object)

We thought about **how you could help us.** (object of preposition)

■ In addition to these noun functions, noun clauses can follow certain adjectives.

I'm sure **that Val will know the answer.**

■ Noun clauses tend to be used with verbs and adjectives that express mental activities.* These verbs include *agree, believe, decide, doubt, feel, forget, guess, hear, hope, imagine, know, notice, realize, remember, see, show, suppose, think, understand,* and *wonder.*** The adjectives include *afraid, angry, aware, certain, clear, convinced, disappointed, glad, happy, pleased, positive, sad, sorry, sure, surprised,* and *worried.*

* Noun clauses can also be used with verbs that report speech (e.g., *ask, say, tell;* see Chapter 21, Grammar Briefing 1).

** Some verbs are used with gerunds and/or infinitives but not noun clauses (e.g., *I want you to help me.* **Not:** *I want that you help me.*).

■ The tense of the verb in the noun clause is affected by the tense of the main clause verb. If a main clause verb is past tense, a noun clause verb

• is past tense if it expresses a situation that occurred at the same time.

I suddenly **realized** that she **wasn't** with us.

• is often past perfect if it expresses an earlier situation.

I **was** afraid that she **had wandered off.**

• uses *would* + the base form of the verb or *was/were going to* + the base form of the verb if it expresses a later situation.

I **wondered** if we **would find** her in that crowd.

GRAMMAR PRACTICE 1: **Noun Clauses**

1 Identifying Noun Clauses: *Two Views of Popular Fiction*

A. Read the following letters sent to a literary magazine (a magazine of fiction and articles about fiction). Underline each noun clause and circle the word that introduces it. Label the function of each noun clause: **S** = subject; **O** = object; **O Prep** = object of preposition; **SC** = subject complement; **adj** + **NC** = noun clause following adjective. (**Hints:** 1. Do not confuse *that* noun clauses with adjective clauses: Adjective clauses modify nouns and usually come right after the noun they modify. 2. Do not confuse *if/whether* noun clauses with conditional clauses.)

Dear Editor:

adj + NC

I am extremely disappointed (that) you included an article about genre fiction in your magazine last month. That this inclusion is highly inappropriate is obvious to any serious reader.

A literary magazine is supposed to be about literature—that is, written works of art.

Literature is fiction that is original and makes readers see the world in a new way. It is fiction that uses poetic language.

It is obvious that genre fiction is the opposite of literature. Genre fiction just follows formulas: for example, boy meets girl, and boy and girl fall in love and get married. Authors of genre fiction are like cooks who just follow recipes instead of inventing new dishes. It's not surprising that some of these authors turn out a hundred books. I wouldn't be surprised if they wrote those things in their sleep. Reading genre fiction is like watching TV.

To summarize, my position is that you should stick to literature from now on.

Professor Harold Burton

Dear Editor:

As a writer of genre fiction, I feel that I must respond to Professor Burton.

(Unfortunately, the professor's attitude is familiar. After a lecture I gave recently, I was

asked about whether I would try writing literature. My reply was that genre fiction **is**

literature.)

First, surveys tell us that 90 percent of all new fiction published is genre fiction. I

wonder whether the professor wants to ignore 90 percent of all new fiction.

Second, I wonder why the professor thinks all great works are fully original. Doesn't he

realize that even Shakespeare got most of his stories from other sources?

Third, genre fiction deals with the same issues that the greatest works of literature deal

with. Undoubtedly, the professor admires Fyodor Dostoyevsky's *Crime and Punishment.*

I'd like to ask him what he thinks mysteries are all about. If you don't know, professor, then

let me tell you: crime and punishment.

Finally, I don't understand why the professor thinks watching TV is so bad. Perhaps he's

a snob. That TV and genre fiction can bring pleasure seems obvious and important.

Roslyn Martyn-Jones

B. Work in a small group. Discuss the letters. What do you think of the two writers'
ideas? Who do you agree with more? Why? Use sentences with *I (don't)
agree/think/believe that . . .*

> **Example:** I think that Professor Burton is right. I think that romances are
> more like soap operas on TV than like real literature.

GRAMMAR BRIEFING 2: Types of Noun Clauses

There are three types of noun clauses: noun clauses introduced by *that*, noun clauses introduced by a *wh-* word, and noun clauses introduced by *if* or *whether*.

FORM AND FUNCTION Types of Noun Clauses

Noun Clauses with *That*

■ Noun clauses with *that* can be used after a wide range of verbs and adjectives—all the adjectives listed in Grammar Briefing 1 and all the verbs listed except *wonder*.

> I think **(that) this book will be interesting.**
>
> I'm sure **(that) this book will be interesting.**
>
> I wonder whether this book will be interesting.
> **Not:** I wonder ~~that this book will be interesting.~~

■ The word *that* is often omitted. However, it cannot be omitted if the *that* clause is in subject position.

> I'm really happy **(that) you could come.**
>
> **That he's late** doesn't surprise me.   **Not:** ~~He's late~~ doesn't surprise me.

■ Although *that clauses* can occur in subject position, more often *it* is put in the subject position and the *that* clause is put after the predicate. The meaning is the same.

> **That she said something** is fortunate. = **It is fortunate that she said something.**

■ *The fact* (or a similar noun phrase, e.g., *the idea, the possibility*) can sometimes be used before a *that* clause. *The fact* is common before noun clauses that are in subject position. It is not used before noun clauses that follow adjectives or that are objects of verbs.

> **The fact** that she said something is important.
>
> It is important that she said something.
> **Not:** It is important ~~the fact~~ that she said something.

■ *That* clauses can be objects of prepositions only if a noun phrase such as *the fact* comes before the *that* clause.

> We are curious **about the fact** that she said something.
> **Not:** We are curious ~~about that she said something.~~

■ If the content of a *that* clause is clear from what has already been said, the clause can sometimes be replaced by *so* or *not*. This is possible only with certain main clause verbs, including *assume, believe, guess, hope, imagine, know, suppose,* and *think,* and with certain other structures, including *be afraid* and *it appears/seems.*

• An affirmative idea is expressed with *so.*

> He's coming with us tonight—at least I **hope so.** (*so* = that he's coming with us tonight)

- A negative idea is expressed with *so* if the main clause includes *not;* otherwise the negative idea is expressed with *not.*

> A: I wonder if class has been canceled.
>
> B: I **don't think so.** (= I don't think that class has been canceled.) OR
>   I **think not.** (= I think that class hasn't been canceled.)

Believe, imagine, suppose, think, and *it seems/appears* can be used with main clause *not* + *so* or with *not.*

Hope and *be afraid* are used only with *not. Guess* is usually used only with *not.*

Know can be used only with *so.*

> **I'm afraid not.**   **Not:** ~~I'm not afraid so.~~
>
> **I don't know so.**   **Not:** ~~I know not.~~

Noun Clauses with *Wh-* Words

■ *Wh-* clauses begin with *wh-* words (*who, what, why, when, where, how*).
Wh- clauses have statement word order, even when they occur within questions.

> I don't know **what he is doing.**   **Not:** I don't know ~~what is he doing.~~
>
> Can you see **where he is?**   **Not:** Can you see ~~where is he?~~

■ *Wh-* clauses are often used in statements that express uncertainty.

> I wonder **how he knows that.**
>
> We don't know **why the sky is blue.**
>
> **Where I put that book** is a mystery to me.

■ *Wh-* clauses can be used as part of indirect requests for information. Such requests are considered more polite than direct requests. In these requests, the *wh-* clause is often preceded by *can/could you tell me* or *do you know.*

> Do you know **how I can get to Union Station?** = How can I get to Union Station?
>
> Can you tell me **when the post office closes?** = When does the post office close?

■ *Wh-* clauses can be used with only some of the verbs and adjectives listed in Grammar Briefing 1. The verbs include *decide, forget, hear, know, notice, remember, see, understand,* and *wonder.* The adjectives include *certain, clear, known,* and *sure.* These verbs and adjectives are often used in negative statements, which in many cases express uncertainty.

> I don't remember **how the teacher solved the math problem.**
>
> I'm not sure **when the assignment is due.**

Noun Clauses with *If/Whether*

■ *If/whether* clauses begin with *if* or *whether*. The two words have the same basic meaning and use. However, *if* may be more common in informal contexts and *whether* may be more common in formal contexts.

> I want to know **if/whether my flight will leave on time.**

■ *If* is generally used only when the noun clause is an object of a verb or follows an adjective. It is not used when the noun clause is a subject, a subject complement, or the object of a preposition. *Whether* can always be used.

> I **wondered whether/if** Jon might want to go.
>
> I thought **about whether** Jon might want to go. (object of preposition— *whether* only)
>
> **The question is whether** Jon might want to go. (subject complement— *whether* only)

■ *If* and *whether* are often followed by *or not*, which makes clear that there is an alternative. *Or not* often comes at the end of the noun clause. It can also immediately follow *whether*, but it cannot immediately follow *if*.

> I don't know **whether he will come or not.**
>
> Do you know **whether or not he's here?**

> I don't know **if he will come or not.**
>
> **Not:** Do you know if ~~or not~~ he's here?

■ *If/whether* clauses are in many ways similar to *wh-* clauses:

- They are used with the same verbs and adjectives, often in negative statements.

> I don't know **if/whether my aunt will visit this year.**

- They can be used in indirect requests for information.

> Can you tell me **if/whether this is the road to Boston?** (= Is this the road to Boston?)

- They are often used in statements that express uncertainty.

> I wonder **if/whether it's going to rain.**

GRAMMAR HOTSPOT!

■ Remember! Use statement word order in *wh-* and *if/whether* noun clauses.

> I wonder **when Mark will get here.** I'm not sure **whether he's coming.**
>
> **Not:** I wonder ~~when will Mark get here.~~ I'm not sure ~~whether is he coming.~~

GRAMMAR PRACTICE 2: Types of Noun Clauses

2 *That* Noun Clauses—Form: *The Rules of the Game*

Use the words in parentheses to complete sentences with *that* clauses. Be sure to include *that* and use appropriate tenses.

It's obvious ___that each genre has its own formula, or "rules."___ (each
                                    1
genre/have/its own formula, or "rules"). For mysteries, a main rule is

_____ (the crime/must/be/important)—
                    2
for example, a murder. Readers opening a mystery book know

_____ (when they read it, they/find/
                    3
clues) but also "red herrings," or false clues.

It's equally obvious, however, _____
                                                        4
(all genres/share/certain rules). An important shared rule is authenticity:

Even details must seem vivid and real. One well-known publisher of Westerns

often refused to publish books because he felt _____
                                                                    5
(they/not/be/authentic enough). In many cases he actually thought

_____ (the books/be/good), but he was
                    6
disappointed _____ (he/can/not/"smell
                            7
the gunsmoke").

3 Forming Sentences with *That* Clauses: *And Then There Are Subgenres—A Tale of Two Detectives*

A. Combine the two sentences to form a sentence with a *that* clause. When possible, write the sentence in two ways. Include *that*. When necessary, include *the fact* or *the possibility* with the noun clause. Do not omit any words other than *this*.

Every genre can be divided into subgenres.

1. For example, readers of mysteries know this. There are "classic" mysteries and there are "hard-boiled" mysteries.

    For example, readers of mysteries know that there are "classic" mysteries and there are "hard-boiled" mysteries.

2. This is obvious. There are great differences between the two kinds of mysteries.

    It is obvious that there are great differences between the two kinds of mysteries.

That there are great differences between the two kinds of mysteries is obvious.

3. There's no doubt about this. Even the tone of the writing is different.

   There's no doubt about the fact that even the tone of the writing is different.

4. The reader of classic mysteries, like Agatha Christie's, expects this. The crime will take place in an upper-class setting, like a mansion in England.

5. The detective in these mysteries, for example, Christie's Hercule Poirot, is sure about this. He'll be able to solve the crime through logical thinking.

6. This is usual and expected. The classic detective is an amateur with an interest in crime.

7. Experts agree on this. The hard-boiled mystery developed in the United States as authors tried to look at crime more realistically.

8. The reader of hard-boiled mysteries expects this. The action will occur in the streets of a city and will involve "lowlifes" as well as the rich.

9. The detective, like Raymond Chandler's Philip Marlowe, is a professional who knows this. He may need to use his weapon as well as his brains.

10. The readers worry about this. The detective will be hurt while investigating the crime.

11. This is not surprising. Many people read one kind of mystery but not the other.

B. Work with a partner. Read the following quotes. Two are from a book by Raymond Chandler (i.e., a hard-boiled detective novel). Two are from stories by Agatha Christie (i.e., classic detective stories). Decide which quotes are from which author. Discuss your reasons. Use noun clauses after verbs such as *think, believe, agree, decide, doubt,* and *guess* and after adjectives such as *certain, clear, convinced,* and *sure.*

   Example: I (don't) think that the quote in *a* is from . . . because . . . AND I (don't) agree that . . . because I'm convinced . . .

a. I went on up the street and parked and walked back. In the daylight it seemed an exposed and dangerous thing to do. I went in through the hedge. She stood there straight and silent against the locked front door. One hand went up to her teeth and her teeth bit at her funny thumb. There were purple smears under her eyes and her face was gnawed white by nerves.

b. "So you're tough tonight," Eddie Mars' voice said.
   "Big, fast, tough, and full of prickles. What can I do for you?"
   "Cops over there—you know where. You keep me out of it?"
   "Why should I?"
   "I'm nice to be nice to, soldier. I'm not nice not to be nice to."
   "Listen hard and you'll hear my teeth chattering."

c. "Mrs. Robinson did not seem to notice anything amiss. Very curious, is it not? Did she impress you as being a truthful woman, Hastings?"
   "She was a delightful creature!"
   "[Evidently,] since she renders you incapable of replying to my question. Describe her to me, then."
   "Well, she's tall and fair; her hair's really a beautiful shade of auburn—"

> d. . . . The side door in question was a small one in the angle of the wall, not more than a dozen yards from the scene of the tragedy. As we reached it, I gave a cry. There, just short of the threshold, lay the glittering necklace, evidently dropped by the thief in the panic of his flight. I swooped joyously down on it. Then I uttered another cry which Lord Yardly echoed. For in the middle of the necklace was a great gap. The Star of the East was missing!
>
> [Sources: Agatha Christie, *Poirot Investigates* (Harper Paperbacks, 1992); Raymond Chandler, *The Big Sleep* (Vintage, 1976)]

4 *That* Clauses—Error Correction: *He Said, She Said*

Correct the errors in the passage. Some errors can be corrected in more than one way. Including the example, there are **eight** errors.

That
Conversation adds interest to our daily life is clear. Similarly, there's no doubting

the fact that dialogue—the conversations of characters in a book—adds interest to

fiction. Dialogue brings characters to life for readers. And every good writer knows

dialogue is a way to introduce information without taking up much space. There are

limits to this use of dialogue to provide information. One writer decided that he will

start a book with the following line (and he was surprised the fact that his book

doesn't get published!): "Oh, uncle, I wish you had come into my life years ago, so I

wouldn't have spent all that time in the orphanage and then have suffered in poverty

before becoming governess to those terrible children in that cruel family. . . ."

Dialogue should be like real conversation—but not too much like real conversa-

tion. Listen to a real conversation. It is filled with *um*s and pauses is the first thing

you will notice. You will probably also notice much of it is dull and hard to under-

stand. Readers would wonder about a book that had lines like this: "Um, . . . you

know those canned tomatoes on the shopping list . . . uh, never mind."

Few writers would argue with that verbs like *say* and *ask* are needed to intro-

duce speech. But many wonder that "colorful" verbs like *scream, whisper, cry,*

threaten, and *plead* should be used. Probably these verbs should be used only when

needed. If writers want that they make their dialogue interesting, they should do it

through the characters' words.

5   Replacing *That* Clauses with *So* or *Not: Fiction and Real Life*

A group of experts discussed the issue of connections between popular fiction and society. Read their discussion. In each item, replace the noun clause with *so* or *not* if possible. If a noun clause can't be replaced, write **NR.** If a noun clause can be replaced in two
ways, show both ways.

Moderator: First of all, is there much connection between popular fiction and society?

Speaker A: (1) Frankly, I ~~don't think that there is much connection between popular~~
            think not/don't think so.

            ~~fiction and society.~~

Speaker B: (2) Well, I think ~~there are many connections between the two.~~ Think
                                      so.

            about some of the social trends that you read about in the newspaper. . . .

Speaker A: That's exactly my point. For example, you read that divorce has become

            common. But this trend isn't reflected in romances. In romances it's

            always "and they lived happily ever after."

Speaker B: (3) I don't agree that higher divorce rates aren't reflected in romances. In
                    NR

            the past, romances were always about young, single women. But today

            there are romances about older, divorced women as well. Actually, I've

            written a book on how changes in our society have affected romance

            fiction. Perhaps you've read my book.

Moderator: (4) I'm afraid I haven't read your book. But that brings up a good point.

            Do you think that genre fiction can mirror—that is, be the same as—life

            in a society?

Speaker B: (5) I don't believe that fiction can mirror life in a society. (6) At least, I

            hope it can't mirror life in a society. If fiction were too much like real life,

            it would no longer be an escape.

Speaker C: (7) No, I suppose that fiction too much like real life wouldn't be an

escape. That's an important social function of fiction. Furthermore,

popular fiction can play an educational role.

Speaker D: (8) Yes, I've heard that popular fiction can play an educational role. For

example, many women who read romances say that they've learned a

lot about relationships from them. And this is true of men, too. (9) At

least, I assume that it is true of men, too. (10) I don't really know that it's

true of men. Men don't like to admit to reading romance fiction.

Moderator: Can changes in society actually bring about new genres of fiction?

Speaker D: (11) I think that changes in society can bring about new genres.

(12) Actually, I know that changes in society can bring about new genres.

When Americans first went out west, readers back east wanted to know

about their lives. So the Western—the story of cowboys—was born.

Speaker A: Genres can also be negatively affected by changes. Did as many

people buy spy novels once the Cold War between Russia and the

United States ended? (13) I imagine that not as many people bought

spy novels. (14) And apparently booksellers noticed that not as many

people bought them.

Moderator: Does anyone here doubt that popular fiction and society influence each

other? (15) After our discussion, I don't think anyone here doubts that

they influence each other!

6 Noun Clauses with *Wh-* Words—Form: *What the Reader Knows and Doesn't Know*

A. Complete the noun clauses with the words in parentheses. Use appropriate tenses.

1. It is obvious _why books like mysteries are called "page turners."_ (why/books
like mysteries/be called/"page turners").

2. When Evelyn recently read her first Agatha Christie book, she was surprised at

_____ (how/she/can/not/put the book down).

3. She knew who was murdered, but she didn't know

_____ (who/be/ the murderer).

4. As she read, she tried to notice _____ (what/be/the clues).

5. But it was hard for her to notice the clues because she kept turning the pages to

find out _____ (how/the book/end).

6. If readers are familiar with the genre, they have insights into

_____ (why/characters/behave/as they do).

7. The heroine in a romance novel is confused about

_____ (why/the hero/seem/unfriendly),
but the reader knows it's because he's falling in love!

B. Work with a partner. In a few sentences, tell your partner the basic plot (story) of a book, movie, or TV program your partner isn't familiar with. Don't reveal any details or the ending.

Example: A man and a woman send each other e-mail messages but have never met. They think they have a lot in common and they want to meet. But they live far from each other.

Your partner should think of some things he or she would like to know about the book, movie, or program and express these in statements beginning *I wonder + wh-word*.

Example: I wonder when they finally meet.

Satisfy your partner's curiosity. Then your partner tells you the plot of a book, movie, or program, and you find out about the things you'd like to know.

7 Noun Clauses with *If/Whether*—Form: *I Wonder Whether I Can Publish a Book?*

A. Use the questions to complete the sentences with noun clauses with *if* or *whether*. Make only necessary changes. If both *if* and *whether* are possible, use *if*.

1. Do I have enough talent to write fiction?

I often think about ___whether I have enough talent to write fiction.___

2. Could I write the story of my own life as a book?

I wonder ___if I could write the story of my own life as a book.___

3. Would my story fit into the romance genre?

I can't decide about _____.

4. Would I find readers who are interested in my story?

I'm not sure _____.

5. Can readers accept something a little bit different?

   _____ is the main issue.

6. Should I use this time to work?

   I have plenty of free time now—the only question is _____.
   (983 pages later . . .) There's a writers' conference coming up. Publishers and
   authors will be speaking there and might even read manuscripts.*

7. Should I go?

   I wonder _____.

8. Will Roslyn Martyn-Jones be there?

   I need to find out _____,
   because she's my favorite author.

9. Would she have time to read the manuscript for my book?

   It's not clear _____.
   I hope so!

* A manuscript is papers intended for publication.

B. Add *or not* to the sentences in **A.** Put *or not* within the noun clause if possible. If this
   is not possible, put it at the end of the noun clause.

                               or not

      Example: I often think about whether I have enough talent to write fiction.
                                           ^

8   Using *If/Whether* and *Wh-* Clauses in Indirect Requests and Statements of Uncertainty: *Do You Know Whether Readers Will Be Interested?*

Use the questions to complete the indirect requests for information. Use *whether* or the
appropriate *wh-* word. Use the words in parentheses to answer with statements
expressing uncertainty.

At the writers' conference:

1. Is Ms. Roslyn Martyn-Jones speaking this morning?

Morton: Excuse me, sir. Do you know ___whether Ms. Roslyn Martyn-Jones is_

    ___speaking this morning?_

Guard: I'm sorry. (don't know) ___I don't know whether Ms. Roslyn Martyn-Jones is_

    ___speaking this morning._ I don't know who she is.

2. When is Ms. Roslyn Martyn-Jones speaking?

   Morton: He doesn't know who she is! Excuse me, ma'am. Can you tell me

    ___when Ms. Rosyln Martyn-Jones is speaking?_

Receptionist: Ask at the information desk. (not sure) <u>I'm not sure when</u>

<u>Ms. Roslyn Martyn-Jones is speaking.</u>

Several hours later:

3. Would you have time to read my manuscript?

Morton: Ms. Martyn-Jones, it's a privilege to meet you. I've written a book. Do you

know _____?

RMJ: (don't know) _____.

4. Does your book belong to the romance genre?

RMJ: Well, can you tell me _____?

Morton: (not certain) _____. I think so.

5. Who is your heroine?

RMJ: Can you tell me _____?

Morton: (haven't decided) _____. What

I mean is my main character is a guy.

6. Why do you think this story would interest readers?

RMJ: Well, can you tell me _____?

Morton: (not sure) _____. Maybe it

would interest them because it's the story of my life. I went to work for a

nice boss. I liked her a lot. But finally she fired me for not doing my job

well. . . . Let me give you my manuscript.

The next day, in Ms. Martyn-Jones's hotel room:

7. Who do these pages belong to?

Hotel maid 1: Do you know _____?

Hotel maid 2: (don't know) _____. But

they're in the trash, so I'm sure you can take them.

8. Why would you want those papers?

Hotel maid 2: Can you tell me _____?

Hotel maid 1: Sure! It's a novel about some guy who goes to work for a nice boss. . . .

It looks really interesting. I'd like to read it.

🔟 Using Noun Clauses: *I Think That. . . . I Wonder If . . .*

A. Work in a small group. Pick **two** of the following topics to discuss. Discuss what you know about the topics, and discuss what you would like to find out. Use *that* clauses, *wh-* clauses, and *if/whether* clauses. Try to use at least one *so* or *not* in place of a *that* clause. Include negatives. Verbs that you can use include *agree, believe, doubt, guess, know, realize, think, understand,* and *wonder.* Adjectives you can use include *certain, clear, convinced, sure,* and *surprised.*

Topics:

1. Why do readers read popular fiction? For what reasons do people like particular genres (romance fiction, mysteries, horror fiction, science fiction, Westerns)? Which genre do you think would be most interesting to you? Why?

2. How is reading genre fiction similar to watching romances, mysteries, etc., on TV? How is it different from watching TV?

3. Do you think fiction can have an educational role? What can people learn by reading fiction?

4. Do you think writing fiction would be hard or easy? Why? Would you want to write fiction? Why or why not?

5. Can popular fiction be considered literature? Why or why not?

B. Write a paragraph on one of the topics that your group discussed. Use all three types of noun clauses. Include one noun clause with *the fact that.*

Noun Clauses with Reported Speech; Quoted Speech

Introductory Task: *Passing Along a Message*

A. Work with a partner. Read the following lines from two telephone conversations.

Claire to Miriam: I will be in San Francisco Wednesday on my way to Tokyo. Can Carlos and you meet me for dinner? I really am sorry I didn't call you sooner, but I have been busy.

The next day:

Miriam to Carlos: Claire said that she would be here tomorrow on her way to Tokyo. She asked if you and I could meet her for dinner. She said that she really was sorry she hadn't called me sooner but that she had been busy.

The lines from the second conversation are reported speech: Miriam reports what Claire said. In the reported speech, some words have been added and others have been replaced or changed.

Underline all the new or different words in the reported speech. Then answer the following questions:

1. a. What words have been added? (do not include words that replace other

    words) _Claire said that,_ _____

    b. What kind of clauses is reported speech given in? _____

2. a. In reported speech, verbs that were present tense in the original speech

    become _____ tense verbs.

    b. Both present perfect and past tense verbs become _____ tense verbs.

3. a. What are the two modals in Claire's original speech? _____

_____

   b. What modals do they become in the reported speech? _____

_____

4. In addition to verbs, modals, and time and place words, what other kind of

   words can change in reported speech? _____

B. Here's what Carlos told Miriam: I'm glad, and I can't wait to see her. I will pick her
   up at the airport. . . .
   Miriam called Claire right back. Complete her message to Claire.

Miriam: Carlos said that _____ and that

_____.

   He said that _____ at the airport . . .

GRAMMAR BRIEFING 1: Overview of Quoted Speech and Reported Speech

Speech can be quoted or reported. Quoted speech uses the exact words of the original speaker. Reported speech, which is generally given in a noun clause, does not use the exact words.

FORM AND FUNCTION Overview of Quoted Speech and Reported Speech

Function

■ Quoted speech (also called "direct speech") is used to give the exact words someone said, wrote, or thought. Quoted speech is most often found in writing, especially in news reports and as dialogue in fiction.

   Jon said, **"I'm very much in love with Mary."**

■ Reported speech (also called "indirect speech") is used to tell what someone said,
wrote, or thought. It generally does not give the exact words. Reported speech is
used much more often than quoted speech.

   Jon said **(that)** he was very much in love with Mary.

Form

■ Quotation marks are used around quoted speech. Quoted speech begins with a
capital letter and may come before or after the words that introduce it (e.g., *Jon
said*).

   • If the introductory words come first, a comma separates them from the quoted
speech. The quoted speech ends with the appropriate punctuation (period,
question mark, exclamation point) inside the quotation mark.

      The police captain asked me**,** **"Could he have escaped through the
window?"**

- If the quoted speech comes first, a comma is used instead of a period to separate a statement from the introductory words. Question marks and exclamation points are used as usual. Notice that more quoted speech can follow.

    "Did you see it happen**?**" he asked.

    "Yes, I did**,**" she replied. "I was there, and I saw the whole thing**."**

    "I thought so**!**" he exclaimed.

■ Reported speech is given in a noun clause. Statements are given in *that* clauses. Questions are given in *wh-* and *if/whether* clauses (see Grammar Briefing 3). As with other noun clauses, no punctuation is added.

    He asked **whether she saw it happen.**

    She replied **(that) she had been there and (that) she had seen the whole thing.**

Verbs Used to Introduce Quoted and Reported Speech

■ *Tell* and *say* are often used to introduce speech. Verbs introducing speech are most often used in the past tense. Other verbs used include the following:

add	complain	insist	recall	state
admit	confess	mention	remark	swear
announce	cry (out)	note	remind	think
answer	declare	object	repeat	warn
ask	exclaim	persuade	reply	whisper
claim	explain	promise	report	wonder
comment	indicate	protest	shout	write

■ *Say* and most of the other verbs listed may be followed by *to* + noun phrase or be followed directly by the speech.

    She **said (to him),** "I am happy."   She **said (to him)** (that) she was happy.

■ *Tell, persuade,* and *remind* must be followed by a noun phrase.

    She **told him,** "I am happy."   She **told him** (that) she was happy.

■ *Ask, answer, promise,* and *warn* may be followed by a noun phrase or be followed directly by the speech.

    He **promised (Joan),** "I'll leave early."   He **promised (Joan)** (that) he'd leave early.

■ *Think* must be followed directly by the speech.

    He **thought,** "I'll leave early."   He **thought** (that) he'd leave early.

GRAMMAR PRACTICE 1: Overview of Quoted Speech and Reported Speech

1 Punctuating Quoted Speech; Identifying Reported Speech: *A Woman from His Past*

A. Add the missing punctuation to the following quoted speech.

Brent grabbed his coat and, glancing at his watch, said , "I'm leaving, Tom. I've

told my clients that they can reach me tomorrow ."

Are you off to another night on the town, Brent   Tom asked   I'd thought that

you'd reformed. Who are you going out with this time

Live your life the way you want   Brent replied   Let me do what I want with

mine

Sure, you're the boss   Tom said   Hey, you know who's back in town? That sec-

retary of yours who left so suddenly. I thought that she was nice. But you said you

were glad she was gone. . . . What was her name

In a strange voice, Brent replied   Katie

B. Underline the sentences in the passage in **A** that include reported speech.

2 Quoted Speech; Verbs Used to Introduce Speech: *Brent and Katie*

A. Work with a partner. Rewrite the following dialogue as quoted speech. Use the verbs in the list. Try to use all of the verbs. Include a noun or pronoun after the verb only if necessary. If a noun or pronoun is possible but not necessary, follow the verb directly with quoted speech. Punctuate carefully.

admit	ask	cry out	explain	promise	tell	~~wonder~~
answer	confess	exclaim	insist	remind	think	

Katie (thinking): What will I do if I run into him? But I couldn't stay away.

> "What will I do if I run into him?" Katie wondered. "But I couldn't stay away."
> OR Katie wondered, "What will I do if I run into him? But I couldn't stay away."

Five minutes later, turning a corner, Katie bumped into Brent.

Katie: Oh, Brent! I didn't expect to see you.

Brent: Katie! It's you! You look as beautiful as ever—but somehow more mature
            and sophisticated.

Katie: I've traveled. I've gone to school.

Brent: Would you have dinner with me tonight, Katie?

Katie: No. I can't. I'm sorry.

Brent: Come on, Katie. You've got to. I won't take no for an answer.

Katie: Remember what I told you the last time we spoke. I said that I never wanted
            to have anything to do with you again.

Brent: I remember.

Katie: I meant it. I still do.

Brent: But I'll never be like that again. I'm a changed man.

Katie (thinking): Can I believe him? I wish I knew!

Brent: I love you, Katie. I've been terribly unhappy without you. Sure, I've gone out
            with other women. But they don't mean anything to me.

B. Look at the sentences in **A.** Add a noun or a pronoun after the verb where possible.
Include *to* if it is needed.

> Example: Katie cried out ~~to Brent~~, "Oh, Brent! I didn't expect to see you."

▣ Writing Quoted Speech: *What Happened? What Will Happen?*

Work with a partner. What will happen next between Brent and Katie? What had happened earlier? How does Brent and Katie's story end? Think of a scene that happens
before or after the conversation in exercise 2. Discuss the scene. What is happening in
this scene and why? What are Brent and Katie thinking, and what do they say? Write a
short conversation for your scene. Use quoted speech introduced by *said, told,* and several other verbs. Each character should speak four or five times.

GRAMMAR BRIEFING 2: Reported Speech

Reported speech often requires some changes in verbs, modals, pronouns, and time and place expressions.

FORM AND FUNCTION Reported Speech

■ Reported speech generally occurs in a different situation from the original speech it reports. For example, the person reporting the speech might not be the original speaker, and the listener(s), time, and place might be different. Because of these differences, some changes in wording are often required.

> **Original:** Josh to Liz, Monday, school: **I'll meet you at The Cafe on Wednesday at eight o'clock.**
>
> **Reported:** Liz to Paul, Wednesday, The Cafe: Josh said that **he would meet me here tonight at eight o'clock.**

Changes in Verb Tense

■ If the reporting verb (*say, tell,* etc.) is in the present or present perfect, there is no change in the tense of verbs in the noun clause.

> Cheryl: I **am** fifteen.   Cheryl **tells/has been telling** everyone (that) she **is** fifteen.

■ Most often the reporting verb is in the past tense. In this case, the tense of verbs in the noun clause shifts to become more past, as follows:

• Present tense verbs become past tense verbs.

> I **write** every day. → She said (that) she **wrote** every day.
>
> I**'m writing** a letter. → She said (that) she **was writing** a letter.

• Present perfect verbs become past perfect verbs.

> I**'ve written** many letters. → She said (that) she**'d written** many letters.

• Past tense verbs become past perfect verbs.*

> I **wrote** a letter last week. → She said (that) she **had written** a letter last week.
>
> I **was writing** a letter at eight o'clock. → She said (that) she **had been writing** a letter at eight o'clock.

* This shift can be optional if there is no possibility of the listener thinking that present tense forms were used in the original speech—that is, if it's obvious that the original also had past tense verbs. (Consider, e.g., *She said she had written a letter last week. Last week* makes it clear that she said "I wrote," not "I write." Therefore, *She said she wrote a letter last week,* without the shift, is also possible.)

■ Some forms do **not** change with past tense reporting verbs.

• Past perfect verbs cannot change and therefore remain past perfect.

> He **had traveled** to India several times before. → He said (that) he **had traveled** to India several times before.

• Verbs in present and past unreal conditionals do not change form.

> If I **loved** her, I **would marry** her. → He said (that) if he **loved** her, he **would marry** her.

■ Sometimes verb forms do not have to change with past tense reporting verbs. Changes are optional when the reported speech:

• expresses a general truth

> Copernicus said (that) the earth **revolves/revolved** around the sun.

• expresses a situation that is still true

> Bob told me (that) he **has/had** a new car.

• is a repetition of something that was just said

> Did you hear that? She said (that) **we're having/we were having** a quiz now.

• is about future events

He said (that) he**'ll start/he'd start** college next fall.

Changes in Modals

■ Most modals also change when the reporting verb is in the past tense.

I **can** try it.	→	She said (that) she **could** try it.
He **may** be there now.	→	She said (that) he **might** be there now.
He **must/ has to** know the answer.	→	She said (that) he **had to** know the answer.
We **will go/are going to go** to the theater next week.*	→	They said (that) they **would go/were going to go** to the theater next week.*

* The change to *would go/were going to go* is optional, because future events are involved.

■ *Might, could, should,* and *ought to* do not change.

We **might** go to the theater.   →   They said (that) they **might** go to the theater.

■ The perfect forms of modals do not change.

We **should have gone** to the theater.   →   They said (that) they **should have gone** to the theater.

■ Changes in modals are optional under the same circumstances as changes in verbs.

Bob told me (that) he **can swim.** (still true)

Changes in Pronouns

■ Subject, object, and reflexive pronouns and possessive pronouns and determiners often change. The changes occur when the speaker(s) and/or listener(s) are not those of the original speech. Changes from first to third person forms are especially common.

John: **I** like **you,** but **I** don't like **your** dog.   →   John said (that) **he** liked **me** but **he** didn't like **my** dog.

Phil: **I**'ll just do it **myself!**   →   Phil said (that) **he**'d do it **himself**.

■ Demonstratives change, especially when objects near the original speaker are not nearby when the speech is being reported.

Maria: I've read **this** book.   →   Maria said (that) she'd read **that** book.

Changes in Time and Place Expressions

■ Time and place expressions change when the time and place of the original speech and reported speech differ.

• Common changes in time expressions include the following: *now* may change to *then; today* may change to *that day; tomorrow* may change to *the next day; yesterday* may change to *the day before; next week* may change to *the following week;* and so on.

• The place expression *here* changes to *there,* and *there* may change to *here.*

■ Many different changes are possible, depending on when and where the reported speech occurs. For example, *today, tomorrow,* and *yesterday* could all become *last Monday.*

Teacher: We're having an exam **two weeks from today.**

Same day—The teacher said (that) we're having an exam **two weeks from today.**

One day later—The teacher said (that) we're having an exam **two weeks from yesterday.**

One week later—The teacher said (that) we're having an exam **next Monday.**

Paula: I'll be **here tomorrow** at **this time.**

Paula said (that) she would be **there/here/in her office today** at **nine o'clock.**

TALKING the TALK

■ In informal speech, present forms of *say* and other reporting verbs are sometimes used.

So Robert **tells** Annie he's really annoyed at her, and Annie **says** she's pretty annoyed at Robert, too. . . .

GRAMMAR PRACTICE 2: Reported Speech

Note for exercises 4–9: On the evening of Monday, May 3rd, in the dining room of her country mansion, old Mrs. Pierson suddenly fell over dead from an apparent heart attack. Present on the sad occasion were:

■ Old Barkley and Mrs. Barkley, butler and housekeeper to Mrs. Pierson for nearly 50 years.

■ John Small, houseguest, a pale and serious young man who ran many charities and had become Mrs. Pierson's "favorite" since meeting her a year ago.

■ Miss Esmeralda O'Connor, houseguest, an old college friend, once wealthy but now very poor, who had shown up several months ago and stayed.

The occasion turned from sad to potentially ugly when Dr. Millwood examined the dead woman and said he feared she'd been poisoned. He immediately contacted the police and Professor Wendell, a retired history professor whose hobby was solving crimes.

In working on exercises 4–9, see if you can arrive at the solution with Professor Wendell. Look for clues and try not to get fooled by red herrings (false clues)!

4 Changes in Verb Tense in Reported Speech: *The Doctor and the Lawyer Speak*

Professor Wendell immediately interviewed Mrs. Pierson's doctor and lawyer, and the following quotes are from those interviews. Finish changing the speech to reported speech by filling in the verbs in the appropriate tenses. Make all changes possible, including those that are optional. Where a change is not possible, fill in the verb as given in the original speech. Use full or contracted verb forms.

1. *Dr. Millwood:* I have been the only doctor in town for decades, and Mrs. Pierson was my patient for most of that time.

   Dr. Millwood said that he ___had been___ the only doctor in town for decades

   and Mrs. Pierson ___had been___ his patient for most of that time.

2. *Dr. Millwood:* We have been having flu epidemics here every year, and yet I don't remember her ever getting sick.

He said that they _____ flu epidemics there every year and yet

he _____ her ever getting sick.

3. *Dr. Millwood:* If everyone were that healthy, I would be out of a job.

He said that if everyone _____ that healthy, he _____ out of a job.

4. *Dr. Millwood:* She'd been really sick only once—about three months ago, she was getting weaker over a period of several weeks, but then suddenly she made a full recovery.

He said that she _____ really sick only once—about three months

ago, she _____ weaker over a period of several weeks but then sud-

denly she _____ a full recovery.

5. *Dr. Millwood:* It was poison. I feel sure of it since her health was so good.

He said that it _____ poison—that he _____ sure of it since

her health _____ so good.

6. *Mr. Torrance:* I am—or rather was—Mrs. Pierson's lawyer.

Mr. Torrance said that he _____—or rather _____—Mrs.
Pierson's lawyer.

7. *Mr. Torrance:* In fact, I've been reviewing her will, which she'd recently changed.

He added that in fact he _____ her will, which she'd recently
changed.

8. *Mr. Torrance:* In the old will nearly all her money had been left to Niles Pierson, who is Mrs. Pierson's nephew, and his wife, Victoria.

He said that in the old will nearly all her money _____ to Niles
Pierson, who is Mrs. Pierson's nephew, and his wife, Victoria.

9. *Mr. Torrance:* In the new will nearly all her money goes to her friend John Small.

He said that in the new will nearly all her money _____ to her friend
John Small.

10. *Mr. Torrance:* Under both wills, Mr. and Mrs. Barkley receive a cottage and a pension.

He said that under both wills Mr. and Mrs. Barkley _____ a cottage
and a pension.

11. *Mr. Torrance:* No mention is made of Miss O'Connor in either will.

He said that no mention _____ of Miss O'Connor in either will.

5 Optional Changes in Verb Tense: *The Money Angle*

If the following statements are reported, tense changes in the underlined verbs are optional. For each statement, decide why the change is optional. Indicate one of the following reasons: *obvious that also past tense in original speech; a general truth; situation still true; future event.*

1. *John Small:* I <u>am not</u> interested in any gain for myself; I want to use the money

    to benefit charities. _____ still true _____

2. *John Small:* The dead woman had her faults, but it <u>is</u> unkind for people to

    speak ill of the dead. _____

3. *Niles Pierson:* When times are hard, people just <u>spend</u> on necessities, you know.

    _____

4. *Niles Pierson:* But John Small <u>won't have to worry</u> about money for his charities

    ever again, will he? _____

5. *Niles Pierson:* I <u>run</u> a very successful art gallery.

    _____

6. *Old Barkley:* Maybe I shouldn't say it now that she's dead, but the old lady <u>was</u>

    never easy to work for. _____

7. *Old Barkley:* Next week, we<u>'ll move</u> into our new cottage.

    _____

6 Changes in Modals in Reported Speech: *More Clues Emerge*

Finish changing the speech to reported speech by filling in each modal + verb. Make all changes, including optional changes. Where a change is not possible, fill in as in the original speech.

1. *Mrs. Barkley:* We had to work hard for all those long years, but now, finally, we can relax.

    Mrs. Barkley said that they ___ had had to work ___ hard all those years but now,

    finally, they ___ could relax ___.

2. *Esmeralda O'Connor:* What a tragedy! I could have stayed for years with my old friend, but now she's gone.

    Esmeralda O'Connor said that she _____ for years with her old friend but now she was gone.

3. *Niles Pierson:* Of course I think my aunt should have left her money to me, but I can live quite well on the income from my gallery.

Niles Pierson said that of course he thought his aunt _____ her

money to him but he _____ quite well on the income from his gallery.

4. *John Small:* I can't talk now because I must meet with the director of the orphanage.

John Small said that he _____ then because he _____ with the director of the orphanage.

5. *Police Inspector:* It seems that Mrs. Pierson must have been poisoned.

The police inspector said that it seemed that Mrs. Pierson _____.

6. *Police Inspector:* As far as we're concerned, anyone could be the murderer.

He said that as far as they were concerned, anyone _____ the murderer.

7. *Mr. Torrance:* As a young man, Niles was a bit wild and did some things he shouldn't have done—mainly gambling.

Mr. Torrance said that, as a young man, Niles had been a bit wild and had done

some things he _____.

8. *Mr. Torrance:* But now he's quite wonderful. He must be disappointed about his aunt's will, but he didn't complain.

Mr. Torrance said that he _____ disappointed about his aunt's will but he hadn't complained.

9. *Niles Pierson:* I may talk to a lawyer about the will—but then again I might not since Mr. Torrance has told me there is nothing I can do about it.

Niles Pierson said that he _____ to a lawyer about the will but that

he _____ not since Mr. Torrance had told him there was nothing

he _____ do about it.

7 Changes in Pronouns in Reported Speech: *Poisoned Grape Juice?*

Professor Wendell's assistant has conducted some interviews and is reporting to the professor. Complete the speech as reported by the assistant to the professor by filling in the pronouns. Where no change is needed, fill in the pronoun from the original speech.

1. *Mrs. Barkley:* I'm sure they all ate everything—especially Miss O'Connor.

Mrs. Barkley said _____*she*_____ was sure _____*they*_____ had all eaten everything—especially Miss O'Connor.

2. *Professor Wendell's assistant:* I would like to hear about anything you or your husband remember only Mrs. Pierson eating or drinking.

I told Mrs. Barkley that _____ would like to hear about anything

_____ or _____ husband remembered only Mrs.
Pierson eating or drinking.

3. *Old Barkley:* You should tell him about the grape juice.

   Mr. Barkley told Mrs. Barkley that _____ should tell _____
   about the grape juice.

4. *Mrs. Barkley:* Mrs. Pierson never had dinner without her special organic grape
   juice from Switzerland, and she never let us or anyone else touch
   a drop.

   Mrs. Barkley said that Mrs. Pierson had never had dinner without

   _____ special organic grape juice from Switzerland and

   _____ had never let _____ or anyone else touch a drop.

5. *Mrs. Barkley:* I poured it for Mrs. Pierson myself from this very same bottle that
   I am showing you.

   Mrs. Barkley told me that _____ had poured _____ for

   Mrs. Pierson _____ from _____ very same bottle that

   _____ was showing _____.

6. *Mrs. Barkley:* Mrs. Pierson asked me to fill her glass.

   Mrs. Barkley said that Mrs. Pierson had asked _____ to fill

   _____ glass.

7. *Old Barkley:* You mean Mrs. Pierson told you—she wasn't very polite to us; we
   put up with a lot from her.

   Old Barkley told his wife that _____ meant Mrs. Pierson had told

   _____—that _____ hadn't been very polite to

   _____ and _____ had put up with a lot from

   _____.

8. *Mrs. Barkley:* I got a new bottle that night from a locked pantry that can be
   opened only with my key.

   Mrs. Barkley said that _____ had gotten a new bottle

   _____ night from a locked pantry that could be opened only

   with _____ key.

9. *Mrs. Barkley:* Oh, no! You'd better call the professor. You need to tell him something important: The new bottle of grape juice had already been
   opened.

Mrs. Barkley cried out to me that _____ had better call

_____ and that _____ needed to tell _____
something important: The new bottle of grape juice had already been opened.

8   Changes in Time and Place Words in Reported Speech: *Getting at the When and Where of It*

The assistant is reporting to Professor Wendell about other interviews. The times and places of this report and the interviews are given below. Read this information. Then complete the reported speech by filling in time and place words. Make appropriate changes (some words could be changed in several ways). If no change is needed, fill in the words as they appear in the original speech.

Person(s)	Day, Time	Place
Interviews with Mrs. Barkley, Miss O'Connor, John Small, Victoria Pierson	Tuesday, May 5, 9:00–9:30 P.M.	Mrs. Pierson's country mansion
Interview with Niles Pierson	Wednesday, May 6, 10:00 A.M.	the city
Report to Professor Wendell	Wednesday, May 6, 10:05 A.M.	the city

1. *Mrs. Barkley:* I'm getting ready to go out now, but I haven't gone out for the past few days.

   Mrs. Barkley said that she was getting ready to go out ____*then*____ but that

   she hadn't gone out for ___*the past few days*___.

2. *Esmeralda O'Connor:* I've been here the past three months. Unfortunately I'm leaving tomorrow.

   Esmeralda O'Connor said that she'd been ___*there*___ ___*the past three months*___ but

   that unfortunately she was leaving ____*today*____.

3. *John Small:* I was here all last weekend and then returned last night for dinner.

   John Small said that he had been _____ all _____ and then

   had returned _____ for dinner.

4. *Victoria Pierson:* My husband and I were here for the weekend and then returned to the city Sunday night after dinner.

   Victoria Pierson said that she and her husband had been _____ for

   the weekend and then had returned _____ _____ after dinner.

5. *Victoria Pierson:* We came back this morning as soon as we heard she had died.

   Victoria Pierson said that they had come back _____ as soon as they'd heard she had died.

6. *Victoria Pierson:* Niles had to leave this evening because he has some important
                         meeting about the gallery tomorrow.

   She said that Niles had had to leave _____ because he had some

   important meeting about the gallery _____.

7. *Mrs. Barkley:* Nothing unusual happened on Sunday evening—except that
                    around this time there seemed to be a thief in the garden.

   Mrs. Barkley said that nothing unusual had happened on _____

   except that around _____ there seemed to be a thief in the garden.

8. *Niles:* I have a meeting, so I can't talk now, but everything seemed fine there
            Sunday evening, although when I came back from my walk they'd all
            been looking for a thief.

   Niles said that he has a meeting so he can't talk _____ but everything

   had seemed fine _____ _____ although when he'd come
   back from his walk they'd all been looking for a thief.

9 Changes That Occur in Reported Speech: *Putting It All Together*

A. Rewrite the sentences as speech that is reported by someone else at a later time in
     a different place. Make all possible changes.

1. *Esmeralda O'Connor:* I came here so I could help my friend when she was so
                          sick.

   Esmeralda O'Connor said ___that she had come there so she could help her friend when she was so sick___.

2. *Professor Wendell:* It may be important for us to learn more about the man in
                         the garden.

   Professor Wendell said that _____.

3. *Mrs. Barkley:* After dinner Mrs. Victoria was helping me put things away in the
                    pantry.

   Mrs. Barkley said that _____.

4. *Victoria Pierson:* Suddenly I saw someone creeping behind the bushes and I
                        screamed.

   Victoria Pierson said that _____.

5. *Mrs. Barkley:* I ran into the garden and I saw someone but I couldn't get a good
                    look at him.

   Mrs. Barkley said that _____.

6. *Old Barkley:* Later that evening we looked through the house but didn't see anything missing.

   Old Barkley said that _____.

7. *Mrs. Barkley:* Maybe the police will find something.

   Mrs. Barkley said that _____.

8. *Police Officer* (to Police Inspector, showing him a small bottle): We might have
found something just now.

   The police officer told the police inspector that _____.

9. *Police Inspector:* This bottle contains nitroglycerin, a medicine that, if taken in
too high a dose, can cause death.

   The police inspector said that _____.

10. *Police Officer:* We found it in the trash can in the bathroom that Miss O'Connor
and Mr. Small have been sharing.

   The police officer said that _____.

B. Who murdered Mrs. Pierson? Work in a small group. Look for clues in exercises
4–9. You might want to take notes on a piece of paper. Discuss why and how the
various characters might have murdered Mrs. Pierson. Use reported speech to talk
about the evidence.

> Example: The Barkleys might have murdered Mrs. Pierson. Mr. Barkley said
> that they had put up with a lot from Mrs. Pierson and that she wasn't very
> polite to them.

As a group, decide who you think murdered Mrs. Pierson. Write down your solution and
explanation, and tell the class what you decided. Then turn to Exercise Page E–5 for
Professor Wendell's solution.

10 Meaning and Use of Reported Speech: *Party Gossip*

You're at a party and overhear the following pieces of conversations. Listen to a
piece of conversation. Read the statements for it. Listen again as many times as you
want. Circle the letter of the statement that gives correct information.

1. a. Alma is referring to present actions.

   (b.) Alma is referring to past actions.

   c. Alma is referring to present and past actions.

2. a. Mercedes said this to the person who is reporting it.

   b. Mercedes said this to someone other than the person who is reporting it.

   c. There is no way to know whether Mercedes said this to the person reporting
   it or to someone else.

3. a. Abigail first says Carmella was talking about present feelings and then says Carmella was talking about past feelings.

   b. Abigail says the same thing in two different ways.

   c. Abigail doesn't report Carmella's speech accurately.

4. a. According to John, Rick should look into the problem.

   b. According to John, John should look into the problem.

   c. There is no way to know from the sentences who John said should look into the problem.

5. a. Phil's thoughts concern present actions.

   b. Phil's thoughts concern past actions.

   c. There is no way to know whether Phil's thoughts concern present actions or past actions.

6. a. Tony made this comment at the place where the party is being held.

   b. Tony made this comment at some place other than the place where the party is being held.

   c. There is no way to know whether Tony made the comment at the place where the party is being held or somewhere else.

7. a. Sue was talking about the present and future.

   b. Sue was talking about the past and present.

   c. Sue was talking about the past and future.

8. a. "Tomorrow" can refer to a time before the time when the speech is being reported.

   b. Paula might have used the word "tomorrow" in her original speech.

   c. Both **a** and **b** are true.

9. a. Sylvia's advice is about the present.

   b. Sylvia's advice is about the past.

   c. Sylvia's advice could be about the present or about the past.

10. a. This person is talking about something that is happening in the present.

    b. This person is talking about something that happens habitually in the present.

    c. This person is talking about something that happened in the past.

GRAMMAR BRIEFING 3: Questions, Commands, and Requests in Reported Speech; Noun Clauses after Verbs or Adjectives of Urgency

Questions are reported in *wh-* and *if/whether* noun clauses. Commands and requests are usually reported using infinitives. Verbs and adjectives of urgency are followed by the base form of the verb in the noun clause.

FORM AND FUNCTION Questions, Commands, and Requests in Reported Speech

- All of the changes discussed in Grammar Briefing 2 (in verbs, modals, pronouns, and time and place expressions) also apply to reported questions.

- *Ask* is the verb most commonly used to report questions; *inquire* and *wonder* can also be used, as can the expression *want to know.* Only *ask* can be followed by a noun phrase. If a noun phrase is used with *inquire,* the noun phrase is preceded by *of.*

- *Wh-* questions are reported in *wh-* clauses.

  > Louis to Carol and Alice: Where are you going?

  > Louis asked Carol and Alice **where they were going.***

- *Yes/no* questions are reported in *if/whether* clauses.

  > Louis to Carol and Alice: Can I go, too?

  > Louis inquired (of Carol and Alice) **if/whether he could go, too.***

* Remember that statement word order is always used in *wh-* and *if/whether* clauses.

- The changes in pronouns and time and place expressions also apply to commands and requests. Commands and requests are reported with infinitives; if the command or request has a negative, *not* precedes *to. Tell* and *ask* are often used to report commands.

  > **Go** home!   → She told us **to go** home.

  > **Don't go** home!   → She told us **not to go** home.

  > **Could** you **help** me? → She asked us **to help her.**

FORM AND FUNCTION Noun Clauses after Verbs or Adjectives of Urgency

- After certain verbs in the main clause, a verb in a *that* noun clause occurs in the base form, regardless of person or tense. The main clause verbs involved generally express urgency or relate to giving advice or suggestions. They include *advise, ask, beg, command, demand, insist, order, prefer, propose, recommend, request, require,* and *suggest.*

  > We insist (that) they **be** here on time.

  > I recommended (that) she **be seen** by a doctor. (passive)

  > I suggested (that) she **not tell** him yet. (negative)

- The verb in the *that* clause must also be in the base form with certain adjectives, generally when the adjectives follow *it + be* (e.g., *It is important . . .*).* These adjectives relate to urgency or advice. They include *advisable, desirable, essential, imperative, important, necessary,* and *urgent.*

  > It is important (that) he **go** with us.

  > It is desirable (that) the meeting **not be postponed.** (negative, passive)

* The *that* clause can also occur in subject position (e.g., ***That he go with us** is important;* see Chapter 20, Grammar Briefing 2).

GRAMMAR PRACTICE 3: Questions, Commands, and Requests in Reported Speech; Noun Clauses after Verbs or Adjectives of Urgency

11 Questions, Commands, and Requests in Reported Speech: *A Class Discussion*

David was absent yesterday, so Carrie is telling him what happened in English class. Using the verbs in parentheses, rewrite the speech as questions, commands, and requests reported by Carrie. Include the original listener if given in parentheses. Make all possible changes.

1. *Mrs. Blair* (to class): Will anyone see David before the next class? (ask)

   Mrs. Blair asked us whether/if anyone would see you before the next class.

2. *Mrs. Blair* (to Carrie): Could you tell David about everything we discussed today? (ask)

   Mrs. Blair asked me to tell you about everything we discussed yesterday.

3. *Mrs. Blair* (to class): Write a paper on a topic related to reading books. (tell)

4. *Mrs. Blair* (to class): First think about questions you have about reading. (tell)

5. *Mrs. Blair* (to class): Could you help me get everyone started by sharing your questions with each other? (ask)

6. *Mrs. Blair* (to class): Use the questions for ideas about topics. (tell)

7. *Paul:* Do more men or women buy books?* (want to know)

8. *Angela:* What kinds of books do people tend to read? (ask)

9. *Tim:* How many books are sold in the United States each year? (want to know)

10. *Carrie:* Can reading books change people's lives? (wonder)

11. *Tanya:* Have people been reading fewer books because of TV? (wonder)

12. *Paul:* What reasons do people give for reading books? (ask)

13. *Carrie:* What can be done to encourage people to read more? (ask)

14. *Mrs. Blair* (to class): Don't use just your own ideas for this paper. (tell)

15. *Mrs. Blair* (to class): Work on the paper in groups. (ask)

16. *Mrs. Blair* (to class): Don't write more than five pages because I don't want to have too much reading to do. (tell)

* See Exercise Page E–6 for brief answers to this question and some of the other questions.

12 Noun Clauses after Verbs or Adjectives of Urgency: *It's Important That We Read!*

Carrie and David's group wrote about the importance of reading and about ways to encourage people to read. Complete the sentences with the correct form of the verbs in parentheses. Use negatives where indicated. Use passives where appropriate.

1. Most people say that their main reason for reading _____is_____ (be) that it gives them pleasure.

2. Some psychologists recommend that a person feeling stress _____read_____ (read) fiction as a way to "escape" for a few hours.

3. It is desirable that a person _____ (learn) about people who think as he or she does and about people who are very different.

4. It is clear that a good work of fiction _____ (teach) us about many kinds of people.

5. It is important that people _____ (not/associate) reading just with school.

6. Experts recommend that a parent _____ (read) to his or her child and _____ (give) the child books.

7. It's urgent that young people _____ (encourage) to read more.

8. It's necessary that TV _____ (not/replace) reading.

9. One study suggested that TV _____ (use) more to advertise books.

10. The study pointed out that movies and TV programs _____ (advertise) much more than books are.

11. It's advisable that teachers and others _____ (not/focus) only on "good" books.

12. Experts are convinced that any book _____ (be) potentially good for someone to read.

13. They propose that genre fiction _____ (use) to get readers interested in "serious" fiction.

14. They insist that books of all sorts _____ (make) available to everyone.

15. We agree that reading _____ (be) a good way to both have fun and learn.

13   Verb + Noun Clause Review: *What Could She Have Said, Asked, . . . ?*

Next to each sentence beginning, write the letters of all the endings, including those on page 402, that are possible. Use the endings as many times as appropriate.

1. She said _____a, c, f, g_____

2. She asked _____

3. She told _____

4. She demanded _____

5. She answered _____

6. She inquired _____

a. to me that she wanted to meet you.

b. that he be home in time for dinner.

c. that they always tell the truth.

d. him that it would be ready in a couple of hours.

e. me whether I'd read that book.

f. what time he would be there.

7. She preferred _____

g. he often watches TV in the evening.

h. the guests to leave.

i. me how long it took to do the homework.

14 Using Noun Clauses and Reported Speech: *A Survey about Reading*

A. Work with a partner. Ask your partner the following questions, and write down your partner's answers.

1. Do you read more often for information or for pleasure?

2. Do you read more often in English or in another language?

3. What have you been reading lately (fiction books, textbooks and other nonfiction books, newspapers, magazines, comic books, other)?

4. Where and when do you read (on the bus? in the library? on weekends? in the evening? before going to bed? other?)?

5. When you were a child, did you read more or less than you do now?

6. Would you like to spend more time reading? Why or why not?

7. In your opinion, should a parent insist that his or her child read? Why or why not?

8. In your opinion, is it important that adults read fiction? Why or why not?

B. Join with two other pairs. Report on some of the questions you asked and on your partner's answers. Use the following verbs or other verbs from the chapter: *ask, add, admit, answer, claim, comment, explain, inquire, mention, say, think.*

> Example: I asked Betty whether she more often reads for information or for pleasure. She said she reads more for information. She explained that she has been reading lots of magazine articles about taking care of babies . . .

Discuss the questions and answers as a group. Were people's answers similar or different?

UNIT WRAP-UP

Error Correction

Find and correct the errors in the noun clauses and quoted and reported speech. Some errors can be corrected in more than one way. Including the example, there are **13** errors.

For my assignment, I decided to interview Alexa Smith, president of Forever

Yours Publishers. I wondered ~~that~~ *whether* I could get an interview with her, because I know

that she's a very busy woman. I was surprised at that her secretary said there would

be no problem.

As soon as I met Ms. Smith, I told to her how much I enjoy reading Forever Yours romances. I added that I had a whole bookcase full of them and asked if or not this was unusual. She answered that some women bought every Forever Yours romance that was published. Then she told me to don't be shy about asking my questions.

I started by asking Ms. Smith how did she decide which books to publish. Computer analyses could be useful seemed obvious to me, so I asked her whether she used computers or not. Ms. Smith replied that she preferred to use Madge. She explained me that Madge was a secretary who always seemed to guess right about if a book would be a success.

I asked her whether she had to read a lot of manuscripts from first-time writers. She nodded and showed me one that began like this: "Oh, uncle, I wish you had come into my life years ago, so I wouldn't have spent all that time in the orphanage" May said. After that first line she wasn't sure if to read any more. But she pointed out that some inexperienced writers had become extremely successful. That is why she demands that each manuscript is read.

When I left, I decided that the business of publishing romance fiction be both interesting and hard.

Task 1: A _____ Story

Work with a partner. Read the paragraphs and think about what kind of story you could turn them into. Write the story with quoted speech, reported speech, and other noun clauses, as appropriate.

All night long, I'd been unable to sleep because I was thinking about

_____. I was worried _____.

Now the phone was ringing and I knew _____. I picked it up. As I'd expected, it was Craig. I wondered _____.

"_____?" I asked.

"_____," he answered.

_____ was obvious to me. Craig said that it was

urgent _____. And he told me not

_____. Trying hard to control my voice, I asked him

_____, but he had hung up. For the first time I

realized _____. I could only hope

_____.

Task 2: Reporting a Scene

Watch a TV show or a video. You can watch a movie or any kind of show where people are talking—a comedy, a drama, a talk show, etc. While you are watching the movie or show, choose a scene or a part of a scene that is about 3–5 minutes long to tell the class about using reported speech. Take notes on what the people say. Don't write everything down—just a few things that are important—and don't try to write down the exact words. If you are watching a video, you can watch the scene again. When the show is finished, use your notes to write a paragraph. In your first two or three sentences, tell what the show was about. Then use reported speech to tell about the scene.

> Example: In the movie I saw, a man wanted to marry a woman he didn't love. She was plain and clumsy, but she had a lot of money. In one scene she spilled coffee all over the rug and said that she was sorry. He said that it didn't matter because only she mattered. He added that he had something to ask her. He wanted to ask her to marry him, but he couldn't quite manage to. So he asked her what time it was. Then he asked her if she'd like more coffee. Finally, he asked her if she would marry him. She answered that she would.

Read your paragraph to the class.

Task 3: Write Your Own Story

Work in a small group. Write a one-page story. It could be a romance, science fiction, horror, or mystery story, or any other kind of story. You can use one of the beginnings below or make up your own beginning. In your story include each of the following: *that*, *wh-*, and *if/whether* noun clauses; quoted speech (start a new paragraph each time a different character speaks); reported speech; a verb or adjective of urgency followed by a noun clause. Plan and discuss your story carefully before you start writing. Who are your characters? What happens and what will they do? How should the story end? When you have written your story, read it to the class.

A. The big house on the hill had been empty for longer than anyone could remember. It was overgrown with plants, and its broken shutters banged in the wind. The people in town all avoided the house. They said it had a terrible secret. But no one seemed to know what that secret was. One day in late summer, my brother and I decided to find out.

B. We were driving home from a movie late one night when we saw it. Edgar saw it first and pointed it out to us. Al brought the car to a screeching stop.

"It's just a weird plane," I said. "It's just some plane from the Air Force base."

But I knew that wasn't true. As we watched, the strangely lit disk became larger and brighter. With a whirring noise, it touched down in the cornfield.

C. Miss Watson looked like a sweet old lady. But everyone knew that she was a great detective—capable of outwitting the most brilliant criminal minds. Mrs. Astor called her as soon as she discovered that someone had replaced her priceless jewels with clever fakes.

"The insurance men said they'll pay, but I don't care about money," Mrs. Astor said. "You must help me get my jewels back."

"I'll do my best, dear," Miss Watson replied, and she hopped on a bus to Mrs. Astor's place.

D. It was Friday night, and Ana was home again. Ana wondered why she was always stuck at home every weekend. She didn't really feel like reading or like watching TV. She wished that her phone would ring and someone would ask her out. Ana thought about that new boy, Kurt.

"But he'll figure out who the popular kids are," Ana thought. "And he'll hang out with them."

Just then, the phone rang.

Adverb Clauses and Phrases; Connecting Ideas

Topic Focus: *Advertising and Consumer Behavior*

UNIT OBJECTIVES

■ **subordinating conjunctions and adverb clauses**
(***Before*** they introduce a new product, most advertisers do research. People buy products ***because they want or need them.***)

■ **adverb phrases**
(***After talking to a friend,*** Haley decided to buy a new car.)

■ **coordinating conjunctions**
(A few commercials are entertaining, ***but*** this one is annoying.)

■ **transitions**
(I want to buy a new computer. ***Therefore,*** I've been paying attention to computer ads.)

INTRODUCTORY TASKS

Reading and Listening

▪▪▪ Read and listen to these advertisements.

A	B	C

Ruben Valas is an artist. He has never followed the crowd. He never will.

Ruben chose the Individualist **because** it expresses his unique personal style.

Joyce Bailey explores the deepest oceans, **and** she climbs the highest mountains.

Joyce needs a durable, accurate watch, **so** she wears the Adventurer.

Edgar Ross is an investment banker. **Furthermore,** he is a director of one of the largest companies in the world.

Edgar wants a watch that reflects the importance of his position. **Therefore,** he wears the Prestige.

Ruben's passion for creating new art forms never leaves him. **After** he spends the day painting in his studio, he moves on to composing experimental music.

Although Ruben's life is complex, his watch is simple.

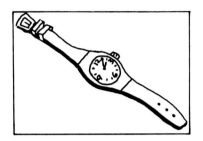

The Individualist is simply the most innovative and stylish timepiece in the world.

Joyce's days are filled with the most extreme physical and mental challenges. In the evening, she writes books about her explorations and figures out new worlds to explore.

Joyce's life is complex, **but** her watch is simple.

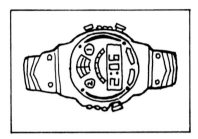

The Adventurer is simply the toughest and most accurate timepiece in the world.

Edgar's typical day is a whirlwind of meetings and decision-making. **Afterward,** in the evening, he usually attends a charity event.

Edgar's life is complex. His watch, **however,** is simple.

The Prestige is simply the most elegant and precise timepiece in the world.

Comprehension Check

Read each sentence. Circle **T** if the sentence is true or **F** if the sentence is false.

1. According to the ad, the reason that Ruben chose the Individualist is that it expresses his unique personal style.   (T)   F

2. Ruben composes music before he paints.   T   F

3. Joyce Bailey explores the deepest oceans. In addition, she climbs the highest mountains.   T   F

4. Edgar Ross is an investment banker but not a director of a large company.   T   F

5. The adjectives *simple* and *complex* have opposite meanings.   T   F

Think about Grammar

Ideas can be connected in different ways. Types of connectors include subordinating conjunctions (as in **A**), coordinating conjunctions (as in **B**), and transitions (as in **C**). These connectors show how ideas are related to each other. Different types of connectors can express the same meaning. Look at the **boldfaced** connectors in the advertisements. Write the connectors that express the following meanings:

Addition: _____*and*_____ _____

Cause and effect: _____ _____ _____

Contrast: _____ _____ _____

Time: _____ _____

Adverb Clauses and Phrases

A. Mark the box that indicates your level of agreement with each of the following statements.

1. I see and hear so many advertisements that I don't pay much attention to them.
   ☐ Strongly agree   ☐ Somewhat agree   ☐ Disagree

2. I often decide to buy a product* because I've seen an advertisement for it.
   ☐ Strongly agree   ☐ Somewhat agree   ☐ Disagree

3. Although a few television commercials are memorable, I've usually forgotten most of them by the next day.
   ☐ Strongly agree   ☐ Somewhat agree   ☐ Disagree

4. When a celebrity (e.g., a sports or television star) is in a commercial for a product, I am more likely to have a positive attitude toward that product.
   ☐ Strongly agree   ☐ Somewhat agree   ☐ Disagree

5. I'm usually not one of the first to try a new product. I wait until other people have tried it and ask them for advice.
   ☐ Strongly agree   ☐ Somewhat agree   ☐ Disagree

6. I buy some products because they are associated with status and prestige.
   ☐ Strongly agree   ☐ Somewhat agree   ☐ Disagree

B. Work in small groups. Compare your responses to the statements in **A.** Did anyone else in the group give responses similar to yours?

C. In your groups, discuss your reactions to television commercials. Which ones do you like? Which do you hate? Which ones are the most entertaining? Which are the most annoying? Which ones are especially informative, persuasive, or memorable? Why? In your discussion, use sentences with *because* clauses.

> Example: I like the computer commercials with people in bunny suits because the suits are cute. OR I hate car dealers' commercials because the announcers talk so loud and fast.

* A product is a good (e.g., a hamburger or a piano) or a service (e.g., dry cleaning or banking).

GRAMMAR BRIEFING 1: Adverb Clauses

Adverb clauses are clauses that function like adverbs.

FORM AND FUNCTION Adverb Clauses

■ Like all clauses, an adverb clause has a subject and a verb. An adverb clause begins with a subordinating conjunction (e.g., *when, where, because, although, if*). The subordinating conjunction links it to the main clause. Like adjective clauses and noun clauses, adverb clauses are dependent clauses: they cannot stand alone but must be linked to a main clause.

> **Main Clause**　　　　**Adverb Clause**
> He closes up the store **because he is the manager.**
> **Not:** He closes up the store. ~~Because he is the manager.~~

■ Some adverb clauses must come after the main clause. Many adverb clauses can come before or after the main clause. Use a comma between clauses when the adverb clause comes first.

> **Main Clause**　　　　**Adverb Clause**
> We will start the meeting　**when he comes.**
>
> **Adverb Clause**　　　　**Main Clause**
> **When he comes,**　　　we will start the meeting.

■ Adverb clauses function like adverbs. They modify the verb or the main clause in a sentence. They answer questions like *when, where, why,* and *how*.

> They worked on the project **before he arrived.** (when)
>
> He opened his business **where he lived.** (where)
>
> She bought the product **because she has seen the advertisement on TV.** (why)
>
> You acted **as though you know her.** (how)

GRAMMAR PRACTICE 1: Adverb Clauses

☐ Identifying Adverb Clauses: *The Research behind the Advertising*

The following passage contains six adverb clauses, including the example. Read the passage. **Underline** each adverb clause and **circle** its subordinating conjunction. (Remember: A clause has a subject and a verb.) Then indicate which question each clause answers by writing *when, where, why,* or *how* above it.

　　　　　　when
(Before) they try to sell a product, advertisers need to know which group of con-

sumers would be most likely to buy it. Advertisers describe these consumers as the

"target market" for the product. The target market for a product may be very large

(e.g., the market for snack foods), or it may be relatively small (e.g., the market for

luxury cars). Because they want to advertise efficiently and effectively, advertisers do a great deal of research on the consumers in the target market. They gather infor-

mation from consumers about their needs and wants. They also try to find out as

much as possible about consumers' habits, interests, attitudes, and buying behav-

ior. Advertisers use various techniques to get information from and about con-

sumers. For example, advertisers often ask consumers to fill out and return a ques-

tionnaire when they purchase a product. They ask consumers to comment on

products or advertisements in telephone surveys or in group interviews. Also, they

interview or observe consumers where they shop. By offering free samples of a

product, advertisers can judge consumers' reactions to it. After advertisers have col-

lected all this information, they analyze it to determine what types of products and

advertising will appeal to the people in the target market.

These days, it seems as though advertising is an inescapable part of life.

Advertising research seems to have become inescapable, too.

GRAMMAR BRIEFING 2: Types of Adverb Clauses

Adverb clauses express time, place, reason, result, contrast and opposition, condition, purpose, and manner.

FORM AND FUNCTION Types of Adverb Clauses

Adverb Clauses of Time

■ Adverb clauses of time tell when the actions or states in the main clause occur. Subordinating conjunctions used in time clauses include *after, before, when, while, as, as soon as, whenever, since, until, once,* and *as long as.* For more on time clauses and tenses used in time clauses, see Chapter 2, Grammar Briefing 2; Chapter 5, Grammar Briefing 1.

We'll wait to start the meeting **until he comes.**

■ *As* means "when, while, at the same time."

I looked up **as** he was coming into the room.

■ *As soon as* means "right after."

As soon as he told us the new plan, we were convinced.

■ *Whenever* means "at any/every time."

> Call me **whenever** you need me.

■ *Once* means "(right) after."

> **Once** you taste our coffee, you won't want any other kind.

■ *As long as* means "during an entire period of time."

> I've known him **as long as** I can remember.

Adverb Clauses of Reason

■ Adverb clauses of reason express a cause for the action or state in the main clause. Subordinating conjunctions used include *because, since,* and *as. Because* and *since* are used more often than *as;* all have the same meaning.

> **Because/Since/As the product is for teenagers,** it will be marketed in stores that cater to teens.

Adverb Clauses of Result

■ *So . . . that* is used with adjectives, adverbs, and nouns to express result:
  - *so* + adjective/adverb + *that*
  - *so* + *many/few* + (adjective +) noun + *that,* for count nouns
  - *so* + *much/little* + (adjective +) noun + *that,* for noncount nouns

> They advertise **so well that they have cornered the market.**
>
> They advertise in **so many places that they have doubled their sales.**
>
> They spend **so much money on advertising that they make little profit.**

■ *Such . . . that* is used with nouns to express result:
  - *such* + noun phrase + *that*

> They sell **such a good product that their business has expanded rapidly.**
>
> The ad campaign had **such poor results that the company dropped it.**

■ Adverb clauses of result must follow the main clause.

Adverb Clauses of Contrast and Opposition

■ Adverb clauses with *while* and *whereas* express a direct contrast or opposition to content in the main clause. *Whereas* is more formal than *while.* With *while* or *whereas* expressing direct contrast or opposition, either idea may be the content of a main clause and the order of the clauses can be reversed without changing the meaning. A comma is used even when the *while/whereas* clause follows the main clause.

> **While/whereas some people like coffee,** others prefer tea. (direct contrast between preferences of the two groups of people)
>
> = Some people like coffee, **while/whereas others prefer tea.**
>
> = **While/whereas some people prefer tea,** others like coffee.
>
> = Some people prefer tea, **while/whereas others like coffee.**

■ Clauses with *although, though, even though, despite the fact that,* and *in spite of the fact that* express a weaker, or partial, contrast or opposition.* They express the idea that their content makes the main clause content surprising or unexpected. *Despite the fact that* and *in spite of the fact that* are more formal than the other subordinating conjunctions.

Although Joan likes the latest fashions, she often wears styles from previous years. (wearing previous years' fashions is in contrast with the idea of liking the latest fashions, but this contrast isn't direct or complete)

Despite the fact that the business was doing well, they closed it after the first year. (since the business was doing well, it's surprising that it closed)

* *While,* but not *whereas,* can also be used to express weak contrast.

Adverb Clauses of Condition

■ Adverb clauses of condition express the conditions for the results expressed in a main clause. Subordinating conjunctions used include *if, unless, provided/providing (that), as long as, only if, whether or not,* and *even if.* Sentences with condition and result clauses are called conditionals and are discussed in Unit 9.

If we advertise well, the product will sell.

Adverb Clauses of Purpose

■ Clauses with *so (that)* and *in order that* express the purpose of the action or state in the main clause. *So (that)* is less formal and more common than *in order that.* Clauses of purpose generally include the modals *will, would, can,* and *could.*

Stores place certain products on shelves at eye level **so (that)/in order that people will buy them on impulse.**

The manager placed the product on a shelf at eye level **so (that)/in order that people would buy it on impulse.**

I turn on the radio every morning **so (that) I can hear the news.**

I turned on the radio last night **so (that) I could hear the news.**

■ Adverb clauses of purpose almost always follow the main clause.

Adverb Clauses of Manner

■ Adverb clauses of manner answer the question of how, describing something in the main clause. The subordinating conjunctions *as if* and *as though* are used.

He looks **as if / as though he is tired.**

■ The content of clauses of manner may be possible or unreal. As in conditionals, if the content expressed is unreal, the past is used for present time and *were* is used for all persons of *be.*

She spends money **as if she were rich.** (unreal—she is not rich)

■ Adverb clauses of manner must follow the main clause.

GRAMMAR HOTSPOT!

■ Keep in mind that some subordinating conjunctions are used in more than one type of adverb clause. These include *as, as long as, since,* and *while.*

Since the product is a good one, it will sell. (reason)

The company has sold the product **since it opened.** (time)

TALKING the TALK

■ *Like* is sometimes used informally in place of *as if* and *as though* in adverb clauses of manner.

He acted **like he owned the company.**

GRAMMAR PRACTICE 2: Types of Adverb Clauses

2   Adverb Clauses of Time: *New Products and Consumer Behavior*

A. Use the subordinating conjunction in parentheses to combine the pairs of sentences in brackets into one sentence containing an adverb clause of time. Use the sentences in the order in which they are given. Punctuate carefully.

1. [People began doing market research in the 1920s. Advertisers have learned a great deal about how trends spread through a group.] (since)
   Since people began doing market research in the 1920s, advertisers have learned a great deal about how trends spread through a group.

2. [A new product is introduced. Only a few people begin using it.] (when)

3. Researchers refer to these interested and adventurous people as "innovators." [Innovators try the new product. They hear that it is available.] (as soon as)

4. [Innovators adopt a new product. Some other people will try it.] (once)

5. Researchers refer to these people as the "early adopters" of the product. [The innovators and early adopters accept the product. They become "opinion leaders" for other consumers in their group.] (after)

6. [Other consumers try the product. They usually ask an opinion leader for information and advice about it.] (before)

7. Researchers refer to people who remain uninterested in the product as "laggards." [Laggards may never adopt the product. They live.] (as long as)

8. Innovators and early adopters often pay attention to advertising for certain new products. [Advertisers introduce new products. They want to attract the attention of people who are likely to be opinion leaders.] (whenever)

9. Opinion leaders have more influence on other consumers than advertising does. [Advertisers keep the interests of opinion leaders in mind. They are planning their advertising strategies.] (as)

10. If opinion leaders do not accept a product, it will probably be unsuccessful. For example, in Norway, opinion leaders had a negative view of microwave ovens. [Microwaves were introduced. Only a few Norwegians have started using them.] (since)

B. The speed with which people adopt a new product depends on the type of product—that is, a person may be an early adopter for electronic equipment but a laggard for sports equipment or clothing styles. Use your ideas about your buying behavior to complete the following sentences.

1. Before I ___buy clothes___, I ___usually look at what others in my group are wearing___.

2. I didn't buy _____ until _____.

3. I will buy _____ as soon as _____.

4. Once someone else has _____, I _____.

5. My friends _____ whenever they _____.

6. I've never bought _____ as long as I

   _____.

7. As I _____, I _____.

3 Adverb Clauses of Reason: *Advertisers Have Reasons for Research*

Use the subordinating conjunction in parentheses to combine each pair of sentences in two different orders. Punctuate carefully.

1. We need to plan our strategy carefully. Advertising is expensive. (because)

   > *We need to plan our strategy carefully because advertising is expensive.*
   >
   > *Because advertising is expensive, we need to plan our strategy carefully.*

2. We don't want to make mistakes. We need to research the target market. (because)

3. We try to predict consumers' future needs and wants. We want to stay ahead of our competitors. (since)

4. We would like to know how viewers react to our commercials. We're going to conduct a telephone survey. (as)

4 Adverb Clauses of Result: *Telephone Survey—Recall and Reaction*

A. To get information about the effectiveness of TV commercials, advertisers telephone people and ask how they feel about the commercials. The following are people's responses to telephone survey questions. Combine the sentences using *so . . . that* or *such . . . that.*

1. The bunny was cute. I wanted to see it again.

   > *The bunny was so cute that I wanted to see it again.*

2. It was a cute bunny. I wanted to see it again.

   > *It was such a cute bunny that I wanted to see it again.*

3. The commercial was effective. I'll always remember the name of the product.

4. It was an effective commercial. I'll always remember the name of the product.

5. The announcer spoke quickly. It was difficult to understand her.

6. Everyone recognizes him. He's a famous athlete.

7. The actors seem to be ordinary people. I can identify with them.

8. The pizza looked delicious. I wanted to order one.

9. They danced well. I'd like to watch them again.

10. The commercial is annoying. The music is played loudly.

11. I didn't notice the name of the product. The actress is beautiful.

B. Use *much/little* or *many/few* and your own ideas to complete the sentences.

1. There are so _____ commercials on television that

    _____.

2. I have so _____ free time that _____.

3. There are so _____ products to choose from

    _____.

4. You get so _____ information from television commercials that

    _____.

5 Using Adverb Clauses of Time, Reason, and Result: *Enter the Contest!*

A. Imagine that you bought one of the watches—the Individualist, the Adventurer, or the Prestige—shown in the advertisements in the Reading and Listening section at the beginning of the unit. Now the advertiser is having a contest. Contestants must write a paragraph about their watch; the best paragraphs will be used in future ads. Write a paragraph about your watch and why you like it. In your paragraph use at least one of each of these types of adverb clauses: time, reason, and result.

> Example: Since I wanted a sports watch, I decided to buy the Adventurer. I've been very satisfied with it because it has everything I want in a watch. The Adventurer is so accurate that I never need to worry about being on time. Also, it's such a stylish watch that all my friends admire it. As soon as they see it, they want one just like it. . . .

B. Read your paragraph to the class. Which paragraphs do you think the advertiser will want to use in future advertisements?

6 Direct Contrast or Opposition: *Information about Consumers*

Complete each sentence and then write it in another way.

1. Whereas some people like shopping, others _____ hate it _____.

> Some people like shopping, whereas others hate it. OR Whereas some people hate shopping, others like it. OR Some people hate shopping, whereas others like it.

2. While females account for 51.2 percent of the U.S. population, _____ account for 48.8 percent.

3. Some people prefer to eat dinner at home, while others prefer to eat

    dinner _____.

4. Some people own their homes, whereas _____.

5. While it takes a short time to decide which brand of toothpaste to buy, it

    takes _____ which brand of car to buy.

6. Whereas very few people had home computers in the 1970s,

    _____ now.

7. Some _____, whereas others _____.

8. While many _____, a few _____.

7 Reason versus Weaker Contrast and Opposition: *Brand Loyalty*

A. A brand is an identifying name on a product. "Brand loyalty" means a consumer's
tendency to keep buying a certain brand of a product. Use one of the subordinating
conjunctions given to complete the sentences. You will need to use some subordinating conjunctions more than once.

because, even though

   Advertisers want to build brand loyalty for products ____*because*____ brand loy-
                                                              1
alty gives companies a long-term advantage over their competitors. Customers who

are loyal to a brand will continue to buy it ____*even though*____ another brand costs less.
                                                    2
Consider two consumers. Mrs. Meyer is loyal to Dentafresh toothpaste. She always

buys Dentafresh _____ she likes its flavor. Mrs. Rossi is not loyal to any
                        3
brand of toothpaste. Yesterday she bought Dentafresh _____ her hus-
                                                              4
band prefers Glisten. She bought Dentafresh _____ it was cheaper than
                                                      5
Glisten.

since, although

   Consumers are more loyal to brands in some product categories than in others.

Coffee is a product with high brand loyalty. Mr. Eaton is loyal to Roma Roast coffee

_____ he's had good experiences with it. Today his supermarket is out of
        6
Roma Roast. _____ there are many other brands, he won't buy any of
                    7
them. Mr. Eaton is going to buy Roma Roast _____ he has to drive five
                                                    8

miles to another store to get it. Batteries are a product with low brand loyalty.

Consumers will buy Super-Pep batteries _____ they've had good experi-
                                                    9
ences with Endura batteries.

as, despite the fact that

_____ children don't have as much money as adults do, many ads are
        10
designed to appeal to children. Appealing to children is important to advertisers

_____ children can persuade their parents to buy products in many cate-
        11
gories. Also, advertisers want to build brand loyalty in children and teenagers

_____ many adults continue buying the brands they learned to like at a
        12
young age.

B. Use your own ideas about different products and brands to complete the sentences.

1. In spite of the fact that _____ is expensive, I

   _____.

2. Because _____ is expensive, I _____.

3. I usually buy _____ because _____.

4. I usually buy _____ even though _____.

5. I don't like _____ because _____.

6. I don't like _____ despite the fact that

   _____.

8 Adverb Clauses of Purpose: *Buying to Fulfill Needs and Desires*

A. Combine the given sentences to form one sentence with an adverb clause of purpose. Use *can* or *could* for ability. Otherwise, use *will* or *would*.

1. Advertisers studied psychological theories. They wanted to be able to learn what
   motivates consumers to buy things. (so that)

   *Advertisers studied psychological theories so that they could learn what
   motivates consumers to buy things.*

2. They make their ads appealing. They want people to be motivated to buy.
   (in order that)

3. Consumers buy products. They want to be able to fulfill their various needs and desires. (so that)

4. Consumers buy food. They want to be able to satisfy a basic survival need. (so that)

5. Scott and Martha bought a car seat. They didn't want their baby to be injured in an accident. (so that)

6. People buy some products. They want other people to accept or admire them. (in order that)

7. Jay drove a luxury car. He wanted other people to know that he had achieved financial success. (in order that)

8. Dolores always wore an unusual style of clothing. She wanted to be able to express her individualism. (so that)

B. Use your own ideas to complete the sentences for a market research survey.

1. I wear certain styles of clothing so that _____.

2. Recently, I bought _____ so that _____.

3. People need _____ so that _____.

4. I _____ so that I will be healthy.

5. I _____ so that I could _____.

6. I _____ so that other people wouldn't

   _____.

🔟 Adverb Clauses of Manner: *Does It Seem As If It's Real?*

Although much of what's in commercials isn't "real," advertisers want to give the appearance of reality. Before commercials are shown on TV, advertisers test them by asking consumers for their impressions. Complete the consumers' responses using adverb clauses with *as if* or *as though*.

1. Q: What's your impression of the restaurant in the pizza commercial?

   A: I think it's possible the restaurant is real. That is, it looks to me _____as if/as though the restaurant is real._

2. Q: What do you think about the actress in the mattress commercial?

   A: I know that the actress isn't asleep, but she looks _____as if/as though she were asleep._

3. Q: What's your impression of the actor in the pain reliever commercial?

   A: I know that the actor doesn't have a cold, but he behaves _____.

4. Q: What do you think about the cat in the pet food commercial?

   A: I think it's possible that the cat likes the food a lot. It eats _____.

5. Q: What's your impression of the dog in the fast food commercial?

A: I know that the dog isn't really talking, but it looks _____.

6. Q: What's your impression of the actress in the laundry detergent commercial?

A: Although I know that the actress isn't a grandmother, she sounds _____.

7. Q: What do you think about the people in the cola commercial?

A: I know that the people in the commercial aren't old friends, but they act _____.

8. Q: What about the speed of the car in the automobile commercial?

A: I think that it's possible that the car is going 100 miles per hour. It seems _____.

10   Subordinating Conjunctions; Adverb Clauses—Meaning: "Coolhunting"

Nowadays, many fashion trends start with certain teenage kids in certain places. Since these kids decide which styles are "cool," they are fashion opinion leaders. Advertisers send researchers known as "coolhunters" to find out what they are wearing and thinking. Listen as a coolhunter talks about her job. Listen a second time and **circle** the letter of the item that better expresses the meaning of the sentence that you hear.

1. a. Terrence has known what's cool from the time he was very young until the present.

   b. Terrence knew what was cool because he was very young.

2. a. During the entire time that I've known Mimi, she's been willing to talk to me about what's cool.

   b. If I knew Mimi, she'd be willing to talk to me about what's cool.

3. a. Because she's wearing a ski parka on the street now, other girls in her group will want to wear one, too.

   b. From the time that she began wearing a ski parka on the street until now, other girls in her group have wanted to wear one, too.

4. a. The kids look at the shoes. In contrast, I listen to what they say about them.

   b. The kids are looking at the shoes. At the same time, I'm listening to what they say about them.

5. a. During the entire time that the kids in Chicago, Detroit, and New York tell me that they like a shoe, I can assume it's going to be a success in other parts of the country.

   b. If the kids in Chicago, Detroit, and New York tell me that they like a shoe, I can assume it's going to be a success in other parts of the country.

6. a. It looks as if the MXR is going to be a popular style.

   b. I'd like the MXR to be a popular style.

7. a. Some cool kids were wearing basketball shoes. In contrast, now they're wearing big leather boots.

   b. Some cool kids are wearing basketball shoes. At the same time, others are wearing big leather boots.

8.   a.   At the same time that kids in New York were shaving their heads, kids in Seattle were dying their hair crazy colors.

     b.   Because kids in New York were shaving their heads, kids in Seattle were dying their hair crazy colors.

9.   a.   I'm going to be talking to them. At the same time, they're going to be starting lots of trends.

     b.   I'm going to talk to them because they've started lots of trends.

▮▮ Subordinating Conjunctions: *Influences on Buying Behavior*

Use the subordinating conjunctions given to complete the sentences. Use each conjunction once.

although   because   so that   ~~when~~   whereas

___When___ advertisers plan their strategies, they look at the various influ-
     1

ences on people's buying behavior. Advertisers gather information on people and

their buying behavior _____ they can design advertising for specific
                    2

groups. They often look at demographic (population) characteristics, including age,

gender, occupation, income, and education. Advertisers use these characteristics

_____ they are easy to obtain and are closely linked to customers' needs
    3

and buying behavior. Consider, for example, occupation. _____ a banker
                                               4

and an electrician may have similar incomes, their different occupations ensure

that they buy some very different products. The banker buys suits, _____
                                                          5

the electrician buys work shirts and jeans.

as   as if   because   even though   unless

     Demographic information also helps advertisers plan for the future.

_____ advertisers have information about population trends, they can't
    6

anticipate changes in markets for products. For example, it looks _____
                                                          7

the average age of the US population will continue to increase. _____ the
                                                   8

age of the population increases, there will be increased demand for health care ser-

vices and retirement housing.

Advertisers are also interested in who influences consumers' buying behavior. _____ family relationships are close, family members probably have
₉

the strongest influence on an individual's buying behavior. These influences work

in all directions. _____ parents may make the final decision to buy prod-
₁₀

ucts, children and teenagers often influence those decisions.

> Adapted from Pride, William M., and O.C. Ferrell. *Marketing: Concepts and Strategies.*
> Boston: Houghton Mifflin Company, 1997, pp. 42, 136–137, 143–144.

12 Using Adverb Clauses: *The Influences on Your Buying Behavior*

A. Work in small groups. Choose **four** of the following kinds of products: toothpaste, shampoo, cola or other soft drinks, coffee or tea, snack chips, fast food, film, blue jeans, shoes, gasoline, and long-distance telephone service. For each of the four, discuss these questions: Who or what influences your choice of brands? Are you influenced more by advertising or by other factors, such as the opinions of family members or friends, past experience with brands, or price? Why? Use adverb clauses in explaining the influences on your buying behavior.

> Example: Price is the main influence on my choice of gasoline. Although I buy a lot of gasoline for my car, I don't pay attention to ads for it. I buy HiPro as it's cheaper than the other brands. All the brands are so similar that it doesn't make any difference. OR Advertising is the main influence on my choice of film. I've used QPV film since I saw an ad for it a couple of years ago. Because the ad gave information about the improved color quality of the film, I was interested in trying it. OR My family is the main influence on my choice of fast food. While I like chicken, my sister likes hamburgers. I go to Lottaburger so that my sister will be happy.

B. Write **three** short paragraphs describing the influences on your buying behavior for **three** of the kinds of products listed in **A.** Use each of the following types of adverb clauses at least twice: time, reason, result, contrast or opposition, and purpose.

GRAMMAR BRIEFING 3: Adverb Phrases

Many kinds of adverb clauses can be reduced to adverb phrases. Like adverb clauses, adverb phrases function as adverbs.

FORM AND FUNCTION Adverb Phrases

■ An adverb phrase doesn't have a subject. When an adverb clause is reduced to a phrase, its subject is omitted. An adverb clause can be reduced only if it has the same subject as the main clause.

> After **they** arrived, **they** unpacked. Reduction possible: After arriving, **they** unpacked.

> After **they** arrived, **we** unpacked. Reduction not possible.

■ Other general rules for reducing adverb clauses to adverb phrases are:*

- If the adverb clause includes *be*, omit *be*.

    When he is hungry, he eats like a horse. (main verb *be*)

    → **When hungry,** he eats like a horse.

    When he is working, he listens to music. (progressive *be*)

    → **When working,** he listens to music.

    When they are marketed right, most good products will make money. (passive *be*)

    → **When marketed right,** most good products will make money.

- If the clause does not include *be*, change the verb to verb + *-ing* (present participle).

    Although it sold well, the product was taken off the market.

    → **Although selling well,** the product was taken off the market.

- If the event or state in the clause occurred before the time expressed in the main clause, the verb can be changed to *having* + past participle.

    After they took the product off the market, they introduced an improved product.

    → **After having taken the product off the market,** they introduced an improved product.

- If the clause includes a *not*, follow the rules above and keep the *not*.

    When it isn't working well, an advertising campaign is canceled.

    → **When not working well,** an advertising campaign is canceled.

    If they don't sell well, they can be returned.

    → **If not selling well,** they can be returned.

■ Adverb phrases tend to come before the main clause.

■ Adverb phrases are often formed from adverb clauses of time, reason, and contrast and opposition. They cannot be formed from adverb clauses of result or purpose.

* These general rules have exceptions. Some of the exceptions are discussed in what follows.

Adverb Phrases of Time

■ Adverb phrases of time can be formed from clauses that begin with *after, before, when, while,* and *since*. The subordinating conjunction generally can be omitted if the meaning will be clear without it.

  Before paying for his new car, Jamie took a test drive.

  (While) looking in the showroom window, Priscilla saw the dress she wanted.

- *Before* and *since* must be kept as the meaning would not be clear without them.

    Before she went to the store, she made a list.

    → **Before going to the store,** she made a list.

    Since we moved to the country, we've been much more relaxed.

    → **Since moving/Since having moved to the country,** we've been much more relaxed.

- When the action in the two clauses occurs at the same time, the subordinating conjunction can be omitted, in the case of *when* and *while,* or must be omitted, in the case of *as.*

> **While she was shopping,** she lost her purse.
>
> → **(While) shopping,** she lost her purse.
>
> **As she left the store,** she noticed it was gone.
>
> → **Leaving the store,** she noticed it was gone.

■ *After* is usually kept. However, with *having* + past participle, it is clear that the action in the phrase occurred first, so *after* can be omitted.

> **After she had shopped for hours,** she went home exhausted.
>
> → **After shopping for hours,** she went home exhausted. OR
>
> **(After) having shopped for hours,** she went home exhausted.

Adverb Phrases of Reason

■ The subordinating conjunction—*because, since, as*—is omitted in adverb phrases of reason.

> **Because it is designed for teenagers,** it is selling well.
>
> → **Designed for teenagers,** it is selling well.

■ Use the *-ing* form of the verb only if the two clauses express simultaneous states or actions. If the state or action in the adverb clause occurred first, use *having* + the past participle.

> **Because I love you,** I want the best for you. (simultaneous)
>
> → **Loving you,** I want the best for you.
>
> **Because they had eaten,** they weren't hungry. (adverb clause action first)
>
> → **Having eaten,** they weren't hungry.

■ In adverb phrases of reason, *be* + adjective or noun changes to *being* + adjective or noun.

> **Because it isn't well-stocked,** the store isn't a good place to shop.
>
> → **Not being well-stocked,** the store isn't a good place to shop.

Adverb Phrases of Contrast and Opposition

■ The subordinating conjunctions most often used in phrases of contrast and opposition are *while, although,* and *though.* These subordinating conjunctions cannot be omitted.

> **While the product sold well,** it never made the company money.
>
> → **While selling well,** the product never made the company money.

■ As in the rule given earlier, clauses of opposition with *be* are reduced by omitting the *be.*

> **Although it is effective,** the product hasn't sold well.
>
> → **Although effective,** the product hasn't sold well.
>
> **Though he was running for political office,** he claimed to hate politics.
>
> → **Though running for political office,** he claimed to hate politics.

GRAMMAR HOTSPOT!

■ Remember! Adverb clauses can be reduced to adverb phrases only when the subject in the adverb clause is the same as the main clause subject. If the subjects are different, the result is an error called a dangling modifier. For example: *When **you're walking down Fifth Avenue, the Empire State Building** looks very impressive* cannot be reduced. The resulting sentence—*When walking down Fifth Avenue, the Empire State Building looks very impressive*—says that the Empire State Building is walking down Fifth Avenue.

GRAMMAR PRACTICE 3: Adverb Phrases

13 Identifying Adverb Clauses and Phrases: *The Beginning of the Decision-Making Process*

A. Work with a partner. Read the sentences and put **C** in the space before the sentences that contain adverb clauses and **P** before the sentences that contain adverb phrases. Then look again at the sentences that contain adverb clauses. Underline the clauses that can be reduced to form adverb phrases.

1. ___P___ When buying a product, a consumer goes through a decision-making process.

2. ___C___ The process begins when the consumer recognizes that he or she lacks a needed product.

3. ___C___ <u>While she was brushing her teeth</u>, Lois realized that the toothpaste tube was almost empty.

4. _____ Since moving away from his parents' home, Jeff has been watching television cooking programs.

5. _____ While Jeff was watching television, a chef showed how to make leeks with cheese sauce.

6. _____ Though he wasn't familiar with leeks, Jeff decided that he would try making the dish.

7. _____ Before going to the store, Jeff added leeks to his list of things to buy.

8. _____ When consumers buy low-cost, frequently purchased items, their decision-making process usually requires very little time.

9. _____ After spending thirty seconds selecting a tube of toothpaste, Lois remembered that she needed some carrots.

10. _____ If they buy an unfamiliar product, consumers may need information from a knowledgeable source.

11. _____ Before Lois got to the produce section, Jeff had spent thirty minutes trying to decide which leeks to buy.

12. _____ Since they met at the supermarket, Jeff and Lois have been seeing a lot
of each other.

B. Look again at the adverb clauses you have underlined. Make the changes necessary
to reduce them to adverb phrases.

> Example: While ~~she was~~ brushing her teeth, Lois realized that the tooth-
> paste tube was almost empty.

14   Adverb Phrases of Time: *The Consumer Decision-Making and Purchase Process*

Reduce the adverb clauses to adverb phrases, if possible. Otherwise, write **NR.** If more
than one form is possible, show all forms.

Consumer buying decision process

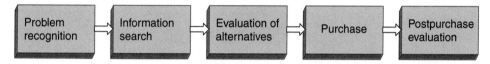

1. Before they purchase a product, consumers go through a decision-making
   process that begins with "problem recognition."

   *Before purchasing a product, consumers go through a decision-making pro-
   cess that begins with "problem recognition."*

2. While she was driving her car, Sarah saw smoke coming from its engine.

   While driving her car,/Driving her car, Sarah saw smoke coming from its engine.

3. After they recognize the problem, buyers enter the "information search" stage.

   *After recognizing the problem,/After having recognized the problem,/Having
   recognized the problem, buyers enter the "information search" stage.*

4. Before she bought a new car, Sarah wanted to make sure that she had all the
   information she needed.

5. When she searched for information, she asked knowledgeable friends and relatives for their opinions.

6. While she was at the library, she read *Consumer Reports* for objective information.

7. After they get enough information, consumers begin to evaluate alternatives.

8. As she thought over the many types of cars, Sarah decided that reliability was an
   important criterion and decided to buy a Jupiter.

9. When Sarah went to the Jupiter dealer, the salesperson was very happy to help
   her with the "purchase" stage of the buying process.

10. When they enter the "postpurchase evaluation" stage, consumers often experi-
    ence a feeling known as "buyers remorse."

11. After she had bought her Jupiter, Sarah felt regretful about spending so much
    money.

12. Since she got over her buyer's remorse, she's been very happy with her Jupiter.

15 Adverb Phrases of Reason: *Whose Opinion Do You Trust?*

Reduce the adverb clauses of reason to adverb phrases, if possible. Otherwise, write **NR.**

1. Since he needed a computer for his school work, Taylor looked at computer advertisements.

   Needing a computer for his school work, Taylor looked at computer advertisements.

2. Because he didn't know much about computers, Taylor also wanted to talk to a knowledgeable person.

3. As she's interested in computers, Jenny keeps up with the latest technological developments.

4. Because she has used different computers, Jenny is able to compare their features.

5. Since Jenny is knowledgeable about computers, many people ask her for her opinion about which one to buy.

6. As they don't have the time to do their own pre-purchase research, they appreciate her advice.

7. Because Jenny gets no financial benefit from her advice, her friends trust her.

8. Because he had talked to Jenny, Taylor felt that he had the information he needed to choose the right computer.

9. Most people choose new products based on the recommendation of an "opinion leader." Because they know this, advertisers of new products design their ads to appeal to opinion leaders.

16 Adverb Phrases of Contrast and Opposition: *Is It Effective?*

Reduce the adverb clauses of contrast or opposition to adverb phrases, if possible. Otherwise, write **NR.**

1. Though they are exposed to many ads, most people pay attention to only a few of them.

   Though exposed to many ads, most people pay attention to only a few of them.

2. While it was entertaining, the commercial didn't persuade many people to try the product.

3. Though they make people aware of new products, ads don't always increase sales.

4. Although it wasn't informative, the advertisement was memorable.

5. While they are used often in advertising, celebrities have little effect on people's decision to try a new product.

6. Though he is admired for his athletic ability, the celebrity probably doesn't know a lot about cars.

7. Although he no longer works as a mechanic, my uncle still knows a lot about cars.

8. Although a great deal of money is spent on advertising new products, most people don't buy them based on advertising alone.

17   Using Adverb Phrases: *Your Buying Decision Process*

A. When they buy a product they have never bought before or make a major purchase, consumers go through a process that usually includes the following stages: (1) recognizing a problem or need, (2) searching for information, (3) evaluating alternatives, (4) making the purchase, and (5) evaluating the purchase. Work with a partner. Find out about a purchase that your partner has made—of a car, a piece of electronic equipment, sports equipment, clothing, or any other significant item. Find out when and why your partner took actions or made decisions and at what stages he or she paid attention to advertising for the product.

B. Using the information you got in **A,** write a description of your partner's buying decision process. In your description, use at least two adverb phrases of time, two adverb phrases of reason, and one adverb phrase of contrast or opposition.

> Example: While reading the student newspaper, Tito saw an ad for calculators. Having seen the ad, he realized that he would need a calculator for one of his classes. Not knowing what kind of calculator to buy, Tito asked the teacher for a recommendation. . . .

Read your description to the class.

Connecting Ideas

Introductory Task: *Is It Fair?*

A. Two adults are having a discussion about advertising. Listen to their discussion once for the main ideas. Then listen again and fill in the missing connectors.

A: Children are fascinated by that commercial for Pixie Puffs cereal,

_____ *but* _____ I think it's outrageous. Pixie Puffs are mostly sugar. They

₁

_____ cause tooth decay _____ make children fat.

₂

_____, that's not the image that the ad presents. _____, it

₃ ₄

shows healthy, active children eating them. _____ it uses animated

₅

"magical" characters, _____ children associate the cereal with a fan-

₆

tasy world. Advertising to young children really shouldn't be allowed.

B: I agree that Pixie Puffs probably aren't the best food for children _____

₇

that advertisers are real experts at _____ tempting _____

₈

persuading them. _____, I think that advertisers have the right to pro-

₉

mote their products to children. _____, television networks can't pro-

₁₀

vide programs for children without the money they get from selling advertising.

A: That may be true, _____ advertising to young children isn't really fair.
                                    11

They have _____ the experience _____ the knowledge to
                            12

make informed decisions about products. _____, they can't always
                                                          13

distinguish the commercials from the programs _____ fantasy from
                                                                14

reality.

B: _____ the problems that commercials cause, I think it's necessary for
         15

children to be exposed to them. _____, they won't learn to resist the
                                              16

persuasive techniques used in advertising.

B. As a class, discuss the conversation. Do you agree with speaker **A** or speaker **B**?
Can you think of other points for or against advertising to children?

GRAMMAR BRIEFING 1: Connectors

Coordinating conjunctions and transitions are used to connect main clauses.

FORM AND FUNCTION Connectors

- There are three types of connectors. Subordinating conjunctions, discussed in
  Chapter 22, connect a dependent clause (an adverb clause) to a main clause.
  They show how the ideas in the two clauses are related. Coordinating conjunctions and transitions, discussed in this chapter, connect main clauses. They show
  the relationships among ideas within sentences and across sentences.

                               dependent clause   main clause
  Subordinating conjunction: **Although** he was late, we waited for him.

                              main clause   main clause
  Coordinating conjunction: He was late, **but** we waited for him.

                    main clause   main clause
  Transition: He was late. **However,** we waited for him.

  By showing how our ideas are connected, connectors make our speech and writing clear to listeners and readers.

- Like subordinating conjunctions, coordinating conjunctions and transitions can
  express different kinds of relationships (result, contrast, etc.). These are discussed
  in Grammar Briefings 2 and 3.*

* Prepositions can also link ideas, by linking a noun phrase to a main clause (e.g., **Despite** *his inexperience, he was offered the
job*). If the prepositional phrase comes at the beginning of the sentence, it is followed by a comma. Some prepositions that link
ideas are discussed in Grammar Briefing 3.

Coordinating Conjunctions

■ The coordinating conjunctions are *and, but, or, nor, so* (indicating result), *for* (meaning "because"), and *yet* (meaning "but").

■ In addition to connecting clauses, *and, but, or,* and *yet* can connect words or phrases.

> The advertising campaign was **successful and memorable.** (words)
>
> The client liked **the general idea but not the specific layout.** (phrases)
>
> **The client was happy, so the advertisers celebrated.** (clauses)

■ When coordinating conjunctions join two main clauses, they come between the clauses and are preceded by a comma. In formal writing, coordinating conjunctions usually do not occur at the beginning of a sentence.

> The new products sold well**, yet** the company's profits did not increase.

■ More than two elements can be joined by *and* or *or.* In such cases, commas are used between each element.

> Tiffany, Suzanne**, and** Andrew will attend the meeting.

■ Content connected by coordinating conjunctions must be parallel—that is, must belong to the same grammatical category (e.g., adjective, adverb, noun phrase, verb phrase, infinitive phrase, or gerund phrase).

> The client likes **to sell her product** and **(to) make a profit.** (infinitive phrases)
>
> **Not:** The client likes ~~to sell her product~~ and ~~making a profit.~~ (infinitive phrase and gerund phrase)

■ In many cases, the content that is joined has some of the same information. When this happens, repeated words are often omitted.

> They can continue with this campaign **or (they can)** try something different.

■ Because repeated words can be omitted, different versions of a sentence are often possible.

> Prices in the United States are rising. + Prices in Europe are rising. =
>
> Prices in the United States are rising, and prices in Europe are (rising), too.*
>
> Prices in the United States and prices in Europe are rising.
>
> Prices in the United States and in Europe are rising.
>
> Prices in the United States and Europe are rising.

■ Paired coordinating conjunctions are special coordinating conjunctions that have more than one part. They are similar in meaning to other coordinating conjunctions but tend to be more emphatic. These conjunctions include *both . . . and, not only . . . but (also), either . . . or,* and *neither . . . nor.* All paired coordinating conjunctions can connect words or phrases. All except *both . . . and* can connect clauses.

> The client wanted **both** quality **and** results.

* If two verb phrases are the same, the second one can be shortened as follows: Verb phrases with *be* can be shortened to *be . . . , too* or *so + be.* For example: *My mother was at the party, and my sister was at the party* becomes *My mother was at the party, and my sister was, too* or *My mother was at the party, and so was my sister.*

If the verb phrase does not include *be* or a modal, *do* is used. For example: *My mother brought a present, and my sister brought a present* becomes *My mother brought a present, and my sister did, too* or *My mother brought a present, and so did my sister.*

Content connected by paired coordinating conjunctions should be parallel.

> You should take either **calculus** or **organic chemistry.** (noun phrases)
>
> **Not:** ~~You should either take calculus or organic chemistry.~~ (verb phrase and noun phrase)

Transitions

- There are many transitions, including *also, in addition, moreover, however, consequently, therefore,* and *for example* (see Grammar Briefings 2 and 3).

- Transitions can connect main clauses in a single sentence or in separate sentences. If the clauses are in a single sentence, they are separated by a semicolon.

  > The product worked well**;** in addition, people liked it. OR
  >
  > The product worked well**.** In addition, people liked it.

- Many transitions can occur at the beginning, middle, or end of a clause. The beginning is the most common position, and nearly all transitions can occur there. Transitions are usually set off from the rest of the clause by commas.

  > We thought the idea was great. **However,** our client was unenthusiastic. OR
  >
  > We thought the idea was great. Our client, **however,** was unenthusiastic. OR
  >
  > We thought the idea was great. Our client was unenthusiastic, **however.**

- Particularly in writing, transitions are often used to connect ideas across units that are larger than clauses and sentences. For example, one paragraph might present one idea, and the next paragraph, beginning with *however,* might present a contrasting idea.

GRAMMAR HOTSPOT!

- Remember! Use a comma before a coordinating conjunction when it connects two main clauses. When a coordinating conjunction is not used, use a period or semicolon, not a comma, between two main clauses. A period or semicolon is, therefore, used before a transition. If a comma is used between main clauses not connected by a coordinating conjunction, the result is an error called a "run-on sentence" or "comma splice."

  > He liked the slogan, but they chose not to use it. (coordinating conjunction)
  >
  > He liked the slogan. They chose not to use it. OR He liked the slogan; they chose not to use it.
  >
  > **Not:** He liked the ~~slogan, they~~ chose not to use it.
  >
  > He liked the slogan. However, they chose not to use it. OR He liked the slogan; however, they chose not to use it. (transition)
  >
  > **Not:** He liked the ~~slogan, however,~~ they chose not to use it.

GRAMMAR PRACTICE 1: Connectors

1 Identifying Types of Connectors: *"Image" Advertising*

Work with a partner. Label the boldfaced connectors in the text. Use **SC** for subordinating conjunctions, **CC** for coordinating conjunctions, **PCC** for paired coordinating conjunctions, and **T** for transitions.

　　　　SC　　　　　　　　　　　　　　　　　　　　　　　　*CC*
　　When consumers buy a product, they are really buying the benefits **and** satisfaction they think the product will provide. **However,** there is generally little or no difference between brands, **so** one brand doesn't really give consumers benefits that they couldn't get from another brand. **For example,** high-quality video recording tape is manufactured by several companies. Consumers can buy **either** Brand X tape **or** Brand Y tape for the same price. The labels look different, **but** the products are essentially the same. **Both** Brand X **and** Brand Y tapes are made of the same materials, **and** both brands are equally long lasting. **Therefore,** the advertisers of Brand X want to distinguish it from its competitors by creating a unique image of Brand X in the minds of consumers. They use "image" advertising to build up a positive image **not only** of the brand **but also** of the kind of people who use it. **Since** research has shown that picture quality is important to the consumers, commercials for Brand X emphasize its excellent picture quality. **In addition,** they show Brand X being used by people who are exceptionally attractive. Brand X isn't different from Brand Y, **yet** consumers believe that it is. They buy Brand X **so that** they can have the special benefits **or** satisfaction associated with its image.

2 Punctuating Sentences with or without Coordinating Conjunctions: *Contrasting Images*

Use commas and periods where necessary to punctuate the following sentences. Make letters capital where necessary, but do not add words. If no changes are needed, write **NC**.

1. Consumers' decisions to buy are made on both rational and emotional grounds.
    NC

2. We buy some products to fulfill our basic needs for food, clothing, and shelter.
    O
    ~~other~~ products fulfill our need for safety or security.

3. Consumers buy some products to fulfill their need for love and affection and they buy others to fulfill their need for self-esteem or achievement.

4. Advertisers know why consumers buy products so they use imagery or music to appeal to consumers' emotions.

5. Sometimes the commercials don't show the product at all they show positive images that advertisers want consumers to associate with the product.

6. Images of freedom youthfulness and friendship are common in American commercials.

7. Consumers associate Michelin tires with protecting family members and a De Beers diamond with a loving and long-lasting relationship.

8. The car seems to be traveling through a fierce storm but the family inside it is safe.

9. The woman in the ad is wearing a diamond necklace but no other jewelry.

10. Hector would like to give his wife a diamond necklace for he loves her very much and hopes that their marriage will last forever.

11. Car commercials often show wild driving scenes advertisers know that consumers want fun adventure and excitement in their lives.

12. Naomi isn't really an adventurous person yet she bought a fast sports car.

13. Alfonso thinks of himself as someone who is both responsible and adventurous so he wants a car that is not only safe but also fast.

3 Parallel Structures: *The Messages the Images Send*

Correct the errors in parallel structure in the following sentences. If a sentence contains no errors, write **NC**. Some errors can be corrected in more than one way.

1. You can be happy, glamorous, and ~~success~~. *successful*

2. If you buy and use this elegant fountain pen, people will admire and respected you.

3. This gold watch expresses wealth, prestige, and achievement to everyone who sees it.

4. Simply by wearing these cosmetics, you not only can become beautiful but also popular.

5. With these tires, your family will travel not only safe but also rapidly.

6. If you suspect that your friends have been either avoiding you or keeping a distance from you, you've probably been using the wrong toothpaste or mouthwash.

7. Whenever either your life seems dull or empty, you can transform it by buying colorful and stylish clothes.

8. As soon as a man buys this car, he begins having exciting adventures and to attract beautiful women.

9. They will know that his car is elegant, powerful, and it costs a lot.

4 Omitting Words: *Making the Messages Concise*

Combine the sentences into **one** sentence with *and*. Make the content in the sentence parallel. Make all sentences as concise as possible—that is, omit repeated words. For items 7 and 8, use your own ideas to complete the sentences before combining them.

1. This car is stylish. This car is fast. This car is maneuverable.

    This car is stylish, fast, and maneuverable.

2. Elegant clothes make you more attractive. Expensive cosmetics make you more attractive.

    Elegant clothes and expensive cosmetics make you more attractive.

3. Calla skin cream prevents the signs of aging. Calla skin cream corrects the signs of aging.

4. By listening to these tapes, anyone can learn to speak Spanish quickly. By listening to these tapes, anyone can learn to speak Spanish correctly. By listening to these tapes, anyone can learn to speak Spanish fluently.

5. When people spend their vacations at the Oasis Resort, they relax on sunny beaches. When people spend their vacations at the Oasis Resort, they feast on superb seafood. When people spend their vacations at the Oasis Resort, they enjoy high-quality entertainment every night.

6. Dentafresh helps prevent tooth decay. Glisten helps prevent tooth decay.

7. Men who wear Summit shirts are handsome. Men who wear Summit shirts are

    self-confident. Men who wear Summit shirts are _____.

8. Children enjoy eating at Burger Heaven. _____ enjoy eating at Burger Heaven.

5 Punctuating Sentences Connected by Transitions: *All Image and No Product?*

Use commas, semicolons, and periods to punctuate the following sentences. Add capital letters where necessary.

1. Advertisers say that image advertising may not "sell" a product however it does influence consumers' emotional response to the product.

    Advertisers say that image advertising may not "sell" a product. However, it does influence consumers' emotional response to the product. OR

    Advertisers say that image advertising may not "sell" a product; however, it does influence consumers' emotional response to the product.

2. The manufacturer of Infiniti automobiles hoped to create excitement and curiosity about them the advertising agency therefore decided on an unusual approach to introducing the cars to consumers.

3. They wanted consumers to associate Infinitis with nature also they wanted consumers to equate the cars with peace of mind and serenity.

4. The commercials consisted of lovely natural scenes in addition they featured a soft-spoken narrator discussing the harmony that exists between nature and man.

5. The commercials showed rocks and trees and rain falling on ponds they didn't show the cars at all however.

6. The announcer talked about the simplicity of nature many people consequently were confused about what was being advertised.

7. The advertisers were convinced that the "no product" commercials were a great success because millions of people were curious about their meaning however the manufacturer decided to hire a new agency.

GRAMMAR BRIEFING 2: Relationships Expressed with Connectors— Addition and Time

A range of relationships between ideas can be expressed with coordinating conjunctions and transitions. These relationships include addition and time.

FORM AND FUNCTION Relationships Expressed with Connectors—Addition and Time

Addition

- Addition connectors show that related information is being added.
- Coordinating conjunctions: *and, or, nor;* paired coordinating conjunctions *both . . . and, not only . . . but (also), either . . . or, neither . . . nor*

  - *Both . . . and* has the same meaning as *and* but is more emphatic. *Not only . . . but (also)* is even more emphatic.

    He's smart **and** athletic. = He's **both** smart **and** athletic. = He's **not only** smart **but also** athletic. (same meaning with more emphasis in each version)

    Remember that *both . . . and* cannot connect clauses; *not only . . . but (also)* is used. If a clause begins with *not only,* the subject and verb are inverted.* When *also* is included, it often follows the subject.

    He is a great athlete, **and** his brother excels at sports. = **Not only** is he a great athlete, **but** his brother **(also)** excels at sports.

  - *Or* and the more emphatic *either . . . or* show that the information being added is an alternative.

    Either the original advertisement **or** the new one would work.

  - *Nor* and *neither . . . nor* show that negative information is being added. That is, *nor* has the same meaning as "and not." When *nor* joins clauses, the subject and verb in the second clause are inverted.*

    Neither my parents **nor** I can come. (= My parents **can't** come, **and** I **can't** come.)

    I don't want to deal with them, **nor** will I deal with them. (= I don't want to deal with them, **and** I **won't** deal with them.)

* If the clause does not have *be* or an auxiliary, *do* is added and inverts with the subject (e.g., *Not only does he speak fluent English, but he also knows French, Spanish, and Arabic.*).

■ <u>Transitions</u>: *also, besides, furthermore, in addition, moreover,* etc.

> I might not be able to get you the materials. I haven't been able to locate distributors. **Furthermore,** prices seem to have skyrocketed.

- *Also* is not set off with commas if in the middle or at the end of a clause.

> I saw Mary there. I saw Nadine also.

Time Connectors

■ Time connectors can show not only the order of events in time, but also the order of the ideas that the speaker or writer is discussing.

> **First,** the kids went swimming. **Then** they had lunch and went to a movie. (order of events)

> **First,** I want to discuss several possible strategies. **Then** I want to examine the consequences of adopting these strategies. (order of ideas)

■ <u>Coordinating conjunctions:</u> *and*
And often implies that the events mentioned first took place before the events mentioned next.

> I went home, had dinner, watched TV, **and** went to bed.

■ <u>Transitions</u>: *before/after that, afterward, meanwhile* (= at the same time or in the time between two events), *next, then; first, second,* etc.; *in the end, finally, in conclusion,* etc.

- Time transitions are not set off by a comma when they come at the end of a sentence.

> The first ad campaign was successful; the problems began **after that.**

- Unlike the other transitions, *in conclusion* is used only to indicate order of ideas. The idea that follows is the speaker's last idea and also comments on or summarizes the ideas that came before.

> . . . **In conclusion,** various economic indicators show the economy is heating up. (The speaker/writer has discussed these indicators and is now summarizing.)

■ As discussed in Chapter 22, subordinating conjunctions used to indicate time relationships include *after, before, when, while, as, as soon as, whenever, since, until, once,* and *as long as.*

GRAMMAR HOTSPOT!

■ Plural verbs are used with subjects joined by *and* or *both . . . and.* If subjects are joined by *or, nor, either . . . or, neither . . . nor,* or *not only . . . but also,* the subject that is closer to the verb determines the form of the verb.

> **Both** Alison **and** Latisha **have** the keys to my apartment.

> **Either** my sister **or my parents have** the keys to my apartment.

> **Neither** my parents **nor my sister has** the keys to my office.

> **Not only** my parents **but also my sister has** the keys to my mailbox.

GRAMMAR PRACTICE 2: Relationships Expressed with Connectors— Addition and Time

6 Addition—Paired Coordinating Conjunctions: *What Are Your Reactions?*

A. Rewrite the statements in brackets using an appropriate paired conjunction— *both ... and, not only ... but (also), either ... or,* or *neither ... nor.* In your sentence, omit repeated words and make the content parallel if possible.

1. *Heather:* Advertising has an important place in our culture. [It influences our attitudes. It reflects our attitudes.]

   It both influences and reflects our attitudes. OR It not only influences but also reflects our attitudes.

2. *Merle:* Advertising is wasted on me. [I don't want most of the products that I see in ads. I don't need most of the products that I see in ads.]

   I neither want nor need most of the products that I see in ads.

3. *Diego:* I like the Space-Lex ad campaign because it's made me aware of a useful product. [Their commercial is informative. Their print ad is informative.]

4. *Beata:* I want to see believable people in ads. [Celebrities don't interest me. Celebrities don't impress me.]

5. *Barry:* The latest sport utility vehicle commercial is a great one. [The fast driving looks exciting. The scenery is amazing.]

6. *Maggie:* Lots of commercials are very sentimental. [They use cute animals to give you a warm, happy feeling, or they use adorable children to give you a warm, happy feeling.]

7. *Melody:* I want to see the new Burger Heaven commercial because everyone is talking about it. [Tyler has mentioned it. My grandmother has mentioned it.]

8. *Bob:* I'd prefer that my children didn't see fast food commercials. [French fries aren't good for them. Soda isn't good for them.]

9. *Sal:* The MYMIX commercial is worth watching. [The commercial is clever. I learned something from it.]

10. *Leon:* Edna, I can't stand to watch the talking animal commercial again. [You are going to change the channel, or I am going to change the channel.]

B. Write **four** statements expressing your opinions on specific advertisements and advertising in general. Use each of the following once: *both ... and, not only ... but also, either ... or,* and *neither ... nor.*

   Example: The ElectriChoice commercials are both creative and amusing.

7 Addition Transitions: *Valuable Information?*

A. Connect the ideas in the following paragraph by inserting addition transitions at the beginning of sentences where they are appropriate. Use each of the following once: *furthermore, in addition,* and *moreover.* Various answers are possible.

Many people have criticisms of advertising. They say that it encourages materialism in our culture. They say that it creates dissatisfaction among people who can't afford the products that it promotes. However, other people point out the benefits of advertising. It provides consumers with information about new goods that they might need or want. Advertising informs consumers about services such as health care and educational programs. It can educate people about important social or political issues. Although I can understand both points of view, I believe that advertising has the potential to do more good than harm.

B. Work with a partner. Write **two** sentences in response to each of the following instructions. Connect the second sentence to the first with an addition connector. Use each of the following at least once: *also, besides, furthermore, in addition,* and *moreover.*

1. Tell two things that people should do to be prepared for a natural disaster.

   Before a severe storm strikes, you should make sure that you have plenty of canned food. Also, it's a good idea to check the batteries in your flashlight and radio.

2. Tell two things that are excellent about the community where you live.

3. Tell two things that people could do to protect the environment.

4. Give two reasons why reading fiction is a better form of entertainment than watching television.

5. Give two reasons why teenagers should not drop out of high school.

6. Tell two advantages of being able to speak more than one language.

7. Give two reasons why people should exercise regularly.

8 Time Connectors: *Unnecessary Consumption?*

A. <u>The order of ideas</u>: Use the time connectors given to connect the ideas in the following speeches. Use each connector once. Various answers are possible.

finally   ~~first~~   first   in conclusion   next   second   then

Mr. Russell: In my comments today, I will tell you why I recommend that we con-

                                         First,

       sider restricting the advertising of gasoline. ∧ I want to talk about how

       advertising encourages unnecessary consumption of gasoline, a prod-

       uct that we should be using less rather than more of. I want to show

       you how the images used in gasoline ads encourage reckless driving. I

       will discuss the fact that the advertisements give no information about

       the negative environmental consequences of using the product.

Ms. Salas: I would like to respond to Mr. Russell's objections to gasoline adver-

       tisements with several points of my own. Gasoline ads try to persuade

       consumers to switch brands, not to buy more gasoline, so they don't

       increase the total amount of gasoline that people buy. Everyone who is

       old enough to drive recognizes that the images used in advertising are

       fantasies, not reality, and that an ordinary car can't be transformed into

       a race car by using a different brand of gasoline. The oil companies

       have provided many public service advertisements that raise aware-

       ness of environmental problems. I recommend that the advertising of

       gasoline not be restricted.

B. <u>The order of events</u>: Think of a process involving several steps that you often fol-low—for example, getting ready to go to school or cooking dinner. Write a para-graph about it. Use at least four time connectors to show the order of events.

    Example: *This is the process that I go through when it's my turn to cook dinner. First, I look at cookbooks and choose a recipe. After that, I . . .*

GRAMMAR BRIEFING 3: Other Relationships Expressed with Connectors

Other relationships that can be expressed with coordinating conjunctions and transitions include reason and result, contrast and opposition, condition, and exemplification.

FORM AND FUNCTION Other Relationships Expressed with Connectors

Reason Connectors and Result Connectors

■ Reason and result connectors show that relationships involve cause and effect. Reason connectors signal that a clause expresses a cause; result connectors signal that a clause expresses an effect.

■ Coordinating Conjunctions: *for, so*
For signals reason. *So* signals result.

> It's better to hold meetings in the morning, **for** people tend to concentrate best then. (reason)

> We met first thing in the morning, **so** we got a lot done. (result)

■ Transitions: *as a result, consequently, therefore, thus,* etc.

- All these transitions express result.

> Their sales have doubled; **consequently,** their profits have been high.

- *Thus* is not used at the end of a clause.

■ As discussed in Chapter 22, the subordinating conjunctions *because, since,* and *as* are used to express reason.

■ The prepositions *because of* and *on account of* are also used in expressing reason.

> We succeeded **on account of** hard work.

Contrast and Opposition

■ As with subordinating conjunctions, coordinating conjunctions and transitions of contrast and opposition either can signal direct opposition or can express weaker, partial, opposition or the idea that the content of one clause is unexpected because of the content of the other clause.

■ Coordinating Conjunctions: *but, yet*
But and *yet* can be used to signal either kind of opposition.

> This product is making money, **but/yet** that product is a failure. (direct opposition)

> The product is making money, **but/yet** we'd like to improve it. (weaker, partial, opposition)

■ Transitions: *however, in contrast, on the other hand, nonetheless, nevertheless*
However may be used to signal either kind of opposition. *In contrast* and *on the other hand* signal direct opposition. *Nevertheless* and *nonetheless* signal weaker, partial, opposition.

> Last year we did well; this year, **however/in contrast/on the other hand,** we have failed miserably. (direct opposition)

> We feel we've already gone over budget on the project. **Nevertheless/ Nonetheless/However,** we are willing to spend more money. (weaker, partial, opposition, unexpected content)

- As discussed in Chapter 22, direct opposition is expressed with the subordinating conjunctions *while* and *whereas* and weak, partial, opposition can be expressed with subordinators like *although, even though, though,* and *despite the fact that.*

- The prepositions *despite* and *in spite of* can also be used to express weak, partial, opposition.

> **Despite** their failures, they were optimistic about the future.

Condition Connectors

- The coordinating conjunction *or (else)* and the transition *otherwise* both mean "if not." That is, the following clause expresses what will happen if the condition in the previous clause isn't met.

> The advertisements must come out soon, **or (else)** the client won't be happy.

> The advertisement must come out soon; **otherwise,** the client won't be happy.

- As discussed in Chapter 22, subordinating conjunctions used in expressing conditions include *if, unless, provided that, only if, whether or not,* and *even if.*

Exemplification

- Transitions including *for example* and *for instance* signal that a clause (or other structure) is an example of something that is stated in another clause.

> The new ad campaign reflects current trends. **For example,** it uses black and white images instead of color images.

GRAMMAR HOTSPOT!

- Be careful! Don't use two connectors for the same idea.

> **Although** it's cold, I didn't wear a coat. OR It's cold, **but** I didn't wear a coat.

> **Not:** Although it's cold, ~~but~~ I didn't wear a coat.

GRAMMAR PRACTICE 3: Other Relationships Expressed with Connectors

Reason and Result Connectors: *The Images versus Reality*

Combine the two ideas using each of the connectors given. Punctuate carefully.

1. This soft drink has a special ingredient. This soft drink gives you energy.

   a. because

   > Because this soft drink has a special ingredient, it gives you energy.

   b. because of

   > Because of a special ingredient, this soft drink gives you energy.

   c. consequently   d. so

2. This soft drink has sugar in it. This soft drink causes tooth decay.

   a. as a result   b. on account of   c. since   d. so

3. These shoes will help you succeed in sports. You should buy these shoes.

   a. because   b. for   c. therefore   d. so

4. Michael Jordan worked hard. Michael Jordan succeeded in sports.

   a. because   b. because of   c. on account of   d. thus

🔟 Contrast and Opposition Connectors: *Contrasts*

For each sentence, use the connectors given to write sentences that express a similar meaning.

1. Even though she has perfect teeth, the model isn't an expert on dental health.

   a. (but) _The model has perfect teeth, but she isn't an expert on dental health._

   b. (however) _____

2. Fresh orange juice contains vitamins, whereas cola contains sugar.

   a. (in contrast) _____

   b. (however) _____

3. Dr. Miller is a real doctor, while that man is an actor.

   a. (but) _____

   b. (in contrast) _____

4. Although he isn't a doctor, he plays the part of one in advertisements.

   a. (yet) _____

   b. (nevertheless) _____

5. Despite the fact that he recommends the product, he has never used it.

   a. (however) _____

   b. (yet) _____

6. Whereas this product is useful, that product is useless.

   a. (but) _____

   b. (on the other hand) _____

▮▮▮ Exemplification: *Can You Support These Ideas?*

Follow each of the ideas with an idea of your own that gives an example. Use *for example* and *for instance.*

1. Advertisers show commercials during the programs that members of their target markets are likely to be watching.

   Fast-food restaurants, for example, are often advertised during children's programs.

2. Sometimes it seems as though advertising is everywhere.

3. If I could control television advertising, I would make some changes.

4. I have positive feelings about some advertisements.

5. However, my response to some advertisements is negative.

▮▮ Expressing Relationships with Connectors: *Both Sides Now*

Use the connectors given to complete the passage. Use each connector once.

also	consequently	for example	or	then
both . . . and	~~first~~	however	so	

My lecture today deals with issues in advertising. (1)_____First_____, I want to

talk about _____ criticisms _____ defenses of advertising.

(2)_____ I will answer your questions.

Advertising is controversial. I believe that it has some benefits for consumers.

(3)_____, it also has negative aspects, _____ there are many

people who are critical of it. Advertising is everywhere. (4)_____, critics

believe that there is simply too much of it. (5)They _____ have specific

criticisms of the nature of advertising and advertisers' practices. (6)_____,

they point out that advertising can deceive _____ mislead people.

for instance	in contrast	nonetheless

In the nineteenth and early twentieth centuries, it was common for advertise-

ments to make false claims. (7)_____, obviously false claims are not com-

mon today, partly as a result of government regulations. (8)_____, many

people feel that there are ways in which advertisers continue to be misleading.

(9)_____, advertisers often use actors to play the parts of "real" people in

television commercials.

because of	despite	not only . . . but also	thus
for example	furthermore	or else	yet

(10)Another criticism of advertising is that it leads to materialism—that is, that it encourages people _____ to want _____ to buy more and more things. (11)You and I may agree that it does, _____ many marketers assert that children learn materialism from their parents and friends, not from advertising.

(12)_____ the many criticisms that they get, advertisers often have to defend their industry by reminding us of the value of advertising to consumers. (13)They say that consumers need the information provided by advertising, _____ they won't be able to make informed purchase decisions. (14)_____, studies have shown that advertising stimulates price competition; _____, it lowers prices for consumers. (15)_____, opticians, who make and sell eyeglasses, were not allowed to advertise prior to 1977. In 1977 the rules were changed, opticians began advertising, and prices for eyeglasses fell 34 percent. (16)_____ these benefits, most people probably feel that they could do with less advertising in their lives.

13   Using Connectors: *Your Turn Now*

Think again about the discussion of advertising to children you heard at the beginning of the chapter. The two kinds of products that are most frequently advertised to children are toys and "junk food," including highly sweetened breakfast cereal, fast food, soft drinks, candy, and other snacks. Do you think that the advertising of one or both of these kinds of products to children should be restricted in some way or prohibited? Why or why not? Write a three- or four-paragraph essay that explains your opinion on this topic. In the introductory paragraph, use time connectors to show the order in which you will present your ideas in the essay. In the rest of the essay, use a variety of connectors to show the relationship of your ideas. Use at least three of the following types of transitions: addition, reason and result, contrast and opposition, condition, and exemplification. Also, use at least three coordinating conjunctions to connect clauses.

UNIT WRAP-UP
Error Correction

Find and correct the errors in the following passage. Some errors can be corrected in more than one way. Including the example, there are **15** errors.

The story of New Coke began in the early 1980s. When Pepsi began using the rock star Michael Jackson in commercials, sales of Pepsi began to soar. Young people were turning away from Coke, therefore the president of Coca Cola Company decided that Coke needed a new image. He instructed the chemists at Coca Cola to develop a new formula for Coke, they produced New Coke, which had a sweeter, less fizzy taste than old Coke. After developing the new product, the company spent $4 million and two years on consumer research. In taste tests, consumers preferred the new taste over the original by 61 to 39 percent. Coke was sure that New Coke would be successful. Because its flavor was so popular in the tests.

In 1985, Coca Cola announced that old Coke would soon be replaced by New Coke. Trouble began, as soon as this announcement was made. Because worrying that it would never be available again, some people began to buy all the old Coke they could find. Coca Cola spent over $10 million on an advertising campaign to introduce New Coke. Nonetheless people remained loyal to old Coke. Not only they hated the flavor of New Coke, but many of them also were emotionally upset about the change. Thousands of people wrote letters to the company. One letter said, "Neither my wife nor I likes New Coke; it's too sweet and flat. We liked drinking old Coke and to feel its tingle in our throats. Bring back old Coke. Otherwise, we'll sue you in court for taking away a cherished symbol of America." Another man felt such strongly that he wrote and performed a protest song. Although the company had spent millions on research and advertising, but they hadn't taken into account people's emotional attachment to old Coke. Because of millions of consumers were angry, Coca Cola backed down. Three months after introducing New Coke, the company announced that it would bring back old Coke as Coke Classic. No one was dis-

appointed. Today you won't find New Coke anywhere, nor Coca Cola plans to

change "the real thing" again.

Task 1: A Print Advertisement

Work with a partner. Choose a product—either a real one or one that you "invent."
Write a one- or two-paragraph ad for the product for a magazine. Make the product
sound desirable, and try to make the ad persuasive. Illustrate your ad with a drawing, if
you'd like. Use a variety of connectors to link the ideas in the advertisement, including at
least five of the following: an adverb clause of result with *so . . . that* or *such . . . that,* an
adverb clause of contrast or opposition with *although* or *whereas,* etc., an adverb clause
of condition with *if* or *unless,* etc., an adverb phrase of time with *after* or *once,* etc., an
adverb phrase of reason, a paired coordinating conjunction (e.g., *both . . . and, neither . . .
nor*), and a transition (e.g., *moreover, for instance*).

Task 2: A Television Commercial

Work in a small group. Choose a real or an imaginary product and write the script for a
commercial for it. Use your imaginations and, if you want, make the commercial humor-
ous. There should be a part for each person in the group in it. In addition to using coordinating conjunctions, use at least four of the following in the script: an adverb clause of
time (e.g., *Allegri softens as it cleans.*), an adverb clause of manner (e.g., *Mom looks as
though she's tired.*), an adverb clause of purpose (e.g., *Let's take mom to Burger Heaven so
that she can have a rest from cooking.*), an adverb phrase of time (e.g., *Before brushing with
Dentafresh, I never realized how fresh my breath could be.*), a paired coordinating conjunction (e.g., *Bambi tissues are both soft and strong.*), and a transition (e.g., *The Steamatic cooks
rice perfectly. In addition, it can be used to prepare delicious puddings.*). Perform your commercial for the class.

Task 3: A Debate on a Controversial Topic

Work in groups of four. Divide your group into two teams of two people. Prepare a
debate on the following topic:

> In general, advertising is helpful and beneficial for consumers.

One team should argue in favor of the statement, and the other team should argue
against the statement. Use a variety of connectors to link your ideas. Present your
debate to the class.

Task 4: An Essay

Write a four-paragraph essay about the topic in Task 3. The first paragraph should introduce the topic.

> Example: Advertising causes controversy in our culture. Some people believe
> that it has benefits for consumers. However, others are critical of advertising
> for several reasons.

The second and third paragraphs should present ideas in favor of and against the statement. The concluding paragraph should tell which side you agree with and why. Use a
variety of connectors to link your ideas, including at least six transitions.

EXERCISE PAGES

Unit Two, Chapter 3

Introductory Task: Quiz: *What Is Your Time Type?* Page 47

Scoring for Quiz

16–18 points = a very "fast" person (tends to be extremely aware of time and speed)

12–15 points = a "fast" person (tends to be somewhat concerned about time and speed)

9–11 points = a "slow" person (tends not to be concerned about time or speed)

6–8 points = a very "slow" person (tends to be extremely relaxed about time and speed)

Exercise 2. Present Perfect—Irregular Past Participles; *Yes/No* Questions: *The Right Experience?* Page 52

Information about Frank

These are the experiences that Frank HAS had (if an experience is not listed here, you can assume that Frank has not had it):

break his leg

build a campfire

catch a fish

fall off a cliff

fight a wild animal with his bare hands

find his way in a snowstorm

fly a helicopter

ride a wild horse

see a mountain lion

send a smoke signal for help

teach a rock-climbing class

write an adventure story

Information about Paul

These are the experiences that Paul HAS had (if an experience is not listed here, you can assume that Paul has not had it):

build a campfire

catch a fish

draw a map

drink water from a rain puddle

drive a bus

eat an insect

feed a wild animal out of his hand

forget to bring a compass

lose his way

read many survival skills books

run away from danger

sleep in a cave

win a prize for physical fitness

Unit Three, Chapter 5

Exercise 11. Future Time with Simple Present Tense: *An Outdoor Vacation—Yellowstone National Park,* Page 93

Yellowstone National Park Association

Here's the information you requested on next year's activities.

Park Information:
    Summer Season: April 15 to _____

Opening and Closing Dates:
    Madison Campground: _____ – October 7
    Visitor Centers and Museum: May 15 – _____

Yellowstone Institute Course Dates:
    Ecology of the Park: June 9 – _____
    Geology and Geysers: _____ – July 2

Tour Departure and Return Dates:
    Wildlife Observation: _____ – July 6
    High-Country Fishing: August 9 – _____

Schedule for Student B

Unit Three, Chapter 6

Exercise 8: Using the Future Perfect with *Be Going To: Are You Going to Have Gone to Mars by Then?* Page 107

Red Planet Travel Services

1. January 1999—the company begins taking reservations for tourist trips

2. December 2003—the engineers finish designing the reusable rocket

3. _____ —the engineers test the first rocket

4. January 2005—the first unmanned mission gathers data

5. _____ —the first supply rocket delivers equipment

6. August 2008—the scientists leave on first human mission

7. _____ —the construction crew builds hotels

8. November 2011—the company invites travel agents to try the service

9. _____ —the travel agents visit Mars

10. January 2013 —the company begins regular trips for tourists

Unit Three, Chapter 7

Exercise 12. Listening to Tag Questions: *Christopher Columbus*, Page 129

Part C: Information about Columbus

Columbus set out on his first voyage in 1492. He and his crew weren't the first Europeans to arrive in North America. The Vikings had landed on the northern coast of the continent around the year 1000. Although Columbus made a contract with the Spanish king and queen to sponsor his expedition, he was actually an Italian. Before he arrived in America, no one in Europe knew that the continents of North and South America existed. In fact, Columbus believed that he could sail directly westward from Europe to Asia, which was his goal. Columbus made a total of four voyages to America. He landed on several islands off the coast of North America, and he reached the coasts of Central and South America on two of his voyages, but he never landed on the mainland of North America. Columbus believed that Cuba was Japan and never realized that he hadn't reached Asia, so he didn't give the land a new name. A German mapmaker named it America after Amerigo Vespucci, who explored the coast of South America. Columbus's contract with the Spanish monarchy made him viceroy and governor of all the lands he discovered and gave him 10 percent of the profits from his discoveries. At first he became rich, but later he had troubles and lost his titles and all his money.

Exercise 13. Using Tag Questions: *Columbus Brought Back More Than Gold, Didn't He?* Pages 130–131

Information for Student A:

From the New World: chocolate, tobacco, vanilla

From the Old World: chickens, oranges, sugar cane

Information for Student B:

From the New World: tomatoes, potatoes, corn

From the Old World: honeybees, horses, wheat

Unit Three Wrap-up Tasks

Wrap-up Task 3: Ask the Oracle, Page 133

Instructions for the oracle: Copy each answer in the following list on a small slip of paper. Put the slips into an empty container, such as a box or jar. After each question is asked, draw out an answer (without peeking) and read it aloud. After each answer, return the slip of paper to the container and mix it in with the rest.

The oracle's answers:

1. Yes, definitely.
2. No, definitely not.
3. It's certain.
4. It isn't certain.
5. It's possible.
6. It's probable.
7. The answer isn't clear yet.
8. It will happen.
9. It won't happen.
10. The chances are good.

Wrap-up Task 4: Acting Out the Verbs, Page 133

Lists of Phrasal Verbs for Skits

Telephoning the travel agent:
        call back, call up, hang up, look up, take down, talk over

At the hotel desk:
        add up, check in, check out, hand over, settle in, show up

In a restaurant:
        fill up, pass around, run out of, take back, think over, sit down

Dressing for an expedition:
        have on, pick out, put on, take off, try on, wear out

On a tour:
        point out, start off, finish up, look over, speak up, find out

Unit Five, Chapter 10

Introductory Task: *Let Me Ask You Some Questions*, Page 185

Scoring for the interview:

1. a. L   b. F
2. a. L   b. F
3. a. F   b. L
4. a. L   b. F
5. a. F   b. L
6. a. F   b. L
7. a. F   b. L

Add up the number of questions to which your partner gave **F** (firstborn) answers and the number of questions to which she or he gave **L** (laterborn) answers. According to the birth-order theory, firstborns tend to be practical and conformist while laterborns are more likely to be creative and nonconformist. If four or more answers are **F,** your partner shows the personality characteristics of a firstborn child; if four or more answers are **L,** your partner shows the characteristics of a laterborn. (An only child usually has characteristics similar to those of a firstborn.)

Now turn back to page 185 and go on to part **B** of the task.

Unit Eight, Chapter 16

Introductory Task: *Sports Trivia*, **Page 298**

1. b, 2. a, 3. e, 4. f, 5. i, 6. h, 7. j, 8. k, 9. g, 10. c, 11. d

Exercise 3. Passive Sentences—Questions and Answers: *Stadiums*, **Page 303**

The Astrodome

1. Houston, Texas
2. 1965
3. football and baseball
4. No. On artificial turf called "Astroturf"
5. No.
6. Yes.
7. because first domed stadium

The Skydome

1. Toronto, Canada
2. 1989
3. football, baseball, basketball, other events
4. No. On artificial turf
5. Yes.
6. with eight miles of zippers

Unit Eight, Chapter 17

Introductory Task: *The Things Fans Do*, **Page 313**

Answers: All the statements are true!

Unit Nine, Chapter 18

Exercise 3. Factual Conditionals with Modals and Imperatives: *Advice about Thunderstorms and Tornadoes*, **Page 332**

Information for Student B

1. (You're inside when a thunderstorm occurs.) Stay inside.
2. (You're using a computer when a thunderstorm starts.) Unplug it.
3. (You're outside when a thunderstorm occurs.) Go into a building or get into a car.
4. (The weather service issues a "flash flood watch.") Listen to the radio for further information.
5. (The weather service issues a "flash flood warning.") Move away from streams or rivers immediately.
6. (You're in a car in a mountain canyon and a flood is coming toward you.) Get out of the car and climb up a canyon wall to safety.

Information for Student A

1. (You live in an area where tornadoes are common.) Make plans in advance for taking shelter during tornadoes.
2. (The weather service issues a "tornado watch.") Listen to the radio for tornado warnings.
3. (The weather service issues a "tornado warning.") Go to a basement or a small interior room immediately.
4. (You're outside and you see a tornado nearby.) Get inside the nearest sturdy building.
5. (You're in a car and a tornado is coming toward you.) Get out of the car and lie flat in the nearest ditch.

Unit Ten, Chapter 21

Exercises 4–9: Professor Wendell's solution, **Pages 390–398**

The Police Inspector was about to arrest John Small for the murder of Mrs. Pierson. He said that Small had poisoned her to obtain money that he otherwise might not have gotten for many years. Professor Wendell stepped in and told the Inspector that he was making a serious mistake. He said that the real murderers had been Mr. and Mrs. Niles Pierson. He explained that Niles Pierson had been in serious financial difficulty: Hard times meant that people were spending less on luxuries like art. Pierson had tried to raise money by gambling and had wound up deeply in debt. Several months before the murder, Pierson had begun to slowly poison his aunt. He thought that it would look like she had died of an illness and that he would inherit her money. Suddenly, however, she had written a new will, leaving her money to John Small. Feeling desperate after Mr. Torrance had told him that there was nothing he could do about the new will, Pierson had come up with another plan. He would poison his aunt in a more obvious way and make it look as if Small had been the murderer. If Small were found guilty and sent to jail, Pierson would inherit the money after all, and his troubles would be at an end. He got his wife to help him, and on Sunday night, he pretended to be an intruder in the garden and when everyone left the house, his wife was able to slip the poison in a new bottle of Mrs. Pierson's special Swiss organic grape juice. On Monday, when Niles Pierson and his wife were miles away, old Mrs. Pierson drank the poisoned juice and died.

Exercise 11. Questions, Commands, and Requests in Reported Speech: *A Class Discussion*, Pages 400–401

7. More women than men buy and read books (about 60% vs. 40%).

9. According to one study, about 2 billion books were sold a year—about the same as the number of movie tickets.

10. Many people told interviewers that a book had changed their life. One man, for example, said that not only had a certain book made him a much better person but he liked it so much that he found and married its author.

11. Books are more popular than ever, and there is no evidence that TV has led to less reading.

APPENDICES

APPENDIX 1. Spelling Rules for the Third Person Singular Form of the Simple Present Tense

- Most verbs: Add -s

    work → works   play → plays
- Verbs that end in -ch, -sh, -s, -x, or -z: Add -es.

    miss → misses   teach → teaches
- Verbs that end in a consonant + y: Drop -y. Add -ies.

    try → tries
- The third person singular forms of *do, go,* and *have* are *does, goes,* and *has.*

APPENDIX 2. Pronunciation Rules for the Third Person Singular Form of the Simple Present Tense

- The -s ending is pronounced three different ways:
  - /s/ after the voiceless sounds /p/, /t/, /k/, and /f/.

    stops   gets   takes   laughs
  - /z/ after the voiced sounds /b/, /d/, /g/, /v/, /th/, /m/, /n/, /ng/, /l/, /r/ and all vowel sounds.

    robs   adds   begs   gives   bathes   seems

    remains   sings   tells   hears   agrees   knows
  - /ɪz/ after the sounds /s/, /z/, /sh/, /zh/, /ch/, /j/, and /ks/.

    passes   freezes   rushes   massages (ge = /zh/)   catches

    judges (ge = /j/)   relaxes (x = /ks/)

APPENDIX 3. Spelling Rules for -*ing* Verb Forms

- Most verbs: Base form of verb + -*ing*

    work → working   play → playing
- Verbs that end in -e: Drop -e. Add -ing.

    write → writing   live → living
- Verbs that end in -ie: Change -ie to -y. Add -ing.

    tie → tying   lie → lying
- Verbs that end in consonant + vowel + consonant: Double the final consonant. Add -ing.

    run → running   begin → beginning

NOTE: Do not double the final consonant when:

  - the last syllable is not stressed.

last syllable stressed		last syllable not stressed
begín → begínning	BUT	lísten → lístening

  - the last consonant is *w, x,* or *y.*

permit → permitting	BUT	allow → allowing
		fix → fixing
		play → playing

APPENDIX 4. Adverbs of Frequency

■ Adverbs of frequency tell how often something happens. They range from all of the time to none of the time. (NOTE: Negative adverbs of frequency are not used with *not*.)

Affirmative

100%   always, constantly, continually
       almost always
       usually, generally, normally
       frequently, often
       sometimes
       occasionally

Negative

       seldom, rarely, hardly ever
       almost never
0%   never

We **always** eat breakfast.   I **almost never** go to bed before midnight.

■ Adverbs of frequency usually occur:
   • before main verbs (except *be*).
       We **often** go on vacation in the summer.
   • after *be*.
       They are **rarely** home in the evenings.
   • after the first auxiliary
       I will **never** go to bed before midnight.   He has **sometimes** had to get up early.
   • after the subject in questions
       Does he **ever** act like that?   Is that police officer **always** so kind?
   • before negatives (except *always* and *ever*, which usually come after the negative)
       He **often** did**n't** get home until late in the evening.
       Our friends **usually** are**n't** late.
       They wo**n't ever** call here again!

■ Some adverbs of frequency can occur in the beginning and end of the sentence. These include *frequently, generally, normally, occasionally, often, sometimes,* and *usually.*
       Sometimes we need to take a break.   You should call me **frequently.**

■ Other adverbs that occur in these positions include *already, certainly, finally, just, likely, possibly,* and *probably.*
       They will **certainly** enjoy studying about Mars.   Spring is **finally** here!

APPENDIX 5. Spelling Rules for the -ed Form of the Verb

■ Most verbs: Add -*ed.*
       work → work**ed**   play → play**ed**
■ Verbs that end in -*e:* Add -*d.*
       live → live**d**   decide → decide**d**
■ Verbs that end in a consonant + *y:* Change -*y* to -*i.* Add -*ed.*
       try → tr**ied**
■ Verbs that end in consonant + vowel + consonant: Double the final consonant. Add -*ed.*
       shop → shop**ped**   permit → permit**ted**
       NOTE: Do not double the final consonant when:

■ the last syllable is not stressed.

last syllable stressed		last syllable not stressed
per**mit** → permi**tted**	BUT	**lis**ten → **lis**ten**ed**

• the last consonant is *w, x,* or *y.*

permit → permi**tted**	BUT	allow → allo**wed**
		box → bo**xed**
		play → play**ed**

APPENDIX 6. Pronunciation Rules for the *-ed* Form of the Verb

■ The *-d* ending is pronounced three different ways:

• /*t*/ after the voiceless sounds /*f*/, /*k*/, /*p*/, /*s*/, /*sh*/, /*ch*/, /*ks*/

laughed	talked	clapped	passed
wished	watched	waxed	

• /*d*/ after the voiced sounds /*b*/, /*g*/, /*j*/, /*m*/, /*n*/, /*ng*/, /*l*/, /*r*/, /*th*/, /*v*/, /*z*/, /*zh*/, and all vowels sounds.

robbed	begged	judged (*ge* = /*j*/)	seemed	remained
banged	called	ordered	bathed	waved
surprised	massaged (*ge* = /*zh*/)	played	enjoyed	cried

• /*ɪd*/ after the sounds /*t*/ and /*d*/.

started   needed

APPENDIX 7. Irregular Verbs

Base Form	Past	Past Participle	Base Form	Past	Past Participle
be	was, were	been	eat	ate	eaten
beat	beat	beaten	fall	fell	fallen
become	became	become	feed	fed	fed
begin	began	begun	feel	felt	felt
bend	bent	bent	fight	fought	fought
bet	bet	bet	find	found	found
bind	bound	bound	fit	fit/fitted	fit/fitted
bite	bit	bitten	flee	fled	fled
bleed	bled	bled	fly	flew	flown
blow	blew	blown	forbid	forbade	forbidden
break	broke	broken	forecast	forecast	forecast
bring	brought	brought	forget	forgot	forgotten
broadcast	broadcast	broadcast	forgive	forgave	forgiven
build	built	built	freeze	froze	frozen
burn	burned/burnt	burned/burnt	get	got	gotten
burst	burst	burst	give	gave	given
buy	bought	bought	go	went	gone
catch	caught	caught	grind	ground	ground
choose	chose	chosen	grow	grew	grown
come	came	come	hang	hung	hung
cost	cost	cost	have	had	had
creep	crept	crept	hear	heard	heard
cut	cut	cut	hide	hid	hidden
deal	dealt	dealt	hit	hit	hit
dig	dug	dug	hold	held	held
dive	dove	dove	hurt	hurt	hurt
do	did	done	keep	kept	kept
draw	drew	drawn	know	knew	known
dream	dreamed/dreamt	dreamed/dreamt	lay	laid	laid
			lead	led	led
drink	drank	drunk	leap	leaped/leapt	leaped/leapt
drive	drove	driven	learn	learned/learnt	learned/learnt

Base Form	Past	Past Participle	Base Form	Past	Past Participle
leave	left	left	sit	sat	sat
lend	lent	lent	sleep	slept	slept
let	let	let	slide	slid	slid
lie	lay	lain	speak	spoke	spoken
light	lit/lighted	lit/lighted	speed	sped	sped
lose	lost	lost	spend	spent	spent
make	made	made	spin	spun	spun
mean	meant	meant	split	split	split
meet	met	met	spread	spread	spread
mistake	mistook	mistaken	spring	sprang	sprung
pay	paid	paid	stand	stood	stood
prove	proved	proved/ proven	steal	stole	stolen
			stick	stuck	stuck
put	put	put	sting	stung	stung
quit	quit	quit	strike	struck	struck
read	read	read	swear	swore	sworn
rid	rid	rid	sweep	swept	swept
ride	rode	ridden	swell	swelled	swelled/swollen
ring	rang	rung	swim	swam	swum
rise	rose	risen	swing	swung	swung
run	ran	run	take	took	taken
say	said	said	teach	taught	taught
see	saw	seen	tear	tore	torn
seek	sought	sought	tell	told	told
sell	sold	sold	think	thought	thought
send	sent	sent	throw	threw	thrown
set	set	set	understand	understood	understood
sew	sewed	sewed/sewn	upset	upset	upset
shake	shook	shaken	wake	woke	woken
shave	shaved	shaved/ shaven	wear	wore	worn
			weave	wove	woven
shine	shined/shone	shined/shone	weep	wept	wept
shoot	shot	shot	wet	wet	wet
show	showed	showed/shown	win	won	won
shut	shut	shut	wind	wound	wound
sing	sang	sung	withdraw	withdrew	withdrawn
sink	sank	sunk	write	wrote	written

APPENDIX 8. Time Expressions and Adverbs of Frequency with the Perfect

■ **Time Expressions**

- *Already, yet* (in questions and negatives), *still, ever, until/up to now* (*then, my eighteenth birthday,* etc.), *before April* (*10:00, I go to sleep,* etc.) and *by this time last year* (*Monday, the year 2020,* etc.), indicate an unspecified time of one action or state before another action, state or time.

    I have **already** gone skydiving. (Unspecified time before now)

    Have you **ever** flown a plane? (Unspecified time before now)

    He hadn't gone abroad **until** he came to the USA. (Unspecified time before coming to the USA)

    By this time next year, they will have visited Egypt. (Unspecified time before this time next year)

- *Just* indicates an action very close in time to another action or time.

    He's **just** completed a course in bungee jumping.

    They had **just** left when we arrived.

- *Once, twice, five times, many times,* etc., indicate the repetition of an action or state before another action, state, or time.

    They've been to Paris **twice.**

    Sheila will have seen that movie **three times** by then.

- *For three minutes* (*a long time, many years,* etc.), *since March* (*Monday, I met you,* etc.), and *all day* (*month, my life,* etc.) are time expressions of duration and indicate the continuation of an action or state to another action, state, or time.

    You've known how to dance **for many** years.

    Sam has tap danced **since 1995.**

- Additional time expressions used only with the present perfect and present perfect progressive include *so far, lately,* and *recently.*

    Jim **hasn't missed** a class so far.

    I **have** recently **been studying** the pyramids of Egypt.

    (With some exceptions, most of these time expressions can also be used with the simple past.)

■ **Adverbs of Frequency**

- Adverbs of frequency such as *always, often, sometimes, rarely,* and *never,* are used with the perfect tenses to indicate the frequency of an action or state before another action, state, or time.

    He's **often** slept in the woods.

    She's **never** been a mountain guide.

- *Ever* is used with the perfect tenses in questions to ask whether something happened and in the negative to indicate that something didn't happen at any time in the past. *Ever* is not used in affirmative statements.

    Have you **ever** caught a fish?

    We haven't **ever** ridden a wild horse.

    Not: They have ~~ever~~ held a snake.

    (See Appendix 4 for the position of adverbs of frequency in a sentence.)

APPENDIX 9. Common Phrasal Verbs and Their Meanings

Phrasal Verbs without Objects

break down	fail to function
catch up	reach the same place
close in	surround
come back	return
come down	continue over time by tradition
come off	happen or occur
come out	result, end up, turn out
come over	visit
come up	appear or arise
drop out	leave an activity or group
go down	sink (like the *Titanic*)
go on	go in advance of others
grow up	become adult
head back	start to return
head out	leave a place
let out	end (like classes)
let up	slow down or stop
pay off	be successful
push on	continue despite difficulty
run out	come to the end
set in	begin to happen
set off	start on a journey
settle down	become comfortable
show up	appear
slow down	become slower
stand out	be better or the best
start out	begin a journey
take off	start (to fly or move)
turn up	come; visit unexpectedly
turn out	end or result
watch out	be careful
work out	exercise

Phrasal Verbs with Objects

blow up	1. express anger
	2. explode
	3. fill with air
	4. enlarge a photograph
break up	separate into smaller pieces
bring back	obtain and return with
bring down	cause to fail
bring in	earn profits or income
bring off	accomplish
bring on	cause to appear or happen
bring out	produce or publish
bring up	educate (a child)
build up	make stronger
burn down	destroy by fire
call off	cancel (a plan)
call up	telephone
carry out	do as planned
check in	have the return of something recorded
check out	find information about
drive back	force to return
find out	discover (an answer)
figure out	discover by thinking
force back	cause to return
get through	finish successfully
give up	stop doing (an activity)
hold up	stop or delay
keep back	discourage
keep on	continue
keep up	continue at the same level
leave behind	abandon
let down	disappoint; not keep a promise
let out	1. come to a close or end
	2. make known; reveal
	3. increase the size

Phrasal Verbs without Objects		**Phrasal Verbs with Objects**	
		look over	examine quickly
		look up	search in a dictionary or other reference
		make up	1. invent
			2. replace; compensate
		mark off	define an area by making marks
		pass over	disregard
		pick up	get; collect
		play down	make something seem unimportant
		play up	make something seem more important
		point out	tell
		pull along	drag something
		put down	insult
		put off	delay; postpone
		put on	host
		put together	assemble
		put up	provide money; invest or pay in advance
		run down	chase and capture
		run off	print or copy
		run up	make an expense larger
		set back	slow down progress
		set off	1. make different from others
			2. cause to explode
			3. make angry
		set up	1. assemble or build
			2. create or establish
		show off	want people to see
		sign up	register; add (a name) to a list
		take off	1. remove
			2. go or leave
			3. rise in flight
			4. make (time) free
		take on	accept responsibility for
		take over	claim control or ownership
		take up	accept a challenge
		think over	consider carefully
		think up	create
		tire out	cause to be exhausted
		try out	test
		turn down	1. make quieter
			2. say no to (an invitation)
		turn in	1. give to an authority
			2. inform an authority about
			3. go to bed
		turn off	stop from working
		turn up	make louder
		work out	solve (a problem)

APPENDIX 10. Common Verb-Preposition Combinations

agree with	dream of	look for	run off
be away	forget about	look up	run up
believe in	happen to	pass over	search for
belong to	hear about	pay for	succeed in
care about	hear of	plan for	talk about
care for	hope for	play with	talk to
check in	know about	prepare for	think about
come from	learn from	prevent from	think of
concentrate on	listen to	protect from	turn off
confide in	live on	read about	wait for
depend on	look after	recover from	write about
die from	look at	rely on	worry about

APPENDIX 11. Common Phrasal Verb-Preposition Combinations and Their Meanings

catch up with	come up from behind and reach the same level
close in on	surround
come up with	discover (an idea)
cut down on	use or have less
drop in on	visit unexpectedly
face up to	confront; meet bravely
get along with	enjoy their company
get back from	return from
get down to	begin (work)
get through with	finish
give up on	admit defeat and stop trying
keep on at	continue
keep up with	go at the same speed as
meet up with	meet unexpectedly
miss out on	lose a chance for something
put up with	tolerate
run out of	use all the supply of
run up against	meet and have to deal with
stand up to	endure
start out for	begin a journey toward a particular place
watch out for	be careful of

APPENDIX 12. Some Proper Nouns with *The*

■ Names of countries and islands

the Bahamas
the British Isles
the Canary Islands/the Canaries
the Cayman Islands/the Caymans
the Czech Republic
the Dominican Republic
the Falkland Islands
the Hawaiian Islands
the Marshall Islands

the Netherlands
the People's Republic of China
the Philippines/the Philippine Islands
the Republic of Ireland
the United Arab Emirates
the United Kingdom
the United States of America
the Virgin Islands

■ Regions

the Crimea
the Everglades
the Punjab
the East/West/North/South

the Near/Middle/Far East
the Midwest
the East/West Coast

■ Geographical features

• map features

the Equator
the Eastern/Western/Northern/
  Southern Hemisphere

the Occident/the Orient
the North/South Pole
the Tropic of Cancer/Capricorn

• canals, channels, gulfs

the Arabian Gulf
the English Channel
the Erie Canal
the Gulf of Aden
the Gulf of Mexico

the Gulf of Oman
the Panama Canal
the Persian Gulf
the Suez Canal

• deserts

the Gobi (Desert)
the Mojave (Desert)

the Sahara (Desert)
the Sinai (Desert)

• mountain ranges

the Alps
the Andes (Mountains)
the Appalachian Mountains (the Appalachians)
the Atlas Mountains

the Caucasus (Mountains)
the Himalayan Mountains (the Himalayas)
the Pyrenees
the Rocky Mountains (the Rockies)

- oceans and seas

  the Adriatic (Sea)   the Indian (Ocean)
  the Aegean (Sea)   the Mediterranean (Sea)
  the Arctic (Ocean)   the North Sea
  the Atlantic (Ocean)   the Pacific (Ocean)
  the Baltic (Sea)   the Red Sea
  the Black Sea   the Sea of Japan
  the Caribbean (Sea)   the South China Sea
  the Caspian (Sea)   the Yellow Sea

- peninsulas

  the Iberian Peninsula   the Monterey Peninsula
  the Florida Peninsula   the Yucatan Peninsula

- rivers

  the Amazon (River)   the Potomac (River)
  the Colorado (River)   the Rio Grande (River)
  the Congo (River)   the St. Lawrence (River)
  the Euphrates (River)   the Seine (River)
  the Hudson (River)   the Thames (River)
  the Mississippi (River) the Tigris (River)
  the Nile (River)

- names with *of* in them

  the Bay of Biscay   the Strait of Gibraltar
  the Bay of Naples   the Strait of Magellan
  the Cape of Good Hope

■ Buildings and other structures

  the Brooklyn Bridge   the Ritz-Carlton Hotel
  the Eiffel Tower   the Statue of Liberty
  the Museum of Modern Art   the White House

■ Ships, trains, and airplanes

  the *Mayflower*   the *Spirit of St. Louis*
  the *Orient Express*   the *Titanic*

■ Some newspapers and periodicals

  The Atlantic Monthly   *The New York Times*
  The Economist   *The Washington Post*

APPENDIX 13. Spelling Rules for Regular Plural Count Nouns

■ Most nouns: Add -*s.*

  room → room**s**   office → office**s**
  day → day**s**   studio → studio**s**

■ Nouns ending in -*ch,* -*sh,* -*ss,* -*x,* or -*z:* Add -*es.*

  lunch → lunch**es**   brush → brush**es**
  kiss → kiss**es**   box → box**es**
  quiz → quizz**es**

■ Nouns ending in a consonant + -*y:* Drop -*y.* Add -*ies.*

  dormitory → dormitor**ies**   story → stor**ies**

■ Nouns ending in -*f* or -*fe:* Drop -*f* or -*fe.* Add -*ves.*

  shelf → shel**ves**   knife → kni**ves**

  Exceptions: belief → belie**fs**   chief → chie**fs**   roof → roo**fs**

■ A few nouns ending in a consonant + -*o:* Add -*es.*

  hero → hero**es**   potato → potato**es**
  mosquito → mosquito**es**   tomato → tomato**es**

APPENDIX 14. Pronunciation Rules for Regular Plural Nouns

■ The -s ending is pronounced three different ways:
  - /s/ after the voiceless sounds /p/, /t/, /k/, /f/, and /th/.

    cups   hats   books   cuffs   paths

  - /z/ after the voiced sounds /b/, /d/, /g/, /v/, /th/, /m/, /n/, /ng/, /l/, /r/ and all vowel sounds.

    jobs   kids   legs   knives   lathes   dreams
    bones   things   bells   bears   days   potatoes

  - /ɪz/ after the sounds /s/, /z/, /sh/, /zh/, /ch/, /j/, and /ks/.

    classes   breezes   massages (ge = /zh/)   churches
    judges (ge = /j/)   taxes (x = /ks/)   dishes

APPENDIX 15. Common Irregular Plural Count Nouns

■ Nouns that have different forms in the singular and plural

Singular	Plural	Singular	Plural
child	children	mouse	mice
foot	feet	ox	oxen
goose	geese	person	people
louse	lice	tooth	teeth
man	men	woman	women

■ Nouns that have the same form in the singular and plural

Singular	Plural	Singular	Plural
deer	deer	series	series
fish	fish	sheep	sheep
means	means	species	species
moose	moose		

■ Nouns from other languages that have kept their original plural forms

Singular	Plural	Singular	Plural
alumnus	alumni	hypothesis	hypotheses
(alumna)	(alumnae)	index	indices (indexes)
analysis	analyses	medium	media
appendix	appendices	memorandum	memoranda
	(appendixes)	oasis	oases
bacterium	bacteria	parenthesis	parentheses
basis	bases	phenomenon	phenomena
cactus	cacti (cactuses)	stimulus	stimuli
crisis	crises	syllabus	syllabi
criterion	criteria		(syllabuses)
curriculum	curricula	thesis	theses
datum	data	vertebra	vertebrae
formula	formulae		
	(formulas)		

■ Nouns with no singular form

    cattle   police

■ Nouns with only a plural form

    belongings   congratulations   groceries
    clothes   goods   tropics

■ Nouns with only a plural form that names things that come in pairs

    jeans   pants   shorts   trousers
    pajamas   scissors   (sun)glasses tongs

APPENDIX 16. Common Noncount Nouns

- **Names of groups of similar items:** baggage, cash, change (referring to money), clothing, equipment, food, fruit, furniture, garbage, hardware, homework, jewelry, junk, luggage, machinery, mail, make-up, money, postage, scenery, silverware, stuff, trash, traffic (Note: these groups often have individual parts that can be counted, e.g., clothing is made up of different pieces—dresses, shirts, coats, etc.)

- **Liquids:** beer, coffee, cream, gasoline, honey, juice, ketchup, lotion, milk, oil, rubbing alcohol, salad dressing, sauce, shampoo, soda, soup, syrup, tea, vinegar, water, wine

- **Solids:** aspirin, bacon, barley, beef, bread, broccoli, butter, cabbage, cake, calcium, candy, carbon, celery, cheese, chicken (as food), chocolate, coal, copper, cotton, detergent, film, fish, food, garlic, glass, gold, hair, hamburger, ice, ice cream, iron, jam, jello, jelly, lead, lettuce, magnesium, meat, nylon, paper, pasta, pastry, pie, pizza, platinum, plutonium, polyester, pork, radium, rope, salsa, seafood, silk, silver, spaghetti, spinach, soap, string, thread, tin, toothpaste, uranium, vitamin (C), wood, wool, yogurt

- **Particles:** cereal, chalk, corn, dirt, dust, flour, grass, gravel, hair, oats, pepper, rice, salt, sand, spice, sugar, wheat

- **Gases:** air, carbon dioxide, fog, helium, hydrogen, nitrogen, oxygen, smog, smoke, steam

- **Natural phenomena:** cold, darkness, dew, electricity, fire, fog, gravity, hail, heat, humidity, light, lightning, mist, rain, scenery, sleet, snow, space, sunshine, temperature, thunder, warmth, weather, wind

- **Abstract ideas:** advice, art, beauty, behavior, business, comfort, competition, confidence, crime, democracy, courage, education, energy, enjoyment, entertainment, freedom, friendship, fun, good, grammar, hate, hatred, happiness, health, help, history, homework, honesty, hospitality, importance, inertia, information, insurance, integrity, intelligence, interest, joy, justice, knowledge, laughter, law, life, love, luck, momentum, music, news,* noise, opportunity, patience, peace, permission, practice, pride, progress, proof, quiet, recreation, responsibility, significance, slang, sleep, space, spontaneity, stupidity, time, tradition, traffic, travel, trouble, truth, unemployment, variety, violence, vocabulary, wealth, weightlessness, work

- **Fields of study:** accounting, art, astronomy, biology, business, chemistry, civics, economics, engineering, geography, geometry, history, journalism, linguistics, literature, mathematics,* music, nutrition, physics,* psychology, science, sociology, speech, writing

- **Activities:** badminton, baseball, basketball, billiards, bowling, boxing, camping, canoeing, cards, chess, conversation, cooking, cycling, dancing, driving, football, golf, hiking, jogging, poker, reading, running, sailing, singing, soccer, shopping, skating, skiing, studying, swimming, surfing, talk, tennis, traveling, volleyball, walking, wrestling

- **Languages:** Arabic, Chinese, English, French, German, Indonesian, Japanese, Korean, Polish, Portuguese, Russian, Spanish, Thai, Turkish, Urdu

* Some noncount nouns, such as *news, mathematics,* and *physics* end in *s*. These nouns look plural, but they are not; they always take a singular verb.

APPENDIX 17. Common Adjective + Preposition Combinations That Are Followed by Gerunds

accustomed to	discouraged about	interested in	successful in
afraid of	enthusiastic about	known for	tired of
angry at/about	familiar with	nervous about	tolerant of
ashamed of	famous for	perfect for	upset about
(in)capable of	fond of	proud of	used to
certain of/about	glad about	responsible for	useful for
concerned about	good at	sad about	worried about
critical of	happy about	sorry about	

APPENDIX 18. Verbs Commonly Followed by Gerunds

acknowledge	discontinue	imagine	quit
admit	discuss	include	recall
anticipate	dislike	involve	recollect
appreciate	don't mind	justify	recommend
avoid	endure	keep (continue)	report
can't help	enjoy	loathe	resent
celebrate	escape	mention	resist
complete	excuse	mind (object to)	resume
defend	explain	miss	risk
defer	feel like	postpone	suggest
delay	finish	practice	support
deny	forgive	prevent	tolerate
detest	go	prohibit	understand

APPENDIX 19. Verbs Commonly Followed by Infinitives

■ Verb + Infinitive

agree	consent	hope	pretend
aim	decide	intend	promise
appear	decline	learn	refuse
attempt	demand	manage	seem
can't/couldn't afford	deserve	offer	struggle
can't/couldn't wait	fail	plan	tend
don't/didn't care	hesitate	pledge	wait
claim			

■ Verb + Noun Phrase + Infinitive

cause	hire	persuade	tell
command	invite	remind	trust
convince	order	teach	warn
force			

■ Verb + (Noun Phrase) + Infinitive

arrange	choose	expect	want
ask	dare	know	wish
beg	desire	need	would like

GLOSSARY

active sentence   A sentence in which the subject is the performer of the action.
   Millions of people watch the World Cup.

adjective   A common modifier that describes a noun.
   He drinks **strong, black** coffee.

adjective clause (also called *relative clause*)   A clause that modifies a noun.
   A scientist **who studies personality** has developed a new theory.

adjective phrase   A phrase that modifies a noun.
   People **living in cities** often see strange things.

adverb   A word that describes or modifies the meaning of a verb, an adjective, another adverb, or a sentence.
   They worked **quickly** and **carefully** on the project.

adverb clause   A clause that functions like an adverb.
   Because they want their product to sell, companies do market research.

adverb of frequency   An adverb that tells how often an action occurs.
   Night owls **usually** do their best work at night.

adverb phrase   A phrase that functions like an adverb.
   Known for its quality, the product sells well.

agent   The doer of the action in a sentence. In a passive sentence, the agent, if included, is in a *by* phrase.
   The goalie stopped the ball.   The ball was stopped by **the goalie.**

article   The words *a/an* and *the,* which are used to introduce or identify a noun.
   a cook   **an** orange   **the** menu   **the** recipes

auxiliary verb   A verb that is used with a main verb to make questions and negative sentences and to help make tenses and express meaning.
   Are you working?   We **did**n't finish the exam.
   She **has** traveled a lot.   They **should** get out more.

base form of a verb (also called *the simple form of a verb*)   A verb without *to* in front of it or any endings after it; an infinitive without *to.*
   play   work   be   do

causative verb   A verb (*get, have, let, make*) that is used to mean to cause or convince someone to do something.
   John **had** us buy the concert tickets.

clause   A group of related words that has a subject and a verb.
   Before he leaves, . . .   We're back!   . . . because it sells well.

collective noun   A noun that refers to a group of people or animals.
   committee   family   audience   team

common noun   A noun that is not a name of a particular person, place, or thing.
   cat   coffee   students   buildings   loyalty

conditional sentence   A sentence that contains a condition clause and a result clause and shows a relationship between the condition and the result of the condition.
   If a storm comes up, you should go inside.

connector   A word that shows how the ideas in two clauses are related.
   because   but   also   nevertheless

coordinating conjunction   A word (*and, but, or, nor, so, for, yet*) that connects clauses, phrases, or words.
   We wrote the proposal, **and** they accepted it. I tried **but** didn't succeed.

count noun   A noun that names a person, place, or thing that can be counted.

      a **restaurant**   two **restaurants**   an **apple**   three **apples**

definite article   *The,* which is used to identify nouns that are known to the speaker and listener.

      The chef in this restaurant wrote a best-selling cookbook.

demonstrative   *This, that, these,* or *those,* which is used to indicate the noun as being close or far in terms of distance (actual physical or more abstract).

      That restaurant over there is good.   **These** days, dining out is popular.

dependent clause   A clause that cannot stand alone but must be linked to a main clause.

      When we met, we discussed the ad campaign.

determiner   A words that comes before a common noun to introduce, identify, or tell the quantity of the noun.

      the salad   **many** desserts   **this** table   **your** order

direct object   A noun, pronoun, or noun phrase that directly receives the action of the verb in a sentence.

      Paul called **us.**   The chef prepared **a delicious meal.**

future perfect   *Will/be going to* + *have* + past participle, which is used to talk about an action or state that will occur before a future action, state, or time or to talk about actions that will continue to a future action, state, or time.

      I **will have finished** my work by then.

future perfect progressive (also called *future perfect continuous*)   *Will/be going to* + *have* + *been* + verb + *-ing,* which is used to talk about an action that will continue to a future action, state, or time.

      They **will have been traveling** for many days when they reach the pole.

future progressive (also called *future continuous*)   *Will/be going to* + *be* + verb + *-ing,* which is used to talk about actions that will be in progress in the future.

      He **is going to be flying** to Hawaii next week.

gerund   The *-ing* form of a verb that functions as a noun.

      We enjoy **dancing** and **singing.**

indefinite article   *A/an* or [0] (the zero article), which is used to introduce nouns that are unknown or indefinite to the speaker and/or listener.

      a banana   **an** author

indefinite pronoun   A pronoun that is used to talk about unspecified people or things or about people or things in general.

      Is **anybody** out there?

indirect information question (also called *embedded question*)   A question inside a statement or other question.

      I don't know **where they went.**   Can you tell me **what time it is?**

indirect object   A noun, pronoun, or noun phrase that indirectly receives the action of the verb in a sentence.

      She baked **her child** a birthday cake.   They gave **her** a present.

infinitive   *To* + base form of the verb that functions as a noun.

      We wanted **to go** to the circus.   **To climb** Mt. Everest is our dream.

intensifier   A word that is used before an adjective or adverb to strengthen the meaning of the adjective or adverb.

      That restaurant is **very** expensive.   We got our food **quite** quickly.

intransitive verb   A verb which cannot have an object.

      We **stood** in line for football tickets.

main clause (also called *independent clause*)   A clause that is, or could be, a complete sentence.

      We arrived late.   When we got there, **he had to leave.**

main verb   The verb that can be used alone in a sentence in the simple present and simple past tense and that carries the primary verbal meaning in the sentence.

      We **traveled** to Japan.   We had **gone** there once before.

modal   An auxiliary verb that expresses ideas related to certainty, necessity, and ability.

>   She **might** be at home.   They **must** leave soon.   We **can** sing well.

modifier   A word that describes and gives more information about another word, phrase, or sentence.

>   You look **happy.**   The man **in white** is the chef.

noncount noun   A noun that names something that cannot be counted.

>   **rain   sand   happiness   physics   swimming**

nonrestrictive adjective clause (also called *nonrestrictive relative clause*)   An adjective clause that provides additional information about a noun or pronoun.

>   Professor Jones, **who teaches biology,** has just published a book.

noun   A word that names a person, place, thing, or idea.

>   **Albert Einstein   ocean   table   advice**

noun clause   A clause that functions like a noun.

>   We think **that they will get married and live happily ever after.**

noun phrase   A noun and its modifiers.

>   We ate at **that very charming new restaurant.**

object of a preposition   A noun, pronoun, or noun phrase that comes after a preposition.

>   for **Mary**   to **them**   with **my best friend's mother**

particle   An adverb that is part of a phrasal verb.

>   The explorers set **off** late.

passive causative   A word that expresses the idea that someone "causes" someone else to perform a service.

>   The players **had** their uniforms **cleaned.**

passive sentence   A sentence in which the subject is the receiver of the action of the verb.

>   **The World Cup is watched by millions of people.**

past perfect progressive (also called *past perfect continuous tense*)   A verb tense that is used to talk about an action that began before and continued to or through another past action, state, or time.

>   They **had been working** for hours when he arrived.

past perfect tense   A verb tense that is used to talk about a past action or state that occurred before another past action or state.

>   I **had read** the book before I saw the movie.

past progressive tense (also called *past continuous tense*)   A verb tense that is used to talk about an action in progress in the past.

>   He **was sleeping** when the phone rang.

personal pronoun   A word that replaces a noun or noun phrase and functions as a subject, object, or subject complement in a sentence.

>   **He** is a business man.   The clients liked **her.**
>
>   Where's the restaurant? This is **it.**

phrasal verb   A verb + adverb (particle). The meaning of a phrasal verb often cannot be predicted from the meanings of its two parts.

>   They **kept on** despite the difficulties.   She **called** him **up.**

phrasal verb with preposition (also called a *three-word verb*)   The combination of a phrasal verb + a preposition.

>   We **ran out of** time.

phrase   A group of related words that does not contain both a subject and a verb.

>   **on the street   the people upstairs   having already gone**

possessive   A word that indicates the noun as belonging to someone or something.

>   **David's** house   **our** homework   It's **theirs.**   the corner **of the table**

predicate   The verb and words that come after it.

>   We **ate lunch** together.   You **have been studying English for a year.**

preposition A function word (*at, from, in, to,* etc.) that takes a noun or pronoun as an object, which often express meanings like time, location, or direction.

    in the classroom   **around** the same time   **with** my friends

prepositional phrase A preposition plus a noun phrase.

    in the classroom   **around the same time**   **with my friends**

present perfect progressive tense (also called *present perfect continuous tense*) A verb tense that is used to express an action that began in the past and continues to the present. It often expresses a sense that the action is ongoing.

    They **have been cleaning** all morning.

present perfect tense A verb tense that is used to talk about actions or states that occurred at an unspecified time in the past or actions that began in the past and continue to the present.

    They **have written** a book.   They **have lived** there for many years.

present progressive tense (also called *present continuous tense*) A verb tense that is used to talk about actions in progress at the moment of speaking or during a period of time extending through the present.

    Look! It**'s snowing.**   He **is studying** in the United States this year.

pronoun A word that replaces a noun phrase that has already been mentioned or that is clear from context.

    I need to talk to **you.**   Al is looking at **himself** in the mirror.

proper noun A noun that names a particular person, place, or thing.

    Molly Brown   **Denver, Colorado**   **the *Titanic***

quantifier A word or phrase that indicates the quantity of a noun.

    some potatoes   **a few** choices   **not much** oil

quoted speech A way of reporting speech that uses the exact words of the speaker.

    "I'll love you forever!" he promised.

reciprocal pronoun A pronoun (*each other* or *one another*) that is used when two or more people or things give and receive the same feelings or actions.

    They stared at **each other** from across the restaurant.

reflexive pronoun A pronoun that is used instead of an object pronoun when the object refers to the same person or thing as the subject of the sentence.

    They bought **themselves** a new car.

relative pronoun A pronoun that begins an adjective clause.

    The author **that** wrote the book came.   I like the book **which** we saw in the store.

reported speech A way of reporting speech that does not use the speaker's exact words.

    He told her **that he would love her forever.**

restrictive adjective clause (also called *restrictive relative clause*) An adjective clause that identifies the noun or pronoun modified.

    The professor **whose class I'm taking** just came in.

    We found the classroom **that we had been looking for.**

simple past tense A verb tense that is used to talk about actions and states that began and ended in the past.

    We **walked** to school.   He **looked** healthy.

simple present tense A verb tense that is used to talk about habitual or repeated actions in the present and about things that are generally accepted as true.

    I **work** in a restaurant.   Water **freezes** at 32° F.

stative passive *-ed* adjectives following *be* or *get* that look like passives. Unlike true passives, they express states rather than actions.

    The door **is closed.**   We **got excited** about the team.

subject The noun, pronoun, or noun phrase that comes before the verb in a statement.

    Kate went to the restaurant.   **The woman in the white hat** ordered coffee.

subject complement A noun, pronoun, noun phrase, or adjective that renames, identifies, or describes the subject of a sentence.

    He is **a superb chef.**   They looked like **professionals.**

subordinating conjunction   A word (*when, where, because, although, if,* etc.) that begins an adverb clause.

      Although they advertised the product, it didn't sell well.

tag question   A statement with a short question ("tag") added at the end.

      You haven't been to London, **have you?**   He lives here, **doesn't he?**

time clause   A clause that begins with a time expression like *when, while, before,* or *after.*

      After this class ends, I'm going home.   They came **while she was working.**

transition   A word (*also, however, moreover, therefore,* etc.) that connects main clauses, sentences, or larger units, such as paragraphs.

      The clients were pleased. **Therefore,** they accepted our design.

transitive verb   A verb that can take an object in an active sentence.

      The golfer **hit** the ball.

verb   A word that shows an action or state.

      do   **come**   **be**   **have**

verb-preposition combination   A combination formed by certain verbs and certain prepositions.

      We **looked for** the cat.   They **heard from** him.

verb with stative meaning   A verb that describes a state, not an action.

      She **has known** him for years.   He **is** a good lawyer.

***wh-* question** (also called *information question*)   A question that begins with a *wh-* word (*who, what, where, when, why, how,* etc.) and asks for information.

      Who will win the game?   **How far did you travel last night?**

***yes/no* question**   A question that can be answered with *yes* or *no.*

      Do you like chocolate?   **Was he at the game?**

INDEX